EXCHANGE AND POWER IN SOCIAL LIFE

* PETER M. BLAU

Exchange and Power

in Social Life

JOHN WILEY & SONS, INC., NEW YORK · LONDON · SYDNEY

SECOND PRINTING, JANUARY, 1967

To Zena

Preface

The ideas and analysis presented in this book have been strongly influenced by the works of other social scientists, and they often have their ultimate source in the insights into social life presented by social philosophers and thinkers of long ago. I have tried to acknowledge my debts to predecessors by reference to, and citations from, their works, but there are undoubtedly notions and conceptions I have borrowed from others without being aware of having done so, and I must apologize for failure to make proper acknowledgment in these cases. Of the many influences on my thinking, one should be singled out for special recognition since it is so pervasive in the first half of this book despite some fundamental differences in approach; namely, that of George C. Homans' *Social Behavior: Its Elementary Forms*.

I am indebted to the Center for Advanced Studies in the Behavioral Sciences for inviting me to spend a year in the intellectually stimulating and physically delightful surroundings it has to offer and for providing me with an opportunity to write this monograph, to my fellow Fellows there in 1962–1963 for many stimulating discussions ranging over a wide variety of topics, and to the National Science Foundation for the grant of a Senior Postdoctoral Fellowship.

A number of colleagues in sociology and related fields have read parts, or all, of the first draft of this manuscript and made extensive comments. I have greatly benefited from their suggestions and criticisms in making revisions, though I unquestionably did not have the sagacity to take full advantage of all their insights and criticisms. I am very grateful for such help to Howard S. Becker, Zena S. Blau, Evsey Domar, Erving Goffman, Ruth V. Heydebrand, Wolf Heydebrand, George C. Homans, Edward E. Jones, Elihu Katz, Duncan MacRae, Arthur L. Stinchcombe, Stanley H. Udy, Jr., and Hans Zeisel. Finally, I want to acknowledge the secretarial assistance of Joan Warmbrunn, Ruth Soltanoff, and Jeanne Randolph, as well as Richard Gilman's assistance in preparing the index.

PETER M. BLAU

Chicago
June, 1964

Contents

Synopses of Chapters

attraction promotes concern with impressing others and with social exchange. Unilateral exchange generates differentiation of power. The exercise of power, as judged by norms of fairness, evokes social approval or disapproval, which may lead to legitimate organization and to social opposition, respectively. Distinctive characteristics of macrostructures.

Reciprocity and Imbalance, 25

Equilibrium forces on one level are disequilibrating forces on another. Reciprocal attraction established by imbalance in exchange. Exchange balanced through imbalance of power. Legitimation reciprocates for just exercise of power, and opposition retaliates for unjust, restoring balance but also creating new imbalances.

Conclusions, 31

Discussion proceeds from simpler processes in interpersonal associations to more complex ones in large social structures. Importance of social context of interpersonal relations illustrated by Simmel's analysis.

CHAPTER TWO. SOCIAL INTEGRATION, 33

Bonds of attraction unite individuals in a group. Processes of attraction.

Impressing Others, 34

Expectation of rewards makes association attractive. Intrinsically rewarding associations and those that produce extrinsic rewards. Intrinsic attraction rests on fused rewards. Strategies to appear impressive; taking risks; role distance; exhibiting strain and ease. The gratification in meeting a challenge.

A Paradox of Integration, 43

Impressive qualities make a man attractive to a group but also pose a status threat for the rest. Competition for social recognition in early stages of group formation, which can be conceptualized as a series of interlocking mixed games, and which serves as a screening test for leadership. Emergent differentiation of status intensifies need for integrative bonds. Reversal of strategy from appearing impressive to self-depreciation. Superior status is reward for instrumental contributions, social acceptance, for contribution to group solidarity.

Testing Some Inferences, 50

Data on informal acceptance among colleagues. Experimental findings support and refine theory; pressure to become integrated promoted self-depreciation. It led low-status subjects, however, to stress that they have some impressive qualities as well as to be self-depreciating in other respects, whereas high-status subjects insisted on their own judgment in status-relevant areas but compensated through conciliatory agreement with the lows in other areas.

Conclusions, 56

Group formation: the interdependence of social integration and differentiation. Incompatible conditions required for group cohesion produce integration paradox. Feedback effects of social processes.

CHAPTER THREE. SOCIAL SUPPORT, 60

Group cohesion strengthens normative control of members and social support. Social approval and attraction are two elements of support.

Social Approval, 62

Significance of social approval depends on its being accepted as genuine. Problems of simony and prostitution. Approval and respect: respect for a man raises value of his approval; indiscriminate approval lowers respect for him. Dilemma of approval: providing support through expressing it, but expressing it freely depreciates its value. Status differences and approval. Feedbacks of praising others on praiser's own standing depend on structural support of his status.

Attractiveness: First and Second Impressions, 69

Approval of opinions and mutual attraction. Attraction as generalized approval of person. Self-defeating first impressions. Self-fulfilling first impressions: creating social reality by investing one's style with value; living up to expectations initially produced; bluffing. Preoccupation with impressing others impedes both expressive involvement and instrumental endeavors. Restraints imposed by social approval are confined to circles of significant others.

Excursus on Love, 76

Polar case of intrinsic attraction, where exchange of extrinsic benefit is merely means for expressing and winning intrinsic attachment. Movement toward commitment; flirtation; testing dependence; advantage of lesser commitment. Although expressions of affection stimulate another's love, freely granting them depreciates their value, which is the dilemma of love. Social pressures to withhold commitment. The challenge of conquest. Alienating demands for commitment. Conditions that encourage the expression of affection. For a lasting attachment to develop commitments must keep abreast.

Conclusions, 85

Parallels between approval and attraction: significance depends on their being genuine, their being scarce, and other's orientation to the bestower. A basic difference between the two.

CHAPTER FOUR. SOCIAL EXCHANGE, 88

Homans' conception. Exchange in simple societies. Principles of exchange; illustrated with associations between professionals.

Unspecified Obligations and Trust, 91

Limits of concept of exchange. Reciprocity as starting mechanism. Unspecified obligations distinguish social from strictly economic exchange. Social exchange depends on and promotes trust. No exact price; fusion of various benefits. Constraints to discharge obligations.

Conditions of Exchange, 97

Significance of initial offer. Commitments and other mechanisms to promote trust. Types of social rewards. Types of cost. Furnishing social rewards at no cost. Social context of exchange: role sets; interdependencies in group structure; impingement of other transactions. Multigroup affiliation resolves exchange conflicts and weakens social control.

Overwhelming Benefactions, 106

Gift exchanges in simpler societies and parallels in ours. Obligation to give, to receive, and to repay. Exchange may engender peer relations or status differences, since bestowing benefactions is a claim to superiority, which is invalidated by reciprocation, but which is validated by failure to do so. Tributes to chiefs are an exception. The role distance expressed by exchange rituals. Institutionalization of exchange as basis of stratification; underlying generic forces.

Conclusions, 112

Social exchange as intermediate case between pure calculation of extrinsic advantage and pure expression of intrinsic affection. Supplying benefits may lead to bonds between peers or superiority over others, depending on reciprocity. Common and conflicting interests in associations.

CHAPTER FIVE. DIFFERENTIATION OF POWER, 115

Power defined as control through negative sanctions. Refinement required by problem of recurrent rewards.

Unilateral Dependence and Obligations, 118

Establishing power by supplying needed benefits. The four alternatives to submission that delineate the conditions of power imbalance: (1) reciprocation; (2) alternative sources of needed benefits; (3) use of force; (4) suppression of need for benefits. This schema can be used to specify the conditions of social independence (strategic resources, available alternatives, coercive force, and ideals lessening needs), the requirements of power, the issues in power conflicts, and basic problems in the analysis of social structure. The case of coercive force.

Competition for Status, 125

The object of competition in discussion groups shifts from speaking time to status, power, and leadership, and similar shifts occur in other competitions, such as that between firms. Exchange relations become differentiated from competitive ones as status becomes differentiated. Consensus crystallizes stratified structure. Distinction between the influence respect commands and compliance resting on obligations; the mixed case of leadership.

Status as Expendable Capital, 132

Status is expended in use but can be expanded by investing it at risk. Secure status is source of social rewards not accessible to insecure status. Power over an entire collectivity permits organizing their endeavors to further the pursuit of various objectives. Doing so entails the risk of loss of power if unsuccessful, but it promises the gain of greater power if successful. The greater a man's scope of power, the easier it is to take such risks, since he can insure himself against them and thus reduce uncertainty. Tolerance is a sign of strength, whereas intolerance is an admission of weakness that may strengthen the opponent.

Conclusions, 140

Imbalances of obligations produce differences in power. The supply of needed benefits creates an undeniable claim to power unless one of four alternatives to submission exists. Competition and differentiation. Influences that replenish and those that deplete obligations. Democracy, status threats, and intolerance.

CHAPTER SIX. EXPECTATIONS, 143

Satisfactions with and reactions to social associations depend on expectations. Past experience and reference standards influence those expectations.

Expectations and Associations, 145

Three types: general expectations of achievements, particular expectations of given associates, and comparative expectations of profiting from social associations. Past attainments increase expectations and thus the significance of further rewards, but the attainment of increasing rewards also eventually diminishes the value (marginal utility) of further rewards. American intellectuals illustrate influence of expectations on reactions to social rewards.

Fair Exchange and Reference Groups, 151

Going rates of exchange for social benefits; possible operational measures. Social norms establish fair rates of exchange, which adjust long-term investments and "production" capacities, analogous to the normal price in economics. These norms superimpose a secondary exchange of fairness for approval upon the primary one. The relative deprivation resulting from comparisons with more highly rewarded group members reflects a principle of diminishing collective marginal utility.

Attachment and Immobility, 160

The commitments to groups and organizations that are expected of men severely restrict their mobility, as exemplified by occupational commitments. Effective endeavors in organized collectivities require such commitments, but the immobility produced by them impedes competitive adjustments and has the unjust result that some individuals must pay the price of these adjustments when they do occur.

Conclusions, 165

Attainments influence expectations, and both influence the value of further rewards. Social experiences, reference groups, and expectations. Required organizational attachments prevent some men from receiving fair returns for their major investments.

CHAPTER SEVEN. THE DYNAMICS OF CHANGE AND ADJUSTMENT IN GROUPS, 168

Application of marginal analysis to study of exchange and differentiation in groups, designed to illustrate how operational hypothesis can be derived from the theory presented. Diminishing marginal utility, exchange, and specialization.

Bilateral Monopoly and Proliferation, 171

Consultation pairs conceptualized as bilateral monopolies, with indifference curves on two pairs of coordinates representing, respectively, problem-solving ability and relative status, which can be exchanged by supplying advice for compliance. Bargaining paths and exchange rates. Proliferation of exchange due to search for alternatives and limitation of resources.

Structural Adjustment to Changing Conditions, 179

Elasticity of demand for advice depends on duties that are not too complex, available substitute sources of information, and significance of task performance relative to that of standing among colleagues. Changes in the number of experts, and hence the supply of advice, are expected to affect the volume of consultation less if the task is complex and demand is otherwise inelastic than if it is elastic. The elasticity of the supply of advice is governed by the time pressure on consultants and the availability of potential consultants in the group. An increase in demand for advice due to the assignment of newcomers is expected to increase the volume of consultation more if consultants are not under much pressure, and if others are ready to join the ranks of consultants than if the opposite conditions make supply inelastic. Another inference, which empirical data support, is that the demand for advice created by newcomers promotes partnerships of reciprocal consultation primarily if supply is inelastic. The addition of new-comers may produce a permanent increase in the amount of consultation, because the contracting supply tends to be less elastic than the expanding one.

Imperfections, 187

The assumptions of resource allocation on the basis of alternative costs and of perfect competition. Major sources of imperfections: heterogeneity of services, which is greatest in multipurpose groups; small size of group, which facilitates the development of monopoly, as does a common purpose even in a large collectivity; and restrictions of free communication, notably as the result of a crystallized structure of differential status.

Conclusions, 194

Proliferation of exchange. Differences in elasticity condition the effects of changes in supply and demand for advice on volume of consultation and on status structure. Self-perpetuating element of power. Collectivities with and without a common purpose.

CHAPTER EIGHT. LEGITIMATION AND ORGANIZATION, 199

Power makes it possible to organize collective efforts. Stable organizing power requires legitimation. Legitimate authority rests on normative constraints of subordinate group.

Leadership, 200

The oppressive exercise of power engenders resistance, whereas collective approval of the leader's contributions legitimates and fortifies his leadership. Stable leadership depends on power and the subordinates' legitimating approval of it; the conflicting requirements for attaining the two pose the dilemma of leadership.

Legitimate Authority, 205

Institutionalized authority and sanctioning power of management. Obligating subordinates by contributing to their welfare transforms managerial power into legitimate authority. The role of cognitive dissonance in legitimation. The defining criterion of authority is that compliance with the superior's commands is enforced by the collectivity of subordinates or its dominant sub-groups. The contrasting problems of managerial authority and informal leadership. Institutionalization of authority. Political authority.

Organizing Collective Effort, 213

The function of authority to organize collective effort. Members and employees of organizations. The uncertain investments made to organize men are rewarded by the profits that accrue to leadership. The great strength of an organization enables its leadership to treat members as if they were employees. Assuming responsibility. The diverse comparisons in complex organizations engender relative deprivation and conflict.

Conclusions, 220

The legitimation of power has its source in the social approval its fair exercise evokes among subordinates. Problems of leadership, and how organizations help solve them for managers. The mobilization of power through organization.

CHAPTER NINE. OPPOSITION, 224

Punishment is a poor reinforcer. Resort to it tends to be prompted by its function as social deterrent and by the wish to retaliate for serious harm done.

Exploitation and Retaliation, 227

The oppressive use of power, as defined by social norms of justice, may engender active opposition to it. The unfair exercise of power tends to evoke anger and a desire to retaliate for the exploitation suffered. Serious deprivations experienced in a collective situation may produce a social surplus by giving rise to a revolutionary ideology, since such ideals make men less dependent on material rewards and thus free their energies to oppose existing powers.

Political Opposition, 234

Limitations of purely rational model of politics, notably that it cannot account for the growth of radical political opposition. Extremist opposition as expressive action signifying antagonism against existing powers. The significance of ideological rewards for small opposition parties. Factors that strengthen the ideological commitment of opposition members. Leftist extremism as response to economic deprivation, rightist extremism as one to relative deprivation of status.

Political Structure and Ideological Conflict, 242

Heterogeneity and partisan conflict. Political institutions govern the number of parties and the chances of radical opposition. The conflict between the militants in the opposition, who want to preserve the extremist ideology, and the realists, who are willing to compromise to widen its appeal. In competing for major groups of voters, parties become interpenetrated by organized elements of these groups. Ideological compromise that does not succeed in promoting the growth of the opposition is likely to hasten its decline.

Conclusions, 250

Opposition to oppressive powers often has expressive significance. Majority rule depends on partisan conflict as well as democratic institutions.

CHAPTER TEN. MEDIATING VALUES IN COMPLEX STRUCTURES, 253

Common values mediate indirect relations in large collectivities, and they legitimate the social order.

Social Norms and Indirect Exchange, 255

The need for normative standards in social life, illustrated by the prisoner's dilemma. Enforced social norms discourage self-interested action that harms the collective interest by changing the reward-cost ratio of such action. Conformity with norms substitutes indirect for direct exchange; it entails refraining from engaging in certain transactions and being compensated by the collectivity for the advantages thereby foregone. Friendship cliques illustrate indirect transactions, as do organized philanthropy, professional service, and bureaucratic relations with clients.

Values as Media of Social Transactions, 263

Value consensus serves as medium for extending the range of social transactions through social space and time. Media of communication illustrate the principle. Four types of mediating values: (1) particularistic values as media of social integration and solidarity; (2) universalistic values as media of exchange and differentiation; (3) legitimating values as media of organization; (4) opposition ideals as media of change and reorganization.

These four are reflected in four facets of social structure and have implications for collective power.

Institutionalization, 273

Institutionalization preserves legitimate organizations through time. Two complementary mechanisms perpetuate institutions from generation to generation, a historical reality external to and independent of particular persons, and internalized values transmitted in the process of socialization. The roots of institutions in the power structure further fortify them. Four types: (1) integrative institutions, notably kinship and religious ones; (2) distributive institutions, the core of which is the economy; (3) political institutions, including organizational administration as well as government; (4) counterinstitutional component of cultural heritage.

Conclusions, 280

Common values extend social processes through large collectivities and through time, the latter as the result of institutionalization. Parallels and contrasts between simple structures, complex ones, and institutions.

CHAPTER ELEVEN. THE DYNAMICS OF SUBSTRUCTURES, 283

Macrostructures composed of substructures and microstructures composed of interrelated individuals. Complex interplay between substructures.

Macrostructure and Substructures, 284

Types of substructures. Social values have contrasting implications for substructures and encompassing structure. Particularistic values integrate substructures internally but create segregating boundaries between them. Diverse universalistic standards are a particularistic standard in the larger social structure, whereas universalistic values in the larger system may become sources of particularism in its subsystems. Conflict between legitimate central authority and unit autonomy. Opposition ideals, though divisive force, unite subgroups in a common cause. The relationships between integration, differentiation, and organization in substructures to the integration, differentiation, and organization in the encompassing structure.

Intergroup Relations and Mobility, 294

Relations between individuals and those between groups. One aspect of the latter is intergroup mobility, prompted by differential rewards. Whether the highs or the lows within a subgroup have most inducements to leave it for other groups depends on the value standards that govern the status structure. Vertical mobility poses the problem of relative size of fish and pond, that is, whether the benefits of superordinate status in ingroup interaction or the greater privileges of membership in a superior stratum are preferable. An alternative to adjustment through mobility is adjustment through new social investments represented by a successful opposition.

Opposition as a Regenerative Force, 301

Opposition movements as countervailing forces against institutional rigidities. Opposition takes many forms, a political revolution being merely an extreme. The significance of cross-cutting conflicts, multigroup affiliations, and overlapping oppositions for stable democracy. Cross pressures protect democracy against being sacrificed in violent partisan conflicts, but they do so at the expense of the most oppressed, whose political influence they diminish.

Conclusions, 309

Requirements of a systematic theory of social structure. Intergroup mobility modifies internal structures and boundaries between them in larger system. Cross-cutting conflicts produce dialectical pattern of change.

CHAPTER TWELVE. DIALECTICAL FORCES, 312

Two dimensions of interpersonal relations. Two dimensions of social structures. Analysis of social dynamics must go beyond such schemas derived from underlying dimensions.

Dilemmas, 314

Social exchange can be considered a mixed game, which poses dilemmas. Dilemmas are also revealed by the analysis of social attraction, approval, love, leadership, and opposition. They have their sources in mixed-game situations, the contradictory forces that affect the impact of rewards on social interaction (often due to the principle of diminishing marginal utility), and incompatible requirements of goal states. Structural differentiation often resolves dilemmas of individuals but produces new ones reflected in dialectical forces of change.

Differentiation, 321

Status securely rooted in the social structure promotes expansion of power. Multiple supports in the social structure make power independent of any one of them by making it possible to insure against the risk of defections. The joint social support of subordinates solidifies dominant status further. The independence resting on multiple supports of superior status promotes tolerance, but it also permits the oppressive use of power should conditions invite it, at least up to the point where the oppressed join in opposition to the oppressor and thus deprive him of multiple supports.

Dynamics, 327

Deriving the four facets of social structure—integration, differentiation, organization, and opposition—from an analysis of social exchange. Indirect exchange in organizations and complex structures. Just as the transactions within collectivities lead to the development of common goals and organizations to achieve them, so do the transactions among organized collectivities stimulate the emergence of an overall political organization to maintain order and further other common interests. The restraints exerted by established organizations and its governing groups often give rise to opposition forces.

Dialectic, 336

The very processes that restore social equilibrium are usually disequilibrating forces in other respects. Since social forces may have contradictory implications, and since rigidities may require opposition forces to gather momentum before they can effect adjustments, structural change tends to assume a dialectical pattern of intermittent reorganizations.

Introduction

All contacts among men rest on the schema of giving and returning the equivalence. The equivalence of innumerable gifts and performances can be enforced. In all economic exchanges in legal form, in all fixed agreements concerning a given service, in all obligations of legalized relations, the legal constitution enforces and guarantees the reciprocity of service and return service—social equilibrium and cohesion do not exist without it. But there are also innumerable other relations to which the legal form does not apply, and in which the enforcement of the equivalence is out of the question. Here gratitude appears as a supplement. It establishes the bond of interaction, of the reciprocity of service and return service, even when they are not guaranteed by external coercion. . . .

Beyond its first origin, all sociation rests on a relationship's effect which survives the emergence of the relationship. An action between men may be engendered by love or greed of gain, obedience or hatred, sociability or lust for domination alone, but this action usually does not exhaust the creative mood which, on the contrary, somehow lives on in the sociological situation it has produced. Gratitude is definitely such a continuance. . . . If every grateful action, which lingers on from good turns received in the past, were suddenly eliminated, society (at least as we know it) would break apart.

GEORG SIMMEL, The Sociology of Georg Simmel

Gratitude is like mercantile credit. The latter is the mainstay of business; and we pay our debts, not because it is right that we should discharge them, but in order more easily to borrow again.

LA ROCHEFOUCAULD, The Maxims

The aim of this book is to contribute to an understanding of social structure on the basis of an analysis of the social processes that govern the relations between individuals and groups. The basic question that is being raised is how social life becomes organized into increasingly complex structures of associations among men.

The intent is not to present a systematic theory of social structure; it is more modest than that. The core of a theory of society has to explain the complex interdependence between substructures of numerous kinds, often intersecting, and on different levels. An approach to such a theory is adumbrated in the last part of the book. The foundation required for a systematic theory of social structure is a thorough knowledge of the processes of social association, from the simplest that characterize the interpersonal relations between individuals to the most complex that pertain to the relations in and among large collectivities. These social processes out of which structures of associations evolve are at the focus of attention in the analysis to be presented. This monograph may be considered a prolegomenon of a theory of social structure.

The problem is to derive the social processes that govern the complex structures of communities and societies from the simpler processes that pervade the daily intercourse among individuals and their interpersonal relations. An attempt is made to provide a connecting link between the study of everyday social life, as represented by the works of Georg Simmel and Erving Goffman, and broad theories of society, such as those of Max Weber and Talcott Parsons. The purpose of the intensive analysis of interpersonal relations that occupies much of the first half of the book is not primarily to investigate the relations between individuals for their own sake, nor is it to search for the psychological roots of human interaction, but it is to derive from this analysis a better understanding of the complex structures of associations among men that develop. It is this fundamental concern with utilizing the analysis of simpler processes for clarifying complex structures that distinguishes the approach here from that of other recent students of interpersonal processes, notably George C. Homans and John W. Thibaut and Harold H. Kelley, from whose perceptive insights the present investigation has otherwise greatly benefited.[1]

Two dangers must be avoided in such derivation of more complex from simpler social processes, and in the study of social structure

---

[1] George C. Homans, *Social Behavior,* New York: Harcourt, Brace and World, 1961; and John W. Thibaut and Harold H. Kelley, *The Social Psychology of Groups,* New York: Wiley, 1959.

generally—the Scylla of abstract conceptions too remote from observable empirical reality and the Charybdis of reductionism that ignores emergent social and structural properties. Attributes of social structures are usually abstractions that reflect combinations of variables describing human conduct or individual characteristics. A typical example is the differentiation along various lines that exists in collectivities, such as in respect to the tasks performed by different members. Although the division of labor in a community refers ultimately to observable patterns of conduct of individuals, it is an emergent property of communities that has no counterpart in a corresponding property of individuals. Age distribution, similarly, is an attribute that exists only on the group level; individuals have no age distribution, only an age. The limitation of psychological reductionism is that it tends to ignore these emergent characteristics of social life and explain it exclusively in terms of the motives that govern individual behavior. The limitation of abstract conceptions of social structure that stress their distinctive "Gestalt," and do not analytically dissect the complex patterns into its simpler components, on the other hand, is not only that testable hypotheses can rarely be derived from such theories but also that the most complex aspects of social life cannot be fully explained without reference to its simpler aspects in which they are rooted.[2]

Emergent properties are essentially relationships between elements in a structure. The relationships are not contained in the elements, though they could not exist without them, and they define the structure. Three nonparallel lines in a plane, or even three points, define a triangle, but none of the lines or points contain constituent parts of the triangle. The study of social life is concerned with the relations among people and thus always with emergent properties in the broadest sense of the term. Often, however, social relations are simply treated as characteristics of individuals, no different from their other characteristics, for instance, when the influences of the friendships of workers and of their technical skills on their performance are examined. In these cases, the fact that a variable—such as the extent of friendships—is an emergent social property poses no special problems since it is actually ignored. In contrast, the analysis of the structure of social relations in collectivities, for example, their differentiated

---

[2] On the danger of oversimplifying the concepts of Gestalt and emergent properties, see Ernest Nagel, "On the Statement 'The Whole Is More than the Sum of Its Parts,'" in Paul F. Lazarsfeld and Morris Rosenberg, *The Language of Social Research,* Glencoe: Free Press, 1955, pp. 519–527.

status structures, deals explicitly with emergent properties. A more complex illustration is the study of the interdependence between the internal structures of subgroups and the relations among them in the larger society. Yet not only complex social structures but also patterns of interaction between individuals reveal emergent properties.

The concept of social exchange directs attention to the emergent properties in interpersonal relations and social interaction. A person for whom another has done a service is expected to express his gratitude and return a service when the occasion arises. Failure to express his appreciation and to reciprocate tends to stamp him as an ungrateful man who does not deserve to be helped. If he properly reciprocates, the social rewards the other receives serve as inducements to extend further assistance, and the resulting mutual exchange of services creates a social bond between the two. To be sure, each individual's behavior is reinforced by the rewards it brings, but the psychological process of reinforcement does not suffice to explain the exchange relation that develops. This social relation is the joint product of the actions of both individuals, with the actions of each being dependent on those of the other. The emergent properties of social exchange consequent to this interdependence cannot be accounted for by the psychological processes that motivate the behavior of the partners.

Exchange is here conceived as a social process of central significance in social life, which is derived from simpler processes and from which more complex processes are in turn derived.[3] Social exchange, broadly defined, can be considered to underlie relations between groups as well as those between individuals; both differentiation of power and peer group ties; conflicts between opposing forces as well as cooperation; both intimate attachments and connections between distant members of a community without direct social contacts. Restricting the concept more narrowly, the reciprocal exchange of extrinsic benefits is distinguished from other social processes, for example, those in associations that have intrinsic significance, or the unilateral transactions in which power becomes differentiated. Exchange and related processes of interpersonal relations, which are directly rooted in primitive psychological processes, such as social attraction, are analyzed in the first third of this book. Next, differentiation of status is

---

[3] Although an attempt has been made to derive the *major* concepts used in the analysis from a few primitive terms, the analysis is not completely restricted to concepts so derived. In other words, some concepts are introduced *ad hoc* at various points, such as the concept of connecting links based on common interests in chapter ii.

derived from exchange under specified conditions, and various aspects of a differentiated group structure are discussed, notably adjustments that occur under changing circumstances and the significance of the legitimation of superior power for stable organization of collective effort. The study of opposition leads to a discussion of complex structures and their dynamics in the last third of the book, which rests on the conception that a secondary exchange is superimposed upon the primary one and indirect transactions become substituted for direct ones as the result of normative expectations and value orientations in collectivities.

Not all human behavior is guided by considerations of exchange, though much of it is, more than we usually think. Two conditions must be met for behavior to lead to social exchange. It must be oriented toward ends that can only be achieved through interaction with other persons, and it must seek to adapt means to further the achievement of these ends. The purview of this study is restricted to such behavior. Excluded from consideration, therefore, is behavior resulting from the irrational push of emotional forces without being goal oriented, for instance, a girl's irrational conduct on dates that is motivated by her unconscious conflicts with her father. But a wide range of behavior is pertinent for a study of exchange, including goal-oriented conduct in love relations, and including particularly "wertrational" as well as "zweckrational" conduct, in Weber's terms. The former does not entail what is conventionally defined as rational action but, as Weber put it, "the action of persons who, regardless of possible cost to themselves, act to put into practice their convictions of what seems to be required by duty, honour, the pursuit of beauty, a religious call, personal loyalty, or the importance of some 'cause' no matter in what it consists."[4] In brief, social exchange may reflect any behavior oriented to socially mediated goals.

The fact that given actions of people have expressive significance and are not calculated to obtain specific advantages does not necessarily mean that their conduct is irrational but may mean that it is wertrational rather than zweckrational, that is, oriented to the pursuit of ultimate values rather than to the pursuit of immediate rewards. This is not simply a hairsplitting distinction. Expressive social conduct oriented to ideals and absolute values is of great importance in social life, but our understanding of it is not at all advanced by the assumption that it merely reflects idiosyncratic and irrational individual

---

[4] Max Weber, *The Theory of Social and Economic Organization*, New York: Oxford University Press, 1947, p. 116.

behavior. Radical political opposition, for example, cannot be explained without taking into account the expressive significance it has for supporters, and failure to do so is a serious shortcoming of formalistically rational models of politics. Such political opposition that expresses the resentment of the oppressed can, however, be derived from a conception of exchange without resort to the assumption that the push of irrational impulses or psychopathic personality traits drive individuals to become radicals. Similarly, in intimate relations of intrinsic significance, individuals often do favors for one another not in the expectation of receiving explicit repayments but to express their commitment to the interpersonal relation and sustain it by encouraging an increasing commitment on the part of the other. There is still an element of exchange in doing favors to strengthen another's commitment that one desires, though only in the broadest sense of the term.

The broad application of the notion of exchange raises the question of tautology. There is a great temptation to explore the fruitfulness of the concept by extending its scope and applying it to all social conduct. But the assumption of exchange theory that social interaction is governed by the concern of both (or all) partners with rewards dispensed by the other (or others) becomes tautological if any and all behavior in interpersonal relations is conceptualized as an exchange, even conduct toward others that is not at all oriented in terms of expected returns from them. To be sure, much conduct that appears at first sight not to be governed by considerations of exchange turns out upon closer inspection to be so governed, as we shall see, but this makes it still more important to specify a criterion that restricts the concept of exchange and precludes its use in tautological fashion. Social exchange as here conceived is limited to actions that are contingent on rewarding reactions from others and that cease when these expected reactions are not forthcoming. Ultimately, however, a negative answer to the question of whether the theoretical principles are tautological depends on the possibility of inferring empirically testable hypotheses from them, and some operational hypotheses will be inferred to illustrate that this possibility exists.

Another issue that should be confronted is whether the principles advanced are culture-bound or apply also to other societies, other cultures, and other times. The objective certainly was to suggest generic principles of social life that are not confined to the historical context of America today. Social exchange in nonliterate societies is compared in some detail with that in contemporary ones, for example. There is, nevertheless, undoubtedly a bias in perspective stressing the experiences that are prevalent in our own culture at the expense of those in others. Two illustrations of this bias might be mentioned. Many of the processes of interpersonal relations discussed probably are more typical of societies like ours, where men have many acquaintances of varying degrees of intimacy, and where groups frequently form and reform, than of cultures dominated by an ascribed kinship system where men tend to classify others as either kin or foe. The analysis of opposition is largely conceived within the framework of democratic values, though not necessarily of democratic institutions, and neglects to consider corresponding conflicts in fundamentally different political climates.

In concluding this introduction, an overview of the contents of the book might be in order to facilitate placing the earlier discussion of interpersonal relations and face-to-face groups into a wider social context, which is systematically discussed only in the later part of the book. The first chapter sets the theme of the analysis by outlining how more complex social processes evolve out of simpler ones and have their ultimate source in psychological dispositions, and by posing the inherent conflict between reciprocity and imbalance in social life. Processes of social attraction, without which associations among men would not occur, give rise to processes of exchange. Unreciprocated exchange leads to the differentiation of power. The exercise of power in collectivities, as judged by social norms of justice, promotes processes of social approval, legitimation, and organization, on the one hand, and forces of opposition, conflict, reorganization, and change, on the other. Although there is a strain toward reciprocity in social relations and a strain toward equilibrium in social structures, the same forces that restore balance or equilibrium in one respect are imbalancing or disequilibrating forces in others, which means that the very processes of adjustment create imbalances requiring further adjustments.

Chapters two and three are concerned with the processes connected with social attraction. The topic of chapter two is the process of social integration in the formation of groups. An analysis of the role of attraction to others and of impressing others to prove oneself attractive to them for social integration is presented, and the emergence of differentiating processes simultaneous with integrative processes is discussed. The thesis that most men seek to win social acceptance in groups to which they are attracted by initially trying to impress others and then reverse their strategy and act with self-depreciating modesty is generally supported by the results of an experiment designed to test it. An analytical distinction is drawn between associations that are intrinsically attractive and those to which men are attracted by the expectation of extrinsic benefits. Chapter three deals with two elements of social support, approval and attraction, the latter serving the function of generalized approval of a person. After discussing romantic love as the polar case of intrinsic attraction and the dynamics of the development of deepening commitments, some parallels and a basic difference between approval and intrinsic attraction are outlined.

Whereas some social exchange occurs even in love relations, the expressive orientation characteristic of intrinsic attachments contrasts with the orientation to obtain extrinsic benefits in calculated exchange, and chapter four turns to a consideration of exchange in this narrower sense. Social exchange is distinguished from strictly economic exchange by the unspecified obligations incurred in it and the trust both required for and promoted by it. Various institutions of gift exchange in simple societies are shown to reveal underlying principles that apply to social exchange in general, notably the principle that reciprocated benefactions create social bonds among peers, whereas unreciprocated ones produce differentiation of status.

Power imbalances are shown to derive from unilateral exchange in chapter five. Four conditions are specified under which persons or groups having scarce services at their disposal can use these resources to make an undeniable claim to power over others. The same four-fold schema is employed to indicate the conditions of social independence, the strategies for attaining and sustaining power, the issues in power conflicts, and basic problems in the analysis of social structure. The relationships between competition and differentiation are examined. Status is likened to capital inasmuch as each is expended in use but can be invested at risk to expand it. Tolerance is considered an expression of strength, and intolerance a sign of weakness that may have opposite effects of those intended.

How social expectations modify reactions to experiences in exchange relations and power structures is discussed in chapter six. The principle of the eventually diminishing marginal utility in social exchange is assumed to have its major source in the dampening effect the attainment of expectations has on further attainments, but the rise in expectations typically resulting from attainments partly counteracts the decline in marginal utility. Going rates of exchange that become established in group interaction are distinguished from fair rates, which rest on normative expectations of a fair return for investments. The immobility produced by commitments to organizations and groups, however, prevents many individuals from realizing fair returns for their occupational and other investments. The standards of expectation examined in this chapter, particularly the norm of fairness, become the baseline for the emergence of new social processes in groups and societies.

The application of principles of marginal analysis from economics, appropriately adapted, to the exchange of advice for status in work groups in chapter seven makes it possible to infer numerous specific hypotheses from the theory. Consultation pairs are initially conceptualized as bilateral monopolies, and reasons for the proliferation of exchange into wider circles are indicated. Conditions that govern the elasticity of supply and demand for advice are stipulated, and the effects of changes in group composition on the amount of consultation and on the status structure under variations in these conditions are predicted. Whereas empirical tests would undoubtedly prove a good proportion of the inferred predictions to be incorrect, these negative findings would provide a basis for refining the theory, whereas no such refinements are possible if a theory fails to yield operational hypotheses that can be negated by empirical evidence.

At this point, the focus shifts to the study of complex structures in large collectivities and societies. Legitimation and opposition, which are considered to be collective reactions to the exercise of power as judged by social norms of fairness, result from a secondary exchange (of social approval for fairness) that is superimposed upon the primary one, and they effect organization and reorganization, respectively. Legitimation, as shown in chapter eight, transforms power into authority and thereby into an important resource for the stable organization of collective endeavors. The defining criterion of legitimate authority suggested is that the normative constraints of the collectivity of subordinates, or its dominant subgroups, enforce compliance with the superior's commands. The problems posed by emergent leadership and by authority in established organizations are contrasted. Opposition to existing powers is conceived in chapter nine as grounded in the unfair treatment experienced by an oppressed collectivity with extensive social communication among themselves and in their desire to retaliate for the injustice and exploitation they have suffered. Radical opposition to an oppressive ruling group could not arise were it not for the expressive significance this manifestation of their collective vengeance has for the exploited, because a ruling group has the power to make opposition to it disadvantageous, which would preclude opposition were subjects to engage in it only on strictly rational grounds. Oppression and deprivation often produce a social surplus, since they tend to make some men willing to sacrifice material welfare for the sake of opposition ideals and hence free human energies to join in opposition to the oppressors. A dilemma a radical opposition party is likely to face is that widening the appeal of its ideology requires compromises that may well weaken the commitment of its most devoted supporters.

Value consensus is looked upon in chapter ten as a medium of social transactions that extends their scope far beyond the range of direct social contact and that is essential for the development of complex structures in large collectivities. After analyzing how normative orientations substitute indirect patterns of exchange for direct transactions, four types of mediating value orientations are distinguished: particularistic standards as media of social integration and solidarity; universalistic criteria as media of exchange and differentiation of status; legitimating values as media of organization; and opposition ideals as media of change and reorganization. Institutions are conceptualized as social arrangements that are perpetuated from generation to generation, partly because their formal manifestations persist as a historical reality independent of particular individuals and partly because the values that are embodied in these external forms and give them continuing meaning are transmitted to succeeding generations in the process of socialization. The roots of institutions in the power structure are indicated, and four types are distinguished.

Chapter eleven calls attention to the interdependence between substructures of diverse sorts in a larger structure, some encompassing others and some intersecting, and it indicates the kind of analysis required for a systematic theory of social structure. The relationships between the integration, differentiation, and organization of the substructures and the same three aspects of the encompassing social structure are traced. A treatment of intergroup mobility represents one of these nine relationships, namely, that between the internal differentiation of substructures and their relative position in the differentiated larger structure. The significance of opposition as a regenerative force and the importance of many crisscrossing oppositions for stable democracy are discussed.

The final chapter extrapolates from the preceding analysis those elements that pertain to the dynamics of social life. Men are frequently confronted by dilemmas posed by conflicting forces and incompatible requirements. While social differentiation, and especially multiple social supports of superior status, resolve dilemmas for individuals, the differentiated status structure tends to give rise to new conflicting forces. The political organization of a society can be derived from the social transactions among the organized collectivities in it, just as the formal organization of a collectivity can be derived from the processes of integration and differentiation, as well as exchange and competition, within it. Since social forces often have contradictory implications, creating new imbalances in the course of restoring some balance, and since rigidities in social structures may require opposition forces to gather momentum before they can effect adjustments, the dynamics of social structure is characterized not so much by continuously adjusted equilibrium states as by intermittent reorganizations in a dialectical pattern.

* ONE

The Structure
of Social Associations

Of course the elementary qualities of which the social fact consists are present in germ in individual minds. But the social fact emerges from them only when they have been transformed by association since it is only then that it appears. Association itself is also an active factor productive of special effects. In itself it is therefore something new. When the consciousness of individuals, instead of remaining isolated, becomes grouped and combined, something in the world has been altered.

EMILE DURKHEIM, *Suicide*

To speak of social life is to speak of the associations between people—their associating together in work and in play, in love and in war, to trade or to worship, to help or to hinder. It is in the social relations men establish that their interests find expression and their desires become realized. As Simmel put it: "Social association refers to the widely varying forms that are generated as the diverse interests of individuals prompt them to develop social units in which they realize these—sensual or ideal, lasting or fleeting, conscious or unconscious, casually impelling or teleologically inducing—interests." [1] Simmel's fundamental postulate, and also that of this book, is that the analysis of social associations, of the processes governing them, and of the forms they assume is the central task of sociology. The title of this first chapter can be considered a free translation of Simmel's basic concept, "Die Formen der Vergesellschaftung."

People's associations proliferate through social space and time.

---

[1] Georg Simmel, *Soziologie*, Leipzig: Duncker und Humblot, 1908, p. 6 (my translation).

Social relations unite not only individuals in groups but also groups in communities and societies. The associations between individuals tend to become organized into complex social structures, and they often become institutionalized to perpetuate the form of organization far beyond the life span of human beings. The main sociological purpose of studying processes of face-to-face interaction is to lay the foundation for an understanding of the social structures that evolve and the emergent social forces that characterize their development.

The objectives of our investigation are to analyze social associations, the processes that sustain them and the forms they attain, and to proceed to inquire into the complex social forces and structures to which they give rise. Broad as this topic is, it is intended to provide a specific focus that explicitly excludes many sociological problems from consideration. Sociology is defined by Weber as "a science which attempts the interpretative understanding of social action in order thereby to arrive at a causal explanation of its course and effects. . . . Action is social insofar as, by virtue of the subjective meaning attached to it by the acting individual (or individuals), it takes account of the behavior of others and is thereby oriented in its course." [2] A concern with social action, broadly conceived as any conduct that derives its impetus and meaning from social values, has characterized contemporary theory in sociology for some years. The resulting preoccupation with value orientations has diverted theoretical attention from the study of the actual associations between people and the structures of their associations. While structures of social relations are, of course, profoundly influenced by common values, these structures have a significance of their own, which is ignored if concern is exclusively with the underlying values and norms. Exchange transactions and power relations, in particular, constitute social forces that must be investigated in their own right, not merely in terms of the norms that limit and the values that reinforce them, to arrive at an understanding of the dynamics of social structures. If one purpose of the title of this chapter is to indicate a link with the theoretical tradition of Simmel, another purpose is to distinguish the theoretical orientation in this monograph from that of Weber and Parsons; not "the structure of social action" [3] but the structure of social associations is the focal point of the present inquiry.

---

[2] Max Weber, *The Theory of Social and Economic Organization,* New York: Oxford University Press, 1947, p. 88.

[3] The title of Talcott Parsons' first major work, *The Structure of Social Action,* New York: McGraw-Hill, 1937, would also be appropriate for some of his later theoretical writings, as he himself has noted in *The Social System,* Glencoe: Free Press, 1951, p. ix.

After illustrating the concept of social exchange and its manifestations in various social relations, this chapter presents the main theme of how more complex processes of social association evolve out of simpler ones. Forces of social attraction stimulate exchange transactions. Social exchange, in turn, tends to give rise to differentiation of status and power. Further processes emerge in a differentiated status structure that lead to legitimation and organization, on the one hand, and to opposition and change, on the other. Whereas the conception of reciprocity in exchange implies the existence of balancing forces that create a strain toward equilibrium, the simultaneous operations of diverse balancing forces recurrently produce imbalances in social life, and the resulting dialectic between reciprocity and imbalance gives social structures their distinctive nature and dynamics.

The Exchange of Social Rewards

By Honour, in its proper and genuine Signification, we mean nothing else but the good Opinion of others. . . .

The Reason why there are so few Men of real Virtue, and so many of real Honour, is, because all the Recompence a Man has of a virtuous Action, is the Pleasure of doing it, which most People reckon but poor Pay; but the Self-denial a Man of Honour submits to in one Appetite, is immediately rewarded by the Satisfaction he receives from another, and what he abates of his Avarice, or any other Passion, is doubly repaid to his Pride. . . .

MANDEVILLE, *The Fable of the Bees*

Most human pleasures have their roots in social life. Whether we think of love or power, professional recognition or sociable companionship, the comforts of family life or the challenge of competitive sports, the gratifications experienced by individuals are contingent on actions of others. The same is true for the most selfless and spiritual satisfactions. To work effectively for a good cause requires making converts to it. Even the religious experience is much enriched by communal worship. Physical pleasures that can be experienced in solitude pale in significance by comparison. Enjoyable as a good dinner is, it is the social occasion that gives it its luster. Indeed, there is something pathetic about the person who derives his major gratification from food or drink as such, since it reveals either excessive need or excessive greed; the pauper illustrates the former, the glutton, the latter. To be sure, there are profound solitary enjoyments—reading a good book, creating a piece of art, producing a scholarly work. Yet these, too, derive much of their significance from being later communicated to and shared with others. The lack of such anticipation makes the solitary activity again somewhat pathetic: the recluse who has nobody to talk to about what he reads; the artist or scholar whose works are completely ignored, not only by his contemporaries but also by posterity.

Much of human suffering as well as much of human happiness has its source in the actions of other human beings. One follows from the other, given the facts of group life, where pairs do not exist in complete isolation from other social relations. The same human acts that cause pleasure to some typically cause displeasure to others. For one boy to enjoy the love of a girl who has committed herself to be his steady date, other boys who had gone out with her must suffer the pain of having been rejected. The satisfaction a man derives from exercising power over others requires that they endure the deprivation of being subject to his power. For a professional to command an outstanding reputation in his field, most of his colleagues must get along without such pleasant recognition, since it is the lesser professional esteem of the majority that defines his as outstanding. The joy the victorious team members experience has its counterpart in the disappointment of the losers. In short, the rewards individuals obtain in social associations tend to entail a cost to other individuals. This does not mean that most social associations involve zero-sum games in which the gains of some rest on the losses of others. Quite the contrary, individuals associate with one another because they all profit from their association. But they do not necessarily all profit equally, nor do they share the cost of providing the benefits equally, and even if there are no direct costs to participants, there are often indirect costs born by those excluded from the association, as the case of the rejected suitors illustrates.

Some social associations are intrinsically rewarding. Friends find pleasure in associating with one another, and the enjoyment of whatever they do together—climbing a mountain, watching a football game—is enhanced by the gratification that inheres in the association itself. The mutual affection between lovers or family members has the same result. It is not what lovers do together but their doing it *together* that is the distinctive source of their special satisfaction—not seeing a play but sharing the experience of seeing it. Social interaction in less intimate relations than those of lovers, family members, or friends, however, may also be inherently rewarding. The sociability at a party or among neighbors or in a work group involves experiences that are not especially profound but are intrinsically gratifying. In these cases, all associates benefit simultaneously from their social interaction, and the only cost they incur is the indirect one of giving up alternative opportunities by devoting time to the association.

Social associations may also be rewarding for a different reason. Individuals often derive specific benefits from social relations because their associates deliberately go to some trouble to provide these benefits for them. Most people like helping others and doing favors for them—to assist not only their friends but also their acquaintances and occasionally even strangers, as the motorist who stops to aid another with his stalled car illustrates. Favors make us grateful, and our expressions of gratitude are social rewards that tend to make doing favors enjoyable, particularly if we express our appreciation and indebtedness publicly and thereby help establish a person's reputation as a generous and competent helper. Besides, one good deed deserves another. If we feel grateful and obligated to an associate for favors received, we shall seek to reciprocate his kindness by doing things for him. He in turn is likely to reciprocate, and the resulting mutual exchange of favors strengthens, often without explicit intent, the social bond between us.

A person who fails to reciprocate favors is accused of ingratitude. This very accusation indicates that reciprocation is expected, and it serves as a social sanction that discourages individuals from forgetting their obligations to associates. Generally, people are grateful for favors and repay their social debts, and both their gratitude and their repayment are social rewards for the associate who has done them favors.[4] The fact that furnishing benefits to others tends to produce these social rewards is, of course, a major reason why people often go to great trouble to help their associates and enjoy doing so. We would not be human if these advantageous consequences of our good deeds were not important inducements for our doing them.[5] There are, to be sure, some individuals who selflessly work for others without any thought of reward and even without expecting gratitude, but these are virtually saints, and saints are rare. The rest of us also act unselfishly

---

[4] "We rarely meet with ingratitude, so long as we are in a position to confer favors." François La Rochefoucauld, *The Maxims,* London: Oxford University Press, 1940, p. 101 (#306).

[5] Once a person has become emotionally committed to a relationship, his identification with the other and his interest in continuing the association provide new independent incentives for supplying benefits to the other. Similarly, firm commitments to an organization lead members to make recurrent contributions to it without expecting reciprocal benefits in every instance. The significance of these social attachments is further elaborated in subsequent chapters.

sometimes, but we require some incentive for doing so, if it is only the social acknowledgment that we are unselfish.

An apparent "altruism" pervades social life; people are anxious to benefit one another and to reciprocate for the benefits they receive. But beneath this seeming selflessness an underlying "egoism" can be discovered; the tendency to help others is frequently motivated by the expectation that doing so will bring social rewards. Beyond this self-interested concern with profiting from social associations, however, there is again an "altruistic" element or, at least, one that removes social transactions from simple egoism or psychological hedonism. A basic reward people seek in their associations is social approval, and selfish disregard for others makes it impossible to obtain this important reward.[6]

The social approval of those whose opinions we value is of great significance to us, but its significance depends on its being genuine. We cannot force others to give us their approval, regardless of how much power we have over them, because coercing them to express their admiration or praise would make these expressions worthless. "Action can be coerced, but a coerced show of feeling is only a show."[7] Simulation robs approval of its significance, but its very importance makes associates reluctant to withhold approval from one another and, in particular, to express disapproval, thus introducing an element of simulation and dissimulation into their communications. As a matter of fact, etiquette prescribes that approval be simulated in disregard of actual opinions under certain circumstances. One does not generally tell a hostess, "Your party was boring," or a neighbor, "What you say is stupid." Since social conventions require complimentary remarks on many occasions, these are habitually discounted as not reflecting genuine approbation, and other evidence that does reflect it is looked for, such as whether guests accept future invitations or whether neighbors draw one into further conversations.

In matters of morality, however, individuals have strong convictions that constrain them to voice their actual judgments more freely. They usually do not hesitate to express disapproval of or, at least, withhold approval from associates who have violated socially accepted stand-

---

[6] Bernard Mandeville's central theme is that private vices produce public benefits because the importance of social approval prompts men to contribute to the welfare of others in their own self-interest. As he put it tersely at one point, "Moral Virtues are the Political Offspring which Flattery begot upon Pride." *The Fable of the Bees,* Oxford: Clarendon, 1924, Vol. I, 51; see also pp. 63–80.

[7] Erving Goffman, *Asylums,* Chicago: Aldine, 1962, p. 115.

ards of conduct. Antisocial disregard for the welfare of the ingroup meets universally with disapprobation regardless of how immoral, in terms of the mores of the wider community, the norms of a particular group may be. The significance of social approval, therefore, discourages conduct that is utterly and crudely selfish. A more profound morality must rest not merely on group pressure and long-run advantage but primarily on internalized normative standards. In the ideal case, an individual unerringly follows the moral commands of his conscience whatever the consequences. While such complete morality is attained only by the saint and the fool, and most men make some compromises,[8] moral standards clearly do guide and restrain human conduct. Within the rather broad limits these norms impose on social relations, however, human beings tend to be governed in their associations with one another by the desire to obtain social rewards of various sorts, and the resulting exchanges of benefits shape the structure of social relations.

The question that arises is whether a rationalistic conception of human behavior underlies this principle that individuals pursue social rewards in their social associations. The only assumption made is that human beings choose between alternative potential associates or courses of action by evaluating the experiences or expected experiences with each in terms of a preference ranking and then selecting the best alternative. Irrational as well as rational behavior is governed by these considerations, as Boulding has pointed out:

> All behavior, in so far as the very concept of behavior implies doing one thing rather than another, falls into the above pattern, even the behavior of the lunatic and the irrational or irresponsible or erratic person. The distinction between rational and irrational behavior lies in the degree of self-consciousness and the stability of the images involved rather than in any distinction of the principle of optimum.[9]

What is explicitly *not* assumed here is that men have complete information, that they have no social commitments restricting their alternatives, that their preferences are entirely consistent or remain constant, or that they pursue one specific ultimate goal to the exclusion of all others. These more restrictive assumptions, which are not made in the present analysis, characterize rationalistic models of

---

[8] Heinrich von Kleist's story "Michael Kohlhaas" is a pathetic illustration of the foolishness inherent in the insistence on rigid conformity with moral standards in complete disregard of consequences.

[9] Kenneth Boulding, *Conflict and Defense,* New York: Harper, 1962, p. 151.

human conduct, such as that of game theory.[10] Of particular importance is the fact that men strive to achieve diverse objectives. The
statement that men select the most preferred among available alternatives does not imply that they always choose the one that yields
them the greatest material profit.[11] They may, and often do, choose
the alternative that requires them to make material sacrifices but contributes the most to the attainment of some lofty ideal, for *this* may
be their objective. Even in this choice they may err and select an
alternative that actually is not the best means to realize their goal.
Indeed, the need to anticipate in advance the social rewards with
which others will reciprocate for favors in exchange relations inevitably introduces uncertainty and recurrent errors of judgment that
make perfectly rational calculations impossible. Granted these qualifications, the assumption that men seek to adjust social conditions to
achieve their ends seems to be quite realistic, indeed inescapable.

Basic Processes

> To reward, is to recompense, to remunerate, to return good for good
> received. To punish, too, is to recompense, to remunerate, though in a
> different manner; it is to return evil for evil that has been done.

ADAM SMITH, *The Theory of Moral Sentiments*

The basic social processes that govern associations among men have
their roots in primitive psychological processes, such as those underlying the feelings of attraction between individuals and their desires
for various kinds of rewards. These psychological tendencies are
primitive only in respect to our subject matter, that is, they are taken
as given without further inquiry into the motivating forces that produce them, for our concern is with the social forces that emanate
from them.

The simpler social processes that can be observed in interpersonal

---

[10] For a discussion of game theory which calls attention to its limitations, see
R. Duncan Luce and Howard Raiffa, *Games and Decisions,* New York: Wiley,
1957, esp. chapters iii and vii. For other criticisms of game theory, notably its
failure to utilize empirical research, and an attempt to incorporate some of its
principles into a substantive theory of conflict, see Thomas C. Schelling, *The
Strategy of Conflict,* Cambridge: Harvard University Press, 1960, esp. chapters
iv and vi.

[11] See on this point George C. Homans, *Social Behavior,* New York: Harcourt,
Brace and World, 1961, pp. 79–80; and Anatol Rapoport, *Fights, Games, and
Debates,* Ann Arbor: University of Michigan Press, 1960, p. 122.

associations and that rest directly on psychological dispositions give rise to the more complex social processes that govern structures of interconnected social associations, such as the social organization of a factory or the political relations in a community. New social forces emerge in the increasingly complex social structures that develop in societies, and these dynamic forces are quite removed from the ultimate psychological base of all social life. Although complex social systems have their foundation in simpler ones, they have their own dynamics with emergent properties. In this section, the basic processes of social associations will be presented in broad strokes, to be analyzed subsequently in greater detail, with special attention to their wider implications.

Social attraction is the force that induces human beings to establish social associations on their own initiative and to expand the scope of their associations once they have been formed. Reference here is to social relations into which men enter of their own free will rather than to either those into which they are born (such as kinship groups) or those imposed on them by forces beyond their control (such as the combat teams to which soldiers are assigned), although even in these involuntary relations the extent and intensity of the association depend on the degree of mutual attraction. An individual is attracted to another if he expects associating with him to be in some way rewarding for himself, and his interest in the expected social rewards draws him to the other. The psychological needs and dispositions of individuals determine which rewards are particularly salient for them and thus to whom they will be attracted. Whatever the specific motives, there is an important difference between the expectation that the association will be an intrinsically rewarding experience and the expectation that it will furnish extrinsic benefits, for example, advice. This difference calls attention to two distinct meanings of the term "attraction" and its derivatives. In its narrower sense, social attraction refers to liking another person *intrinsically* and having positive feelings toward him; in the broader sense, in which the term is now used, social attraction refers to being drawn to another person for any reason whatsoever. The customer is attracted in this broader sense to the merchant who sells goods of a given quality at the lowest price, but he has no intrinsic feelings of attraction for him, unless they happen to be friends.

A person who is attracted to others is interested in proving himself attractive to them, for his ability to associate with them and reap the benefits expected from the association is contingent on their finding him an attractive associate and thus wanting to interact with him.

Their attraction to him, just as his to them, depends on the anticipation that the association will be rewarding. To arouse this anticipation, a person tries to impress others. Attempts to appear impressive are pervasive in the early stages of acquaintance and group formation. Impressive qualities make a person attractive and promise that associating with him will be rewarding. Mutual attraction prompts people to establish an association, and the rewards they provide each other in the course of their social interaction, unless their expectations are disappointed, maintain their mutual attraction and the continuing association.

Processes of social attraction, therefore, lead to processes of social exchange. The nature of the exchange in an association experienced as intrinsically rewarding, such as a love relationship, differs from that between associates primarily concerned with extrinsic benefits, such as neighbors who help one another with various chores, but exchanges do occur in either case. A person who furnishes needed assistance to associates, often at some cost to himself, obligates them to reciprocate his kindness. Whether reference is to instrumental services or to such intangibles as social approval, the benefits each supplies to the others are rewards that serve as inducements to continue to supply benefits, and the integrative bonds created in the process fortify the social relationship.

A situation frequently arises, however, in which one person needs something another has to offer, for example, help from the other in his work, but has nothing the other needs to reciprocate for the help. While the other may be sufficiently rewarded by expressions of gratitude to help him a few times, he can hardly be expected regularly to devote time and effort to providing help without receiving any return to compensate him for his troubles. (In the case of intrinsic attraction, the only return expected is the willingness to continue the association.) The person in need of recurrent services from an associate to whom he has nothing to offer has several alternatives. First, he may force the other to give him help. Second, he may obtain the help he needs from another source. Third, he may find ways to get along without such help.[12] If he is unable or unwilling to choose any of these alternatives, however, there is only one other course of action left for him; he must subordinate himself to the other and comply with his wishes, thereby rewarding the other with power over himself

---

[12] The last two of these alternatives are noted by Parsons (*op. cit.*, p. 252) in his discussion of a person's reactions to having his expectations frustrated by another.

as an inducement for furnishing the needed help. Willingness to comply with another's demands is a generic social reward, since the power it gives him is a generalized means, parallel to money, which can be used to attain a variety of ends. The power to command compliance is equivalent to credit, which a man can draw on in the future to obtain various benefits at the disposal of those obligated to him.[13] The unilateral supply of important services establishes this kind of credit and thus is a source of power.

Exchange processes, then, give rise to differentiation of power. A person who commands services others need, and who is independent of any at their command, attains power over others by making the satisfaction of their need contingent on their compliance. This principle is held to apply to the most intimate as well as the most distant social relations. The girl with whom a boy is in love has power over him, since his eagerness to spend much time with her prompts him to make their time together especially pleasant for her by acceding to her wishes. The employer can make workers comply with his directives because they are dependent on his wages. To be sure, the superior's power wanes if subordinates can resort to coercion, have equally good alternatives, or are able to do without the benefits at his disposal. But given these limiting conditions, unilateral services that meet basic needs are the penultimate source of power. Its ultimate source, of course, is physical coercion. While the power that rests on coercion is more absolute, however, it is also more limited in scope than the power that derives from met needs.

A person on whom others are dependent for vital benefits has the power to enforce his demands. He may make demands on them that they consider fair and just in relation to the benefits they receive for submitting to his power. On the other hand, he may lack such restraint and make demands that appear excessive to them, arousing feelings of exploitation for having to render more compliance than the rewards received justify. Social norms define the expectations of subordinates and their evaluations of the superior's demands. The fair exercise of power gives rise to approval of the superior, whereas unfair exploitation promotes disapproval. The greater the resources of a person on which his power rests, the easier it is for him to refrain from exploiting subordinates by making excessive demands, and consequently the better are the chances that subordinates will approve of the fairness of his rule rather than disapprove of its unfairness.

---

[13] See Parsons, "On the Concept of Influence," *Public Opinion Quarterly*, 27 (1963), 37–62, esp. pp. 59–60.

There are fundamental differences between the dynamics of power in a collective situation and the power of one individual over another. The weakness of the isolated subordinate limits the significance of his approval or disapproval of the superior. The agreement that emerges in a collectivity of subordinates concerning their judgment of the superior, on the other hand, has far-reaching implications for developments in the social structure.

Collective approval of power legitimates that power. People who consider that the advantages they gain from a superior's exercise of power outweigh the hardships that compliance with his demands imposes on them tend to communicate to each other their approval of the ruler and their feelings of obligation to him. The consensus that develops as the result of these communications finds expression in group pressures that promote compliance with the ruler's directives, thereby strengthening his power of control and legitimating his authority. "A feeling of obligation to obey the commands of the established public authority is found, varying in liveliness and effectiveness from one individual to another, among the members of any political society." [14] Legitimate authority is the basis of organization. It makes it possible to organize collective effort to further the achievement of various objectives, some of which could not be attained by individuals separately at all and others that can be attained more effectively by coordinating efforts. Although power that is not legitimated by the approval of subordinates can also be used to organize them, the stability of such an organization is highly precarious.

Collective disapproval of power engenders opposition. People who share the experience of being exploited by the unfair demands of those in positions of power, and by the insufficient rewards they receive for their contributions, are likely to communicate their feelings of anger, frustration, and aggression to each other. There tends to arise a wish to retaliate by striking down the existing powers. "As every man doth, so shall it be done to him, and retaliation seems to be the great law that is dictated to us by nature." [15] The social support the oppressed give each other in the course of discussing their common grievances and feelings of hostility justifies and reinforces their aggressive opposition against those in power. It is out of such shared discontent that opposition ideologies and movements develop—that

---

[14] Bertrand de Jouvenel, *Sovereignty,* University of Chicago Press, 1957, p. 87.

[15] Adam Smith, *The Theory of Moral Sentiments* (2d ed.), London: A. Millar, 1761, p. 139.

men organize a union against their employer or a revolutionary party against their government.

In brief, differentiation of power in a collective situation evokes contrasting dynamic forces: legitimating processes that foster the organization of individuals and groups in common endeavors; and countervailing forces that deny legitimacy to existing powers and promote opposition and cleavage. Under the influence of these forces, the scope of legitimate organization expands to include ever larger collectivities, but opposition and conflict recurrently redivide these collectivities and stimulate reorganization along different lines.

The distinctive characteristic of complex social structures is that their constituent elements are also social structures. We may call these structures of interrelated groups "macrostructures" and those composed of interacting individuals "microstructures." There are some parallels between the social processes in microstructures and macrostructures. Processes of social attraction create integrative bonds between associates, and integrative processes also unite various groups in a community. Exchange processes between individuals give rise to differentiation among them, and intergroup exchanges further differentiation among groups. Individuals become incorporated in legitimate organizations, and these in turn become part of broader bodies of legitimate authority. Opposition and conflict occur not only within collectivities but also between them. These parallels, however, must not conceal the fundamental differences between the processes that govern the interpersonal associations in microstructures and the forces characteristic of the wider and more complex social relations in macrostructures.

First, value consensus is of crucial significance for social processes that pervade complex social structures, because standards commonly agreed upon serve as mediating links for social transactions between individuals and groups without any direct contact. Sharing basic values creates integrative bonds and social solidarity among millions of people in a society, most of whom have never met, and serves as functional equivalent for the feelings of personal attraction that unite pairs of associates and small groups. Common standards of valuation produce media of exchange—money being the prototype but not the only one—which alone make it possible to transcend personal transactions and develop complex networks of indirect exchange. Legitimating values expand the scope of centralized control far beyond the reach of personal influence, as exemplified by the authority of a legitimate government. Opposition ideals serve as rallying points to draw together strangers from widely dispersed places and unite them in a common cause. The study of these problems requires an analysis of the significance of social values and norms that must complement the analysis of exchange transactions and power relations but must not become a substitute for it.

A second emergent property of macrostructures is the complex interplay between the internal forces within substructures and the forces that connect the diverse substructures, some of which may be microstructures composed of individuals while others may themselves be macrostructures composed of subgroups. The processes of integration, differentiation, organization, and opposition formation in the various substructures, which often vary greatly among the substructures, and the corresponding processes in the macrostructure all have repercussions for each other. A systematic analysis of these intricate patterns, which will only be adumbrated in chapters ten and eleven, would have to constitute the core of a general theory of social structures.

Finally, enduring institutions typically develop in macrostructures. Established systems of legitimation raise the question of their perpetuation through time. The strong identification of men with the highest ideals and most sacred beliefs they share makes them desirous to preserve these basic values for succeeding generations. The investments made in establishing and expanding a legitimate organization create an interest in stabilizing it and assuring its survival in the face of opposition attacks. For this purpose, formalized procedures are instituted that make the organization independent of any individual member and permit it to persist beyond the life span or period of tenure of its members. Institutionalization refers to the emergence of social mechanisms through which social values and norms, organizing principles, and knowledge and skills are transmitted from generation to generation. A society's institutions constitute the social matrix in which individuals grow up and are socialized, with the result that some aspects of institutions are reflected in their own personalities, and others appear to them as the inevitable external conditions of human existence. Traditional institutions stabilize social life but also introduce rigidities that make adjustment to changing conditions difficult. Opposition movements may arise to promote such adjustment, yet these movements themselves tend to become institutionalized and rigid in the course of time, creating needs for fresh oppositions.

Reciprocity and Imbalance

Now in these unequal friendships the benefits that one party receives and is entitled to claim from the other are not the same on either side; . . . the better of the two parties, for instance, or the more useful or otherwise superior as the case may be, should receive more affection than he bestows; since when the affection rendered is proportionate to desert, this produces equality in a sense between the parties, and equality is felt to be an essential element of friendship.

ARISTOTLE, *The Nicomachean Ethics*

There is a strain toward imbalance as well as toward reciprocity in social associations. The term "balance" itself is ambiguous inasmuch as we speak not only of balancing our books but also of a balance in our favor, which refers, of course, to a lack of equality between inputs and outputs. As a matter of fact, the balance of the accounting sheet merely rests, in the typical case, on an underlying imbalance between income and outlays, and so do apparent balances in social life. Individuals and groups are interested in, at least, maintaining a balance between inputs and outputs and staying out of debt in their social transactions; hence the strain toward reciprocity. Their aspirations, however, are to achieve a balance in their favor and accumulate credit that makes their status superior to that of others; hence the strain toward imbalance.

Arguments about equilibrium—that all scientific theories must be conceived in terms of equilibrium models or that any equilibrium model neglects the dynamics of real life—ignore the important point that the forces sustaining equilibrium on one level of social life constitute disequilibrating forces on other levels. For supply and demand to remain in equilibrium in a market, for example, forces must exist that continually disturb the established patterns of exchange. Similarly, the circulation of the elite, an equilibrium model, rests on the operation of forces that create imbalances and disturbances in the various segments of society. The principle suggested is that balanced social states depend on imbalances in other social states; forces that restore equilibrium in one respect do so by creating disequilibrium in others. The processes of association described illustrate this principle.

A person who is attracted to another will seek to prove himself attractive to the other. Thus a boy who is very much attracted to a girl, more so than she is to him, is anxious to make himself more attractive to her. To do so, he will try to impress her and, particularly, go out of his way to make associating with him an especially rewarding experience for her. He may devote a lot of thought to finding ways to please her, spend much money on her, and do the things she likes on their dates rather than those he would prefer. Let us assume that he is successful and she becomes as attracted to him as he is to her, that is, she finds associating with him as rewarding as he finds associating with her, as indicated by the fact that both are equally eager to spend time together.

Attraction is now reciprocal, but the reciprocity has been established by an imbalance in the exchange. To be sure, both obtain satisfactory rewards from the association at this stage, the boy as the result of her willingness to spend as much time with him as he wants, and the girl as the result of his readiness to make their dates enjoyable for her. These reciprocal rewards are the sources of their mutual attraction. The contributions made, however, are in imbalance. Both devote time to the association, which involves giving up alternative opportunities, but the boy contributes in addition special efforts to please her. Her company is sufficient reward by itself, while his is not, which makes her "the more useful or otherwise superior" in terms of their own evaluations, and he must furnish supplementary rewards to produce "equality in a sense between the parties." Although two lovers may, of course, be equally anxious to spend time together and to please one another, it is rare for a perfect balance of mutual affection to develop spontaneously. The reciprocal attraction in most intimate relations—marriages and lasting friendships as well as more temporary attachments—is the result of some imbalance of contributions that compensates for inequalities in spontaneous affection, notably in the form of one partner's greater willingness to defer to the other's wishes.

The relationship between this conception and balance theory in psychology may be briefly indicated. Thus, Newcomb's ABX scheme is concerned with an individual A, who is attracted to another individual B, has a certain attitude toward an object X, and perceives B to have a certain attitude toward X.[16] Discrepancies between any of these elements produce a strain toward balance both in individual systems, that is, internal psychological states, and in collective systems, that is, interpersonal relations. For example, if A prefers the Democrats and B the Republicans, there are several ways for A to restore balance: he may become more favorable toward the Republicans; he may misperceive B's attitude as being really not Republican; he may lose interest in politics, making the disagreement inconsequential; or he may cease to associate with B and search for other associates whose opinions he finds more congenial. The focus here is on the implications

---

[16] Theodore M. Newcomb, *The Acquaintance Process*, New York: Holt, Rinehart and Winston, 1961, esp. chapter ii. See also Fritz Heider, *The Psychology of Interpersonal Relations*, New York: Wiley, 1958.

that imbalances in interpersonal relations have for psychological processes that restore balance in the mental states of individuals,[17] on the one hand, and for changes in interpersonal relations on the other. Initially, however, individuals tend to cope with impending imbalances of attraction by seeking to prove themselves attractive to associates they find attractive in order to establish friendly relations and become integrated among them. These processes, rather than those to which Newcomb calls attention, are the main concern of the preceding discussion and of the more extensive one in the next chapter.

The theoretical principle that has been advanced is that a given balance in social associations is produced by imbalances in the same associations in other respects. This principle, which has been illustrated with the imbalances that underlie reciprocal attraction, also applies to the process of social differentiation. A person who supplies services in demand to others obligates them to reciprocate. If some fail to reciprocate, he has strong inducements to withhold the needed assistance from them in order to supply it to others who do repay him for his troubles in some form. Those who have nothing else to offer him that would be a satisfactory return for his services, therefore, are under pressure to defer to his wishes and comply with his requests in repayment for his assistance. Their compliance with his demands gives him the power to utilize their resources at his discretion to further his own ends. By providing unilateral benefits to others, a person accumulates a capital of willing compliance on which he can draw whenever it is to his interest to impose his will upon others, within the limits of the significance the continuing supply of his benefits has for them. The general advantages of power enable men who cannot otherwise repay for services they need to obtain them in return for their compliance; although in the extreme case of the person who has much power and whose benefits are in great demand, even an offer of compliance may not suffice to obtain them.

Here, an imbalance of power establishes reciprocity in the exchange. Unilateral services give rise to a differentiation of power that equilibrates the exchange. The exchange balance, in fact, rests on two imbalances: unilateral services and unilateral power. Although these two imbalances make up a balance or equilibrium in terms of one perspective, in terms of another, which is equally valid, the exchange equilibrium reinforces and perpetuates the imbalances of dependence

---

[17] Processes that restore the psychological balance of individuals by reducing dissonance, that is, by decreasing the significance of an unattainable object or person, are the central focus in Leon Festinger, *A Theory of Cognitive Dissonance,* Evanston: Row, Peterson, 1957.

and power that sustain it. Power differences not only are an imbalance by definition but also are actually experienced as such, as indicated by the tendency of men to escape from domination if they can. Indeed, a major impetus for the eagerness of individuals to discharge their obligations and reciprocate for services they receive, by providing services in return, is the threat of becoming otherwise subject to the power of the supplier of the services. While reciprocal services create an interdependence that balances power, unilateral dependence on services maintains an imbalance of power.

Differentiation of power evidently constitutes an imbalance in the sense of an inequality of power; but the question must be raised whether differentiation of power also necessarily constitutes an imbalance in the sense of a strain toward change in the structure of social relations. Power differences as such, analytically conceived and abstracted from other considerations, create such a pressure toward change, because it can be assumed that men experience having to submit to power as a hardship from which they would prefer to escape. The advantages men derive from their ruler or government, however, may outweigh the hardships entailed in submitting to his or its power, with the result that the analytical imbalance or disturbance introduced by power differences is neutralized. The significance of power imbalances for social change depends, therefore, on the reactions of the governed to the exercise of power.

Social reactions to the exercise of power reflect once more the principle of reciprocity and imbalance, although in a new form. Power over others makes it possible to direct and organize their activities. Sufficient resources to command power over large numbers enable a person or group to establish a large organization. The members recruited to the organization receive benefits, such as financial remuneration, in exchange for complying with the directives of superiors and making various contributions to the organization. The leadership exercises power within the organization, and it derives power from the organization for use in relation with other organizations or groups. The clearest illustration of this double power of organizational leadership is the army commander's power over his own soldiers and, through the force of their arms, over the enemy. Another example is the power business management exercises over its own employees and, through the strength of the concern, in the market. The greater the external power of an organization, the greater are its chances of accumulating resources that put rewards at the disposal of the leadership for possible distribution among the members.

The normative expectations of those subject to the exercise of power, which are rooted in their social experience, govern their reactions to it. In terms of these standards, the benefits derived from being part of an organization or political society may outweigh the investments required to obtain them, or the demands made on members may exceed the returns they receive for fulfilling these demands. The exercise of power, therefore, may produce two different kinds of imbalance, a positive imbalance of benefits for subordinates or a negative imbalance of exploitation and oppression.

If the members of an organization, or generally those subject to a governing leadership, commonly agree that the demands made on them are only fair and just in view of the ample rewards the leadership delivers, joint feelings of obligation and loyalty to superiors will arise and bestow legitimating approval on their authority. A positive imbalance of benefits generates legitimate authority for the leadership and thereby strengthens and extends its controlling influence. By expressing legitimating approval of, and loyalty to, those who govern them subordinates reciprocate for the benefits their leadership provides, but they simultaneously fortify the imbalance of power in the social structure.

If the demands of the men who exercise power are experienced by those subject to it as exploitative and oppressive, and particularly if these subordinates have been unsuccessful in obtaining redress for their grievances, their frustrations tend to promote disapproval of existing powers and antagonism toward them. As the oppressed communicate their anger and aggression to each other, provided there are opportunities for doing so, their mutual support and approval socially justify and reinforce the negative orientation toward the oppressors, and their collective hostility may inspire them to organize an opposition. The exploitative use of coercive power that arouses active opposition is more prevalent in the relations between organizations and groups than within organizations. Two reasons for this are that the advantages of legitimating approval restrain organizational superiors and that the effectiveness of legitimate authority, once established, obviates the need for coercive measures. But the exploitative use of power also occurs within organizations, as unions organized in opposition to exploitative employers show. A negative imbalance for the subjects of power stimulates opposition. The opposition negatively reciprocates, or retaliates, for excessive demands in an attempt to even the score, but it simultaneously creates conflict, disequilibrium, and imbalance in the social structure.[18]

---

[18] Organized opposition gives expression to latent conflicts and makes them manifest.

Even in the relatively simple structures of social association considered here, balances in one respect entail imbalances in others. The interplay between equilibrating and disequilibrating forces is still more evident, if less easy to unravel, in complex macrostructures with their cross-cutting substructures, where forces that sustain reciprocity and balance have disequilibrating and imbalancing repercussions not only on other levels of the same substructure but also on other substructures. As we shall see, disequilibrating and re-equilibrating forces generate a dialectical pattern of change in social structures.

Conclusions

In this chapter the basic processes underlying the structure of social associations were outlined, and some of the emergent forces characteristic of complex social structures were briefly indicated. The principles presented in simplified form to convey an overall impression of the theoretical scheme in this book will be elaborated and refined in subsequent chapters. After discussing processes of social integration, support, and exchange in interpersonal associations in some detail, various aspects of social differentiation in groups will be analyzed, and finally attention will be centered on the implication of these social forces as well as of newly emergent ones for organization and change in complex social structures.

The discussion will proceed, therefore, from the basic processes that govern the social interaction between individuals in microstructures to the increasingly complex processes in macrostructures composed of several layers of intersecting substructures. We shall be concerned with the changes in social processes that occur as one moves from simpler to more complex social structures and with the new social forces that emerge in the latter. Entire countries, for example, cannot rely for social control primarily on social approval and personal obligations, as small groups of friends can, and must consequently give formalized procedures and coercive powers, such as law courts and police forces, a more prominent role. While progressing from the simpler to the more complex seems to be the only logical sequence, it does pose some problems in the study of social life.

The pattern of association between two individuals is, of course, strongly influenced by the social context in which it occurs. Even the analysis of social interaction in dyads, therefore, must not treat these pairs as if they existed in isolation from other social relations. The mutual attraction of two persons and the exchanges between them, for example, are affected by the alternative opportunities of each, with the result that competitive processes arise that include wider circles and that complement and modify the processes of exchange and attraction in this pair and in other pairs. The power of an individual over another depends entirely on the social alternatives or lack of alternatives of the subjected individual, and this fact, as well as some others, makes it mandatory to examine power relations in a wider context than the isolated pair. Simmel's perceptive discussion of the dyad and the triad is instructive in this connection.[19]

Simmel's analysis of the dyad seems to be conceived as a polar case that highlights, by contrast, the distinctive characteristics of group life. To cite only one example, the death or withdrawal of one individual destroys the dyad, whereas groups are not completely dependent on any single member. His discussion of the triad is explicitly concerned with the significance of a multiplicity of social relations in social life, and his use of the triad for this purpose is apparently intended to emphasize the crucial distinction between a pair and any group of more than two.[20] Power can be strengthened by dividing the opposition (*divide et impera*); it can be resisted by forming coalitions (*tertius gaudens*); and power conflicts can be mediated by third parties. All these distinctive processes of the dynamics of power cannot be manifest in a dyad. The legitimation of the power of a superior and the mobilization of opposition to him also do not occur in dyads but only if a superior is confronted by a group of subordinates in communication with each other.

It is essential, in the light of these considerations, to conceptualize processes of social association between individuals realistically as finding expression in networks of social relations in groups and not to abstract artificially isolated pairs from this group context. Crusoe and Friday were a dyad that existed in isolation, but most associations are part of a broad matrix of social relations. Although the analysis of complex structures will be postponed until after interpersonal processes have been examined, the group structures within which the associations between individuals occur will be taken into account from the very beginning.

---

[19] Georg Simmel, *The Sociology of Georg Simmel*, Glencoe: Free Press, 1950, chapters iii and iv.
[20] See *ibid.*, pp. 138–139, 141, 145.

* TWO

Social Integration

Modesty is due to a fear of incurring the well-merited envy and contempt which pursues those who are intoxicated by good fortune: it is a useless display of strength of mind; and the modesty of those who attain the highest eminence is due to a desire to appear even greater than their position.

LA ROCHEFOUCAULD, *The Maxims*

The formation of a group involves the development of integrative bonds that unite individuals in a cohesive unit. These are bonds of social attraction. The greater the attraction of individuals to one another and to the group as a whole, particularly if their intrinsic attraction to the association generates common identification, the more cohesive is the group. For a new member to become integrated into an existing group, similarly, requires that ties of social attraction develop between him and the rest. A person's attraction to a group stimulates his desire to become a member, but only if he proves himself attractive to its other members can he realize this desire and gain social acceptance.

Some groups evolve as individuals with opportunities for social contact become increasingly attracted to each other and establish common bonds that stabilize their social association, as happens in the friendship cliques that form in college dormitories or in the gangs that originate in urban neighborhoods. These emergent groups often have diffuse boundaries and constitute, in effect, overlapping circles, with many individuals being peripheral members, and occasionally even core members, of several groupings; the friendship groups in high

33

schools or neighborhoods typify this pattern. Other groups are part of organizational or institutional systems, such as work groups or families. In these cases, the social association is not the product of the participants' initial attraction but of external conditions established by others; children do not choose their parents, and workers are assigned to sections and required to interact with certain other members of the organization. The integrative bonds that tend to unite the members of work groups, not to speak of families, however, do rest on forces of social attraction that induce members to associate more with each other than the minimum requirement externally imposed upon them. Without such integrative bonds that identify the members as part of a distinct social entity, the work group would not really be a group but an assembly of individuals under a foreman.

The processes of attraction that underlie the development of social integration in a group may be briefly summarized. Social attraction, using the term in its broadest sense, refers to the proclivity to associate with others. A person is attracted to others if he expects associating with them to be rewarding, specifically, to be more rewarding than alternatives open to him at the given time and place (and sometimes the only alternative is no association at all). His attraction to them creates a desire to find social acceptance among them. To be accepted by them, he must prove himself an attractive associate. For this purpose, he will seek to impress them and show that he has qualities that make associating with him rewarding. If he is successful, they will accept him, and if the association brings them and him the expected rewards, the reciprocal advantages solidify the mutual attraction and help him to become an integral part of the group.

These primitive processes give rise to other social processes in the context of group formation where a number of individuals in association exhibit such tendencies. The desire of many individuals to impress each other with their outstanding qualities engenders competitive processes, and social differentiation develops in the course of the ensuing competition. It is in the face of these competitive and differentiating processes, which intensify the need for supportive social bonds, that emergent processes of social integration stabilize and unify the group. The consequent common identification of the members with the group itself, its cohesion and its fortunes, complements their mutual attraction as the foundation of social solidarity.

Impressing Others

The fact that a person is an attractive associate is manifest in the inclination of others to engage in social interaction with him, which can be ascertained in various ways. Sociometric questions can be asked to determine the relative popularity of each group member among the rest, either in general or as an associate in specific endeavors, such as working together or rooming together.[1] If there are no external restrictions on associations, the frequency with which any group member is approached by the rest in the course of social interaction can serve as an index of his comparative attractiveness. More complex measures of attractiveness can be devised. On the assumption that meetings with attractive colleagues are most likely to be remembered, for example, the number of colleagues who named one as a fellow worker with whom they had lunched in the past, but who were not named by him in answer to the same question, has been used as such a measure.[2]

The reason a person is an attractive associate is that he has impressed others as someone with whom it would be rewarding to associate. They may expect his company to be entertaining or intellectually stimulating, to get support for their opinions or help on their problems from him, or to enjoy being seen in his distinguished company. A crucial analytical distinction is that between associations that are intrinsically rewarding and those that furnish extrinsic benefits, which are, in principle, detachable from the association itself. In the first case, another's company as such is the source of attraction, while in the second, specific benefits he supplies are the inducement for associating with him. Conceptualized in abstract terms, discriminations and corresponding generalizations along two different lines can be derived from gratifying social experiences. First, the discrimination is between this attractive individual and others who are not, the generalization is from this pleasurable experience to the expectation that other experiences with him will be gratifying too, and an intrinsic attachment to him develops. Second, the discrimination is between the person and the object or activity that is enjoyable, the generalization is that similar objects from, or activities with, other persons will be gratifying too, and an extrinsic interest in these benefits from any source results.

Deep intrinsic attachments fundamentally alter the social transactions in interpersonal relations. The basic difference is between associ-

---

[1] See J. L. Moreno, *Who Shall Survive?* Washington: Nervous and Mental Disease Publishing Co., 1934, esp. pp. 10–16.

[2] See Blau, *The Dynamics of Bureaucracy* (2d ed.), University of Chicago Press, 1963, pp. 150–152. As noted there, even when these discrepancies are not due to the faulty memory of the person named but to misperceptions of those naming him, they reveal his attractiveness.

ations that are considered ends-in-themselves by participants and those they consider means for some further ends. The salesman's associations with customers are not intrinsically rewarding for him but means for making profitable sales, while his association with the woman he loves *is* intrinsically rewarding and an end-in-itself for him. In intimate relations of profound significance, the mutual supply of rewards is a means for reaffirming and sustaining the association itself, whereas in other social relations the association is a means for obtaining extrinsic rewards of various sorts. The strong commitments of individuals in interpersonal relations that are of intrinsic importance to them tend to make the continuation of the association a supreme value, for the sake of which they are willing to make great sacrifices. Under these conditions of intrinsic attachment, selfless devotion to another's welfare can often be observed, as exemplified by a mother's love for her children and her tendency to make sacrifices for them without any apparent thought of return. Contributions to the welfare of a loved one are not intended to elicit specific returns in the form of proper extrinsic benefits for each favor done. Instead, they serve as expressive symbols of the individual's firm commitment to the relationship and as inducements for the other to make a corresponding commitment and continue the association. If the devotion of a person and his readiness to benefit another without expecting any specific repayments are exploited by that other to gain extrinsic advantages for himself, a serious strain is introduced into the relationship. Although there is no *quid pro quo* of explicit services in these intimate relations of intrinsic significance, each participant does expect his devotion to the other to be rewarded by the other's enduring commitment to the association.

Extrinsic benefits constitute objective criteria for comparing associates, choosing between them, and abandoning one in favor of another. They are independent standards for determining whether a person's choice of associates is rational or not. If a challenging chess game is what we want and nothing else matters, our decision to play with one friend rather than another is demonstrably correct or incorrect, depending, of course, on the relative qualifications of the two as chess players. Associations that are intrinsically rewarding, however, are unique in the sense that they cannot be compared except in the purely subjective terms of the gratifications they provide. Since there are no independent standards, an individual's subjective judgment that an association is intrinsically rewarding for him cannot be considered wrong in any meaningful sense; it is right by fiat. The extrinsic benefits on which the significance of some social associations rests make factual judgments about them possible, but only value judgments apply to associations that are intrinsically attractive.

There are many social relations, however, that cannot be readily classified as being either extrinsically or intrinsically rewarding. Thus, workers participate in unions not only to improve their employment conditions but also because they intrinsically enjoy the fellowship in the union and derive satisfaction from helping to realize its objectives. Indeed, these are the primary inducements for active participation, since the material rewards the union provides are not contingent, for any one individual, on active participation. The problem is not merely that the distinction is an analytical one and actual associations constitute mixed types. Neither is it simply that many ends are means to further ends or that the ends of some people are means to different ends for others. The basic difficulty is rather that of deciding whether or not a certain social reward can be considered detachable from the association in which it is obtained.

Take a dinner party as an illustration. The person who accepts an invitation in order to enjoy the food and drink is an unambiguous case, and so is the one who does so for the sheer pleasure of seeing his old friends—extrinsic rewards motivate the former, intrinsic ones the latter. But consider the third person who comes to have an opportunity to meet high-status people, or the fourth who attends to enjoy the sparkling wit and intellectual sophistication at the dinner table. Compared to food and drink, the stimulating nature of the conversation of individuals is a reward that is intrinsic to the association, as is the enjoyment of their distinguished company. On the other hand, high prestige is evidently a characteristic that can be abstracted from the persons who possess it and used as an independent standard for evaluating the attractiveness of potential associates. The enjoyment of sophisticated conversation, too, implies that the level of sophistication serves as an extrinsic standard of attraction and of choosing between associates. From this perspective, the third and fourth guests are not drawn to the company at the dinner by its intrinsic attractiveness either but by extrinsic benefits it supplies. If not even people's stimulating conversation is considered a reward intrinsic to associating with them, however, what possibly would be a reward that is intrinsic?

One answer to this question centers on the relative nature of the extrinsic-intrinsic criterion. The satisfaction union members derive from participating in joint endeavors to help realize common ideals is more intrinsic than the material benefits they receive as the result of their activities, but this satisfaction from working for union objectives is more extrinsic than their enjoyment of the fellowship among like-minded activists. The pleasure of being seen with persons of prestige is less intrinsic to the association than the pleasure of their interesting conversation, which, in turn, is not as intrinsic as the contentment produced by simply being in the company of good friends.[3] But what makes just being with some people intrinsically gratifying? It is not so much a specific kind of social reward as the fusion of a variety of rewards in a given association that makes these fused rewards inseparable from the associate who is their source and hence creates intrinsic attraction to him. An important implication of this point, finally, is that the initial attraction of individuals to others always rests on extrinsic factors that permit comparisons. Even falling in love is the result of implicit, and partly unconscious, comparisons of specific traits of various girls—their looks and their charm, their supportiveness, and the congeniality of their emotional makeup. The fusion of several such rewarding qualities in one individual is what produces the intrinsic love attachment. Similarly, although men may want to associate together exclusively for the sake of sociable fellowship and have no interest in deriving any extrinsic advantage from their social relations, they must prove themselves attractive to each other by demonstrating qualities that make them preferable to other possible associates, qualities that must be comparable and that consequently are, in a relative sense, extrinsic.

There are many ways in which individuals who seek to gain social acceptance among others try to prove themselves attractive associates. New acquaintances tend to search in their conversations for clues that indicate some shared experiences or characteristics—having fought in the war in Europe, coming from the same state—and they facilitate one another's search by relating incidents that reveal their background or opinions—the Catholicism of one, the socialism of another. Often mere hints are dropped that would indicate one's affiliation solely to the initiated, who would presumably respond, whereas otherwise the search for something else in common continues. Individuals who share attitudes and values provide one another with social support for their opinions, which makes their association attractive, particularly if minor variations in their orientations contribute a challenge to their discussion of the issue. The fact that a person is an American

---

[3] Parsons conceives of universalism-particularism—the abstract dimension underlying the extrinsic-intrinsic distinction—and of other differentiations in social orientations as involving such nesting series of increasingly finer distinctions. See, for example, Talcott Parsons and Robert F. Bales, *Family, Socialization and Interaction Process*, Glencoe: Free Press, 1955, pp. 117–118 and 161–166.

or that he is opposed to Communism, however, hardly makes him a particularly attractive associate in this country, since attributes or values shared by virtually everyone do not differentiate anyone. It requires distinctive opinions or orientations to become differentially attractive as an associate, and such distinctive viewpoints make a person not only attractive to those who share them but also unattractive to those who do not. The fear of antagonizing associates and being rejected by them is the reason individuals tend to confine themselves to subtle hints about their most distinctive traits and opinions in the initial stages of acquaintance. Another method for proving oneself differentially attractive is to impress others with qualities that command their admiration or respect.

The strategies used to impress others vary widely from group to group and from individual to individual, contingent as they are on the values that determine what group members find impressive and on the aptitudes that limit how an individual can impress them. People create impressions, of course, continually and without special design in the process of engaging in activities and interaction with others. But an interest in gaining social acceptance in a new group makes individuals self-conscious and deliberate about making a good impression. "Instead of allowing an impression of their activity to arise as an incidental by-product of their activity, they can [and often do in this situation] reorient their frame of reference and devote their efforts to the creation of the desired impression." [4] This may involve demonstrating their wide knowledge for some individuals and displaying their sophisticated wit for others. Athletic ability may constitute an impressive quality in one group, artistic talent in another. To make a good impression, a person must infer which of his qualities would do so in a given group and adapt his conduct accordingly. Self-conscious concern with impressing others, however, can easily become self-defeating. If an individual is too self-conscious, his awkwardness will leave a poor impression, and if others suspect him of deliberately putting up a front, he also will have made an unfavorable impression. Creating a good first impression is a subtle form of bragging, but its success depends on its being so natural that it does not appear to be bragging at all.

Presenting an impressive image of oneself entails some risks: the risk of appearing boastful or conceited, the risk of repelling others with extreme opinions, and generally the risk of incurring their dis-

---

[4] Erving Goffman, *The Presentation of Self in Everyday Life,* University of Edinburgh Social Science Research Center, 1956, p. 162.

approval. Conversely, taking risks is a method of impressing others in its own right. Superior competence is impressive, and so is outstanding courage. Although a stunt flyer may not be the most skillful we have ever seen, we cannot help admiring his daring. Taking chances, therefore, enables the individual who lacks impressive skills nevertheless to impress others. The person highly competent in an activity can also take advantage of this fact and not reveal his skills in order to command the more admiration by performing feats too daring for anyone with lesser skills. This strategy is caricatured by the tight-rope artist who performs as a clown.

The ability to risk failure and disapproval and successfully meet the challenge commands respect. Goffman's concept "role distance" refers to this method of impressing others.[5] Using the analogy of children on a merry-go-round, he notes that the child at age two typically finds the movement too threatening and cries to be let off, while at four he can master the challenge, is absorbed in the task of riding the wooden horse, and takes it seriously. School-age children, however, no longer are intent on the task of riding the wooden horses but fool around on them—loosening their straps, raising their hands, climbing from horse to horse while they are moving—to show they are beyond the stage when riding on a merry-go-round is an absorbing task that poses a meaningful challenge. Their ostentatious conduct is designed to exhibit distance from the "baby" role of rider on a wooden horse. By displaying role distance, they make a claim to the superior status of older child.

Role distance is an attempt to show that the demands of a role are beneath one's capabilities, as illustrated by Goffman's discussion of the joking and banter that often occurs among the medical staff during surgery. The routine tasks required of interns and junior residents in an operation are below the dignity of a doctor and imply an inferior role. Joking remarks made by junior staff members in the course of performing their duties serve to demonstrate that these tasks do not absorb their full attention and that they are qualified to remain distant from this inferior role. The chief surgeon's responsibility, however, would seem to deserve his full absorption in his task, yet he too expresses role distance by making humorous remarks during an operation. An important function of the jocular tone he adopts toward his staff of subordinates is to ward off the adverse impact his necessarily curt and sometimes critical directives might otherwise have on their equanimity and effective team work. While Goffman does

---

[5] See Goffman, *Encounters*, Indianapolis: Bobbs-Merrill, 1961, pp. 105–132.

not explicitly say so, it would seem that the chief surgeon's jokes also serve to show that he is superior to the demands of his role, just as those of the intern do.

Regardless of the difficulties of a task, full absorption in it implies that it taxes one's capacities to the limit. Indeed, in the most critical stages of an operation, there is undoubtedly no banter.[6] The surgeon who can joke at other stages, which also make considerable demands on him, demonstrates that his abilities are so great he can perform fairly difficult tasks with ease. Generally, tense involvement in a task implies that the limits of an individual's abilities are being approached. Hence, performing a complex task with great ease is particularly impressive, in part because lack of full absorption increases the risk of failure. The more difficult a performance is, the more impressive is it, and the greater is the risk of failure. Role distance, in the form of being at ease and not even fully involved while performing a complex task, is impressive because it increases the risk of failure and simultaneously indicates confidence in one's ability to meet the challenge.

Two opposite tactics make the performance of a difficult act especially impressive. The circus artist, for example, who strains every muscle and nearly fails before he finally succeeds arouses great awe in his audience, but the one who performs his difficult act with ease, as if it were mere child's play for him, also commands profound admiration. Whether exhibiting strain or ease makes a difficult performance still more impressive depends on the sophistication of the audience and ultimately on whether the fact that the performance is difficult must be established or can be taken for granted. If others do not know how very difficult a performance is, manifesting tense concentration and strain in the course of it provides this knowledge and increases their admiration. If they already realize the difficulties involved, however, it is the great ease with which such a hard task can be mastered that is most impressive.

New social situations typically pose a challenge, since there is the risk of failure to impress others. For a social situation to be experienced as a challenge by an individual, the others present must be sufficiently significant for him to make him concerned with impressing

---

[6] Goffman, in a personal communication, noted that while surgeons during the critical stages of operations do not make funny remarks, they sometimes do hum tunes. Humming is not very distracting—much less so than telling jokes—but it does serve to demonstrate that a person is not tense with anxiety even at these critical times; it may well be a form of "whistling in the dark."

them and winning their approval. For it to be experienced as a stimulating challenge rather than a debilitating threat, he must be fairly confident in his ability to earn their acceptance, if not their respect. Insufficient challenge makes a social occasion boring, and excessive challenge makes it distressing. It is the social gathering in which individuals cannot take their success in impressing others for granted but have reasonable chances of success that animates their spirit and stimulates their involvement in social intercourse. Indeed, thorough involvement in any activity—be it a game, a sport, or one's work—seems to depend on such an intermediate challenge, which makes the outcome problematical but limits the threat of failure, either because failure is not too serious (the loss of money in gambling) or because failure is not too likely (the loss of life in ski jumping).[7] If the risk of failure becomes more serious (the stakes in the game are getting too high; a ravine must be jumped in an emergency), the stimulating challenge can quickly turn into an unpleasant threat. The ability to view great dangers as a challenge rather than a threat is rare and impressive.

Why do men risk life, limb, and fortune to meet a challenge? What makes it enjoyable to race a car at great speeds or to solve a chess problem even when nobody is there to offer social approval? It might be the result of a process that could be called reverse secondary reinforcement. Social rewards owe their significance to the psychological process of secondary reinforcement. The primary gratifications of human beings are originally contingent on, and become associated with, certain actions of others in their environment, such as the mother's nurturing or the father's approval. These and related actions of other human beings become, in due course, intrinsic social rewards that act as secondary reinforcers for the individual's behavior; the respect and approval of significant associates are notable examples. Since taking risks earns an individual social approval and respect, these secondary reinforcers stimulate him to look for challenges he can meet. The repeated association of meeting challenges and obtaining these social rewards makes meeting a challenge, through a process of reverse secondary reinforcement, intrinsically rewarding, motivating individuals to seek out challenging situations even when they are alone. Since the process, in which rewards rooted in the individual organism give rise to socially rooted rewards is a type of secondary reinforcement, the process in which social rewards give rise to new

---

[7] See Goffman, *op. cit.,* pp. 66–79.

rewards that inhere in the individual might be designated as reverse secondary reinforcement.

A Paradox of Integration

In a group situation, impressive qualities make a person attractive in one sense and unattractive in another, because they raise fears of rejection and pose a status threat for the rest of the group. Since we are most impressed by qualities that are superior to our own and that other people also find impressive, an individual who possesses such qualities may well find ours unimpressive and know that he can impress many others, giving us good reason to fear his rejection. If he is attracted to our group, there is, of course, no imminent danger of rejection, but there is the well-founded suspicion that such an impressive person cannot be kept in the group without paying the price of superior status to him. The rewards expected from associating with an impressive person that make him attractive also would make us dependent on him and subject to his control. For it is in the nature of rewarding social experiences to produce simultaneously social attraction and social dependence.[8] Paradoxically, the very attributes that make a person an attractive associate for others also raise fears of dependence that make them reluctant to acknowledge their attraction.

This point requires elaboration lest it be oversimplified. A person who establishes unifying links with the members of a group by showing that he has interests in common with them and holds values they share proves himself an attractive companion without posing a status threat. The newcomer to an established group tends to employ precisely these strategies and other unthreatening ones, such as ingratiating himself through flattering remarks, to gain social acceptance. Such strategies, however, can only succeed in eliciting a bare minimum of social attraction. Whereas the insecure newcomer may feel constrained to confine himself to them, the members of a newly forming group, none of whose social position is more insecure than that of the rest (although psychological differences in feelings of security exist, of course), often resort to more aggressive tactics to establish themselves as valuable associates. They seek to differentiate their attractiveness from that of most people by impressing others with qualities that command respect.

---

[8] See John W. Thibaut and Harold H. Kelley, *The Social Psychology of Groups*, New York: Wiley, 1959, pp. 21–24 and 66.

A colleague who commands professional respect, for example, is a more attractive social companion than one who does not, if only because his conversations promise to be more interesting. The mere fact that they respect him does not make others dependent on and subordinate to him. His stimulating discussions of professional problems in front of a group are amply repaid by their expressions of appreciation and respect for his expertness. If some of them should repeatedly ask his advice on their problems, however, they would become obligated to him, and in the long run their dependence on him would probably require them to comply with his requests. The obligation to defer to the wishes of an expert on whose guidance others have come to depend is what detracts from his attractiveness as a sociable companion for them. Deference to another impedes relaxed sociability with him. Although respect for another as such does not, these processes have feedback effects. The respected expert is expected to make important contributions to the group as a whole as well as to its individual members. These impending contributions lead both the others and the expert to anticipate that they will become obligated to him. In anticipation of their future dependence, others may not feel entirely free with a person whom they highly respect even before they have actually become obligated to assume a subordinate role in relation to him.

What poses the paradox of social integration, then, is that the impressive qualities that make a person a particularly attractive and valuable group member also constitute a status threat to the rest. The result is a defensive reluctance to let oneself be easily impressed, and this reluctance is an important strategy in the competition for social recognition characteristic of early stages of group formation. As group members seek to impress each other with their outstanding attractiveness as associates, they enter into competition with each other. In contrast to competition in economic markets, where the competitors of a firm rarely are identical with the customers for whose purchases the firm competes, each group member's competitors in the competition for social recognition are the same individuals for whose attraction and esteem he competes. The more successful A is in impressing B and earning B's high regard, the more displeasure he causes to C whose relative standing in the eyes of B has suffered. All group members simultaneously play the role of A, B, and C in this schema, which greatly complicates the competitive process. Every member has an interest in withholding evidence of having been greatly impressed by the qualities of others, since his manifestations of high regard for their qualities would give them a competitive advantage over him by contributing to their standing in the group.

This competition can be conceptualized as a series of interlocking, mixed games, in which group members have some common and some conflicting interests. If the members are attracted to the group and to each other, they have a common interest in establishing and maintaining social relations. A simplified conception of the forces that sustain a social association is that at least one of the two associates must be highly attracted to the other. If each has high regard for the other, a peer relationship exists; but if only one has high regard for the other, it is the subordinate role he assumes that supports the relationship. It is assumed that each individual's first preference is to have social relations that are based on the high regard of the others, and in this respect they have conflicting interests, although each prefers relationships maintained by reciprocal regard to the termination of social interaction, which would be the result if neither partner were to manifest high regard for the other. The group member must choose between withholding expressions of his regard for the various other members, thereby endangering the continuation of his associations in an endeavor to achieve superordinate status, and expressing high regard for them to safeguard his associations at the cost of possibly having to assume a subordinate role and certainly not being able to attain a superordinate one. The individual's choice, which is not necessarily the same in regard to all other group members, is governed by his estimation of his chances of winning unilateral respect and by the relative value he places on the four possible outcomes. The situation can be schematized in the following pay-off matrix: [9]

	A's choice	
B's choice	*Expressing regard*	*Withholding regard*
Expressing regard	Peer relation (2nd choice of both)	A superior to B (A's first choice)
Withholding regard	B superior to A (B's first choice)	No relation (Last choice of both)

---

[9] For the extensive use of such matrices in two theories of social behavior, see Thibaut and Kelley, *op. cit.*, and Thomas C. Schelling, *The Strategy of Conflict*, Cambridge: Harvard University Press, 1960.

Although such a matrix grossly oversimplifies the social situation, it does highlight the implications of various strategies. If each individual chooses the strategy that can yield him his first preference (withholding expressions of high regard, since only it can produce superior status), both end up with their least preferred choice (no relation). If each adopts the strategy that averts the danger of maximum possible loss (no relation), both express regard for the other and a peer relation becomes established. The most dynamic elements of the group processes under consideration, however, escape this type of schematization. Group members do not decide on strategies a priori without any knowledge of the strategies of others, but they are in continual interaction and recurrently modify their behavior in response to the preceding actions of others.[10] Social communication furnishes clues about the chances of achieving superior status in a group, and it provides opportunities for reaching agreements that maximize joint advantage. Moreover, the existence of many such interlocking games—there would be forty-five in a group of ten—alters the situation as the outcomes in some affect the conditions in others. The individual who has succeeded in commanding the respect of some group members, for example, has improved his chances of success in impressing others. Finally, there is not merely a series of interlocking pair relations but a group structure with its own dynamics. Processes of association between individuals, such as their endeavors to impress one another, leave their imprint on the social structure, often in unanticipated ways, and the emergent structural conditions, in turn, modify subsequent processes of association.

The competition for social recognition in the early stages of group formation serves as a screening test for leadership and generally for the ability to make various contributions to the group. Although not all groups have specific objectives that require instrumental contributions, all do require some contributions to survive. Even such a fleeting grouping as a dinner party depends on some participants capable of stimulating the conversation. The competition that ensues when group members seek to prove themselves attractive to each other motivates them to reveal their most impressive qualities. This display of potential permits the group to discover the abilities different mem-

---

[10] Thibaut and Kelley qualify game theory in this important respect, as well as some others, by calling attention to the significance of successive moves and exploration, *op. cit.*, pp. 24–25, but their decision nevertheless to ignore sequential effects in the matrices that constitute the core of their analysis (p. 19) constitutes a serious limitation of their theory.

bers have for making needed contributions and to draw upon them. The competitive rivalry also motivates group members to question claims to superior abilities that seem unrealistic and to require evidence to back them up or to belittle attempts to appear impressive they suspect of being unwarranted. These competitive tactics improve the effectiveness of the screening test by discouraging exaggeration and deception and by making it unlikely that misleading impressions remain undetected.

Men who make essential contributions to a group as a whole, or to its members individually, have an undeniable claim to superior status. Interested as members are in withholding social recognition from others to protect their own standing in the group, they have an even greater interest in obtaining needed contributions, because the benefits they derive from group membership are contingent on these contributions. Without men to strengthen a union or organize a gang, to assist fellow workers or score for a basketball team, the members of these groups would be deprived of valued benefits. The obligations of group members to those who make such benefits possible are discharged by according them superior status. They command respect and compliance, which serve as rewards for having made contributions in the past and as incentives for continuing to make them in the future.

The emergent differentiation of status in the group intensifies the need for integrative bonds, particularly for those who do not command respect for their ability to make important contributions. Having to acknowledge the superior status of others undermines their own security and casts doubt on the impressive image they have attempted to convey. They have yet to gain full social acceptance, and their subordinate status increases their need for supportive bonds to secure their position in the group and bolster their self-confidence. Lack of success in proving themselves attractive by demonstrating outstanding abilities constrains them to turn to other means for doing so, and the fact that a number of group members find themselves in the same situation provides opportunities that make this possible.

In the course of impressing each other, these group members have shown that they have attractive qualities, although not the kind of superior qualities that promise great benefits for associates and thus force them to override their own defensive reluctance against acknowledging a former peer as their superior. The defensive reactions aroused by the claim to superior status implicit in appearing impressive can be overcome not only by making this claim undeniable but also by withdrawing it. Completely reversing their earlier strategy of revealing only their impressive qualities, these group members now flaunt their weaknesses. Whereas an individual usually conceals his shortcomings and less desirable traits on first acquaintance, he often readily admits them soon afterwards in sociable intercourse, long before the association has become intimate. Having first impressed us with his Harvard accent and Beacon Hill friends, he may later tell a story that reveals his immigrant background. After having talked only of the successes in his career, he may let us in on the defeats he has suffered. He no longer carefully protects himself against the slightest ridicule but may now tell some jokes at his own expense.[11]

Such self-depreciating modesty is disarming—literally so since it obviates the need for defenses. As the listeners sympathize with a person's troubles or smile at his blunders, they feel drawn to him because he ceases to be a status threat against which they must protect themselves. By calling attention to his weaknesses, a person gives public notice that he withdraws from the competition for superior standing in the group and that he considers acceptance as a peer sufficient reward for his attractive qualities and for whatever contribution they enable him to make. When many group members surrender their claim to superior status and appeal for peer group acceptance, their latent feelings of attraction—inasmuch as they were initially attracted to and discovered further attractive traits in each other—are freed from the restraints imposed by fear of loss of status. They consequently are prone to establish mutual bonds, which meet their needs for social acceptance and support and constitute the basis of social integration.

To be sure, self-depreciation does not always promote sympathy and social acceptance; under some circumstances, it has the opposite effect of producing discomfort and rejection. If an individual whose outstanding qualities we appreciate modestly admits some shortcomings, it will strengthen our regard for and attraction to him and not cause us any discomfort. But if an individual whom we do not find attractive insists on telling us about his shortcomings, it tends to embarrass us and incline us to withdraw from his company. The reason is that his exhibition of modesty is a claim for acceptance but our lack of attraction to him prevents us from honoring this claim, and

---

[11] This reversal of strategy is nicely illustrated by a passage of Evelyn Waugh in which the speaker describes his wife as adept in "first impressing the impressionable with her chic and my celebrity and, superiority once firmly established, changing quickly to a pose of almost flirtatious affability." *Brideshead Revisited,* New York: Dell, 1956. p. 220.

when the expectations of one person are not fulfilled by others, embarrassment arises, as Goffman has pointed out.[12] A display of his deficiencies does not make a person attractive; such self-effacement can only activate already existing feelings of attraction that have been suppressed. Hence, unless the weaknesses to which a group member calls attention are less significant than the attractive qualities he has exhibited, he will not have succeeded in demonstrating to others that he is approachable as a peer as well as attractive but only in convincing them that he is fundamentally not an attractive associate at all.

Group members who have achieved high status also tend to engage in self-depreciation. While their abilities and contributions earn them respect and obligate others to follow their suggestions, these obligations are experienced as restraints, which inhibit sociable interaction and create some social distance between the leading group members and the rest. Rewarding as high esteem is, it is still more rewarding to be not only esteemed but liked and fully accepted as well. Besides, leaders in small groups depend on their followers for supportive bonds because there are no distinct leadership subgroups that can provide them. The modest leader, who freely admits his inferiority to others in some respects, rewards them by acknowledging their superior abilities and mitigates the burden of their subordination by not insisting on maintaining superiority over them in every way. It is easy to exhibit such modesty for the person whose status is securely anchored, since doing so cannot endanger his position. On the contrary, his modesty is likely to earn the leader the approval and loyalty of his followers to complement the respect his abilities command, and thus to increase the effectiveness of his leadership. As long as several members of superior status compete for leadership in the group, moreover, their appealing modesty is, in fact, a strategy to win group support in this competition.

Frankness is often infectious, especially when it proves effective in gaining acceptance in a peer group. An individual who ceases to try to appear impressive invites others to follow his example, and the more group members do so, the easier it becomes for the rest to do the same. The first person in a circle with intellectual pretensions who admits that he prefers watching television to going to the symphony modestly admits a weakness. His frankness may well encourage others to acknowledge their low-brow tastes. Now for still others to join in and tell of their fondness for Westerns or wrestling or comics no

---

[12] Goffman, "Embarrassment," *American Journal of Sociology*, 62 (1956), 264–271.

longer involves self-depreciating modesty but represents attempts to establish common links with the rest, which permit group members to relax and enjoy each other's company. The common interests discovered in this process—be they baseball, art, or pacifism—are an important source of the integrative bonds that unite the group. To be sure, the ideals and purposes that initially bring men together constitute the unifying bonds of the groups they form. In groups without explicit objectives of this kind, however, the discovery of common links is essential for the development of social integration, and this discovery tends to be made when group members withdraw from the competition for status.

In brief, processes of competition and social differentiation create strains that increase the need for integrative ties in groups. As some group members find it necessary to withdraw from the competition for superior status, they establish integrative bonds which become the foundation of group solidarity. Social solidarity rooted in bonds of fellowship makes important contributions to groups that have instrumental objectives as well as to those that are primarily sociable in character. Large-scale participation in a union or a political party, for example, which promotes the effectiveness of the organization, and without which it cannot be democratically governed, is contingent on such integrative ties. Unless active participation is motivated not only by the prospect of commanding respect and attaining positions of leadership but also by gratifications derived from working with like-minded men in a common cause, it will be inevitably restricted to a small minority. Associations have to be intrinsically attractive for large-scale participation to occur, and integrative bonds of fellowship make them so. Some group members must compete for superior status to furnish a screening device for effective leadership, but to maintain social integration there must be many who do not participate in this competition. The members who cease to compete for superior status win social acceptance in the group in exchange for the contribution they thereby make to group solidarity.

Testing Some Inferences

Outstanding attributes are not an unambiguous asset for establishing friendly relations in a group, because they tend to make an individual a status threat and somewhat unapproachable as well as attractive. Common sense would lead one to expect that the group member two of whose attributes others find attractive is more likely to be befriended by the rest than the member who has only one of these two positive qualities, and that the one without either is least likely to attain friendly acceptance in the peer-group fellowship. The inference derived from the theory presented, in contrast, is that group members who have positive characteristics on a salient attribute, which make them attractive, but *negative* ones on a less salient attribute, which also make them approachable, have the best chance to win informal acceptance; correspondingly, those who are negative on a more salient and positive on a less salient attribute should have the least chance. Interview data from twelve work groups in a welfare agency were used to test this inference.[13]

The sixty caseworkers in these twelve groups were classified, for each comparison made (that is, in each table), on the basis of two characteristics as the independent variables and their informal acceptance as the dependent variable, the measure of the dependent variable being whether others in his own group were on a first-name basis with a given individual. Sociometric measures, such as popularity and being respected among colleagues, were used to indicate the more salient attribute, and background characteristics, such as seniority and class origin (father's occupation) as the indications of the less salient attribute. The prediction implied by the theory is that first-name informality is most prevalent among individuals who have a positive quality on the more salient and a negative one on the less salient factor and that first-name informality is least prevalent among those positive on the less and negative on the more salient attribute. Of 18 cross-tabulations examined, 15 confirmed this prediction.[14]

Of special interest is an experiment by Jones and his colleagues that was explicitly designed, in part, to test some inferences of the theory presented, a version of which had been previously published.[15] The experimenters wanted to test the tendency to ingratiate oneself as affected by differences in status between individuals and in the amount of pressure to achieve mutual compatibility or, in our terminology, social integration. For this purpose, seventy-nine Naval R.O.T.C. students at Duke University were used as subjects in pairs composed of one upperclassman and one freshman, the high-status and low-status individual, respectively. In the experiment, each subject sat in

[13] Blau, "A Theory of Social Integration," *American Journal of Sociology,* 65 (1960), 550–553.

[14] Since not all 18 tests were independent of each other, however, the finding furnishes only suggestive support for the inference

[15] Edward E. Jones, Kenneth G. Gergen, and Robert G. Jones, "Tactics of Ingratiation Among Leaders and Subordinates in a Status Hierarchy," *Psychological Monographs,* 77 (1963), whole No. 566.

a private booth and received standardized, written communications presumably from his partner and sent to his partner written evaluations of himself, opinions on various issues, and evaluations of the partner. The experimental variable, which was, in effect, pressure to become integrated, was introduced through instructions given in advance. All subjects were told that each pair consists of a commander (the senior) and a subordinate (the freshman) and that their partner had expressed a preference for working with them. The central sentence in the talk to the experimental group was: "After forming the pairs, in other words, we want to find out whether the commander ends up thinking highly of the subordinate and whether the subordinate ends up liking and respecting the commander." The talk to the control group, on the other hand, stressed: "We are not especially concerned with whether you end up liking each other or not. . . . We are interested only in how well you can do in reaching a clear impression of the other person." [16]

To measure self-presentation and self-depreciation, subjects were given a list of twenty-four pairs of antonyms, such as forceful-weak, and asked to check their own characteristics, and also to indicate those they considered most important, the ratings being presumably sent to the partners. Separate scores for the important and unimportant items were computed. Most subjects, notably those in the control condition, rated themselves more highly on the important than on the unimportant attributes, which suggests that they tried to impress their partners. By and large, the self-ratings of the subjects were more modest in the experimental than in the control condition, which implies that pressure toward integration promotes self-depreciation. A specific hypothesis tested was that superiors are more likely than subordinates to rate themselves lower on unimportant than on important items under pressure to become integrated, since by doing so they prove themselves approachable associates while maintaining respect, and the results confirmed this hypothesis. But what is of particular interest is the overall pattern of findings.

Pressure to win social acceptance made both superiors and subordinates more modest about those of their qualities they considered important; it lessened the tendency to appear very impressive. This pressure, however, had opposite effects on superiors and subordinates in unimportant areas. Whereas the experimentally introduced integra-

---

[16] *Ibid.*, p. 5. Although limitations of the experimental design, to which the authors call attention in a concluding "Apologia," make the implications of findings somewhat equivocal, the results are very suggestive for the theory presented.

tion pressure made superiors more modest about their unimportant qualities too, it made subordinates less modest in regard to qualities they considered not important. As a result, subordinates under integration pressure presented self-ratings in unimportant areas that were not only less modest than those of subordinates in the control condition but also less modest than those of superiors under integration pressure. Apparently, concern with winning social acceptance and approval prompted subjects in inferior positions to depreciate their own important qualities, as a demonstration that they did not seek to challenge their partner's superior status; and it led them simultaneously to emphasize that they have some impressive qualities, albeit not in the most important areas, in order to prove themselves sufficiently attractive associates. The secure status of the superiors, which was firmly grounded in their advanced standing as naval trainees and college students, permitted them to be more modest in all areas. On issues relevant to their superordinate position, however, superiors exhibited little conciliatory modesty in their judgments.

Agreeing with the opinions of others is a way of making oneself attractive to them. The authors of the experimental report reasoned plausibly that this method is more congenial for subordinates than for superiors and hence hypothesized that the low-status subjects would conform to the opinions of the highs more than the high-status subjects would conform to the opinions of the lows and that such conformity would generally increase under integration pressure. To measure conformity with the partner's opinions, twelve statements that presumably came from the partner and that differed considerably from the opinions known to be prevalent among these college students were presented to every subject, and he was asked to indicate his agreement with each opinion on a twelve-point rating scale for transmission to the partner. Inasmuch as subjects were expected actually to disagree with most of the opinions presented, the degree of agreement expressed was taken as the measure of conformity to the partner's opinions. Some of the statements pertained to the Navy, some to academic life, and some to general issues.

Generally, the subjects were influenced by the statements they attributed to their partners, that is, they checked statements that were closer to the bogus opinions they had received than were the opinions known to have prevailed in the student population from which they were drawn. On the average, subjects conformed more under integration pressure than without, and subordinates expressed more agreement with the opinions of superiors than superiors did with those of subordinates, confirming the hypotheses. Here again, however, these average differences conceal the most interesting interaction effects. The subordinates did not conform in all respects to the opinions of superiors; indeed, in some areas the superiors were the ones who expressed most conciliatory agreement with the opinions of subordinates.

On items concerned with naval problems, which are directly relevant to the status difference between subjects, superiors insisted on their own judgment, and even integration pressure hardly induced them to move toward closer agreement with subordinates. Subordinates were considerably more likely than superiors to conform with the bogus opinions on naval issues in the control condition, and the experimentally induced integration pressure moved their statements still further away from what probably was their own viewpoint toward increasing conformity. On academic items, however, the difference was small, and on general items it became reversed, that is, the superiors had a somewhat *greater* tendency to conform to the opinions of subordinates on miscellaneous topics than the subordinates had to conform to the opinions of superiors. In matters irrelevant to the status hierarchy, then, superiors were willing to compromise their own beliefs in a conciliatory gesture of moving toward closer, although not full, agreement with subordinates. High status requires firm judgments on issues that directly pertain to the basis of the superior position, in disregard of the contrary opinions of subordinates and of the pressure to court their approval. To compensate for this insistence on contradicting their ideas, superiors made concessions to subordinates in other areas, modifying their opinions to bring them into greater harmony with that of subordinates, and modestly depreciated their own important as well as unimportant qualities in response to the pressure to win the approval of subordinates.

These findings go beyond the hypothesis that conformity with the opinions of others is a means for proving oneself attractive that is more often employed by low-status than by high-status individuals. As a matter of fact, the experimental data are not particularly well suited to test this hypothesis. Since superior status in a given area implies that a person's judgments in this area will prevail over those of subordinates, the finding that this is the case does not constitute specific evidence that low-status individuals are more likely than high-status individuals to conform in order to ingratiate themselves and gain social acceptance. To test the hypothesis that lows are more likely to conform than highs *because* doing so is a more appropriate method of winning social approval and for becoming integrated for low-status than for high-status individuals, it is necessary to isolate the significance of conformity as a strategy for earning approval from the tendency to agree with the statements of a person whose status and presumed competence are the inverse of one's own. This can be done by comparing the conformity of the highs and the lows to the same general group pressure rather than to one another's opinions. Several studies that made such comparisons found that individuals with low informal status were more likely to conform to group pressures than those whose informal status was high,[17] confirming the hypothesis. Low status in a group constrains an individual to conform lest he antagonize others, whereas the contributions and power high status implies permit a person greater latitude, since the dependence of others on him restrains them from penalizing him for minor deviations.[18]

A final method of ingratiating oneself examined by Jones and his colleagues was flattery. They hypothesized that the superiors would be more prone to resort to flattery than the subordinates, arguing that subordinates would be reluctant to flatter superiors for fear of appearing to be sycophants, and they expected integration pressure to increase this tendency. On a form identical to that used for self-ratings subjects were asked to rate their partners, the assumption being that the form would be sent to their partners. Favorability scores derived from these forms served as index of flattery. The results did not confirm the hypothesis. The ratings of partners were more favorable in the experimental condition of integration pressure than in the control condition, but this was particularly so for the low-status subjects, and the lows were more flattering in their ratings of the highs than the highs were in their ratings of the lows. It seems that the imposing nature of superior status and its halo-effect exert more influence on the orientations of subordinates than the fear of giving the appearance of a sycophant. Indeed, unsparing approval of others

---

[17] See, for example, Harold H. Kelley and M. M. Shapiro, "An Experiment on Conformity to Group Norms Where Conformity is Detrimental to Group Achievement," *American Sociological Review*, 19 (1954), 667–677; and Blau, "Patterns of Deviation in Work Groups," *Sociometry*, 23 (1960), 245–261.

[18] Some studies, however, obtained a direct relationship between high status and conformity (see *ibid.* for references to them), perhaps because conformity with basic values, as distinguished from conformity to the prevailing climate of opinion, is mandatory and only outcasts are likely to deviate from them. In any case, there is a need for further clarification of the relationship between status and conformity and the conditions that affect it (such as the type of norm and the type of status under consideration).

is incompatible with superior status, whereas inferior status encourages giving approval freely, as will be seen in chapter three.

In sum, the experimental results indicate that pressure to establish integrative bonds promotes the tendency of individuals to please others by making favorable comments about their characteristics and by conforming with their opinions and that it fosters self-depreciating modesty. Under this pressure, individuals whose status is inferior depreciate those qualities of theirs that might be interpreted as a status threat and simultaneously try to demonstrate that they do have some impressive qualities in order to prove themselves attractive associates. Individuals whose status is superior hold to their own judgments on status-relevant matters in disregard of group pressures, whereas inferiors do not, but the superiors seek to pacify others, whose opinions in these matters they have rejected, through conciliatory agreement with their other opinions and through modest self-depreciation under pressure to maintain social integration. These findings generally support the theory presented and refine it, notably by suggesting that the person whose status is secure is the one who depreciates his own qualities most extensively, probably in part because his evident superiority obviates any need to stress that he has attractive qualities and in part because he must counteract the antagonism his insistence on his own judgment in status-relevant areas may well arouse.

Conclusions

In the course of group formation processes of social integration give rise to differentiating processes, and social differentiation, in turn, stimulates the development of social integration. The attempts of individuals to prove themselves attractive associates in a newly forming group promote competition for being highly esteemed among them. Their competitive endeavors to impress each other reveal that some have qualities that enable them to make essential contributions to the group, and these abilities to make contributions become the source of superior status in the group. The emergent differentiation of status intensifies the need for social integration, which is met when most group members withdraw from the competition for status and establish mutual ties of fellowship. These integrative bonds, reinforced by the shared interests discovered in the process of establishing them and by the common objectives or ideals that brought group members together, are the basis of group cohesion.

Social integration in groups poses a paradox. For social acceptance requires some outstanding qualities that make an individual a differentially attractive associate, but outstanding qualities raise fears of dependence that inhibit acceptance as a sociable companion. Even group members who are interested only in being accepted as peers—and many are, of course, also interested in attaining superior status—have strong inducements to display impressive qualities to which others react with ambivalence. The individual with superior abilities can make important contributions to the group as a whole, but by doing so he displaces other members from a superior position. The rewards they obtain collectively from his contributions and the rewards they forego individually as the result of his superior status combine to produce their ambivalent attitude toward him, which is likely to be most pronounced among those of relatively high status, whom he directly threatens to displace. Although contributions of undeniable significance constrain others to accord superior status to a person, doing so leaves a residue of resentment. Superiors often depreciate their own abilities and express conciliatory agreement in order to lessen the resentment of group members forced to occupy subordinate positions. Group members whose abilities do not command great respect also depreciate some of their qualities, in their case to demonstrate they have surrendered any claim to superior status, but they simultaneously emphasize that they have some impressive qualities, though less important ones, to prove themselves attractive. This double strategy of appearing both impressive and self-depreciating in order to win social acceptance reflects the paradox of social integration.

Group cohesion depends on somewhat incompatible conditions, and this is what produces the paradox. Acceptance as a sociable companion requires that an individual have attractive qualities and that he not pose a status threat, but outstanding qualities that make him especially attractive also pose a status threat. Similarly, the solidarity of the group depends on contributions to its goals and on integrative bonds among its members, but the differentiation of status necessary to provide incentives for making contributions is detrimental for integrative bonds of fellowship. Many social phenomena rest on incompatible conditions that pose a paradox and create dilemmas, as will be seen in the discussion of such topics as social approval, love, leadership, opposition, and substructures in the following chapters. These dilemmas rooted in incompatible requirements of social phenomena are the source of much of the dynamics of social life.

Social processes often have a variety of feedback effects, since human beings anticipate the consequences of social interaction on the basis of previous experience and take them into account even before they occur. Thus a person whose superior abilities command respect is expected to make contributions that obligate others to him, and the anticipation of their dependence may inhibit easygoing sociability with him in advance of having actually incurred obligations to him. The experience of winning social approval for the ability to take risks and meet difficult challenges appears to make, through a process of reverse secondary reinforcement, the meeting of a challenge intrinsically gratifying. If others do not know how difficult a task is, we impress them by conveying the difficulty through appearing tense and strained while performing it, but once they do appreciate the difficulty, we impress them more by performing it with ease. In parallel fashion, as long as the great talent of a man is not known to others he can impress them only by directing attention to it, but once they do know of it he can impress them more by modestly depreciating it.[19] The fact that a baseline for expectations has been established has a feedback effect on behavior in social associations, as will be more fully discussed in the analysis of the implications of first impressions in chapter three.

Finally, an individual may be attracted to others either because associating with them is intrinsically gratifying or because the association furnishes extrinsic benefits for him. This distinction between intrinsically and extrinsically rewarding social associations, which is of fundamental importance, can be considered a special case of Parsons' more general distinction between particularism and universalism.[20] The basic criterion is whether individuals are oriented toward an association as a means to some further end, as when they request a neighbor's help, or as an end-in-itself, as when they simply socialize with him. Extrinsic benefits constitute standards for comparing associations and deciding between them, whereas no such independent criteria of comparison exist for intrinsically rewarding associations.

---

[19] Aristotle already called attention to the use of modesty as a means of impressing others: "and sometimes such mock humility seems to be really boastfulness, like the dress of the Spartans, for extreme negligence in dress, as well as excessive attention to it, has a touch of ostentation. But a moderate use of self-depreciation in matters not too commonplace and obvious has a not ungracious air." *The Nicomachean Ethics*, London: William Heinemann, 1926, p. 245 (Book IV, vii, 15–16).

[20] For an early reference, see Parsons, *Essays in Sociological Theory*, Glencoe: Free Press, 1949, pp. 185–199 (originally published in 1939). The most systematic discussion is in Parsons and Edward A. Shils, *Toward a General Theory of Action*, Cambridge: Harvard University Press, 1951, pp. 76–88.

Since any aspect of a social association that is experienced as rewarding, however, can be analytically distinguished from the association itself, the significance of an association is purely intrinsic only when a variety of rewards that it provides have become fused and thus inseparable from it. Hence, the initial attraction between individuals always rests on the expectation of rewards that are, analytically, extrinsic and that make comparisons between potential associates possible. But once social relations have become established, they often rest primarily on either intrinsic or extrinsic rewards, as exemplified by the supportive and the exchange relations, respectively, to be discussed in the next two chapters.

THREE

Social Support

But Swann said to himself that, if he could make Odette feel (by consenting to meet her only after dinner) that there were other pleasures which he preferred to that of her company, then the desire that she felt for his would be all the longer in reaching the point of satiety. . . .

He made what apology he could and hurried home, overjoyed that the satisfaction of his curiosity had preserved their love intact, and that, having feigned for so long, when in Odette's company, a sort of indifference, he had not now, by a demonstration of jealousy, given her that proof of the excess of his own passion which, in a pair of lovers, fully and finally dispenses the recipient from the obligation to love the other enough.

MARCEL PROUST, *Swann's Way*

Integrative bonds of social cohesion strengthen the group in the pursuit of common goals. Group cohesion promotes the development of consensus on normative standards and the effective enforcement of these shared norms, because integrative ties of fellowship enhance the significance of the informal sanctions of the group, such as disapproval and ostracism, for its individual members. Cohesion, therefore, increases social control and coordination, as a number of studies have shown. One experiment, for example, demonstrated that integrative bonds between individuals make it more likely for them to reach consensus in discussions after initial disagreement.[1] A field study

---

[1] Kurt W. Back, "Influence through Social Communication," *Journal of Abnormal and Social Psychology*, 46 (1951), 9–23.

of two student housing projects found that once distinctive group norms had formed, cohesion, as measured by ingroup sociometric choices, was inversely related to the proportion of deviants from these norms, which indicates that cohesion promoted group control.[2] Although cohesion in work groups is not consistently related to high productivity, since some groups encourage and others restrict high output, a study of 228 industrial work groups obtained an inverse correlation between a group's cohesion and the variation in the productivity of its members, which suggests that the members of cohesive groups conformed more closely to common output standards.[3]

Group cohesion is an important source of social support as well as of normative control. To be sure, these two implications of cohesion are related, since it is the threatened loss of extensive social support that serves as an effective control mechanism in cohesive groups. But social support exerts an independent influence on conduct, which is distinct from that of the enforcement of conformity. Whereas social control strengthens the group as a whole, social support strengthens its members individually, particularly in relation to outsiders. The results of one experiment, for instance, indicate that peer group support facilitates expressing aggression and opposition against an interfering power figure.[4] In a study of a welfare agency, the social support in cohesive work groups was found to make caseworkers more independent of clients and more impersonal in their approach to them than were workers in less cohesive groups.[5] In unity lies strength, for the collectivity as a whole and for its individual members, and it is the social support unifying bonds furnish that is an important source of this strength.

This chapter is concerned with two related elements of social support—social approval and intrinsic attraction. The conditions that determine expressions of approval and attraction in interpersonal relations will be examined, as will the processes in which these two components of social support manifest themselves. These are social rewards that, although they enter into reciprocal transactions, cannot

[2] Leon Festinger, Stanley Schachter, and Kurt Back, *Social Pressures in Informal Groups,* New York: Harper, 1950, chapter v.

[3] Stanley E. Seashore, *Group Cohesiveness in the Industrial Work Group,* Ann Arbor: Institute for Social Research, University of Michigan, 1954.

[4] Ezra Stotland, "Peer Groups and Reactions to Power Figures," in Dorwin Cartwright, *Studies in Social Power,* Ann Arbor: Institute for Social Research, University of Michigan, 1959, pp. 53–68.

[5] Blau and W. Richard Scott, *Formal Organizations,* San Francisco: Chandler, 1962, pp. 107–108.

be directly bartered in exchange without losing their intrinsic value. The analysis, therefore, will help to indicate the boundary of explicit social exchange and to distinguish social transactions of intrinsic from those of primarily extrinsic significance.

Social Approval

Men are anxious to receive social approval for their decisions and actions, for their opinions and suggestions. The approving agreement of others helps to confirm their judgments, to justify their conduct, and to validate their beliefs. Factual decisions, which are either true or false in terms of an outside criterion, often engender doubts and anxieties regarding their correctness, which are dispelled if associates whose judgment is respected concur in the decision. The values of men that govern their opinions and behavior cannot be considered true or false on the basis of any objective criterion, but this makes it even more important to receive the confirming approval of others. For it is the stamp of approval social agreement bestows on our values that validates them.[6] Social consensus defines beliefs as right or wrong. Although it is possible for men to maintain convictions in the face of contrary public opinion, it is most difficult to do so; and the more at odds a man's beliefs are with prevailing values, the more important it is for him to receive some social support to sustain them.

Since social approval is of great significance, it constitutes an important social reward and a basic source of social influence. To earn social approval, men often modify their opinions, change their conduct, seek to improve their judgment, and devote efforts to making contributions to the welfare of others. The rewarding experience of receiving social approval for one's opinions encourages men to express opinions more freely.[7] But the significance of social approval depends on its being accepted as genuine. In contrast to many other social rewards, therefore, social approval is not expected to be bartered in exchange for other rewards. Whereas it is quite proper for an individual to be prompted to offer help or accede to another's wishes, for example, by the gratitude or other benefits he receives in return, he

---

[6] See Leon Festinger, "A Theory of Social Comparison Processes," *Human Relations*, 7 (1954), 117–140.

[7] Thus an experiment by William S. Verplank found that subjects with whose opinions others regularly agreed increased the rate of stating opinions; "The Control of the Content of Conversation," *Journal of Abnormal and Social Psychology*, 51 (1955), 668–676.

is not expected to be motivated to give approval by a desire to make others grateful or obligated to him.[8] If others suspect that he furnishes approval merely to please them and not because it reflects his actual judgment of their behavior, his approval loses its significance.

Valuables that are not for sale create the problems and temptations symbolized by simony and prostitution. Salvation cannot be bought, nor can love, but its great significance may prompt men to seek to buy at least its appurtenances. Priceless spiritual benefits are worth much to men, and this exposes those who have the power to dispense them to the temptation of offering them for a price. By supplying goods that moral standards define as invaluable for a price in the market, individuals prostitute themselves and destroy the central value of what they have to offer, leaving only some by-products—not love but merely sex, not spiritual blessing but merely spiritual office. The importance of approval produces social pressures to give it more freely. As a result, some individuals simulate approval of others and flatter them to ingratiate themselves. Even those who do not yield to the temptation of simulating approval to gain advantage, however, are under pressure to relax their standards and not restrict expressions of approval to behavior that meets their highest ideals.

Social approval is the general term, whereas respect or esteem refers to a specific type of approval. The distinguishing characteristics of respect are that it entails *unilateral* approval of *abilities* presumably judged by objective standards. Approval of beliefs and opinions is frequently reciprocal, since we tend to approve of the orientations of others whose values are similar to our own and they tend to approve of ours. The abilities of a person command the respect of others, however, if his abilities are superior to theirs, which implies that the others' abilities do not command his respect, at least not as far as the same abilities are concerned. Respecting a person means looking up to him, and if his standing requires others to look up to him, theirs cannot require him to look up to them, too, although he may admire their skills in debating, while they admire his as a quarterback. Finally, the term respect denotes a positive evaluation of a person's ability in a given area or his abilities in general, whereas the term approval is more appropriate for a positive evaluation of specific

---

[8] Even compliance with a person's suggestions, which has extrinsic significance and may be bartered, is apparently valued more if it is assumed to be genuine, that is, to be motivated by internal reasons rather than primarily by external pressures. See John W. Thibaut and Henry W. Riecken, "Some Determinants and Consequences of Social Causality," *Journal of Personality,* 24 (1955), 113–133.

judgments or actions. We approve of given decisions, while we respect the ability to make correct decisions regularly.

The significance that a person's approval has for others depends not only on their acceptance of it as genuine but also on two other conditions, namely, their respect for his judgment and the discrimination he exhibits in furnishing approval. These factors are related. If rather poor decisions as well as very good ones receive a man's approval, his approval does not provide incentive for learning to make better decisions, and it loses much of its significance. Such lack of discrimination in offering approval leads others to question a person's judgment, with the result that their respect for him suffers. The recurring disapproval expressed by superiors who adhere to strict standards protects the value of their approval from becoming deflated. To command respect for his judgment and safeguard the value of his approval, a person must use it sparingly.

Superior status, whether it rests on the respect a person commands or on his official position of power, makes his approval important for others. The high value of his approval permits him to use it sparingly despite group pressures for greater leniency, although there are, of course, individual differences in the tendency to yield to these pressures. The individual who neither occupies a superior official position nor is highly respected is under constraints to use his less valuable approbation more freely. His approval is not in great demand, particularly not by those whose competence enables them to receive praise from more respected persons. Hence, for his approval to have any impact at all, he must be willing to furnish it for decisions of only mediocre quality. The fair artist's praise is not particularly salient for Picasso, nor is the junior executive's very important for the senior executive. To make their approval a salient influence, persons of lower rank themselves must grant it for less outstanding performances than do those of higher rank. Besides, the golfer who shoots in the eighties, to alter the illustration, cannot gracefully withhold admiration for the one whose score is close to par, while the champion golfer can. The lower a man's status, consequently, the more incentive he has to express his approval freely, and his doing so further decreases respect for his judgment. Empirical support for these principles is provided by two research findings. One study indicated that the most respected members of discussion groups were less likely to agree with others, that is, approve of their decisions, and somewhat more likely to disagree, than the rest.[9] Another set of studies found that the most

---

[9] Philip E. Slater, "Role Differentiation in Small Groups," *American Sociological Review*, 20 (1955), 305.

effective informal leaders discriminated in their approval of followers more than others.[10] Initial differences in respect and social standing promote tendencies in the expression of approval that are likely to intensify these differences.

Since people greatly value the approval of others whom they respect, they can hardly help being displeased when they fail to receive it, not only with themselves but also with those who withheld approval. The person who husbands his approval to protect its value against depreciation, therefore, does so at some cost to his popularity. This is the dilemma of judging associates and their performances, which is related to the paradox of integration discussed in chapter two. Men who explicitly or implicitly present something they have done to a close associate for his evaluation expect both supportive approval for their performance and assistance with further improving it from him, but the two are not compatible. The associate's approval furnishes social support and dispels their anxieties about their performance, and it is likely to increase their positive feelings for him. His penetrating criticism helps them to improve their performance, and it may well augment their respect for his judgment. Either alternative, however, also has negative implications for both parties. Supportive approval does not furnish the instrumental help they need, and it gives them no reason to increase their respect for his expert abilities. Criticisms, even constructive ones, are threatening inasmuch as they cast doubt on the ability to perform satisfactorily, and the defensive psychological reactions against being criticized can easily turn into negative attitudes toward the critic.[11] Our attempts to compromise by prefacing our criticisms with some soothing praise merely highlight the existence of the dilemma.

Furnishing support and supplying assistance are somewhat incompatible, as are winning affection and earning respect, not only in a

---

[10] Fred E. Fiedler, *Leader Attitudes and Group Effectiveness*, Urbana: University of Illinois Press, 1958.

[11] One of the many aspects of the negative implications of both alternatives is illustrated in this passage from "Within a Budding Grove": "But as there is always something to be said on both sides, if the pleasure, or at least the indifference shewn by our friends in repeating something offensive that they have heard said about us, proves that they do not exactly put themselves into our skin at the moment of speaking, but thrust in the pin-point, turn the knife-blade as though it were gold-beater's skin and not human, the art of always keeping hidden from us what might be disagreeable to us in what they heard and said about our actions, or in the opinion which those actions have led the speakers themselves to form of us, proves that there is in the other kind of friends, in the friends who are so full of tact, a strong vein of dissimulation." Marcel Proust, *Remembrance of Things Past*, New York: Random House, 1934, Vol. I, 692.

single encounter but still more so in the total pattern of associations between individuals. The person who applies strict standards of judgment that command respect displeases others by rarely offering supportive approval, and the one whose ready approval makes him a more congenial companion undermines respect for his judgment. Only after role expectations have become crystallized can men judge the performance of others without being greatly concerned over how their judgments will reflect on their own reputations. A leader whose expertness is widely acknowledged does not endanger respect for his judgment by praising the performance of followers, but a man whose status is not so secure does. The mutual support in close friendships is not threatened if one criticizes a friend's work, but in less firmly entrenched social relations critical assistance and social support are incompatible, and individuals usually obtain one from some associates and the other from different associates.[12] Professional or bureaucratic detachment has the function of preventing decisions on cases from being distorted by a concern with how these evaluations will affect one's own reputation, since it is designed to make the reactions of clients insignificant for, and sometimes entirely unknown to, the professional or official who has the responsibility of making judgments about them.

The differentiation of status in groups is accompanied by differences in the nature of the social approval that sustains the various social positions. Mutual approval of opinions and of conformity to group norms suffices as the basis for mere acceptance as a group member, but superior status requires that a member's abilities command unilateral respect. The social approval of a person's beliefs and values, regardless of how profound its significance is for him, does not help raise him to a superordinate position; only respect for his superior qualities does that. While moral superiority as well as superior instrumental competence command respect, sheer conformity with prevailing values does not. It only earns approval because, as Homans has noted, "what is important about conformity is not just that it is valuable but that it is in ample supply. Any old fool, so to speak, can conform, for many in fact do conform—including the very people that are giving approval in return." [13]

---

[12] For empirical data that suggest this conclusion, see Donald C. Pelz, "Some Factors Related to Performance in a Research Organization," *Administrative Science Quarterly*, 1 (1956), 310–325.

[13] George C. Homans, *Social Behavior,* New York: Harcourt, Brace and World, 1961, p. 146.

An individual's endeavors to gain social acceptance in a group are furthered most by the approval of highly respected group members, since their approving opinions of him influence the opinions of others and thus have a multiplier effect. Highly respected persons, however, tend to reserve their approval for outstanding qualifications and not to express it for mere conformity. To win their approbation, consequently, an individual must show that he has some superior abilities. The fact that even social acceptance is expedited by making an outstanding impression on others reinforces the tendency of new group members to demonstrate their impressive qualities, although acceptance as a peer does not require outstanding abilities and can be won, if more slowly, by establishing common links with other members, expressing opinions they share, and conforming to the prevailing norms among them.

Men do not necessarily accept as valid the evaluations others make of them and their performance. The appraisals of superiors are more likely to be accepted at face value than those of inferiors.[14] Whether men grant or question the accuracy of an evaluation of themselves governs their reactions to the evaluator. If they question the validity of another's approval, it tends to make them contemptuous of his attempt at flattery or his lack of discernment rather than pleased with his support. If they question the validity of another's disapproval, it tends to make them annoyed with his lack of appreciation for their abilities rather than grateful for his helpful suggestions for improvement. Since the judgments of a person who commands respect are more likely to be accepted as correct than those of one who does not, superiors have a better chance to earn gratitude with either their supportive approval or their critical suggestions for improvement, whereas inferiors take a greater risk of incurring contempt by their approving agreement or of provoking annoyance by their critical disagreement. Moreover, the displeasure caused by disapproval makes it more likely for negative than for positive evaluations to be rejected.[15] The expectation is, therefore, that individuals generally, and inferiors

---

[14] For a study that shows that suggestions of superiors, even if incorrect, are accepted in disproportionate numbers and those of inferiors, even if correct, are rejected in disproportionate numbers, see E. Paul Torrance, "Some Consequences of Power Differences on Decision Making in Permanent and Temporary Three-Man Groups," in A. Paul Hare, Edgar F. Borgatta, and Robert F. Bales, *Small Groups*, New York: Knopf, 1955, pp. 482–492.

[15] In the cynical words of François La Rochefoucauld, "Few men are wise enough to prefer helpful censure to treacherous praise." *The Maxims*, London: Oxford University Press, 1940, p. 49 (#147).

in particular, are less prone to express disapproval than approval, and empirical data on discussion groups confirm this expectation.[16]

Generalized approval of a person's performances becomes respect for his abilities. If nearly every task a person performs elicits our strong approval, we express, in fact, high regard for his competence. Such positive evaluations of another's abilities, however, may imply either that the evaluator has a superordinate status that qualifies him as a judge, as is the case when an instructor praises the talent of a student, or that the evaluator acknowledges that the other's abilities are superior to his own, as is the case when the scholarly expertness of a colleague commands the instructor's respect. The question arises as to what conditions determine whether a person's praise of another's skills reaffirms or negates the praiser's superiority. Actual differences in skills are important, provided that they are clearly evident, and so are pronounced differences in status that are presumed to rest on corresponding differences in abilities. But differences in abilities often cannot be readily measured, as illustrated by the difference between art experts in contrast to that between long-distance runners. In these cases, the crucial factor is the relative respect the abilities of the two parties command among others who are qualified to judge them. If a widely respected scientist highly praises the competence of a colleague with lesser standing in the scientific community, it may help raise this colleague's standing but does not threaten the widely respected scientist's. If, on the other hand, most scholars regularly express great admiration for the work of a colleague, the common respect they accord him establishes his professional standing as superior to theirs.

Superior status that is firmly rooted in the social structure—in a man's generally acknowledged expertness, his superior power, or his position of official authority—cannot be endangered by free expressions of approval of others, whereas insecure status that yet needs to be solidly anchored must be protected against the loss of respect entailed in the lack of discrimination in judgments. The inference is that persons whose superior status is secure give praise *more* freely

---

[16] In discussions scored in terms of the Bales interaction categories, agreements with others, which imply approval, are about ten times as frequent as disagreements, which imply disapproval, but social status affects this ratio. In one study, for example, the ratio of agreements to disagreements was 7.7 for the highest and 14.1 for the lowest status category. See Edgar F. Borgatta and Robert F. Bales, "Interaction of Individuals in Reconstituted Groups," *Sociometry*, 16 (1953), 302–320 (the two ratios were computed from the data in the upper half of Table 3).

than those whose status is not. On the other hand, the greater value with which superior status endows a man's approval enables him to use it more sparingly than the man of inferior status can easily do, as pointed out in the previous discussion. The inference here is that persons of superior status give praise *less* freely than those of inferior status. The two inferences appear contradictory, but actually they are not, although they do refer to two conflicting forces, which account for the observation that many persons of high status express approval less readily but some express it more readily than do persons of low status. If the two aspects of status under consideration are analytically separated, however, two unambiguous hypotheses are implied by the foregoing analysis: first, the higher a man's status, the less free he will be in offering approval; second, among those with equally high status, the more securely grounded a man's status—that is, the less subject it is to modification by the impressions he makes—the freer will he be in offering approval.

Attractiveness: First and Second Impressions

Expressions of intrinsic attraction to an individual, just as expressions of approval of him, are expected to be spontaneous reactions to his qualities; they lose their significance for him if it becomes apparent that they are calculated to have a certain effect on him, though it be only to give him pleasure. A man who seeks affection does not want kindness. Approval is expected to be governed by internalized normative standards of judgment, and intrinsic attraction, by an internal emotional reaction. The simulation of either is condemned. Approval of an individual's specific qualities that becomes diffuse approval of his composite qualities as a person is the source of intrinsic attraction to him.

Your opinions of which we approve and your approval of our opinions both increase your attractiveness for us. Individuals who share values and interests provide each other with support for their beliefs and have a basis for engaging in common endeavors. Homogeneous orientations and attitudes, therefore, draw individuals together, whereas disagreements in important matters make each an unattractive companion for the other. On initial acquaintance, individuals may deceive themselves about the differences in outlook between them and perceive more agreement than actually exists—Newcomb found such autistic distortion to be most prevalent among individuals with authoritarian personalities—but in the long run significant disagreements are usually discovered and motivate individuals to turn to other associates with whom they have more in common. As a result, bonds of mutual attraction are typically found among associates who are in essential agreement on basic issues.[17]

The support an individual's opinions receive from associates who share his values is rewarding for him, particularly if the opinions are important to him but he is not entirely sure that they are right, because their agreement helps to confirm his beliefs and to silence his disturbing doubts. An individual's self-image is such a belief that is of vital significance for him and that simultaneously raises doubts concerning its accuracy in his mind. To have his favorable self-evaluation confirmed by the approval of others implicit in their attraction to him is thus especially rewarding for him, as Thibaut and Kelley have pointed out.[18] The more attracted others are to an individual, consequently, the more attractive companions they become for him.[19] In brief, the rewards furnished by supportive approval of common beliefs make associates increasingly attractive to one another, and the rewarding experience for each of having his favorable self-image confirmed by the fact that the other finds him attractive further increases their mutual attraction.

Serious and persistent conflicts of opinions lead, in corresponding manner, to personal rejections. Some differences of opinions are important conditions for a stimulating discussion. In a discussion of a topic in a companionable group, each participant typically concedes points of lesser significance for him, making himself agreeable and inviting others to do likewise, and closer agreement on the issue is reached. Sometimes, however, a participant refuses to surrender an opinion with which most or all others strongly disagree. What tends to happen in such cases, as an experiment by Schachter indicates, is that the others address themselves increasingly to him and seek to overwhelm him with arguments, but if he resists their efforts to influence him and persists in his deviant opinions, they reject him and no longer want to associate with him.[20]

Extreme opinions and characteristics of individuals are conceived of not merely as qualifying attributes but as status-defining traits. The difference is exemplified by the contrast between a neighbor who

---

[17] See Theodore M. Newcomb, *The Acquaintance Process,* New York: Holt, Rinehart and Winston, 1961, chapters iv, v, and vii.

[18] John W. Thibaut and Harold H. Kelley, *The Social Psychology of Groups,* New York: Wiley, 1959, pp. 42–43.

[19] Newcomb, *op. cit.,* chapter viii.

[20] Stanley Schachter, "Deviation, Rejection, and Communication," *Journal of Abnormal and Social Psychology,* 46 (1951), 190–207.

has progressive political ideas and a Red who lives next door. The progressive neighbor is a man with whom one can discuss politics and whose opinions on various issues carry some weight. One is inclined to grant some of his points in the expectation that he will reciprocate and make concessions too. If his viewpoint is somewhat more extreme and less flexible, however, he is defined as a Red, and his arguments no longer have to be taken seriously, which averts the necessity of continually having to defend one's opinions against fundamental criticisms. When a person's social values put him beyond the pale, there is no basis for the give and take of a debate. The situation is similar to that where a person's greatly superior or far inferior resources discourage enduring relations of reciprocal social exchange with him. Simmel called attention to this contrast between attributes that modify an individual's status in the ingroup and traits that exclude him from it in his analysis of the difference between a poor man and a pauper.[21]

The attraction of associates to an individual and their approval of him are affected in complicated ways by the first impression he makes on them. Their initial impressions give rise to expectations, and these expectations influence his behavior, sometimes inspiring him to perform with extraordinary skill and sometimes inhibiting his faculties in front of them. As others judge his performance, moreover, in terms of the expectations his earlier impressions have created, their evaluation is likely not to be the same as it would have been in the absence of these expectations. First impressions may be self-defeating, for example. The high expectations they raise of a person's brilliant wit or outstanding horsemanship may make others disappointed with his actual performance, although they might have appreciated his adroitness had they not expected so much more; and as his awareness of their disappointment disconcerts him, he may make a still worse impression. The diffident person benefits from this process, since his unimpressive initial demeanor makes it easy for him to exceed the expectations of others and prove himself a surprisingly attractive associate. He gains this advantage, however, at the cost of having to remain on the side lines in the early phases of social interaction.

First impressions may be self-fulfilling as well as self-defeating. One reason for this is that the impressions people make on others are in some areas not merely reflections (which may be distorted) of an underlying reality but the only reality there is. What are the characteristics, for instance, of a sophisticated man or of a fascinating

---

[21] Georg Simmel, *Soziologie,* Leipzig: Duncker und Humblot, 1908, pp. 490–491.

woman? Although a sophisticated man's conversation cannot entirely consist of platitudes and a fascinating woman's conduct cannot entirely lack charm, a content analysis of what they say and do would undoubtedly not reveal a distinctive difference between their behavior and that of others who are not considered sophisticated or fascinating. There must, of course, be subtle differences between others and them, otherwise they could not convey the impression they do. But the crucial point is that the woman who succeeds in inspiring men to conceive of her as a glamorous and exciting enchantress is actually a fascinating woman for them, and that the man who impresses others as the pinnacle of worldly wisdom and *savoir-faire* defines and represents for them what sophisticated conduct really is. If only one person is impressed and others are not, he may check his impression with that of others and revise it. If, however, most associates are convinced that a man is not just intelligent but sophisticated and that a woman is not just beautiful but fascinating, that is what they actually are.

The difference between these impressions, which are intrinsically significant, and those that reflect traits of extrinsic import, such as athletic prowess, parallels that between artistic creation and economic production. Both generate valuables, but in fundamentally different ways. Economic goods and services are produced and supplied because they are valuable in terms of existing standards of utility or value. Artistic creation, in contrast, does not involve so much producing something that is already valuable as it does investing something with new value. The creative artist makes us enjoy a picture or a poem, a song or a play, and since we could not have imagined the experience before, we cannot, in any meaningful sense, be said to have valued it. We do know what we miss when we do not own a car, but we did not know what we missed before we first read Hamlet, saw Chartres, or heard a Brandenburg concerto.[22] The creative genius, in particular, establishes a new style in art and succeeds in making us value entirely new experiences that at first often seemed displeasing. In similar fashion, if on a less exalted plane, the woman who can convince men that her distinctive style makes being in her company a more desirable experience than being with other women has made

---

[22] To be sure, we did not know what we missed by not having cars before they were invented. In terms of the analytical distinction made here, successful invention contains an element of artistic creation, because it produces not only new products but in the long run also new needs for them, and so does advertising, inasmuch as it sometimes makes us value things we did not miss or value before.

herself attractive by the creative act of investing her style with value.

Another reason why impressions may be self-fulfilling is that the expectations they arouse in others influence the individual's conduct. In this case, an external standard for evaluating accomplishments exists, but the expectations an individual has created in others either serve as incentives for living up to them or have a dampening effect on his performance. The poor impression the self-conscious and awkward person makes leads others to expect to be bored in his company, and their apparent lack of interest causes him discomfort and makes his conversation less stimulating than it otherwise would be. The anticipation raised in his audience by a man who gives the impression of a brilliant conversationalist that they will find him entertaining, and their resulting appreciative attentiveness when he talks, may inspire a versatility and adroitness in him of which he is not capable under ordinary circumstances. There is no sharp line of distinction between these self-fulfilling impressions and the ones discussed above. The woman who impresses men as an enchanting companion also is emboldened by their expectations of her actually to behave in an especially alluring manner, just as the one who impresses them as a model matron may feel required by their different expectations to live up to these. "The desire to be worthy of the praise we receive fortifies our virtue; praise accorded to wit, courage, or beauty tends to enhance those qualities." [23] Even physical skills are affected by the expectation of associates, because it fortifies or disturbs the self-confidence of individuals. A well-known illustration is Whyte's case of a bowling contest, in which a gang's leading group, who were expected to excel, won over the followers, some of whom made higher scores than the leaders in practice sessions.[24] A tragic example of a self-fulfilling prophecy, as Merton calls it, is the Negro in the United States; the assumption that Negroes are intellectually inferior helps to justify the lack of adequate educational provisions for them that makes the assumption come true.[25]

Bluffing is another mechanism that makes early impressions self-fulfilling, for the cost of calling the bluff may be too high. The large bet in poker is designed to convey the impression that a man has a good hand, and the great loss possibly entailed in covering his bet

---

[23] La Rochefoucauld, *op. cit.,* p. 49 (#150).

[24] William F. Whyte, *Street Corner Society* (2d ed.), University of Chicago Press, 1955, pp. 14–25.

[25] Robert K. Merton, *Social Theory and Social Structure* (2d ed.), Glencoe: Free Press, 1957, pp. 421–436.

may restrain others from forcing him to show his hand to determine whether he is bluffing. Similarly, the swaggering bully lays a claim to superior status in the gang, and the fear of his possible strength may inhibit other members from testing it, because if they were to test his strength and fail, they would be likely to suffer his retribution. The costlier it is to test the claims a person makes through his impressive demeanor, even if they can in principle be validated, the better are the chances that false claims of his remain undetected. Bluffing in group situations, however, involves great risks, since there are recurrent opportunities for discovering deceptions, and since their discovery engenders distrust as well as loss of respect. Hence, outright bluffing is undoubtedly more prevalent in casual encounters than in enduring groups, although more subtle forms of trying to present initially a too favorable image of oneself to others are probably ubiquitous.

The challenge of impressing associates in social intercourse greatly adds to its enjoyment, but continuing preoccupation with the impression one makes is an impediment, inasmuch as it requires an individual to forego various advantages. Concern with the impression he makes on associates may prevent him from asking for their advice for fear of appearing ignorant; or constrain him to spend much money entertaining them lest he seem insufficiently affluent; or induce him to compromise his integrity and agree with extremist opinions in order not to sound like a Philistine. Moreover, preoccupation with making a favorable impression keeps a person from becoming fully involved in the ongoing activities; it precludes full absorption in his play and full concentration on his work.

A preoccupation with impressing others contrasts with two alternative orientations—expressive involvement in the situation and instrumental concern with securing benefits. "When an individual becomes engaged in an activity, whether shared or not, it is possible for him to become caught up by it, carried away by it, engrossed in it—to be, as we say, spontaneously involved in it," noted Goffman, adding in regard to sociable experiences of this sort: "By this spontaneous involvement in a joint activity, the individual becomes an integral part of the situation, lodged in it and exposed to it, infusing himself into the encounter in a manner quite different from the way an ideally rational player commits his side to a position in an ideally rational game." [26] The enjoyment produced by such involvement in games or other sociable encounters—or, indeed, in work on a common task of

---

[26] Erving Goffman, *Encounters,* Indianapolis: Bobbs-Merrill, 1961, p. 38.

great interest—is enhanced by the opportunities it provides for impressing others, whether it is with being a good loser in poker, an entertaining companion at a party, or an effective speaker at a political rally. Nevertheless, as long as the concern with the impression he makes *dominates* the individual's thinking, he cannot become completely involved in the social situation or fully enjoy it, and neither can he thoroughly concentrate on his tasks.

The reason that an individual is not particularly anxious to appear impressive to his associates is either that he is quite sure of their approval or that their approval is of no significance for him. The person whose previous social experiences make him self-confident, as well as the one who is already accepted in a group, can cease to worry about impressing others. The security derived from acceptance in a peer group that is of great importance for a person not only enables him to relax in the ingroup but also makes the approval and respect of outsiders, especially those of lower status, less significant for him. His consequent lesser concern with impressing outsiders of little importance to him permits him to concentrate on the performance of his task in interaction with them. Agents in a federal office who were highly integrated in their own work group, for example, were found to be less disturbed by the presence of stenographers when composing difficult reports and able to dictate these reports more often instead of writing them out themselves than their less integrated colleagues, probably because the less integrated agents were more concerned with the impressions they made on stenographers.[27] Uneasiness about the impression he makes in social interaction interferes with an individual's instrumental endeavors.

Concern with impressing others and earning their social approval generally limits heedless pursuit of personal advantage in social situations. Yet often men can be observed to pursue their instrumental self-interests in apparent disregard of the reactions of others and of incurring disapproval. This conduct would seem surprising in view of the great significance that social approval has. Men, however, do not aim for the approval of everybody or just anybody. They strive to prove themselves attractive and win approbation and respect in the social circles that are most significant for them. The reactions of persons outside these circles have little intrinsic value for them, both because their secure position obviates the need for further social support and because they are oriented in their interaction with out-

---

[27] Blau, *The Dynamics of Bureaucracy* (2d ed.), University of Chicago Press, 1963, pp. 155–156.

siders to gaining instrumental benefits that they can use to fortify their position in the important circles. A worker may be willing humbly to request assistance with his tasks from fellow workers, particularly those not in his ingroup, to be able to receive his superiors' approval for his performance. An employer may be willing to exploit his workers in disregard of their disapproval, as long as it is not strong enough to alienate them completely from their jobs, to make profits that enable him to impress his own social circle as an affluent and generous man. Apparent disregard for social approval, including such extreme forms as exploitation and oppression, typically entails indirect attempts to earn social approval by using some people to obtain the resources needed to impress others who are more significant. Hence, the restraints imposed by social approval on conduct are largely confined to circles of significant associates.

Excursus on Love

Love is the polar case of intrinsic attraction. Whereas it finds undoubtedly its purest expression in the relation between mother and child, its development as the result of the increasing attraction of two independent individuals to one another can best be examined in a romantic relationship. Love appears to make human beings unselfish, since they themselves enjoy giving pleasure to those they love, but this selfless devotion generally rests on an interest in maintaining the other's love. Even a mother's devotion to her children is rarely entirely devoid of the desire to maintain their attachment to her. Exchange processes occur in love relations as well as in social associations of only extrinsic significance. Their dynamics, however, are different, because the specific rewards exchanged are merely means to produce the ultimate reward of intrinsic attraction in love relations, while the exchange of specific rewards is the very objective of the association in purely instrumental social relations. In intrinsic love attachments, as noted earlier, each individual furnishes rewards to the other not to receive proportionate extrinsic benefits in return but to express and confirm his own commitment and to promote the other's growing commitment to the association. An analysis of love reveals the element of exchange entailed even in intrinsically significant associations as well as their distinctive nature.

A man falls in love if the attractiveness of a woman has become unique in his eyes. "All that is necessary is that our taste for her should become exclusive." This happens, Proust continues, when we start to experience an "insensate, agonising desire to possess her."[28] The woman who impresses a man as a most desirable love possession that cannot be easily won and who simultaneously indicates sufficient interest to make ultimate conquest not completely beyond reach is likely to kindle his love. His attraction to her makes him dependent on her for important rewards and anxious to impress and please her to arouse a reciprocal affection that would assure him these rewards.

In the early stages of falling in love, the fears of rejection and dependence engendered by the growing attraction motivate each lover to conceal the full extent of his or her affection from the other and possibly also from himself or herself. Flirting involves largely the expression of attraction in a semi-serious or stereotyped fashion that is designed to elicit some commitment from the other in advance of making a serious commitment oneself. The joking and ambiguous commitments implied by flirting can be laughed off if they fail to evoke a responsive cord or made firm if they do.[29] But as long as both continue to conceal the strength of their affection for the other while both become increasingly dependent on the other's affection, they frustrate one another. In the lovers' quarrels that typically ensue, as Thibaut and Kelley have pointed out, "each partner, by means of temporary withdrawal or separation, tests the other's dependence on the relationship."[30] As both are threatened by these quarrels with the possible end of their relationship, they are constrained to express sufficient commitment for it to continue. Of course, one may not be ready to do so, and the conflict may terminate their relationship.

Human beings evidently derive pleasure from doing things for those they love and sometimes make great sacrifices for them. This tendency results partly from the identification with the other produced by love, from the desire to give symbolic expression to one's devotion, from the function providing rewards has for strengthening a loved one's attachment to oneself, and perhaps partly from the process previously termed reverse secondary reinforcement. The repeated experience of being rewarded by the increased attachment of a loved one after having done a variety of things to please him may have the effect that giving pleasure to loved ones becomes intrinsically gratifying.

---

[28] Proust, *op. cit.*, p. 177.

[29] For the analysis of a special case of this strategy, see James D. Thompson and William J. McEwen, "Organization Goals and Environment," *American Sociological Review*, 23 (1958), 29–30.

[30] Thibaut and Kelley, *op. cit.*, p. 66.

Further feedback effects may occur. Since doing favors and giving presents are signs of love, a man's gifts and efforts for a woman may stimulate his own affection for her as well as hers for him, and a woman may encourage a man to give her things and do things for her not primarily out of interest in the material benefits but in order to foster his love for her. "Benefactors seem to love those whom they benefit more than those who have received benefits love those who have conferred them," said Aristotle.[31]

The more an individual is in love with another, the more anxious he or she is likely to be to please the other.[32] The individual who is less deeply involved in a love relationship, therefore, is in an advantageous position, since the other's greater concern with continuing the relationship makes him or her dependent and gives the less involved individual power. Waller called this "the principle of least interest."[33] This power can be used to exploit the other; the woman who exploits a man's affection for economic gain and the boy who sexually exploits a girl who is in love with him are obvious examples.[34] Probably the most prevalent manifestation of the principle of least interest, however, is that the individual whose spontaneous affection for the other is stronger must accede to the other's wishes and make special efforts to please the other. Such an imbalance of power and extrinsic rewards is often the source and remains the basis of lasting reciprocal love attachments. Hence, the lover who does not express unconditional affection early gains advantages in the established interpersonal relationship. Indeed, the more restrained lover also seems to have a better chance of inspiring another's love for himself or herself.

Costly possessions are most precious, in love as elsewhere. A man's intrinsic attraction to a woman (and hers to him) rests on the rewards

---

[31] Aristotle, *The Nicomachean Ethics*, London: William Heinemann, 1926, p. 545 (Book IX, vii, 1).

[32] Providing extrinsic benefits may be a substitute for proving oneself intrinsically attractive, as Proust has noted (*op. cit.*, p. 205): "For the moment, while he lavished presents upon her, and performed all manner of services, he could rely on advantages not contained in his person, or in his intellect, could forego the endless, killing effort to make himself attractive."

[33] Willard Waller and Reuben Hill, *The Family*, New York: Dryden, 1951, pp. 190–192.

[34] For a discussion of exploitation in courtship, see *ibid.*, pp. 159–173. See also the fictional account of the game of making another dependent in order to derive pleasure from exercising power over him or her, played actually as a game and in real life, in Roger Vailland, *The Law*, New York: Knopf, 1958, esp. pp. 42–52, 196–198.

he expects to experience in a love relationship with her.[35] An analytical distinction can be made between his actual experiences—resulting from her supportiveness, her charming talk, her kisses, and so forth—and the value he places upon these experiences with her compared to similar experiences with other women. His gratifications are the product of the experiences themselves and the value he places on them. The ease with which he obtains the rewards of her love, however, tend to depreciate their value for him. This is the dilemma of love, which parallels the previously discussed dilemma of approval. Just as a person is expected to give approval to his associates, but his doing so too freely will depreciate the value of his approval, so is a woman under pressure to give evidence of her love to her admirer, but if she does so too readily the value of her affection to him will suffer.

How valuable a woman is as a love object to a man depends to a considerable extent on her apparent popularity with other men. It is difficult to evaluate anything in the absence of clear standards for doing so, and individuals who find themselves in such an ambiguous situation tend to be strongly influenced by any indication of a social norm for making judgments.[36] Evaluating the intrinsic desirability of a woman is an ambiguous case of this kind, in which any particular man is strongly influenced by her general popularity among men that socially validates her value as a love object. Of course, a girl can only become generally popular by being attractive to many particular boys, but her attractiveness to any one depends in part on evidence that others find her attractive too. Good looks constitute such evidence, and so does her behavior on dates.

A woman whose love is in great demand among men is not likely to make firm commitments quickly, because she has so many attractive alternatives to weigh before she does. The one who is not popular is more dependent on a man who takes her out and has more reason to become committed to him. A woman who readily gives proof of her affection to a man, therefore, provides presumptive evidence of her lack of popularity and thus tends to depreciate the value of her affection for him. Her resistance to his attempts to conquer her, in contrast, implies that she is in great demand and has many alternatives

---

[35] To make the following discussion less burdensome, it will refer largely to men's orientations to women, but it is assumed to apply, in principle, also to women's orientations to men, although there are, of course, sex role differences in specific practices, as will be noted.

[36] See Muzafer Sherif, "Group Influences upon the Formation of Norms and Attitudes," in Eleanor E. Maccoby, Theodore M. Newcomb, and Eugene L. Hartley, *Readings in Social Psychology* (3d ed.), New York: Holt, 1958, pp. 219–232.

to choose from, which is likely to enhance her desirability in his eyes. Her reluctance to become committed helps to establish the value of her affection, partly because he takes it as an indication of her general desirability, notably in the absence of any direct knowledge of how desirable she appears to other men. To be sure, men sometimes discuss women among themselves, their desirability and even their behavior on dates, the social taboo on doing so notwithstanding, but these discussions only increase the importance a woman's restraint has for protecting the value of her affection. If a woman has the reputation of readily engaging in sexual affairs, the value of this expression of her affection greatly declines, largely because her sexual favors entail less commitment to, and ego support for, a man than those of a woman who very rarely bestows them.

To safeguard the value of her affection, a woman must be ungenerous in expressing it and make any evidence of her growing love a cherished prize that cannot be easily won. Ultimately, to be sure, a man's love for a woman depends on her willingness and ability to furnish him unique rewards in the form of sexual satisfaction and other manifestations of her affection. The point made here is *not* that a woman who fails to provide a man with sexual and emotional gratifications is more likely to win his love than one who does. The opposite undoubtedly is the case, since such gratifications are the major source of a lasting love attachment. The point made is rather that a man's profound love for a woman depends not only on these rewarding experiences themselves but also on the value he places upon them and that a woman who refrains from bestowing expressions of her affection freely increases the value of these expressions *when she does bestow them.* Of course, unless she finally *does* bestow these rewards, she does not profit from their increased value. This is precisely the reason for the dilemma. A woman promotes a man's love by granting him sexual and other favors, as demonstrations of her affection and as means for making associating with her outstandingly rewarding for him, yet if she dispenses such favors readily—to many men or to a given man too soon—she depreciates their value and thus their power to arouse an enduring attachment.

Social pressures reinforce the tendency to withhold early evidence of great affection. If most girls in a community were to kiss boys on their first dates and grant sexual favors soon afterwards, before the boys have become deeply committed, it would depreciate the price of these rewards in the community, making it difficult for a girl to use the promise of sexual intercourse to elicit a firm commitment from a boy, since sexual gratifications are available at a lesser price. The interest of girls in protecting the value of sexual favors against depreciation gives rise to social pressures among girls not to grant these favors readily. Coleman's study of high schools shows that these pressures tend to take the form of making a girl's social standing contingent on her reputation in regard to her sexual behavior with boys.[37] This social pressure, which helps to maintain the sexual favors of girls worthy of permanent commitments of boys, strengthens the position of girls in their exchange relations with boys in the courtship market.[38] The situation among boys is complementary, which means that the social pressures here discourage early commitment. The aim of both sexes in courtship is to furnish sufficient rewards to seduce the other but not enough to deflate their value, yet the line defined by these two conditions is often imperceptible.

The challenge of conquest is an important element in the formative stages of a love relationship, and its significance as a catalyst for the development of a lasting attachment is dissipated by making conquest too easy. A basic function of the casual dating among young people is to provide opportunities for them to ascertain their own attractiveness as lovers and their chances in the competition for desirable mates. In dating—and to some extent in intimate sociable intercourse generally—an individual places the attractiveness of his own self on the market, so to speak, which makes success of extreme importance for his self-conception. The girls or boys who are successful in making many conquests of the other sex validate their attractiveness in their own eyes as well as those of others. In casual dating, therefore, girls and boys use each other to test their own attractiveness through conquests. A girl's resistance to being easily conquered constitutes a refusal to let herself be used as such a test object and a demand for a minimum commitment as a condition of her affection. By prolonging the challenge of the chase until a boy has become intrinsically attracted to her, a girl exploits the significance of conquest to promote a more fundamental attachment that makes this incentive for dating her superfluous. Since an interest in conquest may be a boy's primary initial reason for courting a girl, an easy conquest robs him prematurely of this inducement for continuing the relationship.

A girl's demonstrations of affection for a boy, moreover, imply a commitment by her and a demand for a countercommitment from him. If he was satisfied with the previous level of involvement and is not yet ready to commit himself further, such a demand for greater commitment may alienate his affection for her. Love is a spontaneous

---

[37] James S. Coleman, *The Adolescent Society,* Glencoe: Free Press, 1961, pp. 118–123.

[38] See Waller and Hill, *loc. cit.*

emotion that cannot be commanded, and the command to love her more implicit in the girl's expressions of increasing affection for him may act as an external restraint that withers the boy's existing affection for her. A boy's growing love for a girl he pursues is typically accompanied and spurred by an anxiety lest he lose his love object, but the fear of becoming too deeply involved that her great involvement arouses in him is incompatible with and corrodes the anxiety of losing her and the affection associated with it. Although he can take advantage of her greater commitment to obtain sexual favors from her, his exploitative orientation in doing so is not likely to stimulate an intrinsic attachment; and if his superego prevents him from exploiting her, he is likely to terminate the relationship under these circumstances. The jealousy characteristic of the more deeply involved lover constitutes an explicit demand for a more exclusive commitment on the part of the other, and it frequently provides the final stimulus for the less involved lover to withdraw from the relationship. The growth of love is often stifled by the pressure put on it by the other lover's too great affection.

Whereas the processes just considered discourage the free expression of affection in early courtship, lovers also experience pressures to express their feelings. If an individual is in love, he or she obtains gratification from declaring his love to the beloved and even "to shout it from the treetops." Identification with the person one loves makes rewarding him enjoyable, and rewarding him tends to involve some expressions of love for him. Besides, many actions of a girl that reward a boy and express her feelings for him are simultaneously rewarding for her, such as her willingness to kiss him. Flirting, moreover, gives rise to expectations that must later be fulfilled to maintain the love relationship. The conduct of the flirtatious girl implies that, although she may not yet be ready to let the boy hold her hand, continued association with her would ultimately bring these and much greater rewards. The implicit promises made in the course of flirting put subsequent pressure on lovers to live up to the expectations they have created and begin to provide at least some of the rewards promised. The result is a dynamic force of increasing rewards and commitments, since each new commitment creates further expectations, lest frustrated expectations lead to the termination of the relationship. The girl lets the boy kiss her, he takes her to the "prom," she permits some sex play, he ceases to date others, so does she, and he ultimately gives her the ring that formalizes their relation—unless, of course, these pressures toward stepped-up rewards and increasing commitments induce one of the lovers to discontinue the affair.

Finally, the gratifications a woman experiences as the result of being loved by a man are greatly enhanced if she loves him too, and this may unconsciously incline her to return his love. The love of a man animates a woman and makes her a more fascinating and attractive person. Going out with a man who is in love with her enhances her self-image as a captivating woman and thus probably affects her behavior to make her actually more charming and appealing. For a man's loving admiration to have pronounced effects on her self-image and conduct, however, his estimation of her must be of great significance for a woman, and the more she loves him the greater is its significance for her. A woman's love for a man who loves her, therefore, helps to make her a more charming and self-confident person, because it magnifies, as it were, the mirror that reflects and partly shapes her personality as a lover. Although a woman cannot will herself to love a man who loves her, the advantages she gains from reciprocating his love may unconsciously motivate her to do so.

Lovers, then, are under pressure to express affection for one another as well as under pressure to withhold expressions of affection. The basic dilemma is that a woman who freely provides evidence of her affection for a man in order to make associating with her more attractive to him thereby depreciates the value of her affection. The generic processes are the same for both sexes, although cultural sex role differences determine their specific forms. The willingness to enter into sex relations, for example, entails less of a commitment for a boy than for a girl in our culture, and he can more easily declare his love first, since this too tends to imply less of a commitment for a boy than for a girl. But those acts of a boy that signify his commitment to a girl, such as his introducing her to his parents or his giving her his fraternity pin, have essentially the same implications as her acts of commitment. If both lovers are interested in continuing the relationship, both are also interested in having the other commit himself or herself first and more deeply. Hence, there is an element of "brinkmanship" in courtship, with both partners seeking to withhold their own commitment up to the point where it would endanger the relationship, because courtship is a mixed game with some common and some conflicting interests, just as is the establishment of other social relations discussed in chapter two (see chart on p. 45).[39]

---

[39] Another dilemma posed by this mixed game is that the lover who expresses his eagerness to spend time with his beloved enables her to enjoy dates with him without revealing how eager she is to do so and without making the commitment implicit in such revelations.

One lover's apparent affection and increasing commitment sometimes stimulate the growth of the other's love for him, while they
sometimes inhibit the other's love and cause the other to lose interest
in the relation. What determines which is the case? The personality
structure of the lovers is unquestionably the most important factor,[40]
but the social condition in the developing love relation also exerts an
influence. Since lovers tend to suppress the strength of their growing
affection for one another, a lover's own deepening involvement produces a state of tension. This state makes him anxious to receive
evidence of the other's increasing affection for him, which would avert
the danger of rejection and of one-sided dependence and permit him
to cease suppressing his strong feelings of attraction. In this situation
the eagerly anticipated expressions of affection of a woman tend to
relieve a man's distress and intensify his love for her. If, on the other
hand, there is no such reservoir of suppressed feeling and a lover is
no more involved than is manifest, a woman's demonstrations of great
affection for him are likely to alienate his affection for her, because
they depreciate the value of her love, undermine the challenge of
pursuing her, and make demands for stronger commitments than he
is ready to undertake. In parallel fashion, a man's expressions of
affection that meet a woman's suppressed desires tend to intensify
her love for him, but if his affection far exceeds her feelings and
desires it is likely to alienate her.

In brief, it seems that commitments must keep abreast for a love
relationship to develop into a lasting mutual attachment. If one lover
is considerably more involved than the other, his greater commitment
invites exploitation or provokes feelings of entrapment, both of which
obliterate love. Whereas rewards experienced in the relationship may
lead to its continuation for a while, the weak interest of the less committed or the frustrations of the more committed probably will sooner
or later prompt one or the other to terminate it. Only when two lovers'

---

[40] Generally, this discussion has not attempted to deal with the psychological
forces and motivational structures underlying the socio-psychological processes
analyzed. Waller and Hill's comment concerning their analysis is also appropriate
for the one presented here (*ibid.*, pp. 172–173): "It happens that we have
directed our own analysis at the interaction process in courtship; we recognize
the necessity of supplementing this analysis by pointing out how these processes
are related to the inner nature and developmental history of the participants.
Here the psychoanalytic contributions are much in point." Special attention should
be called to the neglect of emotional conflicts and the resulting irritational tendencies of individuals, that is, tendencies produced by unconscious drives that
defeat the individual's own objectives.

affection for and commitment to one another expand at roughly the same pace do they tend mutually to reinforce their love.

Conclusions

Social approval and personal attraction are basic sources of support for an individual's opinions and judgments, for his values and self-conception. The significance of another's approbation or admiration depends on its being accepted as genuine. In contrast to the services of an associate or his compliance, where his actions count rather than his underlying attitudes, the underlying orientation is what counts in expressions of approval and affection. Simulated approval and feigned affection have little value.

The significance of a person's expressions of approval or affection also depends on their being scarce. Individuals who hardly ever disapprove or who readily demonstrate affection for others thereby depreciate the value of their praise or their love. Whereas the simulation of approval and affection is highly condemned, their dissimulation is not seriously censured. False praise stamps a person as a sycophant; false agreement, as a liar; false show of affection, as dishonorable; but the person who fails to express approval when he could or who withholds evidence of affection that he feels is much less severely rebuked and is merely accused of being unappreciative or cold. Only simulation, not dissimulation, makes approval and affection unauthentic. Given this asymmetry, there is no conflict between the requirements that expressions of approval must be genuine and that they must be rare to be of importance for others.

A man's willingness to provide social support by giving approval makes his associates appreciate him, but if he freely offers praise he depreciates its value. Similarly, a woman's expressions of affection for the man who loves her make him appreciate her the more, but if she too readily gives evidence of her love she depreciates its value. This poses a dilemma, since individuals risk either antagonizing significant associates by withholding expressions of approval and affection or depreciating the value these expressions have for them. The dilemma is more pronounced in the case of love than in the case of approbation, because the significance of approbation rests to a greater extent on alternative foundations than that of love. A person's ability to contribute to the welfare of others, which commands their respect, and his power over them govern the value his approval has for them, and the effect of his lack of discrimination in bestowing approval on its value does not completely obliterate these other effects. A person's lack of restraint in demonstrating affection, on the other hand, is much more intimately bound up with the impression he makes as a lover and thus with the value of his love for another.

The significance of a person's approval or affection for others depends, furthermore, on their orientation to him. The respect of others for a man greatly increases the significance of his approval for them, and the adoration of others for a woman greatly enhances the significance of her affection for them. Men whose performance receives the commendation of highly respected persons care little about the approval of less respected persons, and women who are adored by the most desirable men care little about the admiration of less desirable ones. For his approval to be appreciated at all, the less respected person must be relatively undiscriminating in expressing it and praise performances of only mediocre quality, thereby further decreasing the value of his approval. Correspondingly, for her affection to be appreciated at all, the woman who is not greatly admired among men must be comparatively indiscriminate in expressing it and readily give evidence of her love for a man, thereby further decreasing the value of her affection.

The very endeavor to impress others in order to win their approval or admiration makes a person less impressive. The man whose eminence in his field is renowned can dispense with such endeavors. He can act naturally and be matter-of-fact, and he can even minimize his own accomplishments, since doing so does not detract from their evident importance but only increases the others' estimation of him. The man whose equally great achievements are not known in a particular group cannot impress them in the same fashion. Unless he tells them of his accomplishments, they have no basis for respecting him or for appreciating his modesty in speaking of his attainments in a deprecatory manner, yet his having to tell them that he is a man of distinction, however subtly, makes him less impressive. Similarly, the raving beauty's evident attractiveness frees her from the necessity to demonstrate that she is a captivating woman and permits her to be charming and unpretentious and thus to prove herself still more attractive. Once a baseline of social standing is established, it is relatively simple to make further gains, but establishing it is not so easy.

There are, then, numerous parallels between expressions of affection in love relations and expressions of approval in social associations generally. There are also some contrasts, however. The main source of the difference is that the conditions in a collective structure largely govern the significance of social approval while the conditions established by a pair of lovers themselves primarily govern the significance of their affection for one another, although pair relations modify the significance of approval and the broader social situation affects the significance of affection, too. The baseline of prestige that makes others appreciate an individual's approval and the baseline of attraction that makes others appreciate an individual's affection rest on different foundations, since prestige is typically more firmly rooted in the social structure than is attraction.

Although a woman's beauty and popularity make her initially attractive to a man, the significance of her love for him depends ultimately on his personal feeling of attraction for her, whereas the significance of the approval of a person of superior status is inherently greater than that of others, whatever an individual may think of him for idiosyncratic reasons. The judgment of his superior or of an expert in his field cannot rationally be dismissed by an individual, but there is nothing irrational about not being attracted to a woman who is beautiful and whom other men consider desirable. Finally, with the exception of the special case of physical beauty, what makes a woman a desirable love object is the impression she makes of being desirable, while the respect commanded by a man—or a woman, for that matter—is governed by his actual abilities and evaluated in terms of objective criteria. To be sure, the relevance of these abilities rather than others depends on the social standards of evaluation that prevail in the social structure, but this fact does not affect the fundamental distinction. The attractiveness of a person as a lover, or generally as a sociable companion, is primarily a function of the orientations of his particular associates to him, whereas the multiple supports on which status in a social structure rests—especially, though not only, in areas of instrumental achievement—make it comparatively independent of the orientations of particular associates.

✳ FOUR

Social Exchange

The moral type on the other hand is not based on stated terms, but the gift or other service is given as to a friend, although the giver expects to receive an equivalent or greater return, as though it had not been a free gift but a loan; and as he ends the relationship in a different spirit from that in which he began it, he will complain. The reason of this is that all men, or most men, wish what is noble but choose what is profitable; and while it is noble to render a service not with an eye to receiving one in return, it is profitable to receive one. One ought, therefore, if one can, to return the equivalent of services received, and to do so willingly. . . .

ARISTOTLE, *The Nicomachean Ethics*

Processes of social association can be conceptualized, following Homans' lead, "as an exchange of activity, tangible or intangible, and more or less rewarding or costly, between at least two persons." [1] Social exchange can be observed everywhere once we are sensitized by this conception to it, not only in market relations but also in friendship and even in love, as we have seen, as well as in many social relations between these extremes in intimacy. Neighbors exchange favors; children, toys; colleagues, assistance; acquaintances, courtesies; politicians, concessions; discussants, ideas; housewives, recipes. The per-

---

[1] George C. Homans, *Social Behavior*, New York: Harcourt, Brace and World, 1961, p. 13. This entire book has been an important source of inspiration for the analysis presented here, as noted in the preface. For Homans' first statement on the subject, see his "Social Behavior as Exchange," *American Journal of Sociology*, 63 (1958), 597–606.

vasiveness of social exchange makes it tempting to consider all social conduct in terms of exchange, but this would deprive the concept of its distinctive meaning. People do things for fear of other men or for fear of God or for fear of their conscience, and nothing is gained by trying to force such action into a conceptual framework of exchange.

Mauss and other anthropologists have called attention to the significance and prevalence of the exchange of gifts and services in simpler societies. "In theory such gifts are voluntary but in fact they are given and repaid under obligation. . . . Further, what they exchange is not exclusively goods and wealth, real and personal property, and things of economic value. They exchange rather courtesies, entertainments, ritual, military assistance, women, children, dances, and feasts; and fairs in which the market is but one element and the circulation of wealth but one part of a wide and enduring contact." [2]

The institutionalized form the exchange of gifts frequently assumes in simpler societies highlights the two general functions of social, as distinct from strictly economic, exchange, namely, to establish bonds of friendship and to establish superordination over others. The creation of friendship bonds is typified by the ceremonial Kula exchange in the Western Pacific, where "the Kula partnership provides every man within its ring with a few friends near at hand, and with some friendly allies in the far-away, dangerous, foreign districts." [3] A polar example of the establishment of superordination over others is the potlatch in the American Northwest, in which "status in associations and clans, and rank of every kind, are determined by the war of property. . . ." [4] What is most interesting, however, is that the exchanges in the same institution serve sometimes to cement peer relations and sometimes to produce differentiation of status, contradictory as these two consequences appear to be.

The basic principles underlying the conception of exchange may be briefly summarized. An individual who supplies rewarding services to another obligates him. To discharge this obligation, the second must furnish benefits to the first in turn. Concern here is with extrinsic benefits, not primarily with the rewards intrinsic to the association itself, although the significance of the social "commodities" exchanged is never perfectly independent of the interpersonal relation between the exchange partners. If both individuals value what they

---

[2] Marcel Mauss, *The Gift,* Glencoe: Free Press, 1954, pp. 1, 3.

[3] Bronislaw Malinowski, *Argonauts of the Western Pacific,* New York: Dutton, 1961, p. 92.

[4] Mauss, *op. cit.,* p. 35.

receive from the other, both are prone to supply more of their own services to provide incentives for the other to increase his supply and to avoid becoming indebted to him. As both receive increasing amounts of the assistance they originally needed rather badly, however, their need for still further assistance typically declines.

"The profits from exchange decrease with the number of exchanges;" [5] in technical terms, the marginal utility of increasing amounts of benefits eventually diminishes. If we need help in our work, for example, five minutes of an expert's assistance are worth much to us, and another five minutes are perhaps just as valuable, but once he has aided us for half an hour another five minutes of his time are undoubtedly less significant than were the first five. Ultimately, the declining marginal utility of additional benefits is no longer worth the cost of obtaining them, and the point at which this happens for both partners, often after some adjustment in the ratio at which they exchange services, governs the level of transactions most advantageous for both at which the volume of exchange between them presumably becomes stabilized./ Although personal considerations—for instance, the desire not to antagonize a colleague— modify these rational decisions, such factors also can be taken into account in more complex versions of the basic model, at least in principle.

Take the association of a new member of a profession with a respected senior colleague as an illustration of these processes. The junior is rewarded by the senior's stimulating expert discussions of professional matters and by the senior's willingness to treat him as a colleague, which symbolizes acceptance as a full-fledged professional. He reciprocates by his deferential admiration, which is rewarding for the senior. The gratification the senior derives from being listened to with great respect prompts him to devote some of his, limited time to the association, but his gratification is not proportionately increased if he extends the period in which the other admires his expert opinions from half an hour every few days to several hours daily. Moreover, the more time the senior devotes to the association, the costlier it becomes for him to further restrict the time available to him for other activities. Hence, he will be inclined to limit the time he spends in discussions with the junior to the level at which the support he receives from his admiration still outweighs in significance the advantages foregone by taking time from other pursuits. At this point, however, the junior may still profit from

---

[5] Homans, *Social Behavior*, p. 70.

further association with the senior. Since his admiration does not suffice to increase the association time, the junior must endeavor to furnish supplementary rewards, for example, by doing odd jobs for his senior colleague, thereby obligating him to reciprocate by devoting more time to the association than he otherwise would. Eventually, the marginal advantages for the junior of associating still more with the senior will no longer outweigh the marginal cost of providing more services for him, and the exchange will tend to level off. The assumption is not that individuals make these calculations explicitly but that such implicit calculations underlie the feelings of boredom or pressure from other work that prompt their decisions to spend only a certain amount of time together.

Unspecified Obligations and Trust

The concept of exchange can be circumscribed by indicating two limiting cases. An individual may give another money because the other stands in front of him with a gun in a holdup. While this could be conceptualized as an exchange of his money for his life, it seems preferable to exclude the result of physical coercion from the range of social conduct encompassed by the term "exchange." An individual may also give away money because his conscience demands that he help support the underprivileged and without expecting any form of gratitude from them. While this could be conceptualized as an exchange of his money for the internal approval of his superego, here again it seems preferable to exclude conformity with internalized norms from the purview of the concept of social exchange.[6] A social exchange is involved if an individual gives money to a poor man because he wants to receive the man's expressions of gratitude and deference and if he ceases to give alms to beggars who withhold such expressions.

"Social exchange," as the term is used here, refers to voluntary actions of individuals that are motivated by the returns they are expected to bring and typically do in fact bring from others. Action

---

[6] Ludwig von Mises refers to this type as autistic exchange. "Making one-sided presents without the aim of being rewarded by any conduct on the part of the receiver or of a third person is autistic exchange. The donor acquires the satisfaction which the better condition of the receiver gives to him. The receiver gets the present as a God-sent gift. But if presents are given in order to influence some people's conduct, they are no longer one-sided, but a variety of interpersonal exchange between the donor and the man whose conduct they are designed to influence." *Human Action,* New Haven: Yale University Press, 1949, p. 196.

compelled by physical coercion is not voluntary, although compliance with other forms of power can be considered a voluntary service rendered in exchange for the benefits such compliance produces, as already indicated. Whereas conformity with internalized standards does not fall under the definition of exchange presented, conformity to social pressures tends to entail indirect exchanges. Men make charitable donations, not to earn the gratitude of the recipients, whom they never see, but to earn the approval of their peers who participate in the philanthropic campaign. Donations are exchanged for social approval, though the recipients of the donations and the suppliers of the approval are not identical, and the clarification of the connection between the two requires an analysis of the complex structures of indirect exchange, which is reserved for chapters eight and ten. Our concern now is with the simpler direct exchanges.

The need to reciprocate for benefits received in order to continue receiving them serves as a "starting mechanism" of social interaction and group structure, as Gouldner has pointed out.[7] When people are thrown together, and before common norms or goals or role expectations have crystallized among them, the advantages to be gained from entering into exchange relations furnish incentives for social interaction, and the exchange processes serve as mechanisms for regulating social interaction, thus fostering the development of a network of social relations and a rudimentary group structure. Eventually, group norms to regulate and limit the exchange transactions emerge, including the fundamental and ubiquitous norm of reciprocity, which makes failure to discharge obligations subject to group sanctions. In contrast to Gouldner, however, it is held here that the norm of reciprocity merely reinforces and stabilizes tendencies inherent in the character of social exchange itself and that the fundamental starting mechanism of patterned social intercourse is found in the existential conditions of exchange, not in the norm of reciprocity. It is a necessary condition of exchange that individuals, in the interest of continuing to receive needed services, discharge their obligations for having received them in the past. Exchange processes utilize, as it were, the self-interests of individuals to produce a differentiated social structure within which norms tend to develop that require individuals to set aside some of their personal interests for the sake of those of the collectivity. Not all social constraints are normative

---

[7] Alvin W. Gouldner, "The Norm of Reciprocity," *American Sociological Review*, 25 (1960), 161–178, esp. p. 176.

constraints, and those imposed by the nature of social exchange are not, at least, not originally.

Social exchange differs in important ways from strictly economic exchange. The basic and most crucial distinction is that social exchange entails *unspecified* obligations. The prototype of an economic transaction rests on a formal contract that stipulates the exact quantities to be exchanged.[8] The buyer pays $30,000 for a specific house, or he signs a contract to pay that sum plus interest over a period of years. Whether the entire transaction is consummated at a given time, in which case the contract may never be written, or not, all the transfers to be made now or in the future are agreed upon at the time of sale. Social exchange, in contrast, involves the principle that one person does another a favor, and while there is a general expectation of some future return, its exact nature is definitely *not* stipulated in advance. The distinctive implications of such unspecified obligations are brought into high relief by the institutionalized form they assume in the Kula discussed by Malinowski:

> The main principle underlying the regulations of actual exchange is that the Kula consists in the bestowing of a ceremonial gift, which has to be repaid by an equivalent counter-gift after a lapse of time. . . . But it can never be exchanged from hand to hand, with the equivalence between the two objects being discussed, bargained about and computed. . . . The second very important principle is that the equivalence of the counter-gift is left to the giver, and it cannot be enforced by any kind of coercion. . . . If the article given as a counter-gift is not equivalent, the recipient will be disappointed and angry, but he has no direct means of redress, no means of coercing his partner. . . .[9]

Social exchange, whether it is in this ceremonial form or not, involves favors that create diffuse future obligations, not precisely specified ones, and the nature of the return cannot be bargained about but must be left to the discretion of the one who makes it. Thus, if a person gives a dinner party, he expects his guests to reciprocate at some future date. But he can hardly bargain with them about the kind of party to which they should invite him, although he expects them not simply to ask him for a quick lunch if he had invited

---

[8] This is not completely correct for an employment contract or for the purchase of professional services, since the precise services the employee or professional will be obligated to perform are not specified in detail in advance. Economic transactions that involve services generally are somewhat closer to social exchange than the pure type of economic exchange of commodities or *products* of services.

[9] Malinowski, *op. cit.*, pp. 95–96.

them to a formal dinner. Similarly, if a person goes to some trouble in behalf of an acquaintance, he expects *some* expression of gratitude, but he can neither bargain with the other over how to reciprocate nor force him to reciprocate at all.

Since there is no way to assure an appropriate return for a favor, social exchange requires trusting others to discharge their obligations. While the banker who makes a loan to a man who buys a house does not have to trust him, although he hopes he will not have to foreclose the mortgage, the individual who gives another an expensive gift must trust him to reciprocate in proper fashion. Typically, however, exchange relations evolve in a slow process, starting with minor transactions in which little trust is required because little risk is involved. A worker may help a colleague a few times. If the colleague fails to reciprocate, the worker has lost little and can easily protect himself against further loss by ceasing to furnish assistance. If the colleague does reciprocate, perhaps excessively so out of gratitude for the volunteered help and in the hope of receiving more, he proves himself trustworthy of continued and extended favors. (Excessive reciprocation may be embarrassing, because it is a bid for a more extensive exchange relation than one may be willing to enter.) By discharging their obligations for services rendered, if only to provide inducements for the supply of more assistance, individuals demonstrate their trustworthiness, and the gradual expansion of mutual service is accompanied by a parallel growth of mutual trust. Hence, processes of social exchange, which may originate in pure self-interest, generate trust in social relations through their recurrent and gradually expanding character.

Only social exchange tends to engender feelings of personal obligation, gratitude, and trust; purely economic exchange as such does not. An individual is obligated to the banker who gives him a mortgage on his house merely in the technical sense of owing him money, but he does not feel personally obligated in the sense of experiencing a debt of gratitude to the banker, because all the banker's services, all costs and risks, are duly taken into account in and fully repaid by the interest on the loan he receives. A banker who grants a loan without adequate collateral, however, does make the recipient personally obligated for this favorable treatment, precisely because this act of trust entails a social exchange that is superimposed upon the strictly economic transaction.

In contrast to economic commodities, the benefits involved in social exchange do not have an exact price in terms of a single quantitative medium of exchange, which is another reason why social obligations are unspecific. It is essential to realize that this is a substantive fact, not simply a methodological problem. It is not just the social scientist who cannot exactly measure how much approval a given helpful action is worth; the actors themselves cannot precisely specify the worth of approval or of help in the absence of a money price. The obligations individuals incur in social exchange, therefore, are defined only in general, somewhat diffuse terms. Furthermore, the specific benefits exchanged are sometimes primarily valued as symbols of the supportiveness and friendliness they express, and it is the exchange of the underlying mutual support that is the main concern of the participants. Occasionally, a time-consuming service of great material benefit to the recipient might be properly repaid by mere verbal expressions of deep appreciation, since these are taken to signify as much supportiveness as the material benefits.[10] In the long run, however, the explicit efforts the associates in a peer relation make in one another's behalf tend to be in balance, if only because a persistent imbalance in these manifestations of good will raise questions about the reciprocity in the underlying orientations of support and congeniality.

Extrinsic benefits are, in principle, detachable from the source that supplies them, but their detachability is a matter of degree. At one extreme are economic commodities, the significance of which is quite independent of the firm that supplies them. The value of a share in a corporation is not affected by the broker from whom we buy it. At the other extreme is the diffuse social support we derive in a love relationship, the significance of which depends entirely on the individual who supplies it. The typical extrinsic benefits socially exchanged, such as advice, invitations, assistance, or compliance, have a distinctive significance of their own that is independent of their supplier, yet an individual's preferences for them are also affected by his interpersonal relations with the supplier. Although the quality of advice determines its basic value for an individual, regardless of who furnishes it, he tends to prefer to consult a colleague whose friendly relations with him make it easy for him to do so rather than a more expert consultant whom he hardly knows.[11] The ease with which he can approach a colleague, the jokes and conviviality that surround the consultation, and other rewards he obtains from the association combine with the quality of the advice itself to determine

---

[10] See Erving Goffman, *Asylums*, Chicago: Aldine, 1962, pp. 274–286.

[11] See Blau, *The Dynamics of Bureaucracy* (2d ed.), University of Chicago Press, 1963, pp. 129–131.

the value of the total transaction for him. Indeed, the exchange of instrumental assistance may sometimes largely serve the function for participants of providing opportunities for exchanging these other more salient rewards. Going over and helping a fellow worker with his task might simply be an excuse for chatting with him and exchanging social support.

Since social benefits have no exact price, and since the utility of a given benefit cannot be clearly separated from that of other rewards derived from a social association, it seems difficult to apply the economic principles of maximizing utilities to social exchange.[12] The impersonal economic market is designed to strip specific commodities of these entangling alliances with other benefits, so to speak, and thus to make possible rational choices between distinct alternatives with a fixed price. Even in economic exchange, however, the significance of each alternative is rarely confined to a single factor, which confounds rational decision-making; people's job choices are affected by working conditions as well as salaries, and their choices of merchants, by the atmosphere in a store as well as the quality of the merchandise. Although the systematic study of social exchange poses distinctive problems, the assumptions it makes about the maximization of utilities implicit in choice behavior are little different from those made by the economist in the study of consumption.

In production and in marketing, profit is at a maximum "when the marginal cost and the marginal revenue are equal,"[13] and since both these quantities are defined in dollars, an unequivocal criterion for maximizing exists. But in consumption maximizing involves equating the marginal utilities obtained from expending an extra dollar in alternative ways, and this comparison of utilities poses, in principle, the same problem the study of social exchange does. Indeed, economists typically do not attempt to measure utilities directly to ascertain whether they are equated but simply infer that they are from the distribution of consumer expenditures or from other economic decisions. Thus, if a scientist accepts an academic job at a lower salary than he could command in industry, the so-called psychic income he obtains from his university position is assumed to equal or exceed in utilities the difference in salary. Similar inferences can be made from the observable conduct in social exchange. Moreover, these inferences about the value the social rewards exchanged have for

---

[12] See Homans, *op. cit.*, p. 72.

[13] Kenneth E. Boulding, *Economic Analysis* (3d ed.), New York: Harper, 1955, p. 552.

individuals can be used to derive testable hypotheses concerning the group structures that will emerge among them and the structural changes that will occur under various conditions, as will be exemplified in chapter seven.

Impressionistic observation suggests that people usually discharge their social obligations, even though there is no binding contract that can be enforced, in contrast to the contractual obligations in economic exchange, which can be enforced through legal sanctions. The reason is that failure to discharge obligations has a number of disadvantageous consequences, several of which do not depend on the existence of a norm of reciprocity. Suppose an individual to whom a neighbor has repeatedly lent some tools fails to reciprocate by doing his neighbor a favor when an opportunity arises. He can hardly borrow the tools again next time he needs them, and should he be brash enough to ask for them the neighbor may be reluctant to lend them to him. The neighbor is also likely to become less friendly toward an individual who refuses to do favors after he accepts some. Besides, the neighbor will probably distrust him in the future and, for example, be disinclined to trust him to repay for having their common fence painted but ask him for payment in advance. Chances are, moreover, that the neighbor will tell other neighbors about the ingratitude of this individual, with the result that this person's general reputation in the community suffers. Specifically, the neighbor's complaints will prompt numerous others to think less well of him, to hesitate to do him favors, and generally to distrust him. The first neighbor and the others have reason to act in this manner even if they were only concerned with protecting their own self-interest. The existence of a norm of reciprocity among them further reinforces their disapproval of him and their disinclination to do favors for him, now as a punitive reaction against a violator of a moral standard as well as to protect their own interest. Finally, an internalized norm of reciprocity would make him feel guilty if he fails to discharge his obligations, subjecting him to sanctions that are independent of any actions of others. The multiple penalties that failure to discharge social obligations evokes constitute pressures to discharge them.

Conditions of Exchange

A variety of conditions affect processes of social exchange: the stage in the development and the character of the relationship between exchange partners, the nature of the benefits that enter into the transactions and the costs incurred in providing them, and the social context in which the exchanges take place.

The initial offer of a favor to a stranger or an acquaintance is of special significance, whether it takes the form of a few friendly words, a cigar, the first invitation to one's home, or some helpful suggestions. It entails the risk of rejection of the offer itself and the risk of rejection of the overture implied by it through failure to reciprocate and enter into a friendly relationship. By taking these risks, an individual brings to an end the complete indifference between himself and another and forces on the other a choice of two alternatives, as Lévi-Strauss has noted: "From now on it must become a relationship either of cordiality or hostility." [14] The offer cannot be refused without being insulting, and acceptance of it invites some friendly exchange, if only of greetings and a few cordial words. Simmel took the extreme view that the first kindness of a person can never be fully repaid, because it alone is a spontaneous gesture of good will for another, whereas any future favor is prompted by the obligation to reciprocate. [15]

The establishment of exchange relations involves making investments that constitute commitments to the other party. Since social exchange requires trusting others to reciprocate, the initial problem is to prove oneself trustworthy. We have already seen how the gradual expansion of exchange transactions promotes the trust necessary for them. As individuals regularly discharge their obligations, they prove themselves trustworthy of further credit. Moreover, the investments an individual has made by fostering a friendly relation with another, in which it is easy to exchange services of various sorts, and by neglecting to cultivate other associates, who might constitute alternative sources of such services, commit him to the relationship. His commitment, which would make it disadvantageous for him to abandon the partnership in favor of another, gives the other additional reasons to trust him not to evade his obligations in their relationship. [16] Both partners gain advantages from a stable exchange partnership, but the greater commitment of one constitutes a particu-

---

[14] Claude Lévi-Strauss, "The Principle of Reciprocity," in Lewis A. Coser and Bernard Rosenberg, *Sociological Theory,* New York, Macmillan, 1957, p. 90.

[15] Georg Simmel, *Soziologie,* Leipzig: Duncker und Humblot, 1908, pp. 595–596.

[16] Commitment has been conceptualized as a side bet that promotes trust by making it disproportionately disadvantageous for a person to violate an agreement; see Thomas C. Schelling, *The Strategy of Conflict,* Cambridge: Harvard University Press, 1960, Chapter ii; and Howard S. Becker, "Notes on the Concept of Commitment," *American Journal of Sociology,* 66 (1960), 32–40.

lar advantage for the other. Here again we find, as we did in the discussion of social integration and in that of love, a situation that resembles a mixed game with some common and some conflicting interests—the common ones in the partnership and the conflicting ones concerning who makes the greater commitment. The partner with fewer alternative opportunities tends to be more dependent on and committed to the exchange relation than the other.

Since trust is essential for stable social relations, and since exchange obligations promote trust, special mechanisms exist to perpetuate obligations and thus strengthen bonds of indebtedness and trust. In the Kula expeditions of the Trobriand islanders, for example, the ceremonial gifts received cannot be returned until the next expedition many months later,[17] and while exchanges between partners who live in proximity to one another are more frequent, hasty reciprocation here too is condemned as improper.[18] In our society, similarly, the custom of giving Christmas gifts prevents us from reciprocating for an unexpected Christmas present until a year later or, at least, until another suitable occasion arises. Although an invitation to a party can be repaid any time, it is not proper to do so too promptly. Generally, posthaste reciprocation of favors, which implies a refusal to stay indebted for a while and hence an insistence on a more businesslike relationship, is condemned as improper. "Excessive eagerness to discharge an obligation is a form of ingratitude." [19] Social bonds are fortified by remaining obligated to others as well as by trusting them to discharge their obligations for considerable periods.

The nature of social rewards can be distinguished along several lines. First, some social rewards cannot be bartered in exchange, notably intrinsic attraction to a person, approval of his opinions and judgments, and respect for his abilities, because their significance rests on their being spontaneous reactions rather than calculated means of pleasing him. These evaluations of a person or his attributes reward him only if he has reason to assume that they are *not* primarily motivated by the explicit intention to reward him. Rewarding actions, in contrast to evaluations, can be bartered in social exchange since the fact that they are intended as inducements does not infringe on their inherent value as rewards. Social acceptance in a group to which a person is attracted, instrumental services of various kinds, and

---

[17] Malinowski, *op. cit.*, pp. 210–211.

[18] *Ibid.*, p. 96.

[19] François La Rochefoucauld, *The Maxims*, London: Oxford University Press, 1940, p. 73 (#226).

compliance with his wishes constitute rewards for him even if he knows that they are furnished in exchange for benefits expected of him. Second, within each of these two categories, rewards that are intrinsic to the association between individuals, such as personal attraction and social acceptance, can be distinguished from extrinsic ones, such as approval of decisions or opinions and instrumental services. Third, rewards that individuals may mutually supply for each other, as the four types just mentioned, can be distinguished from those that are necessarily unilateral, which are manifest in the general respect for a person that bestows superior prestige on him and in the prevailing compliance with his requests that bestows superior power on him. The six types of rewards delineated can be presented in this schema:

	Intrinsic	*Extrinsic*	*Unilateral*
Spontaneous Evaluations	Personal attraction	Social approval*	Respect– prestige †
Calculated Actions	Social acceptance*	Instrumental services*	Compliance– power †

* Entails investment costs for suppliers in addition to those needed to establish the social association.

† Entails the direct cost of subordination for suppliers.

The person who receives rewards from associating with another has an incentive to furnish inducements to the other to continue the association, and this is also the case if the rewards are spontaneous reactions that must not be bartered in exchange. Since it is rewarding for an individual to associate with others who accord him high respect, he is likely to provide sufficient inducements for them to continue the association unless he suspects them of simulating respect in order to obtain benefits from him. Positive evaluations of a person must not be bartered lest they cease to be accepted as genuine and thus lose their significance, but they do make social associations rewarding and worth some cost to the recipient and consequently enable the evaluator to reap some benefits from associating with him. Men sometimes take advantage of this fact and express approval of another in a calculating manner to obtain benefits from him in exchange, but this strategy of the sycophant can succeed only as long as its calculating intent remains hidden.

The cost incurred in providing social rewards in exchange for others may be thought of as "investment cost," "direct cost," and "opportunity cost." Investments in time and effort are necessary to acquire the skills required for furnishing many instrumental services, and such investments are also necessary to command respect for one's approval and thereby make it valuable for others. A group's investments that benefit its membership determine the value of social acceptance in the group and the contributions it can demand in exchange for acceptance. The supply of other social rewards usually entails no investments beyond those needed to establish the exchange relations. The most distinctive direct cost in social transactions is the subordination involved in expressing respect or manifesting compliance, that is, in rewarding another with prestige or with power. The most general cost incurred in supplying any social reward is the time required to do so in social associations. Since the significance of this time depends on the alternatives foregone by devoting it to a given exchange relation, it may be considered an opportunity cost. Time is not the only limited resource that may have to be withdrawn from alternative uses, thereby engendering opportunity costs, although it is probably the most widely significant one in social life.

The rewards an individual obtains from a social association cost him the opportunity to devote the time (and other limited resources) spent to another association where he could have obtained rewards. The mutual support in a love relationship and the social acceptance in an artistic circle, the endeavors made to court the approval of others or to command their respect, the efforts devoted to providing benefits to others in exchange for needed services or for compliance with one's wishes—all entail the cost of alternatives foregone as the result of the decision to expend time and energy in these associations rather than elsewhere. This time and effort could have been spent to obtain the same kinds of rewards from another source, possibly at less cost or of a better quality, and it could have been spent to obtain different rewards. As long as these alternatives appear tempting, individuals are inclined to explore them, but once they decide on what they consider the best alternative, they are likely to become committed to an exchange partnership and stop further exploration, with the result that they may not be able to take advantage of better opportunities that do become available.

If an individual obtains gratification from doing something in social interaction that is also gratifying for his associate, he provides the associate with a social reward without any cost to himself. Although there is a cost in time for him, this cost should be allocated to the reward he himself experiences rather than to the one he simultaneously furnishes the other. Such costless rewards are typical of mutual love, where each individual derives gratification in the very process of furnishing it to the other, but they also can be observed in instrumental associations. Giving advice to a colleague costs time and effort, and the colleague is expected to recompense the consultant for this cost, at least by expressing appreciation and respect for his expert counsel. Instead of asking for advice, however, a competent individual who encounters complex problems may tell his colleagues about his interesting case, as was actually often observed in a study of government officials.[20]

Such discussions of intricate problems in the presence of fellow experts can be considered consultations in disguise. The attentive listening and appreciative comments of his colleagues provide the speaker, in effect, with needed advice and confirmation by indicating to him whether he is on the right track while "thinking out loud," thus helping him to arrive at decisions that he might not have been able to make when alone. Since listening to and commenting on an interesting presentation of a complex case is instructive and enjoyable, the implicit advice of the listeners does not entail any cost to them for which the speaker would be obligated to recompense them. He obtains advice free, except for the indirect cost of his investment in his competence, without which he could not present complex discussions others find stimulating enough to want to hear.[21]

What exactly is it that enables a person to obtain social rewards from associates without incurring obligations to reciprocate? It is basically the fact that their actions that reward him are experienced by them not as a net cost but as a net gain, that is, as sufficiently rewarding to themselves to motivate them to engage in these actions.[22] The perception of relative advantage of the exchange partners, however, may complicate the situation. For example, if one neighbor

---

[20] Blau, *op. cit.*, pp. 132–135.

[21] He also incurs a cost in time but not an obligation to reciprocate. Individuals who ask advice pay, at least, respect to the superior ability of others implicitly by requesting their advice. In contrast, individuals who present discussions on the complex problems in their cases *earn* respect by doing so successfully, although they do incur the risk of losing respect should their analysis prove incorrect, and this discourages the less competent individuals from resorting to this practice.

[22] Although I emphasized in my study the significance of a person's *intention* of rewarding another in this connection (*ibid.*, p. 134), I now think that the crucial factor is not his intent but whether he himself profits in the very process of rendering a service to the other.

enjoys chopping wood and another wants to have his wood chopped, the first can provide the other with a service by an action from which he directly profits himself (chopping wood), and vice versa (letting wood be chopped), so that initially neither is indebted to the other. But if either or both should come to think that the advantages one gains from the transaction are greater than those of the other, one will feel obligated to supply additional favors to the other, who will feel justified in accepting or even requesting favors. The *comparative* net advantage one person gains from an action that also rewards another is what frees the other from the obligation to reciprocate for the rewards he receives.

In the analysis of the cost in an exchange transaction, it is important to differentiate between the cost to A of obtaining a given reward and the cost to B of supplying it. If B's cost in alternatives foregone are amply repaid by the gratification he receives in the very process of rewarding A, he can supply these rewards at no net cost to himself. Nevertheless, obtaining these rewards may be costly for A, because the disproportionate benefits he derives obligate him to make a return to B at some expense to himself. An individual can cut his costs by obtaining rewards from actions of others that are profitable rather than costly to them, if this is possible.[23] Thus, consulting others indirectly by telling them about difficult problems is a more economical method of receiving help with decision-making than directly asking for advice, but only experts whose discussions of problems others find stimulating can avail themselves of this method of obtaining help without becoming obligated to reciprocate for it. Social exchange can also be made less costly and more profitable by supplying social rewards that simultaneously benefit and obligate several others. The person who makes important contributions to an entire group illustrates this way of multiplying the benefits produced by one's actions and so does, to a lesser extent, the individual who mediates disagreements between friends. A manipulative case of this type is illustrated by Proust:

> He would now and then agree to act as an intermediary between two of his friends who had quarrelled, which led to his being called the most obliging of men. But it was not sufficient for him to appear to be doing a service to the friend who had come to him to demand it; he would represent to the other the steps which he was taking to effect a reconciliation as undertaken not at the request of the first friend but

---

[23] He will cut his cost, although not to nothing, even if they profit less than he does from these actions.

in the interest of the second, an attitude of the sincerity of which he had never any difficulty in convincing a listener already influenced by the idea that he saw before him the "most serviceable of men." In this fashion, playing in two scenes turn about, what in stage parlance is called "doubling" two parts, he never allowed his influence to be in the slightest degree imperilled, and the services which he rendered constituted not an expenditure of capital but a dividend upon some part of his credit.[24]

The social context in which exchange transactions take place affects them profoundly in several respects, which must be briefly adumbrated in this discussion of the conditions of exchange, although a more complete analysis of the interrelations between exchange processes and social structure is reserved for later chapters. First, even if we abstract the exchange transactions in a single pair, they are influenced by the "role-set" of each partner,[25] that is, by the role relations either has by virtue of occupying the social status relevant to the exchange, since these role relations govern the alternative opportunities of the two. The larger circle of acquaintances of the members of a clique who exchange invitations, for example, or the dating opportunities of two lovers, define the alternatives foregone by each and hence affect the cost each incurs in order to obtain rewards from his present association.

Second, the entire exchange transactions in a group determine a prevailing rate of exchange, and this group standard puts pressure on any partnership whose transactions deviate from it to come into line. These are not normative pressures in the sense of moral standards supported by group sanctions that enforce conformity but pressures resulting from existing opportunities. The demand for and supply of certain mechanical skills in a group of factory workers, for instance, influence how much respect and other benefits a highly skilled worker can command on the average for helping others with their tasks. Considerable departures from this average in a given exchange partnership create strong inducements for one of the partners to abandon it, inasmuch as more profitable opportunities for social interaction are elsewhere available to him. Third, potential coalitions among the weaker members of a collectivity tend to restrain its stronger members from fully exploiting their advantageous position in exchange transactions. Fourth, the differences in power to which

---

[24] Marcel Proust, *Remembrance of Things Past,* New York: Random House, 1934, Vol. I, 703.

[25] For the concept of role-set, see Robert K. Merton, *Social Theory and Social Structure* (2d ed.), Glencoe: Free Press, 1957, pp. 369–370.

exchange processes typically give rise in a group subsequently modify these processes, since established power enables an individual to compel others to provide services without offering a fair return, although the danger of the formation of coalitions to destroy his power may discourage its exploitative use.

Finally, the social situation exerts a subtle but important influence by making the transactions in a given exchange relation part of other exchanges that occur in the background and that may, nevertheless, be the more salient ones. A person may give a waiter a large tip to elicit the approval of his companions at the table for his generosity, not primarily to earn the waiter's gratitude. A worker may kindly help a newcomer and refuse any return offered because he wants to impress his supervisor or senior colleagues. If we look only at the apparent exchange in these cases, the individual appears to be uninterested in profiting from it, but the reason is that he is oriented toward a different exchange, and his unselfish behavior in one exchange is designed to profit him in another by winning him the approval of significant others. The opposite type of case is that of the individual who fully exploits every advantage to extract maximum instrumental benefits from some exchange relations in disregard of the disapproval he thereby incurs, because he needs these benefits to court the approval of other parties who are more significant for him. In either case, the immediate exchange processes cannot be understood without taking into account other exchange transactions that impinge on them.

People want to gain approval and they want to gain advantage in their social associations, and the two desires often come into conflict, since heedless pursuit of advantage tends to elicit disapproval. The multigroup affiliations of individuals in modern societies help to resolve this conflict. The resources needed to win social approval in some groups are typically acquired in other groups whose approval is less significant and can be dispensed with, as mentioned earlier. The money the businessman earns driving hard bargains that make him more feared than liked among his business associates enables him to earn the approval of his friends with his generosity. The politician humbly ingratiates himself with voters in order to achieve a position where he can wield power. The miserly secretary saves all year despite the ridicule of her companions in the hope of impressing another social circle with her affluence during her vacations. The juvenile delinquent willingly draws upon himself the condemnation of the larger community for acts that command respect in his gang. Multigroup affiliation entails social costs, as shown by the last illustration, particularly. It enables individuals in modern society to make the informal, and partly even the formal, sanctions of the community at large ineffective by organizing themselves into subcollectivities whose social approval alone is considered important.

Overwhelming Benefactions

The exchange of gifts and services in simple societies, which frequently assumes a ceremonial form, serves not only to create bonds of friendship and trust between peers but also to produce and fortify status differences between superiors and inferiors. The pervasive exchange processes in modern society, which are typically not institutionalized, have the same paradoxical twofold implication. Indeed, there are many parallels between the exchange rituals in simpler societies and social exchange in ours.

Malinowski has pointed out that the ceremonial objects used in the Kula are virtually pure objects of exchange. Although these armshells and necklaces are sometimes worn on festive occasions, the great pride the islanders take in them is neither due to their value as possessions to be displayed—they are readily lent to others for ceremonies—nor to their significance as heirlooms, since they must not be kept in possession for more than a year or two at the most. It is rather due to the renown an individual achieves from the success in the ceremonial exchange that his temporary possession of a fine Kula object indicates.[26] Other permanent possessions are greatly valued, and "wealth is the indispensable appanage of social rank and attribute of personal virtue. But the important point is that with them to possess is to give—and here the natives differ from us notably. A man who owns a thing is naturally expected to share it, to distribute it, to be its trustee and dispenser. And the higher the rank the greater the obligation. . . . Thus the main symptom of being powerful is to be wealthy, and of wealth is to be generous." [27]

Perhaps our orientation to wealth is really not as different from that of the Pacific islanders as Malinowski claimed in this passage. We too value wealth primarily for the uses to which it can be put to strengthen our power and to win us approval by dispensing it generously. The miser who secretly hoards his wealth gains no social advantages from it and can be considered a pathological case. To be sure, wealth is undoubtedly employed much more often to maintain

---

[26] Malinowski, *op. cit.*, pp. 86–87, 94.
[27] *Ibid.*, p. 97.

power over people in the complex economic structures in modern society and much less often to be generous to people than it is among the islanders. The reason for this, however, is the segmental nature of modern society, which makes the approval of most of the persons with whom we come into contact of little significance for us, as repeatedly noted. In the narrow circle of intimates whose approval is highly salient for modern man, the main function of his wealth is that it enables him to be generous in dispensing rewards that help win their approval and sustain their affection.

"Total prestation," as Mauss called any form of exchange, "not only carries with it the obligation to repay gifts received, but it implies two others equally important: the obligation to give presents and the obligation to receive them. . . . To refuse to give, or to fail to invite, is—like refusing to accept—the equivalent of a declaration of war; it is a refusal of friendship and intercourse." [28] Giving a present or doing a favor demonstrates trust in another; the other's reciprocation validates this trust as justified. A refusal to give a present or invite a person when the occasion arises implies distrust of him, and so does a refusal to accept a present or an invitation, since acceptance would involve an individual in an exchange relation in which he would have to trust the other to reciprocate at some future date. Distrust in simple societies is the equivalent of hostility; while distrust in economic relations in our society is expected, distrust in sociable relations here too is a sign of unfriendliness. The offer of a present or a favor is an invitation to become friendly; the rejection of such an overture is an insult, and failure to make one when it seems called for is only slightly less insulting.

The acceptance of an overture and the reciprocation of the present or favor received tend to become the starting point of a budding exchange relation and possibly a lasting friendship.[29] The expanding exchange of benefits of various sorts between individuals makes them increasingly interdependent, establishes mutual trust, and fortifies their social bond. A person's interest in the extrinsic benefits that are being exchanged, however, may lead him to accept a favor although he cannot properly reciprocate, or to fail to reciprocate for one

---

[28] Mauss, *op. cit.*, pp. 10–11.

[29] The significance of small favors as an invitation to engage in more significant exchanges is illustrated by the Kula practice of soliciting gifts. The partners of an islander who has a particularly valuable Kula object give him soliciting gifts of various kinds, trying to obligate him to give this object to them rather than another partner; see Malinowski, *op. cit.*, pp. 98–99, 354–355.

although he could. Failure to reciprocate engenders loss of credit and loss of trust, and it ultimately brings about exclusion from further exchanges and a general decline in social status, particularly as a person's reputation as one who does not honor his obligations spreads in the community.

There is a conflict between the obligation to reciprocate and the obligation to accept favors, since the only way an individual who is not in a position to reciprocate appropriately for benefits offered to him could protect himself against the dire consequences of lack of reciprocation would be not to accept the offers. Yet this combination of two apparently incompatible conditions is what makes it possible for largess to become a source of superordination over others, that is, for the distribution of gifts and services to others to be a means of establishing superiority over them. One of the important functions of social exchange is, in the words of Lévi-Strauss, "to surpass a rival in generosity, to crush him if possible under future obligations which it is hoped he cannot meet, thus taking from him privileges, titles, rank, authority, and prestige." [30]

A person who gives others valuable gifts or renders them important services makes a claim for superior status by obligating them to himself. If they return benefits that adequately discharge their obligations, they deny his claim to superiority, and if their returns are excessive, they make a counterclaim to superiority over him. If they fail to reciprocate with benefits that are at least as important to him as his are to them, they validate his claim to superior status. (In simple societies this status difference is typically due to the institutionalized significance of one-sided gifts, while in modern societies it is typically the result of unilateral dependence on recurrent needed services.) If others refuse his offer, it may imply that they cannot afford to repay him for it, and this admission of their inability to be his equal in social exchange also entails a loss of status. But if their rank and affluence are beyond dispute, their refusal of his offer implies something else, namely, that they do not consider him worthy of being their companion in exchange, and in this case their refusal creates animosity. [31]

The ability to distribute valuable possessions becomes a socially

---

[30] Lévi-Strauss, *op. cit.*, p. 85.

[31] See the discussion in Homans, *op. cit.*, pp. 318–319, from which this analysis derives, except that Homans does not make the distinction between the two different implications that the refusal to enter into an exchange relation may have, depending on the refuser's rank and resources. The distinction is implicit in Mauss, *op. cit.*, pp. 10–11, 39–40.

defined mark of superiority. The extreme illustration of this process is found in the institution of the potlatch among the Kwakiutl and other Indian tribes. These ceremonies are, to quote Mauss, "above all a struggle among nobles to determine their position in the hierarchy to the ultimate benefit, if they are successful, of their own clans." [32] For this purpose, feasts are given in which the host not only distributes but actually destroys huge quantities of valuable possessions in order to shame others who cannot match his extravagance into submission. "In some potlatch systems one is constrained to expend everything one possesses and to keep nothing. The rich man who shows his wealth by spending recklessly is the man who wins prestige." [33] The seemingly senseless dissipation and destruction of wealth as a means for asserting superior status, which is institutionalized in the potlatch, can also be observed in our society, where it is not institutionalized and takes the form of "conspicuous consumption." Veblen has emphasized that visible achievements, once thought of as indications of a man's skills and capacities to make productive contributions, have come to be emulated and looked up to in their own right, and that conspicuous consumption and even conspicuous waste have become major strategies for asserting superior status by displaying outward signs of achievement.[34] A reason for this might be that conspicuous waste indicates that a person's resources are so great he has no need to husband them, and as it demonstrates his ample potential for rewarding others and obligating them to accede to his wishes, it may lead them to accord him superior status even in anticipation of his actual use of this potential.

The distribution and destruction of valuables at public ceremonies is, moreover, held by many peoples to constitute a sacrifice to the gods in behalf of the entire community, and giving alms to the poor and gifts to children sometimes has similar significance.[35] The rest of the tribe confers high status on those who make these sacrifices, partly in exchange for the good will they are assumed to create among the spirits and gods toward the whole tribe. The benefits a modern community derives from charitable and philanthropic donations correspondingly help to sustain the high status of those who make them.

---

[32] *Ibid.,* pp. 4–5.

[33] *Ibid.,* p. 35. See also Ruth Benedict, *Patterns of Culture,* Boston: Houghton Mifflin, 1934, chapter vi.

[34] Thorstein Veblen, *The Theory of the Leisure Class,* New York: Viking, 1931, chapter iv.

[35] See Mauss, *op. cit.,* pp. 12–16.

Tributes to chiefs constitute a notable exception to the principle that unilateral giving establishes superordination. In the Kula, for example, the initial gift always goes to the chief. "So that the chief sometimes owes a gift to a commoner, but a commoner never owes a gift to a chief." [36] A chief maintains his superiority over commoners despite his temporary indebtedness to some in the ceremonial Kula exchange and despite his dependence on the contributions of many to support his household and staff.[37] The explanation probably is that commoners owe tribute to a chief, and the goods and services they furnish him are not considered favors that obligate him to them but returns for obligations they owe him. The underlying assumption is that the chief's leadership provides important benefits to the community, and their tribute to him, both in the form of valuables and in the form of deference, is a repayment of their continuous indebtedness to him. Institutionalized power commands services which a superior can use to provide benefits to subordinates that fortify his power. Such power makes the services of subordinates insufficient for establishing equality with the superior. Unilateral giving produces status differences between former peers, but once superior status is securely grounded in the social structure its occupant can demand unilateral services without endangering his superordinate position.

An examination of the ritualized behavior in the actual exchange of Kula objects is also instructive: "The native term 'to throw' a valuable describes well the nature of the act. For, though the valuable has to be handed over by the giver, the receiver hardly takes any notice of it, and seldom receives it actually in his hands. The etiquette of the transaction requires that the gift should be given in an off-hand, abrupt, almost angry manner, and received with equivalent nonchalance and disdain." [38] These conventions symbolize the exchange interests of the partners, which they are prohibited from manifesting directly through bargaining, as Malinowski indicates; the recipient's disdain implies that the object is of little value, and the donor's display of anger serves "to enhance the apparent value of the gift by showing what a wrench it is to give it away." [39] In addition, the recipient's nonchalance expresses a lack of need for the valuable, and the donor's off-hand manner of throwing it down similarly expresses a lack of need for it.

---

[36] Malinowski, *op. cit.*, p. 473.

[37] *Ibid.*, pp. 64–65.

[38] *Ibid.*, p. 352.

[39] *Ibid.*, p. 353.

This exchange etiquette can be considered an institutionalized form of role distance, which provides each actor with an opportunity to impress the audience at the ceremony as well as his partner by showing that he can easily rise beyond the demands of the role of Kula partner and that neither the rewards it brings nor the sacrifices it requires involve him deeply in this role.[40] By expressing role distance, a Kula partner implicitly claims that his resources warrant superior status in the exchange structure. This interpretation is indirectly supported by Malinowski's observation that a commoner does show appreciation when he receives a Kula object from a chief,[41] since a commoner would be expected to seek to claim superiority over other commoners but not over a chief. The etiquette that surrounds the giving of presents in our society reveals some parallels with that in the Kula exchange. We too tend to display role distance by depreciating the value of the presents we give—"It's really nothing!"—and, while the recipient is supposed to show his appreciation for the gift, the stereotyped forms of gratitude prescribed by conventions function to conceal any strong interest he may have in the object itself. Gifts are tokens of friendship and social bonds, and the requirement not to exhibit an interest in their inherent value as objects helps to preserve their pristine significance as symbols of interpersonal sentiments.[42]

In sum, overwhelming others with benefactions serves to achieve superiority over them. The ritual stance assumed when conferring benefits on others reveals the claim to superiority made by doing so. In many simple societies, exchanges of gifts and services have become institutionalized as the basis for status distinctions, and the institutionalized pattern of approval and deference bestows superior status on those who are able to dispense valuables with most largess. "Where we have institutionalized the market, they have institutionalized the gift."[43] But underlying these institutionalized forms are generic social forces that are manifest in the most complex as well as the simplest societies. Whatever is defined as valuable in a society, those who possess much of it can easily reward others and thus gain ascendancy over them. Their dispensation of these valuables, whether in the

[40] Erving Goffman's concept of role distance was discussed in chapter ii.

[41] Malinowski, *op. cit.*, p. 352.

[42] Simmel has noted (*op. cit.*, pp. 488–489) that giving something useful to a poor relative or friend who needs it humiliates him, because the evident instrumental value of the gift robs it of its sentimental value, thus emphasizing that he is being treated as a needy person rather than as an intimate.

[43] Homans, *op. cit.*, p. 319.

form of actual rewards or in the form of conspicuous waste that demonstrates their potential to reward, constitutes a claim to superiority most others tend to acknowledge. The recurrent unilateral supply of benefits that meet important needs makes others obligated to and dependent on those who furnish them and thus subject to their power.

Conclusions

People's positive sentiments toward and evaluations of others, such as affection, approval, and respect, are rewards worth a price that enter into exchange transactions, but they must not be explicitly bartered in exchange lest their value as genuine feelings or judgments be compromised. The actions of people that benefit others, however, remain significant whatever the underlying motive; hence their value as rewards is not jeopardized if they are explicitly used for bargaining in exchange transactions. This is particularly so for instrumental services, which constitute extrinsic rewards, including the generic instrumental service of compliance with another's wishes. But the distinction between rewards that are intrinsic to a social association and those that are extrinsic and, in principle, detachable from it is an analytical and relative one.

Social exchange always entails elements of intrinsic significance for the participants, which distinguishes it from strictly economic transactions, although its focus is on benefits of some extrinsic value and on, at least, implicit bargaining for advantage, which distinguishes it from the mutual attraction and support in profound love. The taboo on explicit bargaining in the exchange of gifts is designed to protect their significance as tokens of friendship, that is, as signs of intrinsic attraction, from being obliterated by the inherent value of the objects themselves. Social exchange, then, is an intermediate case between pure calculation of advantage and pure expression of love. However, even economic transactions and love relations rarely express the polar processes in entirely pure form, since the multiple gains and costs typically involved in any economic transaction prevent unambiguous calculation of advantage, and since extrinsic benefits are exchanged in love relations and often help to produce mutual affection. Economic institutions, such as the impersonal market and the contract that stipulates the precise terms of the exchange, are designed to separate concern with distinct objects of exchange from other considerations and to specify the exact obligations incurred in a transaction, thus maximizing the possibility of rational calculation. Social exchange, in contrast, involves unspecified obligations, the fulfillment of which depends on trust because it cannot be enforced in the absence of a binding contract. But the trust required for social exchange is generated by its own gradual expansion in a self-adjusting manner.

Furnishing benefits to others may lead to the development of bonds of fellowship with them or to a position of superiority over them. A person who distributes gifts and services to others makes a claim to superior status. By reciprocating and, particularly, by making excessive returns that now obligate the first to them, others invalidate his claim and invite further transactions in expanding exchange relations of mutual trust between peers. Their failure to reciprocate, on the other hand, validates his claim to superiority, and so does their failure to accept his offer, unless their evident affluence proves that their rejection is not due to their inability to enter into egalitarian exchange relations with him but to their unwillingness to do so, in which case it is likely to produce hostility. A person can establish superiority over others by overwhelming them with benefits they cannot properly repay and thus subduing them with the weight of their obligations to him. But once superiority is firmly rooted in political or economic structures, it enables an individual to extract benefits in the form of tribute from subordinates without any peril to his continued superiority over them.

It seems to be typical of social associations that the individuals who establish them have some common and some conflicting interests. A stable social relationship requires that individuals make some investments to bring it into being and maintain it in existence, and it is to the advantage of each party to have the other or others assume a disproportionate share of the commitments that secure their continuing association. Hence the common interest of individuals in sustaining a relation between them tends to be accompanied by conflicting interests as to whose investment should contribute most to its sustenance. We have seen that the first choice of group members who are attracted to each other is typically to have their position in the group buttressed by the unilateral respect of others for them, although most of them are willing to settle for a position in which they must pay respect to others in preference to being excluded from the group. Similarly, lovers gain advantage from having the other more committed, but their interest in maintaining the love relationship often induces them to make the greater commitment if necessary. In parallel fashion, exchange partners derive most advantage from having the other make the bulk of the investment needed to stabilize their relationship, although their interest in the continuing partnership gives each of them an incentive to make the major investment himself rather than let the profitable association fall apart. In every exchange transaction, finally, each participant hopes to gain much at little cost, yet to profit at all both must come to some agreement. The coexistence of conflicting and common interests in all these social associations means that associates always have first choices that conflict but last choices that are identical, and the first choice of either is the second-last of the other, though it may still be preferable to any available alternative.[44] These preferences, however, are continually modified in the process of maneuvering between partners and exploring alternative opportunities until stable social relations have become crystallized.

Aside from these interpersonal conflicts, there is also the intrapersonal conflict between the individual's desire to gain social approval and support and his desire to gain instrumental advantage in his social associations. This conflict is usually resolved by obtaining intrinsic support primarily from some associates and extrinsic benefits largely from others. The multigroup affiliations of individuals in modern society facilitate this solution, permitting them to pursue their advantage without regard for approval in one social context and to elicit approval and support by their generosity and supportiveness in another, for example, in their business and in their family, respectively. Social approval has less pervasive significance as a restraining force in complex societies than in simpler ones, because the multiplicity of groups and the possible mobility between them in complex societies enables deviants of nearly all sorts to escape from the impact of community disapproval by finding a subgroup of like-minded persons where they can gain approval. Impersonal restraints are, therefore, of special importance in modern societies, and a basic source of impersonal restraint is power.

---

[44] See the chart on p. 45.

✳ FIVE

Differentiation of Power

[Power] is thus both awful and fragile, and can dominate a continent, only in the end to be blown down by a whisper. To destroy it, nothing more is required than to be indifferent to its threats, and to prefer other goods to those which it promises. Nothing less, however, is required also.

R. H. TAWNEY, *Equality*

" 'Power' (*Macht*) is the probability that one actor within a social relationship will be in a position to carry out his own will despite resistance," according to Weber.[1] Tawney's definition similarly centers on imposing one's will on others, except that he explicitly directs attention to the asymmetry of power relations: "Power may be defined as the capacity of an individual, or group of individuals, to modify the conduct of other individuals or groups in the manner which he desires, and to prevent his own conduct being modified in the manner in which he does not."[2]

Broadly defined, power refers to all kinds of influence between persons or groups, including those exercised in exchange transactions, where one induces others to accede to his wishes by rewarding them for doing so. Neither Weber nor Tawney, however, used the term that broadly. Although the customer technically imposes his will upon the jeweler when he makes him surrender a diamond ring by paying for it, this situation clearly should not be confused with that of the

---

[1] Max Weber, *The Theory of Social and Economic Organization*, New York: Oxford University Press, 1947, p. 152.

[2] R. H. Tawney, *Equality*, London: Allen and Unwin, 1931, p. 229.

115

gangster who forces the jeweler to hand over the ring at the point of a gun. Physical coercion, or its threat, is the polar case of power, but other negative sanctions, or the threat of exercising them, are usually also effective means of imposing one's will on others. People can be made to do things for fear of losing their jobs, of being ostracized, of having to pay fines, or of losing social standing. This suggests a distinction between coercive power, which rests on the deterrent effect of negative sanctions, and influence based on rewards, as that characteristic of exchange transactions.[3]

Defining power as control through negative sanctions implies that an individual exercises power when he gets another to perform a service by threatening to take 100 dollars from him if he refuses, whereas he does not when he gets the other to perform the same service by promising him 100 dollars for it. The objection may be raised that the net difference is the same in both cases—the other is 100 dollars better off if he performs the service than if he does not— but this objection does not seem valid. The crucial factor is the base-line from which an individual starts when another seeks to influence him, and the only difference between punishments and rewards is in relation to this initial baseline, whether he is worse or better off than he was before the transaction started. The necessity to avert a loss is probably also experienced as more of an external compulsion than the temptation to make a gain. A more serious objection, however, is that the baseline itself is obscured once rewards become recurrent.

Regular rewards make recipients dependent on the supplier and subject to his power, since they engender expectations that make their discontinuation a punishment. A person who has a job is rewarded for performing his duties by his earnings, and as his wages are positive sanctions it seems at first that no power is involved in terms of the definition presented. However, being fired from a job cannot plausibly be considered to constitute merely the absence of rewards; it clearly is a punishing experience. The threat of being fired is a

[3] This corresponds to John P. R. French, Jr., and Bertram Raven's distinction between coercive and reward power, in addition to which they specified three types not contingent on external sanctions (legitimate, referent, and expert power); "The Bases of Social Power," in Dorwin Cartwright, *Studies in Social Power,* Ann Arbor: Institute for Social Research, University of Michigan, 1959, pp. 150–167. Talcott Parsons makes a parallel distinction between coercive power that rests on deterrence through negative sanctions and inducements in exchange transactions that rest on positive sanctions; "On the Concept of Influence," *Public Opinion Quarterly,* 27 (1963), 43–45, and "On the Concept of Political Power," *Proceedings of the American Philosophical Society,* 107 (1963), 238–239.

May remarks

negative sanction that gives an employer power over his employees, enabling him to enforce their compliance with his directives. Regular rewards create expectations that redefine the baseline in terms of which positive sanctions are distinguished from negative ones. The air we breathe is not conceived by us to be a special reward, nor is the freedom to move about the streets as we please, but being suffocated or imprisoned is experienced as a punishment. Correspondingly, a man who has reason to expect to remain in his job does not think of his regular earnings as distinctive rewards, and the loss of his income is a punishment for him. Only a raise in income is a specific reward, although even raises that occur regularly come to be expected, and in these cases failure to receive a raise tends to be experienced as a punishment and may be so intended by the employer.

The definition of power should be amplified, therefore, to read that it is the ability of persons or groups to impose their will on others despite resistance through deterrence either in the forms of withholding regularly supplied rewards or in the form of punishment, inasmuch as the former as well as the latter constitute, in effect, a negative sanction.[4] Three further implications should be noted. First, following Parsons, the concept of power is used to refer to an individual's or group's ability *recurrently* to impose his or its will on others, not to a single instance of influencing a decision of theirs, however important.[5] Second, the punishment threatened for resistance, provided it is severe, makes power a compelling force, yet there is an element of voluntarism in power—the punishment could be chosen in preference to compliance, and it sometimes is—which distinguishes it from the limiting case of direct physical coercion.[6] Finally, power is conceptualized as inherently asymmetrical and as resting on the *net* ability of a person to withhold rewards from and apply punishments to others—the ability that remains after the re-

---

[4] A technical problem of definition, to which Arnold Kaufman has called my attention, arises if there is disagreement between superior and subordinates as to whether a given reward is regularly supplied or not. For example, an employer may think of a Christmas bonus as a special reward, whereas his employees have come to think of it as part of their regular income and to consider not receiving the bonus a penalty. It is necessary to decide, depending on the purpose at hand, whether the defining criterion is the subordinates' expectation or the superior's intent.

[5] *Ibid.*, pp. 237–238.

[6] Parsons' emphasis on legitimacy in this connection (*ibid.*, pp. 236–244), however, seems to confound the distinction between power and the special case of authority, which will be discussed in chapter viii.

straints they can impose on him have been taken into account. Its source is one-sided dependence. Interdependence and mutual influence of equal strength indicate lack of power.

Unilateral Dependence and Obligations

By supplying services in demand to others, a person establishes power over them. If he regularly renders needed services they cannot readily obtain elsewhere, others become dependent on and obligated to him for these services, and unless they can furnish other benefits to him that produce interdependence by making him equally dependent on them, their unilateral dependence obligates them to comply with his requests lest he cease to continue to meet their needs. Providing needed benefits others cannot easily do without is undoubtedly the most prevalent way of attaining power, though not the only one, since it can also be attained by threatening to deprive others of benefits they currently enjoy unless they submit. The threat of punishment, although it exerts the most severe restraints, creates the dependence that is the root of power indirectly, as it were, while recurrent essential rewards that can be withheld do so directly. The government that furnishes needed protection to its citizens, the employer who provides needed jobs to his employees, and the profession that supplies needed services to the community, all make the others dependent on them and potentially subject to their power.

Emerson has presented a schema for examining "power-dependence" relations and their consequences, which can be reformulated to specify the conditions that produce the imbalance of power itself.[7] Individuals who need a service another has to offer have the following alternatives: *First, they can supply him with a service* that he wants badly enough to induce him to offer his service in return, though only if they have the resources required for doing so; this will lead to reciprocal exchanges. *Second, they may obtain the needed service elsewhere,* assuming that there are alternative suppliers; this also will lead to reciprocal exchanges but in different partnerships. *Third, they can coerce him to furnish the service,* provided they are

---

[7] Richard M. Emerson, "Power-Dependence Relations," *American Sociological Review,* 27 (1962), 31–41. Suggestive as the underlying conception is, the focus on balancing operations is unfortunate and somewhat confusing inasmuch as it diverts attention from the analysis of power imbalance. His schema deals with the balancing operations consequent to given differences in power-dependence, whereas the reformulation derives power imbalances from the conditions of exchange.

capable of doing so, in which case they would establish domination over him. *Fourth, they may learn to resign themselves to do without this service,* possibly finding some substitute for it, which would require that they change the values that determine their needs. Finally, if they are not able or willing to choose any of these alternatives, they have no other choice but to comply with his wishes, since he can make continued supply of the needed service contingent on their compliance. In the situation specified, the supply of services inevitably generates power. The absence of the first four alternatives defines the conditions of power in general.

This schema can be employed to indicate the conditions of social independence, the requirements of power, the issues in power conflicts, and their structural implications. The conditions of social independence are characterized by the availability of the first four alternatives, which enables people to evade the fifth one of dependence on services from a given source. First, strategic resources promote independence. Specifically, a person who has all the resources required as effective inducements for others to furnish him with the services and benefits he needs is protected against becoming dependent on anyone. The possession of generalized rewards, such as money, is evidently of major significance in this connection, although wealth is not a perfect safeguard against dependence, since many benefits a person may want, such as fame or love, cannot be obtained for money but only with other resources.

The fact that there are alternative sources from which a needed service can be obtained is a second condition that fosters independence. If there is only one employer in a community, or only one expert consultant in a work group, others are likely to become dependent on him. The situation, however, does not have to be that extreme. As a matter of fact, any commitment to a social relationship entails a degree of dependence by excluding alternatives. An employee presumably remains in a job either because alternative employment opportunities are less attractive to him or because his investment in this job is so great that moving to another would be too costly for him. Whatever the reason, his lack of equally preferable alternatives makes him dependent on his employer.[8] The degree of dependence

---

[8] The counterdependence of the small employer on the employee's services may create interdependence and neutralize the small employer's power, but the large employer is not so much dependent on single employees as on a labor force whose turnover can and must be taken into account in management, and his independence of any one employee sustains his power over all of them, unless it is reduced by their collective action.

of individuals on a person who supplies valued services is a function of the difference between their value and that of the second-best alternative open to them. The more employees prefer their own job to any possible alternative, the more dependent are they on their employer and the more power does he have over them. The employer can cut the salary of employees who are very dependent on their job, assign them unpleasant duties, or force them to work harder, and they have no choice but to accept the decisions and to comply. Yet by doing so the employer makes the job less attractive to the employees and other employment opportunities relatively more attractive, decreasing the difference between the present job and alternatives, and thus reducing his employees' dependence on him and his power over them. Generally, the greater the difference between the benefits an individual supplies to others and those they can obtain elsewhere, the greater is his power over them likely to be. Hence, others can increase their independence of a person who has power over them simply by accepting fewer benefits from him—no more than they can get for their services elsewhere—except that this is often not so simple for them.[9]

A third condition of independence is the ability to use coercive force to compel others to dispense needed benefits or services. The inability to use force may be due to weakness or to normative restraints that effectively prohibit resort to coercion, or it may be due to the fact that the desired benefit loses its significance if given under duress, as is the case for love and for social approval. Superior coercive power makes people relatively independent of others inasmuch as power includes the ability to prevent others from interfering with one's conduct. Since there is strength in numbers, independence can be won through forming coalitions capable of enforcing demands.[10]

A lack of need for various services constitutes the fourth condition of independence. The fewer the wants and needs of an individual, the less dependent he is on others to meet them. Needs, however, do not remain constant. By providing individuals with goods and services that increase their satisfaction, their level of expectations tends to be raised, and while they were previously satisfied without these benefits,

---

[9] Accepting a job at a higher salary than one can command in the market, buying from an acquaintance at wholesale prices, gaining acceptance in a more eminent group than one's achievements warrant, and generally obtaining any recurrent benefit that is superior to what could be obtained elsewhere entails dependence and loss of power.

[10] Emerson, *op. cit.*, p. 37.

they are now desirous of continuing to obtain them. The development of new needs in this fashion underlies the increasing consumer demand that is an essential element in an expanding economy. But emergent needs serve this function by strengthening the dependence of people on those who can supply the resources required to meet these needs, notably employers. Religious and political ideals derive their driving force in large part from imbuing adherents with values that make the satisfaction of material wants comparatively unimportant and that, consequently, lessen men's dependence on those who can supply material benefits. By reducing material needs, revolutionary ideologies become a source of independent strength and resistance to power.

The fourfold schema can also help to delineate the strategies required to attain and sustain power, which are complementary to the conditions of independence just discussed. To achieve power over others with his resources, a person must prevent others from choosing any of the first four alternatives, thereby compelling them to comply with his directives as a condition for obtaining the needed benefits at his command. This requires, first, that he remain indifferent to the benefits they can offer him in exchange for his. The strategies of power designed to preserve this indifference include denying others access to resources that are vital for the welfare of a group or individual, for example, by fighting attempts of working-class parties to take over the government; securing needed benefits from outside sources rather than subordinates, as illustrated by the gang leader's disinclination to borrow money from his more affluent followers; [11] and encouraging competition among the suppliers of essential service, for instance, by opposing the formation of unions that would restrict competition for jobs among workers.

A second requirement of power is to assure the continued dependence of others on the services one has to supply by barring access to alternative suppliers of these services. Monopolization of needed rewards is the typical means of achieving this purpose. The only firm in town where jobs can be found, the only child on the block who has a bicycle, the political society that is the sole source of national security and glory, the church that is the only avenue to salvation, and the police that alone can offer protection against violence—all these have power due to their monopoly over important benefits.

The ability to prevent others from resorting to coercive force to

---

[11] William F. Whyte, *Street Corner Society* (2d ed.), University of Chicago Press, 1955, pp. 257–258.

effect their demands is a third prerequisite of maintaining power. Discouraging coalitions among subordinates that would enable them to extract demands is a strategy that serves this end, as is blocking their access to political power. Such organizations as unions and working-class parties have two analytically distinct, though actually inseparable, functions in the fight against existing powers. Their success threatens those in positions of power, on the one hand, by making them dependent for essential services on these organizations (for example, for labor supply) and, on the other, by subjecting them to their coercive power (for instance, the union's sit-down strike or the executive power of the labor-party government). Obstructing such coalitions, therefore, protects power against being undermined either by withholding vital services or by employing coercive force. Probably the most important strategies for safeguarding the power that rests on the possession of important resources, however, are support for law and order and resistance against political control of exchange processes. These defenses protect the power potential that resides in superior vital resources not only from the threat of violence but also from being curbed by the legitimate power of the state.

Fourth, power depends on people's needs for the benefits those in power have to offer. Materialistic values, which make money and what it can buy of great significance, strengthen the power of employers. Patriotic ideals, which identify people with the success of their country in war and peace, fortify the power of the government. Religious convictions, which make the blessings of a church and the spiritual counsel of its representatives rewards of great saliency, reinforce the power of church dignitaries. Revolutionary ideologies, which define the progress of a radical movement as inherently valuable for its members, bestow power on the movement's leadership. Groups and individuals in power have a stake in helping to perpetuate and spread the relevant social values and in opposing counterideologies that depreciate these values. Dominant groups whose power rests on different social values have some conflicting interests, therefore, although their common interest in preserving the existing power structure may well override these differences.

The conflict between the powerful (who have an interest in fortifying their power) and the people over whom they have power (who have an interest in strengthening their independence) centers around four types of issues, which again correspond to the four alternatives outlined. First, there is the issue of the resources of subordinates. If their resources were sufficient to obtain the benefits they need in exchange for them, they would cease to be subject to the power of the others. Granted that every single subordinate's resources are inadequate for this purpose, the issue becomes that of pooling the resources of all subordinates who confront a superior or group of superiors to extract demands from him or them. The second issue is that of the alternative opportunities available to subordinates for obtaining needed benefits. Competition among superiors for the services of subordinates increases the subordinates' independence, whereas monopolistic practices increase the superiors' power. These two conflicts are complementary, since the question in both cases is the degree of collective organization permissible to restrain free competition, although it is the organization of the powerless that would husband their resources in one case, and the organization of the powerful that would monopolize needed benefits in the other.

The third conflict is political. At issue here is the use of coercive force in the fight against powers based on superior resources. The prototype is the conflict over the use of the legitimate coercive power of the state to regulate exchange transactions and restrict power that rests on economic strength. Fourth, there is the ideological conflict between social values that intensify the need for the services the powerful have to offer and counterideologies that mitigate this need. In the process of decreasing the need for some services, however, radical ideologies increase the need for others—namely, those that contribute to the reform movement—with the result that ideologies make adherents less dependent on the power of some but more dependent on the power of others.

Finally, tracing the implications of each of the four alternatives leads to the analysis of basic problems of social structure. First, the fact that benefits can be obtained by reciprocating for them with others directs attention to the study of exchange processes and the distribution of resources. Second, the exploration of alternative opportunities points to the investigation of the emerging exchange structures, the competitive processes in them, the going rates of exchange, and the normative standards that tend to develop. Third, the study of coercive power raises questions concerning the establishment of coalitions and organizations to mobilize power, the differentiation of power in social structures, and the processes that govern the struggle over political power in a society.[12] Fourth, the ability to get along without something originally needed calls attention to the modifica-

---

[12] These could also be considered to be implications of the fifth alternative. The third and fifth alternatives are complementary, as they are concerned with power from the perspectives of the two different parties.

tions of social values that occur under various conditions, the formation of new ideologies, and conflicts between ideologies.[13]

The main points of the entire discussion presented are summarized in this schema:

Alternatives to Compliance	Conditions of Independence	Requirements of Power	Structural Implications
1. Supply inducements	Strategic resources	Indifference to what others offer	Exchange and distribution of resources
2. Obtain elsewhere	Available alternatives	Monopoly over what others need	Competition and exchange rates
3. Take by force	Coercive force	Law and order	Organization and differentiation
4. Do without	Ideals lessening needs	Materialistic and other relevant values	Ideology formation

Dependence on the benefits a person can supply does not make others subject to his power but gives him only potential power over them. Realization of this power requires that he actually supply the benefits or commit himself to do so. In a technical sense, we are dependent on all employers who are in a position to offer us better jobs than those we have, but these employers have no power over us, while our employer has the power to command our compliance with his directives, because the salary and other benefits he furnishes obligate us to comply lest we cease to continue to receive them. He alone can withdraw from us benefits to which we have become accustomed, whereas other employers can only tempt us with greater rewards.

---

[13] Some aspects of the first problem have been discussed in chapter iv; some of the second will be discussed in this chapter and in chapters vi and vii; of the third, in chapters viii and ix (as well as in the present one); and of the fourth, in chapters ix and xi.

The ability to provide superior benefits than are available elsewhere, in a situation where these benefits are needed and cannot be extracted by force, constitutes a very strong claim to power, although not a completely inescapable one. If the power demands are too severe, relinquishing these benefits may be preferable to yielding to the demands. Moreover, a person's or group's resources may not be adequate to obligate others to comply. For these reasons coercive force, which can hardly be resisted, is important as a last resort for exercising power over individuals who cannot otherwise be made to yield. Whereas physical force is a perfect protection against power—killing a man or incarcerating him disposes of his threat—it is an imperfect tool for exercising power, since people can choose even death over compliance. Hence, coercive force differs only in degree from the power that rests on the supply of needed benefits, albeit an important degree.

Competition for Status

Competition arises in the process of social integration and gives rise to differentiation of status in groups, as noted in chapter two. At this point processes of social differentiation in groups will be traced in greater detail, focusing on the ultimate differentiation of power and drawing attention to some parallels between the differentiating processes in face-to-face groups and those in complex structures.

The initial competition in newly forming groups is for participation time. Whatever attracts individuals to the group, whether they seek to gain simply acceptance, social support, respect, or positions of leadership and power, obtaining these social rewards requires opportunities for proving oneself worthy of them. Others must devote time to interact with and listen to an individual to enable him to impress them with his outstanding qualities, but time is scarce since not everyone can be attended to at once. Time, then, is a generalized means in the competition for a variety of social rewards, equivalent in this respect to profitable sales in economic competition, which also are needed whether the aim is to distribute profits, increase assets, buy new equipment, or achieve a dominant position in the market. The unequal distribution of speaking time produces an initial differentiation that gives some an advantage in subsequent competitive processes, just as the unequal distribution of sales among firms does.

The group allocates time among various members in accordance with their estimated abilities to make contributions to its welfare based on the initial impressions. In a discussion group confronted with the task of resolving some issue or solving some problem, for example, most speaking time is allocated to those who appear most likely to advance the solution. Having speaking time available, however, is not sufficient for an individual's purpose, whatever it is; he must properly use the opportunity it provides to obtain social rewards from the rest of the group. The member who makes important contributions to the discussion is first rewarded by the approval of others, by having them increasingly turn to him for his suggestions and for his approval of theirs, and if his suggestions continue to prove viable, he is further rewarded by their respect for his abilities. The group member who makes lesser contributions—for instance, relieving the tensions generated by conflicts of opinions through his good humor and congeniality—is likely to earn the approval and acceptance of others, though not their high respect.

The object of competition shifts in this process from having time made available for originating interaction with others first to receiving interaction from them that express their positive evaluation of oneself, and then from there to commanding their respect and compliance or, at least, earning their acceptance and social support. Lack of success in the earlier competition for speaking time puts an individual at a disadvantage in the later competition for respect and leadership. Once competition has become refocused on social status, however, speaking time is no longer of central concern and there are even occasions when it is most advantageous to refrain from talking. These processes reveal again some close parallels to economic competition. Firms must compete for sales to maximize profits, and great profits are necessary to compete for a dominant position in the industry. But once a dominant position is the central focus of competitive endeavors considerations other than profitable sales must be taken into account, such as possible anti-trust action of the government. Indeed a situation may arise in which the maintenance of a firm's dominant position is best served by refraining from further increasing sales. Gary's management of United States Steel is reported to have followed such a policy of restraint, in sharp contrast to Carnegie's earlier management under which the firm achieved its dominant position.[14]

Earning superior status in a group requires not merely impressing others with outstanding abilities but actually using these abilities to make contributions to the achievement of the collective goals of the

---

[14] Charles H. Hession, S. M. Miller, and Curwen Stoddart, *The Dynamics of the American Economy*, New York: Knopf, 1956, pp. 193–208.

group or the individual goals of its members. It requires, for example, suggestions that advance the solution of the common problem of a discussion group or advice that helps individual colleagues in a work group to improve their performance. Having his suggestions usually followed by others is a mark of respect that raises an individual's social standing in a group, while others' social standing simultaneously suffers for two reasons, because they often follow his suggestions and because their own are rarely accepted. Initially, the high respect of the rest of the group may be sufficient reward for the contributions a group member makes, and short-term discussion groups in laboratories may never advance beyond this stage, but in the long run it is likely to prove insufficient. Since the value of a person's approval and respect is a function of his own social standing, the process of recurrently paying respect to others depreciates its value. Hence, respect often does not remain an adequate compensation for contributions that entail costs in time and effort to the one who makes them, such as assistance with complex problems. Those who benefit from such instrumental help, therefore, become obligated to reciprocate in some other way, and deferring to the wishes of the group member who supplies the help is typically the only thing the others can do to repay him. As a result of these processes in which the contributions of some come to command the compliance of others, a differentiated power structure develops.

Exchange relations become differentiated from competitive ones concurrently with the differentiation of social status that emerges in the course of competition. In rudimentary social structures, all members compete with each other for the output of each other. Thus, each group member competes with all the other members for the respect of these same other members. As status begins to become differentiated, those whose abilities win the respect of others go on to compete among themselves for positions of power and leadership, whereas those who must acknowledge inferiority by paying respect have no chance in this continuing competition. In consequence, exchange relations are no longer identical with competitive ones. The high-status members furnish instrumental assistance to the low-status ones in exchange for their respect and compliance, which help the high-status members in their competition for a dominant position in the group. Without the contribution of the highs to the performance of collective or individual tasks, the lows would be deprived of the benefits that accrue to them from improved performance and joint achievements. Without the compliance and support of the lows, the highs cannot attain positions of power and leadership. Sometimes the members of work groups compete in their performance. If this is the case, the exchange relations between the highs and the lows that develop out of competitive relations as the result of status differentiation help both the highs in their competition for superior status and the lows in their competition for better performance.

These processes, in which competitive and exchange relations become differentiated in the course of the development of increasing status differences, are also manifest in entire communities, as the class structure of the Ifugao in the Philippines illustrates.[15] There are three broad classes, and class position depends primarily on wealth. Everybody competes for wealth as a means of improving his social status. The middle class is composed of property holders who work on the land, ranging from those with such poor land that they are continually threatened by bankruptcy, which would put them into the propertyless lower class, to those with such large holdings and surplus incomes that they have some chance to move into the upper class. In effect, families in the lower-middle class compete for staying in the middle class, while families in the upper-middle class compete for entry into the upper class, and since they are too far apart to compete, exchange relations develop between these two strata that serve the members of each in their distinct competitive struggles. Members of the upper-middle class often furnish loans, at interest, to those of the lower-middle class, which help them to retain their land and thus stay in the middle class, and which increase the wealth of the upper-middle class and thus their chances of moving into the upper class. It is evident that the situation in Western societies, though more complex, is strikingly similar.

In sum, the development of structural differentiation occurs along several different lines, partly in succession, and in part concurrently. The initial competition for participation time in newly forming groups turns into endeavors to prove oneself attractive to others and ultimately into competition for respect, power, and leadership. The group first allocates participation time differentially, then centers interaction disproportionately on some members, and successively differentiates respect, power, and dominance. Success at each step of differential allocation constitutes a competitive advantage for the next. Simultaneous with the increasing differentiation of social status, exchange relations become differentiated from competitive ones, be-

---

[15] Irving Goldman, "The Ifugao of the Philippine Islands," in Margaret Mead, *Cooperation and Competition Among Primitive Peoples,* New York: McGraw-Hill, 1937, pp. 153–179.

cause only those successful in the earlier competition for respect continue to compete for dominance, while the unsuccessful ones cease to compete with the successful members and instead offer compliance and support for their competition in exchange for instrumental services from them. Furthermore, role specialization develops, particularly in complex social structures, where a great variety of contributions are needed. Individuals who have been unsuccessful in their attempts to earn respect and power have incentives to find new ways of making contributions that would gain them superior status, and individuals in dominant positions have the power to assign specialized tasks to various others, both of which processes promote specialization.

A stratified system of differential status, however, involves more than differences in the respect and compliance various individuals command among others. The fact that one individual's ability and judgment are more widely respected in a group than another's means that the one is more highly esteemed than the other, but for these evaluations to crystallize into status differences requires that they be publicly acknowledged and that consensus is reached regarding them. As Homans put it: "In the early stages of the development of a group, several members may give one of their companions much social approval so that he is in fact enjoying high esteem, and yet no single member may have come to recognize what the others are doing." [16] Only the consensus that emerges among the rest of a group that the qualities of one member are worthy of high respect transforms their personal esteem of him into social status rooted in shared valuations, which implies that newcomers would be expected to accord him high respect even before they personally have acquired a high estimation of his qualities. Public recognition of the relative respect deserved by various members of the group makes the prestige structure a social reality independent of the attitudes of specific individuals. Our behavior to the President of the United States would undoubtedly reflect the high prestige he generally commands, whatever we personally may think of him. Consensus concerning the obligation to comply with the requests of a person similarly transforms his personal power into authoritative leadership, but analysis of this problem is deferred to chapter eight.

The stratification systems of entire communities, which consist of ranked classes rather than ranked individuals, exhibit still another

---

[16] George C. Homans, *Social Behavior*, New York: Harcourt, Brace and World, 1961, p. 150.

way in which social status is grounded in public consensus that reflects the social structure, and so do organized hierarchies of authority. Once an individual is not only accepted by the members of a social class but is also recognized by outsiders as belonging to it, and perhaps even as having more or less social standing within it, the existing social agreement on the class ranking further secures his social status by rooting it in the class structure. For sheer membership in a social class, if generally acknowledged, bestows a certain prestige upon an individual.[17] Correspondingly, the institutionalized authority in a hierarchical order gives officials some authority simply on the basis of occupying a given office, as illustrated by military rank, although this authority is usually fortified and expanded in actual processes of interaction, as we shall see. In contrast to prestige and authority structures, power structures rest not primarily on social consensus concerning the privileges or rights that must be granted to the members of various strata but on the distribution of resources with which compliance with demands can be enforced.

A person of superior status in a group, who usually commands respect as well as compliance, exerts two types of influence, only one of which should be designated properly as power to impose his will on others. The respect others have for his judgment prompts them to follow his advice. The obligations they incur by accepting his contributions to their welfare induce them to reciprocate by complying with his directives. While these constitute two types of influence a person with superior status exerts, exception may be taken to Homans' conclusion concerning them: "In both cases, whether he gives them advice they take or orders they obey, the important point is that he controls their behavior; and the fact that a new occasion may call for his advising them jointly is a nonessential detail." [18] There is a crucial distinction between following advice and following orders, and orders are not simply joint advice, although there is a mixed case that involves both joint advice and directives.

If others follow a person's advice he influences them by enabling them to do something that is to their advantage, but if they follow his orders he influences them to do something that is to his advantage. Although their interests are served in both cases, they profit directly

---

[17] The existence of ranked social classes makes even low standing in any class except the lowest something for which people compete. Hence, most exchange relations between high status and low status individuals contribute to two different competitive systems—that among the highs, and that among the lows.

[18] *Ibid.*, p. 372.

from taking his competent advice, whereas they incur a cost by complying with his directives in order to profit from services he renders
them in exchange, such as advice on their problems. The individual
whose advice is accepted does not impose his will on others—if he
were to advise them to do what he wants rather than what corresponds to his best judgment, his poor advice would soon be ignored—
but the one whose orders are obeyed does; only the latter exercises
power. Indeed, giving advice and issuing orders have opposite consequences; advising another creates obligations, while ordering him to
do something uses them up, as it were, by enabling him to discharge
his obligations through his compliance.[19]

The status implications of asking a person to perform a task depend
largely on its effect on the imbalance of obligations. Homans conceptualized this differently: "If I ask you to do something I cannot do,
I recognize you as my superior. . . . But if I ask you to do something
that I can also do, and there are other valuable things I can do but
you cannot, you are my inferior. . . ."[20] However, although I cannot
clean house or iron or cook as well as our maid, I do not acknowledge
her superiority by asking her to do it, since I pay her for it. If a person repeatedly asks another to do something that benefits himself,
he becomes obligated to comply with the other's wishes, which means
that he implicitly subordinates himself to the other's power by asking,
unless he repays him for it, financially or otherwise. The assumption
is that the maid's wages, given her needs, obligate her to perform
services for and comply with the directives of her employer, and
asking a person who is under obligation to one to do something does
not imply subordination, or equality, for that matter.

If a group of individuals who work on a collective task regularly
follow the good suggestions of one of them, thus marking him as their
leader, a mixed situation exists. Carrying out his suggestions that
advance their work benefits the entire group, those who accept them
as well as the one who gives them. They are apt to continue to
follow his lead, not only because his suggestions are respected, but
also because the others become obligated to him for his contribution
to their welfare, enabling him to make them accede to his wishes
even when this is not to their immediate advantage. Since the leader

---

[19] On separate occasions Homans made essentially each of these two points:
that his rewarding advice entitles a man later to tell others what to do (*loc. cit.*),
and that their doing what he tells them reduces their debt to him (*ibid.*, p. 298).
But the two points together conflict with his statements quoted above.

[20] *Ibid.*, p. 151.

benefits as much as the rest do from their following his good suggestions, rather than somebody else's poorer ones, the compliance his contributions earn him constitutes a surplus profit of leadership.

Status as Expendable Capital

Status can be considered as capital, which an individual can draw on to obtain benefits, which is expended in use, and which can be expanded by profitably investing it at interest. Thus, sociable intercourse tends to occur predominantly among people whose social standing is roughly equal.[21] This is due in part to differences in style of life between social classes, which impede relaxed sociability between widely different classes, and in part to the deference owed superiors, which too hampers easy socializing. Sometimes, however, individuals are willing to put up with these discomforts, because they find it gratifying to be accepted by superiors as sociable companions. The striver is an extreme example of this tendency, although it should be noted that the individual who appears a striver is a poor one indeed, but few of us are entirely free of it. The person is rare who would not enjoy an invitation to a dinner at the White House. The fact that many people find it rewarding to associate with superiors means that those of superior status can furnish rewards, and expect a return for them, merely by associating with others of lower status.[22]

The same principle holds for power. The subordination of a person who has power over many others is more valuable than the subordination of one with little or no power, just as acceptance by a prestigeful person is usually more highly valued than acceptance by one with little prestige. The subordination of a powerful person has a multiplier effect on the power of the one to whom he submits, since it usually carries with it the subordination of those over whom he has power. This is how power hierarchies that are not formally instituted emerge. In political conventions, for example, the delegate who has the power to deliver a large block of votes is a more valuable supporter of a candidate—that is, contributes more to a candidate's power

---

[21] *Ibid.*, pp. 320–331, where several empirical findings in support of this statement are cited.

[22] *Ibid.*, pp. 366–370, and Blau, *The Dynamics of Bureaucracy* (2d ed.), University of Chicago Press, 1963, pp. 146–150. Similarly, since inferiors usually take the initiative in approaching superiors, "if you can get another man, hitherto considered your equal, to come to your office rather than your going to his, to discuss some problem, you are to that extent one-up on him." Homans, *op. cit.*, p. 202.

—than the one who can only offer his own vote. The process may be more subtle and thus have still wider repercussions. The powerful delegate's reputation and the weight of his support may influence other delegates who are not pledged to him and who are not directly under his power to vote for the candidate to whom he throws his support.[23] Inasmuch as a powerful person's willingness to accept a subordinate position is more valuable than that of a powerless one, the powerful can expect more rewards for doing so than the powerless.

Status, like capital, is expended in use. An individual's prestige depends largely on his class position, that is, on the prestige of those who accept him and socialize with him as an equal. If he associates with persons of superior prestige on an egalitarian basis, this helps to raise his own, which is the reason it is rewarding to associate with prestigeful people. By the same token, an individual who regularly socializes with others of inferior prestige is in danger of being considered by the community to be on their level and, hence, of losing prestige. The rewards he can obtain from socializing with social inferiors who prize associating with him—for instance, from the deference they accord him in social interaction—entails the possible cost of losing social standing. Correspondingly, the person who submits to another's power is not only no longer his own master but also indicates to others that his strength is not as great as they might have thought, which may well encourage them to comply less strictly with his requests in the future. These losses, in addition to his submission itself, are the price he pays for using his power over subordinates to obtain benefits from a superior.

There is, however, a more direct expenditure of power. By directing others to do what he wants, a person enables them to discharge their obligations to himself for whatever services he has rendered them, thereby depleting his power over them, although continuing services to them would replenish his power. Moreover, people submit to a superior's power because all other alternatives they have are still less attractive to them. By exercising power and making demands on subordinates, a superior makes remaining under his power less attractive and alternatives to it relatively more attractive than they were before, thus decreasing his subordinates' dependence on which his power rests.

---

[23] For an analysis of the circulation and expansion of influence and power, see Parsons, "On the Concept of Influence," and James S. Coleman's "Comment," *Public Opinion Quarterly*, 27 (1963), 37–92, esp. pp. 72–73.

A person with a large capital can live on its interest without using up any of it, and the case of the person whose superior social status is pronounced and secure is analogous. The upper-class Brahmin can freely associate with middle-class friends should he find it rewarding, since his secure social position is not in the least endangered by doing so. But the parvenue who still seeks to prove that he belongs to the upper class must do so by socializing with others who evidently do belong and thus tends to be reluctant to risk his insecure social standing by being seen with middle-class associates. An interviewing study of psychiatrists (who were generally acknowledged to be the superior group), psychologists, and social workers found that psychiatrists of high status (measured by self-perceived power) thought more highly of psychologists and social workers and showed more interest in associating with them than low-status psychiatrists did.[24] Although the medical degree makes the position of psychiatrists immune to any threat by psychologists or social workers, it tends to require a secure status in the superior stratum to feel free to express approval of, and associate with, the members of the subordinate strata.

Superiors obtain much satisfaction from associating with inferiors, who usually look up to them and follow their suggestions. The rewards that high status yields are undoubtedly an incentive for engaging in social intercourse, which may be a main reason why socioeconomic status has been consistently found to be directly correlated with social participation, specifically, with membership in voluntary associations, active participation within them, and participation in discussions of various sorts.[25] But insecure superior status, which can be jeopardized by social contacts with others of lower status, puts pressure on individuals to forego these satisfactions. Only firmly grounded social standing enables a person to benefit from such social contacts without the risk of losing his superior status or some of it.

The case of power is again closely parallel. If an individual has

---

[24] Alvin Zander, Arthur R. Cohen, and Ezra Stotland, "Power and the Relations Among Professions," in Cartwright, *op. cit.*, pp. 15–34.

[25] On voluntary associations, see Mirra Komarowski, "The Voluntary Associations of Urban Dwellers," in Logan Wilson and William Kolb, *Sociological Analysis,* New York: Harcourt, Brace, 1949, pp. 378–392; on unions, see William Spinrad, "Correlates of Trade Union Participation," *American Sociological Review,* 25 (1960), 237–244; on participation in discussions, see Fred L. Strodtbeck, Rita M. James, and Charles Hawkins, "Social Status in Jury Deliberations," *American Sociological Review,* 22 (1957), 713–719, William A. Caudill, *The Psychiatric Hospital as a Small Society,* Cambridge: Harvard University Press, 1958, pp. 243–252, 295–296, and Blau, *op. cit.*, p. 154.

much power over others, which means that they are obligated to and dependent on him for greatly needed benefits, they will be eager to do his bidding and anticipate his wishes in order to maintain his good will, particularly if there are still others who compete for the benefits he supplies them. If an individual has little power over others, however, they will be less concerned with pleasing him, and he may even have to remind them that they owe it to him to follow his requests.[26] Such reminders demonstrate to them that he really needs the services they render him, just as they need his services, which implies that the relation between him and them is not one of unequal power but one of egalitarian exchange. The power of accumulated obligations is depleted by asking others to repay their debts, because doing so transforms, at least in part, the power relations into exchange relations, which presume relative equality of status. Great inequality of power typically obviates the need for such reminders, and the profound obligations on which it rests cannot be fully repaid by the services furnished at any one time, thus keeping the others continually indebted. The great power produced by a large asset of obligations permits a person to live on its interest without depleting it. Indeed, if he is willing to risk some of it, he can increase it further.

An individual who has power over an entire group can coordinate their activities in the pursuit of various ends by telling each what to do. This principle underlies political government, formal organizations generally, and also the organizing activities of informal leaders. By giving orders to others and imposing his will upon them, the ruler or leader cashes in on some of the obligations they owe him for whatever services he has rendered and thus depletes his power. Actually, coordination often entails credit, that is, compliance with demands in excess of obligations.[27] But if the coordination is effective, it furthers the achievement of some goals, that is, it brings rewards that would not have been obtained otherwise. These rewards may be indivisible—a country's national strength, the trophy of the winning team—or allocated by outside authority—the earnings of the workers in a unit under the group incentive system. In these cases the benefits group members derive due to the leader's effectiveness more than

---

[26] Homans, *op. cit.*, pp. 298–299; on a gang leader's reluctance to call in the debts of his followers to him lest his dominant position suffer, see Whyte, *op. cit.*, pp. 106–107.

[27] "Force alone can establish Power, habit alone can keep it in being, but to expand it it must have credit—a thing which, even in its earlier life, it finds useful and has generally received in practice." Bertrand de Jouvenel, *On Power*, New York: Viking, 1949, p. 25.

replenish his credit and their obligations to him, which were partly used up by their compliance with his directives. If the rewards are divisible, as illustrated by the income of the firm or the political offices of the winning party, the leader can distribute some of the extra benefits resulting from his contribution to his subordinates and still maintain a surplus for himself, increasing his power over subordinates while making special profits besides, whether they are financial or the highest political office. Should his guidance prove unrewarding, however, he will lose power over followers. If the leader has used up their obligations to him and they have nothing to gain by remaining under his direction, he will even cease to be their leader. Without having money to pay employees a person cannot remain their employer; without having patronage to dispense to "ward heelers" he cannot remain their political boss; without winning some contests for the gang he cannot remain its leader. It is by taking this risk of losing some or all his power that the superior earns surplus profits, in the form of increased power and other rewards, if the chances he takes pay off.[28] A person with great power can more easily risk some of it to gain more; hence the rich in power tend to get richer in power.

Very high status, firmly rooted in large resources and in the social structure, is a signal asset, the implications of which differ from those of slight superiority qualitatively as well as quantitatively. Superior status that empowers a person to command a variety of services from others enables him to gain many advantages. But if securing these advantages requires making too stringent demands, he depletes his power and endangers his status for several reasons. The costly services he forces others to supply to him may make it profitable for them to relinquish the benefits on which his power rests in favor of the lesser benefits that can be had from another person at lesser cost. If he must often prod others into furnishing services to him, moreover, it shows them that he is dependent on them and thus reduces his power over them. Finally, his exploitation of subordinates, though they may not be able to escape from it, may draw upon him community disapproval and weaken his position in the community at large. The distinctive asset of vast power is that it obviates the need for making excessive demands that undermine power. This means not merely that individuals or groups with much power still have a great deal left after using some of it, by commanding services, but that their exercise of power usually does not deplete it at all and often

---

[28] Homans, *op. cit.*, pp. 296–297.

actually helps them further to enhance it. For highly superior status and resources facilitate making profits by risking investments under conditions of uncertainty.

Great achievements are usually the result of having taken risks in striving for them. It is precisely when success is uncertain that it tends to be most highly valued and most generously rewarded. Knight has emphasized that profit, strictly speaking, is due to uncertainty and is the reward for assuming responsibility for uncertainty, that is, for risking investments whose return cannot be predicted with accuracy in advance.[29] People seem to prefer to be sure of the rewards they receive for the services they render and to be willing to pay a price for such security.[30] The entrepreneur provides this security by guaranteeing his employees certain rewards for their services and by assuming the responsibility for deciding on investments under conditions of uncertainty. The profits he reaps from the enterprise are his reward for having taken these risks. Leadership generally involves making decisions whose outcome is uncertain and furnishing services expected to (but not certain to) further the attainment of collective objectives. The increment in power the successful leader earns is his reward for having made these risky decisions and investments.

The larger the initial scope of a man's power, the easier it is for him to take the risks that are likely to augment his power. An important reason for this is the principle of insurance.[31] Although the outcome of any single decision may be quite uncertain, it is often possible to predict with a high degree of accuracy the statistical probability of the outcome of a large number of decisions of a given kind. For example, while it is difficult to estimate in advance whether a single employee is going to quit or not, the proportion of several thousands of employees who are likely to quit in any one year can often be predicted rather accurately on the basis of past experience. Whereas there is uncertainty concerning the single event or decision, there is virtually none concerning many events or decisions that can be grouped under a general category, since the proportion of unsuccessful ones can be predicted in advance and taken into account as part of the cost through some form of insurance. Given a knowledge of the proportion of unsuccessful outcomes—for example, warehouses annually destroyed by fire or quitting rate of experienced employees—

[29] Frank H. Knight, *Risk, Uncertainty and Profit* (2d ed.), Boston: Houghton Mifflin, 1933, esp. chapters i, ii, and viii.
[30] See Herbert A. Simon, *Models of Man*, New York: Wiley, 1957, pp. 183–195.
[31] Knight, *op. cit.*, chapter vii.

the man with a large number of investments can completely assure himself against loss and does not operate under uncertainty at all, but this knowledge does not relieve the man with a single investment of uncertainty (unless he buys insurance from another with sufficiently large investments to provide it). The man with one investment risks it and may lose all, while the man with many investments discounts a proportionate loss and assumes, in fact, no risk. In other words, the sheer scope of a man's operations or power decreases the risk involved in assuming what is, in absolute terms, the same amount of risk. The consequent security of individuals with much power and resources makes them less responsive to social pressures but also more tolerant toward inferiors and outsiders than are those whose superior status rests on less secure foundations.

"In the South the master is not afraid to raise the slave to his own standing, because he knows that he can reduce him in a moment to the dust at his pleasure. In the North the white no longer distinctly perceives the barrier that separates him from the degraded race, and he shuns the Negro with the more pertinacity since he fears lest they should some day be confounded together." [32] If this observation of de Tocqueville does not exactly correspond to the situation any more, it is because Negroes are no longer slaves and the advances they have made in the last century, disappointingly small though they are in view of our democratic values, have made them a threat to the superior status of the whites in the South, except to those in the highest social strata, who are generally more tolerant toward Negroes than lower-class Southerners. A group's tolerant attitude toward, and encouragement of, the efforts of another group to raise its power and social standing requires that the first group's secure social status is not endangered by these efforts.[33] There is something smug about tolerance, despite best intentions, since it implicitly asserts one's own superiority.[34] Our attitudes toward opponents and deviants, too, can

---

[32] Alexis de Tocqueville, *Democracy in America,* New York: Vintage, 1954, Vol. I, 374.

[33] See de Jouvenel, *op. cit.,* pp. 345–346.

[34] John Updike illustrates this aspect of tolerance nicely in a story about a conversation the only white woman resident on an island has with the husband of one of the few white tourist couples there. Thus, the woman talks about his wife and the attitude of the Negro inhabitants to her: " 'You see how dark she is,' she explained. 'How tan. . . . They say your wife's being part Negro has kept you out of the hotels on the better islands.' " Later, wondering about his defensiveness in answer to this remark, the husband reflects what the attitude of his progressive wife would have been: "His seriousness had been unworthy of her.

remain permissive only as long as we do not feel threatened by them; once their actions are experienced as a threat, we can hardly help becoming intolerant toward them, often fiercely so.

The social conditions of tolerance can be illustrated by the difference between what might be called the "psychiatric" and the "political" orientation toward offenders of basic values. The psychiatric orientation toward delinquents conceives of them as individuals with personality problems who should be helped and not punished. Although such an orientation is most appropriate for the sex deviant, the parents of children immediately threatened by his activities can rarely muster such a tolerant attitude toward him, not to speak of the parents of children who have actually been attacked by him. Hitler was undoubtedly a person who, though not insane, had serious personality defects that deserved psychiatric treatment. But the Jews, and later most of the world, could not and did not think of him as a pitiful neurotic who should be cared for but as a dangerous foe who should be crushed. The power he held to subjugate people had to be taken seriously, which made any psychiatric understanding of his maladjusted personality completely irrelevant and required instead a political orientation to him as an opponent. This extreme illustration serves to highlight the principle that for people to be tolerant of the actions of others, the latter must not have the power to subjugate them or to endanger their security; if they do, intolerance is required to avert the threat.

Intolerance is an admission of weakness that acknowledges the power of another, just as tolerance is a sign of strength that confirms the other's inferiority. Power over others is greatly desired by many men, since it is a generalized means with the aid of which a large variety of objectives can be accomplished, and since the ability to impose one's will on others often comes to be valued in its own right. A man can demonstrate his power to himself and to the world by forcing others to take his threats seriously. By treating the juvenile delinquent as a boy in need of rehabilitation, we deny his claim to being a strong man through our condescending tolerance. We cannot remain equally permissive in the face of the gangster or fascist

---

She would have wanted him to say yes, her grandfather picked cotton in Alabama, in America these things are taken for granted, we have no problem. But he saw, like something living glimpsed in a liquid volume, that the comedy of this response depended upon, could only live within, a vast unconscious pride of race." "The Doctor's Wife," in *Pigeon Feathers*, New York: Knopf, 1962, pp. 208–209.

hoodlum, who poses a more serious threat to our lives and fortunes and freedom, yet our intolerant opposition to him in attempts to suppress him serves to validate the power that he craves. The gangster's or fascist's power over followers has its source in the rewards they derive from following him, whether these are material or ideological, and their willingness to do his bidding gives him coercive power in the community. Endeavors to suppress his power, as long as they are unsuccessful, confirm and reinforce it, for they show others the apparent futility of resistance and tempt them to submit to him. Power is undeniable, and its serious threats must be opposed, but unsuccessful opposition further strengthens it.

Conclusions

Imbalances of obligations incurred in social transactions produce differences in power. Unreciprocated, recurrent benefits obligate the recipient to comply with the requests of the supplier and thus give the latter power over the former. The conditions of power are defined by the four basic alternatives to it. One method for obtaining needed benefits from a person who can furnish them is to provide services he needs in return. This raises the problems of the exchange processes that develop and of the distribution of resources in a community that governs them and is modified by them. A second possibility is to obtain the needed benefits from another source. Tracing the implications of this alternative leads to the study of competitive processes, of the exchange rates that become established in social structures, and of monopolization. Third, benefits can be secured by force. This fact calls attention to the differentiation of power in a group or society, to the organizations in which power is mobilized, and to political processes and institutions. Fourth, benefits can be renounced and the need for them can be overcome, notably when identification with profound ideals makes material satisfactions appear relatively insignificant. The implications here point toward the analysis of common values, changing needs, and the emergence of ideologies in various social situations.

The four conditions of power are circumscribed by the absence of these four alternatives. If men have insufficient resources, if no satisfactory alternatives are available to them, if they cannot use coercive force, and if their needs are pressing, a person or group who can supply benefits that meet these needs attains power over them. Under these conditions, their subordination to his power is inescapable, since he can make the fulfillment of essential needs contingent on their compliance.

Differentiation of power arises in the course of competition for scarce goods. In informal groups, the initial competition is for participation time, which is scarce, and which is needed to obtain any social reward from group membership. In communities the primitive competition is for scarce means of livelihood. At first, all members of the collectivity compete against all others, but as status differences emerge in consequence of differential success in the initial competition, the object of the competition changes, and exchange relations become differentiated from competitive ones. Those successful in the earlier stages of competition tend to compete later for dominant positions and, in communities, for movement into higher social classes, while the unsuccessful ones cannot compete with them for dominance but become their exchange partners, who receive instrumental benefits in exchange for subordination and status support. In class structures of communities, the exchange relations between members of different classes or substrata complement and support their respective competitive struggles for social status. Public recognition that a person belongs to a given stratum in the hierarchy of classes consolidates his social status.

Not all types of influence reflect power to impose one's will on another. Inducing a person to render a service by rewarding him for doing so does not involve exercising power over him, unless continuing rewards obligate him not only to furnish services but also to comply with directives. Moreover, a person whose advice others follow influences them without imposing his will on them. In contrast, the person whose orders others follow does exercise power over them. His orders prompt them to do what he wants, whereas his advice permits them to do better what they want. His advice benefits them and thus obligates them to him; it does not entail the exercise of power, though it may well be a source of power. On the other hand, their compliance with his orders benefits him and thus discharges their obligations to him; it does entail an exercise of power, and it depletes the power in the process.

Power is expended in use, but it can be invested at some risk to yield more power. A person who calls on others to discharge their obligations to him reveals his dependence on their services and weakens his power over them. But if a man has much power, he need not remind subordinates, who are eager to maintain his good will, to discharge their obligations, and he can use his power to organize their activities more effectively to achieve various objectives. The benefits that accrue to them due to his effective leadership further obligate others to him and strengthen his power over them. This increment in power is his reward for taking the risks of leadership, for leadership entails the danger of losing power should its guidance fail to bring additional rewards.

A firmly established, secure social status that is not endangered by efforts of others to improve theirs is a prerequisite for tolerant encouragement of these efforts. To be sure, democratic values demand that all people have the opportunity to improve their social status and that they are free to organize political opposition in attempts to achieve political power. Institutional restraints are needed to protect these opportunities and freedoms, however, because groups whose social standing and power is endangered by the economic and political endeavors of others cannot be expected to look upon them with tolerant benevolence but are likely to meet these threats to themselves with intolerant opposition. It is the duty of those citizens of a democratic society who are not immediately involved in particular power struggles to help safeguard equality of opportunity and political tolerance, since the involvement of the participants makes them incapable of doing so.

✳ SIX

Expectations

Oft expectation fails, and most oft there
Where most it promises.

SHAKESPEARE, All's Well that Ends Well

The satisfactions human beings experience in their social associations depend on the expectations they bring to them as well as on the
actual benefits they receive in them. The man who expects much
from his associates is more easily disappointed in them than the one
who expects little, and the same degree of friendliness might attract
the first man to other people and discourage the second from associating with them. These expectations of social rewards, in turn, are
based on the past social experience of individuals and on the reference standards they have acquired, partly as the result of the benefits
they themselves have obtained in the past and partly as the result of
learning what benefits others in comparable situations obtain.

The fact that an individual derives outstanding rewards from associating with others increases his attraction to them, his dependence
on them, and, in the long run, his level of expectation concerning
what constitutes satisfactory social relations. The superior gratifications that attract an individual to some associates simultaneously
make other associates comparatively unattractive, thereby making
him dependent on those who provide superior gratifications. The
group whose acceptance is more rewarding than any other's creates
such dependence, as does the girl whose love is most rewarding, and
the employer whose job is most rewarding. As people become accustomed to a certain level of social gratification, which they may have

initially considered extraordinary, they come to take it for granted and to expect at least that much gratification from their associates in the future. The emotional support in early love relations, the congenial camaraderie with previous companions, the salary of the present job become minimum standards of expectations that define future satisfaction.[1]

The groups with which an individual is in contact furnish another set of reference standards that influence these expectations of social rewards. Human beings learn not only from their own experience, as animals do, but also by acquiring knowledge through symbolic communication, as animals do only in very rudimentary form. Individuals compare themselves with others like themselves whom they know or whom they know about, in their own groups and sometimes also in groups to which they aspire to belong, and their knowledge of the rewards these others receive in social life affect the level of social reward they expect to be able to claim. Given such comparisons, individuals who receive high rewards in groups where others do too are likely to be less satisfied with their attainment than individuals who are no better off, or perhaps even worse off, but who find themselves in groups where others receive fewer rewards.

The study of exchange processes in social associations must take into account the ways in which the values of the rewards being exchanged are modified by the expectations of the participants and, ultimately, by the previous distribution of rewards that governs these expectations. This chapter is concerned with these problems. After distinguishing various types of expectations, the influence of accumulated rewards on the anticipation of, and satisfaction with, future rewards will be analyzed. Not only the rewards an individual has received himself in the past but also the prevailing rate at which rewards are obtained for services in his groups and reference groups tend to influence the rewards he expects for his services. The relationship between these expectations based on going rates of exchange and social norms of fairness will be discussed. Finally, the problems posed by social attachments to groups and organizations and the

---

[1] In the conception of John W. Thibaut and Harold H. Kelley, the difference between these comparison standards and the rewards obtained in a given social relationship determines satisfaction with and attraction to it, whereas the difference between the rewards obtained and those available in alternative social relations determines dependence on the given relationship. The definition of an involuntary social relationship is that a person is dependent on but not attracted to it. *The Social Psychology of Groups,* New York: Wiley, 1959, pp. 21–24, 81–82.

immobility they produce will be examined. The central focus of the chapter, then, is the impact of past rewards, received by individuals themselves or others in their environment, on the expectations of and reactions to subsequent rewards.

Expectations and Associations

Three types of expectations of social rewards can be distinguished. The first is the "general expectation" an individual has of the total benefits he will achieve in various aspects of his social life—the income he expects in his career, the emotional support he expects from his family, the social status he hopes to attain in his community. General expectations distinguish achievements that are experienced as success from those that are experienced as failure, and differences between these expectations make the same achievement a success for one person and a failure for another. Usually, however, general expectations range from a level of minimum need, without the attainment of which an individual will be dissatisfied and frustrated, to a level of maximum aspirations, without the pull of which he would cease to strive for improvements once his minimum needs have been met.

General expectations, which define achievement needs and aspirations, are governed by prevailing values and social standards, and by the previously experienced attainments of individuals. Research on levels of aspirations illustrates these two influences. One consistent finding is that most individuals who successfully attain their level of aspiration in the performance of a task raise their aspiration level, whereas most of those who fail to attain their level of aspiration lower it.[2] Besides, the known social standards of achievement in a group typically affect the level of aspiration of its members, and so does knowledge of the prevailing standards of other groups. Specifically, a given standard of attainment of another group tends to raise aspiration levels if that group is considered inferior and tends to lower them if it is considered superior.[3] A strong cultural emphasis on achievement, such as that manifest in the ideology that any good man can achieve financial success and should try to do so, creates high general expectations, with impending frustrations for many

---

[2] Kurt Lewin, Tamara Dembo, Leon Festinger, and Pauline S. Sears, "Level of Aspiration," in J. McV. Hunt, *Personality and the Behavior Disorders*, New York: Ronald Press, 1944, Vol. I, 337–340.

[3] *Ibid.*, pp. 340–343.

whose achievements might have been satisfactory had it not been for their high expectations.[4] The impact of failure on the individual's effort probably depends on the duration of the experience in relation to his capacity to cope with frustration for extended periods. Initially, dissatisfaction with achievements and rewards is likely to be a spur to greater effort, but continuing inability to attain important objectives tends to lead to resignation and embitterment. In other words, prolonged failure to reach general expectations is apt to produce a drop in them, which is often accompanied by permanent dissatisfaction and alienation.

A second type is the "particular expectation" an individual has of a given other person, his behavior and the rewards that associating with him would bring. These role expectations contain two distinct elements: the expectation that the other's conduct conform to accepted social standards, otherwise he would not make an enjoyable companion, and the expectation that associating with him would furnish particular rewards, more or less than associating with someone else. The early impression an individual makes on others determines what social benefits, if any, they anticipate deriving from associating with him and thus their initial attraction to him. Their expectation of benefits as well as their expectation of conformity constitute standards that he must live up to in order to gain their approval. The strength of the initial attraction of individuals to another depends on the difference between their particular expectations of him and their general expectations. If they expect him to furnish all the advice they need, for example, they will be highly attracted to him as a consultant. If they expect some advice from him, but not all they need, and he lives up to their expectations, they will be satisfied, although they will continue to seek other opportunities to consult and not develop an exclusive attachment to him as a consultant.

The term "comparative expectation," finally, might be used for the profits individuals expect to realize in social associations, that is, their rewards minus their costs. The continuing attraction of individuals to social relations depends not simply on the rewards they derive but also on the costs they incur and, specifically, on the ratio between the two, which determines how profitable the social relations are for them. Whereas particular expectations differ for various associates, depending on one's estimation of their ability and willingness to furnish rewards, comparative expectations constitute a common

---

[4] See Robert K. Merton, *Social Theory and Social Structure* (2d ed.), Glencoe: Free Press, 1957, chapter iv.

standard that is independent of the persons to whom it is applied and makes comparisons between them possible. The more profitable social relations are in terms of this standard, the more committed will individuals be to them.[5] These expectations of return relative to investment—how much income individuals with a given level of skill expect, how much compliance is expected for advice, how much status can be claimed for certain achievements—are governed by social norms that define what fair rates of exchange are. Before analyzing these social standards of exchange, the ways in which past attainments of individuals and groups influence their expectations in general will be discussed.

The attainments of people modify their general expectations of what rewards can be realized and, indeed, what rewards need to be realized to maintain satisfaction, and these altered expectations, in turn, affect the significance of future rewards. The achievement of individuals raises their expectations and consequently makes the absence of a certain level of reward a deprivation for them, while it previously was not. The worker whose wages were raised from $100 to $120 might have been quite satisfied with $110, but when his income is later cut by $10 he will feel deprived with earnings of only $110, which means that the minimum expectations aroused by his higher income increased the significance of the difference between $110 and $120 for him. Similarly, the girl who was very popular in high school probably suffers more from lack of popularity in college than the girl who was not popular in high school either.[6] Since current reward levels tend to define minimum expectations, they affect satisfactions with and reactions to a given level of reward in the future.

Two studies of new top managers in factories, one by Gouldner and one by Guest, illustrate how the past experiences of groups, by affecting social expectations, influence their members' reactions to the treatment they receive from others.[7] Gouldner found that a new plant manager, under pressure to improve productivity in order to impress his superiors in the corporation, felt that he had to resort to

---

[5] The expectation of relative profit in particular partnerships might be considered a fourth type.

[6] To avoid the interpersonal comparison of utilities in the example, the purist might want to change the comparison to read "than the same girl did before she had become popular in high school."

[7] Alvin W. Gouldner, *Patterns of Industrial Bureaucracy*, Glencoe: Free Press, 1954, chapters iii, iv, and v; and Robert H. Guest, "Managerial Succession in Complex Organizations," *American Journal of Sociology*, 68 (1962), 47–54.

bureaucratic procedures for this purpose, such as elaboration of rules and close supervision, because he was unable to command the loyalty of the workers. In contrast, Guest found that a new plant manager, who also was under pressure from superiors to improve productivity, did so by relaxing bureaucratic rules and thus promoting worker loyalty. A crucial difference between the two situations was that the predecessor of Gouldner's manager had been very lenient and had commanded much loyalty, whereas the predecessor of Guest's manager had been authoritarian and unpopular with workers. The inference that might be drawn is that the minimum expectations aroused by the treatment of the predecessor had to be met, if not exceeded, by the new manager to gain the approval of the workers, and differences in these expectations made it difficult for the first but easy for the second manager to command the loyalty of his subordinates.

Since expectations govern satisfaction, the attainment of rewards that meet expectations tends to be more significant than further increments that exceed them. Individuals who expect an income of $10,000, assuming for the moment that their expectations and other conditions remain constant, are likely to obtain more gratification from the $1000 raise from $9000 to $10,000 than from the next $1000 raise. This is a manifestation of the economic principle of the ultimately diminishing marginal utility: "As a consumer increases the consumption of any one commodity, keeping constant the consumption of all other commodities, the marginal utility of the variable commodity must eventually decline." [8] The principle is similar to that of satiation—the hungry man wants food, but once he is full he no longer wants any more—but the physiological analogy seems less appropriate than the economic one for the declining significance of increasing social rewards.

When a man is satiated he wants no more; if food were forced upon him, he would reject it; he might vomit; he cannot possibly eat any more. Men are not satiated in this sense with prestige or money or power, regardless of how much they have. Social rewards do not have a point of complete satiation; instead, as more of them are obtained, their significance declines, either gradually or more abruptly. The shape of the marginal utility curve of social rewards—specifically, whether it drops gradually or sharply—depends on the nature of the expectations. If individuals expect to attain a certain goal, for example, earn a medical degree or earn enough money to get married, the

---

[8] Kenneth E. Boulding, *Economic Analysis* (3d ed.), New York: Harper, 1955, pp. 682–683.

significance of increments in attainments probably rises to the point where the goal is reached and then drops sharply. (Despite this abrupt drop there is no satiation; the individual who had decided he can get married on an income of $6000 will not therefore refuse a job that pays him $6500.) If, however, individuals expect greater achievements without having specific goals that set bench marks for them, for example, to achieve wealth or fame or power, the decline in the significance (marginal utility) of increasing rewards tends to be more gradual.

The differences between the principle previously discussed, concerning the implications of "changing expectations," and the "marginal principle" should be well noted. The marginal principle refers to the eventually *declining* significance of rewards consequent to increasing attainments, whereas the first principle refers to the *growing* significance of rewards consequent to rising expectations resulting from increasing attainments. Implicit in the marginal principle is the assumption that general expectations remain constant, although there are different levels ranging from minimum expectations to high or virtually unlimited aspirations. Given this assumption, the significance of growing achievements, although it may first rise, declines as successive levels of expectation are reached and surpassed. Removing the restrictive assumption of constant expectation requires taking into account the fact that increasing attainments raise levels of expectations. This rise in expectations, notably in minimum expectations, makes the attainment of sufficient rewards to meet the new expectation level more significant than attaining that amount of reward was before. This has an effect opposite to that of the principle of diminishing marginal utility and mitigates its influence.

The cost incurred in obtaining social benefits also affects the significance they have for individuals, because costly possessions are most precious, as indicated in some detail in chapter three. Thus, the value of social approval depends on its being scarce, and scarce approval can be obtained only with costly effort. Generally, rewards that are in high demand are highly valued and are difficult to attain. As a result, the cost entailed in attaining social rewards that do not have an objectively measurable value, such as group acceptance or approval, becomes a sign of their social value. This process is exemplified by some findings concerning the significance of colleague approval among caseworkers in a welfare agency.[9] Newcomers to the

---

[9] Blau and W. Richard Scott, *Formal Organizations*, San Francisco: Chandler, 1962, pp. 99–100.

agency who were not yet popular among colleagues were more likely than popular newcomers to state that it was more important for them to be highly thought of by fellow workers than by either clients or the supervisor. But among those with more than one year of seniority, the relationship was reversed, that is, the popular were more inclined than the unpopular to value colleague approval most highly. The implication is that easy attainment of colleague approval depreciated its value (the minority of workers who earned it, as indicated by their popularity, in less than a year valued it comparatively little), while colleague approval that was obtained only after considerable effort had more significance (workers who needed more than a year to earn it, as most did, valued it comparatively much).

A final illustration of the influence of expectations on satisfaction with social rewards and on consequent reactions is taken from Lipset's analysis of the political attitudes of American academicians and intellectuals generally.[10] Intellectuals in the United States often complain that their prestige in our society is lower than elsewhere, and their consequent identification with the underprivileged probably contributes to the prevailing left-of-center and egalitarian political beliefs among them. Lipset cites empirical evidence to show that the prestige of American academicians, although they themselves consider it to be low, is actually about as high as that of major businessmen in this country and that their relative social standing is about as high as that of academicians in other countries. Whereas American academicians have misconceptions about their relative prestige ranking, they perceive correctly that the European professor and intellectual is treated with more honor and respect than they are. "This difference is no more or less than the difference between a fairly rigid class society and a society which emphasizes equality. In Europe, open deference is given to *all* those with higher status, whether engineers, factory owners, or professors, while in this country it is not given to *any* to the degree that it is abroad."[11] But what Lipset leaves implicit is that the lesser deference that high status as such commands in this country has quite different implications for intellectuals from those it has for the economic and political elite.

The emphasis on equality in the American value system does not mean that we have no differences in wealth and power or even that we have less of those differences than other societies. What it does

---

[10] Seymour M. Lipset, *Political Man*, Garden City: Doubleday, 1960, pp. 313–330.

[11] *Ibid.*, p. 327 (italics in original).

mean is that high status is not, or hardly, ennobled by distinctive titles, symbols, and honors, and that it does not bestow upon its bearer special privileges and rights to claim deference *aside from those* that rest on the wealth and power from which high status typically derives. In Europe, by contrast, high status does carry with it rights to claim deference from others that are independent of the wealth and power usually, but not consistently, associated with it. The high prestige of top businessmen and politicians is accompanied by much wealth or power or both, which gives these men in the United States great status privileges, just as it does their counterparts in Europe. But the prestige status of ministers, academicians, and other intellectuals is not similarly founded on considerable wealth or power, with the result that men in these occupations enjoy fewer social rewards here than in countries whose cultural norms require that deference be paid to anybody with superior social status.

Europe, moreover, with its great traditions in the arts and sciences, is an important reference group for American intellectuals, whereas this is not the case in business and politics. His orientation to his European colleagues leads the American intellectual to expect more deference than he receives here, and the frustrations due to his too great expectations foster his identification with underprivileged classes and with the very egalitarian ideologies that help cause his frustrations. To quote Lipset again: "Ironically some of the reasons why American intellectuals do not get the signs of respect which they crave spring from the strength of the egalitarian standards which they espouse." [12]

Fair Exchange and Reference Groups

In the course of social exchange, a going rate of exchange between two social benefits becomes established. This going rate is governed by supply and demand, though only in rough fashion, since considerations other than the two benefits in question influence exchange transactions, notably other benefits that simultaneously enter into exchange relations, such as social support and companionship. Thus, if the demand for advice in a work group is high and there are only few experts who can supply it, others will be under pressure to comply with the wishes of an expert to a considerable extent in order to induce him to devote his scarce time to consultations with them rather than someone else. The resulting high price of advice is likely

---

[12] *Ibid.*, p. 320.

to motivate experts to devote more time to giving it, thereby increasing supply. Should the supply of advice come to exceed the demand for it, experts will be under pressure to offer it for less compliance, because others can choose among many available consultants. This process can also be viewed from the perspective of the experts' varying demand for compliance, that is, superior status, and the degree of compliance the others are willing to supply in exchange for advice.

The competition among experts for superior status, which furnishes incentives to supply advice, and the competition among others for advice, which furnishes incentives to supply respect and compliance, are governed by supply and demand, giving sometimes one party the greater advantage and sometimes the other. These two competitions simultaneously adjust supply and demand to one another through the mechanism of changing rates of exchange and establish the going exchange rate as determined by supply and demand at any one time. The assumption is that the amount of advice actually requested ("demanded") by those in need of some *decreases* the higher the price in compliance they would have to pay for it and the amount of advice supplied by those who can offer some *increases* the higher the price in compliance they would obtain for it.[13] On a coordinate system with units of advice on the horizontal axis and its price in compliance on the vertical axis, the demand curve slopes downward from left to right, and the supply curve slopes upward from left to right. Exchange tends to move toward the rate at which demand equals supply, that is, toward the point on the coordinate system where the two curves intersect, which indicates the equilibrium price or exchange ratio as well as the quantities exchanged in the hypothetical state of equilibrium.

The ratio of exchange between two types of social benefits is affected by the hypothetical equilibrium defined by existing conditions of supply and demand in a manner parallel to the effect of the equilibrium price on the actual price in economic exchange. Boulding explains this process in the following way:

> The equilibrium price is not necessarily the actual price existing at a given instant of time. A price may exist—i.e., there may be transactions taking place at a certain ratio of exchange—and yet there may be forces operating in the market which tend to bring about a change in that

---

[13] An alternative conceptualization of the same facts is that the "demand" for superior status (or compliance) depends inversely on its price in terms of advice and that the supply of the compliance needed for superior status depends directly on its price in terms of advice.

price. . . . It is possible, even, that we may *never* reach the equilibrium price, that in fact no actual price is ever an equilibrium price. Before the forces which would bring together the actual and the equilibrium prices have had time to work themselves out, it is quite possible—indeed, almost inevitable—that the circumstances will have changed and with them the equilibrium price.[14]

Similarly, the going rate at which advice is exchanged for compliance and superior status in a group depends on conditions of supply and demand, but the continual changes in these conditions, partly produced by the changes in the exchange rate they themselves have produced, make it likely that the actual rate of exchange never catches up with the hypothetical rate toward which supply and demand pull it. In contrast to economic exchange, moreover, there is no exact price in social exchange but only an approximate exchange ratio between two social benefits, as other rewards experienced by exchange partners in their social association become implicated in the exchange of the two benefits under consideration and impede precise calculation of the worth of one in terms of the other. Hence, the actual rate of exchange in a specific transaction often differs from the prevailing rate in a group as various pressures induce members, for example, to offer more compliance for advice or more advice for compliance than the going rate indicates. But the going rate sets approximate standards of social expectations that influence the actual rates of exchange between particular partners.

To apply these conceptions in empirical research requires that operational measures for them be devised. The first problem is that of constructing indices for the benefits to be exchanged, for instance, for compliance and advice. A measure of the degree of compliance of one individual with the requests and suggestions of another could be obtained through sociometric questions, using either general questions referring to relative status or specific questions asking respondents how they usually do or would react to various requests from given colleagues. Alternatively, social interaction could be directly observed, if this is possible, and the net compliance of one individual with the directives and suggestions of another could be derived from such a record. (A prerequisite for doing so would be to classify requests in terms of the degree of compliance involved lest minor acts of compliance be given the same weight in the index as very major ones.) In order to obtain a valid index of advice furnished, which takes into account its quality as well as its quantity, a measure of

---

[14] Boulding, *op. cit.*, pp. 55–56 (italics in original).

competence, possibly derived from evaluations of superiors, should be used to weigh the minutes of advice a man gives to a colleague. These measures would make it possible to ascertain the rate at which advice is exchanged for compliance in each pair and the average exchange rate in a group, provided one is willing to make the assumption that advice and compliance are the only salient benefits being exchanged in the situation under consideration. If this assumption is not warranted, the other important benefits that enter into exchange transactions would also have to be measured and included in the calculation of exchange rates.[15]

The empirical study of the equilibrium state toward which the going rate of exchange moves would require some further operations. For this purpose, it would be necessary to determine how changes in the price of advice in compliance affect variations in its supply and its demand. A market schedule would have to be made for each individual to show how much advice of a given quality he would be willing to supply at various prices in compliance and how much advice he would demand at various prices. Such a schedule could be based on answers to hypothetical questions or, preferably, on observation in situations in which the compliance received per unit of advice is experimentally varied and subjects are permitted to supply and request as much advice as they wish. By summing the schedules of all members of a group, a total demand-and-supply schedule would be obtained, which would show how much demand and how much supply for advice there is at varying prices.[16] The price at which demand and supply are equal is the "equilibrium price," which clears the market, and toward which the going rate is presumed to move.

There are also social norms of fair exchange, and the going rate of exchange in a group is not necessarily, or even typically, identical with what is considered a fair rate of exchange. To clarify this difference, it is necessary to extend the scope of the analysis from the social conditions in specific groups to those in the larger community and from narrow spans of time to extended periods in the lives of individuals. Thus, the expert advice available in the various groups in a community depends on the efforts individuals have made in the

---

[15] For a general scheme for recording exchange processes, see Richard Longabaugh, "A Category System for Coding Interpersonal Behavior as Social Exchange," *Sociometry,* 26 (1963), 319–345.

[16] See Boulding, *op. cit.,* pp. 49–55. A possible procedure for dealing with the problem of differences in the quality of advice would be to have separate schedules for different categories of quality.

past to acquire the knowledge and develop the skills needed to furnish competent advice of diverse sorts to colleagues, friends, and neighbors. The more that individuals profit from being experts, the greater are their incentives to achieve expertness. In the long run, therefore, the community's ability to "consume" expert knowledge, that is, to return adequate social rewards for it, tends to equal the "production" of expertness by its members, since otherwise there are insufficient incentives to make the necessary investments to produce it. The situation corresponds to the relationship between economic production and consumption, though again with notable differences. The intersection between the two curves showing the quantity of a commodity produced at varying prices and the quantity consumed at varying prices defines the normal price of the commodity. This is a hypothetical state of equilibrium, at which production and consumption would be equal, and which indicates the long-term trends of supply, demand, and price.[17] So, too, the relationship between the expertness acquired and the expertness utilized in a community can be envisaged as governing, in the long run, the supply of, and demand for, advice in different groups and the degree of status superiority that can be earned with it. The crucial distinction is that the intervening mechanisms in social exchange are social norms of fairness.

Common norms develop in societies that stipulate fair rates of exchange between social benefits and the returns individuals deserve for the investments made to produce these benefits. These normative standards of what a fair return for a given service is have their ultimate source in the society's need for this service and in the investments required to supply it. They have the function of relating consumption needs to production capacities by providing varying incentives for the investment of time and effort in diverse pursuits. Individuals who have invested much of their resources in order to be able to supply services in great demand by the community ought to receive proportionately high social rewards, according to these norms.

The relationship between the fair rate and the going rate of social exchange is somewhat parallel to that between the normal price and the average price in economic markets. But the fair and going rates both rest on social expectations, though of different kinds. The going rate of exchange in a group gives rise to expectations that certain returns will be received for certain services. Whereas these standards

---

[17] *Ibid.*, pp. 107–114.

of expectation are not moral norms but merely anticipations that influence conduct, the normative expectations that a service that required a certain investment deserves a certain return are moral standards, the violation of which evokes social disapproval. Nevertheless, the going rates in many groups depart from the fair rates, making it impossible for some individuals to realize a fair return on their investments. Some individuals cannot even realize the going rate in their exchange transactions, because factors other than these social norms and standards also affect exchange processes, notably the conditions of supply and demand in particular groups and the power relations that have developed.

The concept "fair exchange" is fundamentally similar to Homans' rule of "distributive justice," which he formulates as follows: "A man in an exchange relation with another will expect that the rewards of each man be proportional to his costs—the greater the rewards, the greater the costs—and that the net rewards, or profits, of each man be proportional to his investments—the greater the investments, the greater the profit." [18] The main difference is that Homans does not emphasize explicitly that social norms, which function to promote socially significant investments, underlie this notion of fairness or justice; indeed, he seems to imply that it is a natural sentiment. An important implication of this principle of justice is that people compare themselves in terms of their investments as well as in terms of their rewards and expect differences in the rewards to correspond to differences in the investments, and their satisfaction with their own rewards depends just as much on the fact that these expectations are not disappointed as on the actual quantity of the rewards.

A study by Patchen of workers in an oil refinery provides some empirical support for this inference from Homans' principle.[19] The investigator asked workers to name the occupations of some others whose earnings differed from their own, being either higher or lower, and he asked them how satisfied they were with the way their own earnings compared with those of these others. The most relevant finding was that workers, in comparing their own earnings with others who had higher earnings, were on the average more satisfied if these others were professionals than if they were blue-collar workers like themselves (and comparisons with nonprofessional white-collar occupations yielded an intermediate level of satisfaction). These occupa-

---

[18] George C. Homans, *Social Behavior,* New York: Harcourt, Brace and World, 1961, p. 75.

[19] Martin Patchen, "A Conceptual Framework and Some Empirical Data Regarding Comparisons of Social Rewards," *Sociometry,* 24 (1961), 136–156.

tional comparisons were implicit comparisons of educational invest-ments. The finding suggests, therefore, that men, as Homans stipu-lated, expect rewards to be positively related to investments and do not seriously object if the rewards of others exceed their own *provided* that the investments of those others are correspondingly superior to their own.

Another implication of the principle of justice is formulated by Homans as a major proposition: "The more to a man's disadvantage the rule of distributive justice fails of realization, the more likely he is to display the emotional behavior we call anger." [20] People whose standards of justice are violated feel angry as well as dissatisfied and give vent to their anger through disapproval of and sometimes hos-tility and hatred against those who caused it. *Mutatis mutandis,* people whose standards of fairness are met or possibly even exceeded by the magnanimity of others express their appreciation through approval of them. The power of a person and the significance of the advantages he can extract from another may make him disregard the other's approbation. However, since fairness is a social norm that prescribes just treatment as a moral principle, third parties in the community will disapprove of a person who deals unfairly with others under his power, whereas the one whose dealings are just and fair earns general social approval. Finally, internalized moral standards may make men feel guilty for treating others unjustly. [21]

Inequitable treatment and, particularly, exploitative use of power, therefore, evoke social disapproval, which makes it costly to take such unfair advantage of others. Group or community disapproval of individuals who deal unfairly with others over whom they have competitive advantages in exchange relations, or of those who use their power over others oppressively, constitutes social pressures to refrain from actions of this kind. Correspondingly, the social approval received by individuals who are generous in their treatment of those dependent on them provides incentives for such benevolent actions. Research findings on work groups in two organizations suggest that expert consultants who took advantage of their superior status were less likely than those who did not to win their colleagues' approval and acceptance as sociable companions. [22]

Norms of fairness superimpose a secondary exchange, of fairness

---

[20] Homans, *loc. cit.* (original in capitals).

[21] See *ibid.*, pp. 75–76 for a slightly different conceptualization of the relation-ship between lack of justice and guilt.

[22] Blau, *The Dynamics of Bureaucracy* (2d ed.), University of Chicago Press, 1963, pp. 163–164.

for approval, on the primary one. In a sense, the unrewarding social disapproval provoked by unfairness and the rewarding social approval bestowed for fairness and unselfishness tend to restore equity by reducing the excessive profits in the case of unfair dealings and by raising the possibly insufficient rewards in the case of unselfish ones. Does this mean that all social transactions are necessarily equitable? Not really. To be sure, men, regardless of their power, have no control over the sentiments of others, which means they cannot prevent others from retaliating for exploitative oppressions with disapproval and animosity. But great power may enable men to prevent those subject to it from expressing their negative feelings, and it may immunize men against disapproval and dislike if they do find overt expression. Moreover, the exploited and oppressed continue to receive inequitable treatment in terms of prevailing standards of fairness, though they and others express their disapprobation and hostility, as long as they remain subjugated to the dominant power.[23]

People belong to many groups, and potentially to still others, which constitute reference groups with which they compare themselves. The members of a group compare how profitable various social experiences are not only among themselves but each also compares the returns he gets for his investments with persons in other groups of which he is a member or aspires to be one. Since the various members of a given group compare themselves with others in different reference groups, whose investments they consider similar to their own, their diverse expectations create differences in satisfaction with the same rewards. Thus, American soldiers who had graduated from high school were less satisfied with the promotions they had received in the army than those who had not, since the high school graduates' different reference group, with its higher educational attainment, led them to expect greater social rewards, expectations that were not unjustified, given the fact that high school graduates generally achieved higher ranks than nongraduates.[24] Stouffer and his colleagues

---

[23] The model of exchange can be used with varying degrees of inclusiveness. If only specific services are taken into account, some partnerships are characterized by unilateral services. If power is also taken into account, these are seen as also involving reciprocation, but power is used in some relations exploitatively, entailing inequitable transactions. If social disapproval too is taken into account, these again can be encompassed by an exchange conception. The independent standards of fair rates and going rates should prevent the analyst from employing these models in tautological fashion.

[24] Samuel A. Stouffer, Edward A. Suchman, Leland C. DeVinney, Shirley A. Star, and Robin M. Williams, Jr., *The American Soldier*, Princeton University Press, 1949, Vol. I, 254–256, 246–247.

referred to such dissatisfactions produced not by one's own meager rewards but by comparisons with more highly rewarded others as "relative deprivation." [25]

Social rewards have an invidious significance that depends on their scarcity as well as an inherent one that does not. Since reference groups serve as standards of comparison and expectation, the average reward received by their members becomes a baseline for evaluating what is a relatively gratifying or a relatively depriving experience. Men derive gratification from the amount of money they earn, but they also derive gratification from earning more than their associates and feel deprived if they earn much less, regardless of how high their absolute income is. Scarce approval is most valuable, as repeatedly noted, which means the approval a few get and most do not. The best empirical illustration of this phenomenon of relative gratification and deprivation is the finding from the Stouffer research that soldiers in outfits with few promotions, such as the Military Police, were *more* satisfied with promotion opportunities than those in outfits with many promotions, such as the Air Corps.[26] The noncommissioned officer in the MP's (where only a quarter of the enlisted men had this status) received a comparatively higher social reward than his counterpart in the Air Corps (where nearly half of the enlisted men were noncommissioned officers), and the private in the MP, sharing this fate with the large majority, was less deprived than the private in the Air Corps.[27]

The principle of relative deprivation is, in effect, a principle of diminishing *collective* marginal utility. According to the principle of marginal utility (for individuals), a person who has much of a benefit tends to value a further increment less than he did when he had only a little. Relative deprivation implies that in a group where a benefit, such as superior military rank, exists in abundance those who possess it value it less and those who do not value it more than they would were they in a group where it is scarce. (We infer from the empirical fact that promoted soldiers express comparatively low satisfaction with promotions that they value the promotions they have received *less,* and from the fact that nonpromoted soldiers express comparatively low satisfaction that they value the promotions withheld from

---

[25] *Ibid,* p. 125.

[26] *Ibid.,* pp. 250–253. For a somewhat similar finding, see Nigel Walker, *Morale in the Civil Service,* Edinburgh: University Press, 1961, pp. 205–207.

[27] A formal model of this conception of relative deprivation is presented in James A. Davis, "A Formal Interpretation of the Theory of Relative Deprivation," *Sociometry,* 22 (1959), 280–296.

them *more.*) Since these two differences in valuations are opposite in direction, they indicate nothing about a general trend produced by increasing rewards (promotions).

However, from the perspective of the organization as a whole (and in this case, there is no need to make complex inferences), the more benefits in the form of promotions that have been received by a collectivity, the less impact another increment of promotions makes. Although promoted soldiers were generally more favorably disposed toward promotion chances than privates—promotions were rewards that produced satisfaction—a growing number of promotions in an outfit did not proportionately, in fact not at all, raise these expressions of satisfaction. This corresponds closely to the principle that the more income an individual already has, the less difference in his satisfaction another dollar makes. In brief, the marginal utility of increasing rewards eventually declines for entire collectivities as well as for individuals, though the mechanisms are different; the effect for collectivities is produced by processes of social comparison, while that for individuals is produced by psychological reactions to meet needs and expectations.

Attachment and Immobility

Men are expected to commit themselves to their social relations, groups, and organizations. The investments they make in fostering social relations and in qualifying for membership in groups and organizations entail commitments to them. Many exchange transactions depend on, or are facilitated by, the investments made in them by at least one party—the inservice training without which a man could not do his specialized job, or the railroad spur to transport goods from manufacturer to purchaser. To protect the investment of one party against loss as the result of the other's withdrawal from the exchange relation, the other is expected to make a commitment to it also. Commitments themselves constitute opportunity costs, both "actual" and "virtual." The rewards obtained in the social associations or organizations abandoned in favor of the present one are actual opportunity costs, and the rewards not obtained from other affiliations that could have been established are virtual opportunity costs. These alternative opportunities foregone strengthen commitments, and together with the investments made sometimes produce firm attachments.

Memberships in groups and organizations involve such attachments of varying degrees. The stronger the attachments, the more rigid is the larger social structure of groups and organizations. Firm attachments strengthen groups and organizations, but weak attachments are required to maintain individual mobility and a fluid, adaptable social structure. Strong attachments prevent individuals from exploring alternative opportunities and taking advantage of them to increase their rewards and improve their positions—from turning to a better consultant, taking a more promising job, moving to a more desirable community, or switching to a more profitable occupation. The immobility resulting from firm attachments precludes the adjustments in the social structure required for exchange transactions to yield fair returns to all parties.

Occupational life provides a prototype of commitments that generate immobility. Individuals are attracted to occupations by the rewards they expect from becoming members of them. To become eligible for membership, they must invest resources to acquire the necessary qualifications and skills. This entails sometimes a long process of education, training, and selection. Aspirants to professional occupations must compete with other candidates for acceptance in professional schools, which requires that they impress selection committees with their potential for making professional contributions. Subsequently, they must devote time and effort to their training and to demonstrating to teachers and prospective colleagues their qualifications and worthiness of becoming a professional colleague. The superior rewards consequent to accreditation constitute, in part, returns for these investments. Were it not for superior rewards, individuals would have no incentives to make the greater investments needed to become a professional, although it is entirely conceivable that the higher prestige and more interesting work of professionals, even if their incomes were no higher than those in other occupations, would furnish sufficient rewards for recruiting an adequate number of aspirants.

The investments made in occupational training are irrevocable and create strong occupational commitments. The adult manual worker as well as the adult professional can rarely afford the new investment in time and resources necessary to enter into a completely different occupation. If the demand for the services of a given occupation should decline, and with it the rewards received for them, fewer and less able young people will be attracted to the occupation, and possibly less training will be required to enter it. In the long run, these processes may adjust the investment of resources made, as a prerequisite for furnishing occupational services, to the returns received for them, though the superior power of some occupational groups often impedes these adjustments when they are to their disadvantage. In any case, the persons in the declining occupation at the time do not benefit from these long-run adjustments. Quite the contrary, they pay the cost of the process of adjustment. Their commitment to the occupation, which precludes mobility to other occupations for most of them, means they receive unfair returns for their investments as the result of the process in which rewards for supplying occupational services become adjusted to the decreasing demand for them. The imbalance these persons suffer is the human cost that helps equilibrate the system of occupational supply and demand. For them, their inability to obtain a fair deal in terms of social norms owing to forces beyond their control is a punishing experience, to which they are likely to react with bitterness and perhaps belligerence. But theirs is only a more extreme example of the inequities widely generated by social attachments.

Organizations and other collectivities require membership attachment, and the adjustment of exchange rates by supply and demand depends on mobility, but social attachments inevitably restrict social mobility. Turnover of membership is costly to an organization. Lasting attachments further organizational efficiency, and they are promoted by various mechanisms used by organizations, ranging from employment contracts and pension plans in firms to ideological identifications in political parties. Competition among organizations has ideally the result that those who supply services in demand by the public prosper while others decline or fail to survive altogether. The assumption is that competition, and the failure of some organizations to prosper or to survive that it necessarily entails, contribute to the common welfare. Some firms must decline if there is serious economic competition, and so must some parties if there is serious political competition. Economic and political rivalry as well as other forms of contests and competitive conflicts have important functions and are encouraged in societies like ours.

Mobility of various types makes it possible for competitive conflicts to persist and serve their functions without permanent, serious injury to the individuals innocently caught up in them. The businessman who risks his fortune in order to increase it is not an innocent victim of circumstances should he fail, but his employees are and need social protection against being irremediably harmed by his failure. As a matter of fact, the businessman himself needs protection against technological and economic forces beyond his control, if only to encourage him to take the risks of innovation. Mobility—using the term in its most general sense to include all kinds of movements and readjustments—offers such protection and attenuates the deleterious impact that competitive conflict between groups and organizations otherwise has on individuals, as Boulding has pointed out.[28]

One type of mobility that reduces conflict is group mobility. The upward mobility of the different socio-economic classes in a society, made possible by an expanding economy, mitigates the severity of the conflict of economic interests. In a stationary society the capacity of the rich to increase their wealth and power necessarily means that the poor get poorer and more powerless, with the result that class conflict is usually acute. In a growing economy, however, "the rich can get richer without the poor getting poorer; indeed anybody can get richer, up to a point, without anybody else getting poorer. There is still economic conflict, in the sense that some get richer faster than others. This is very different, however, from the conflict in a stationary society, where one only rises by pushing another down." [29] Similarly, once ethnic groups have improved their socio-economic positions, as the successive waves of immigrants to this country have done,[30] the conflict between them abates, while continuing conflict is associated with the absence of group mobility, as illustrated by the difference between Negroes and other ethnic groups in the United States.

The involuntary and inevitable mobility between age groups, too, lessens the conflict between them. The adults of a society must share the product of their labor, in the words of Boulding, "with the young, who must be fed, clothed, sheltered, and educated in the nonproductive years, and also with the aged, who must be supported when they are not producing anything. The conflict is a very real one; the more of the product goes to one group, the less is currently available for the others." [31] Yet with rare exceptions, such as the Townsend movement and the opposition to it, age groups are not engaged in open conflict (the conflicts between parents and children are an entirely different matter). A major reason for this is that young adults, who are likely to become parents of children who benefit from educational institutions and later old people who benefit from pension plans, are not a lasting group with enduring interests distinct from those of other age groups.

---

[28] Boulding, *Conflict and Defense,* New York: Harper, 1962, chapter x.

[29] *Ibid.,* p. 192.

[30] W. Lloyd Warner and Leo Srole, *The Social System of American Ethnic Groups,* New Haven: Yale University Press, 1945, chapter v.

[31] Boulding, *op. cit.,* p. 199.

Another type of mobility that mitigates the adverse effects of conflict is that of organizations and, specifically, their resources. As products become obsolete or the demand for them falls off sharply for some other reason, the firms that produce them decline. If firms are committed to a particular line of production and incapable of turning to other lines, this worsening of their terms of trade threatens their survival. But if they can adapt to the new situation and if their resources are mobile, they can start producing, for example, bodies for cars instead of horsedrawn carriages, and the reverses they have suffered will have been only temporary and not permanent. In parallel fashion, the political party whose program is rejected by the voters may be able to recoup its losses by modifying its program, but it cannot do so if strong commitments to the old ideals preclude such mobility of ideological resources, so to speak. Even when an organization's resources are immobile and its lack of adaptability to changing conditions leads to its decline, its individual members suffer only temporary setbacks if they themselves are mobile.

The mobility of individuals between organizations and groupings, finally, is the most important protection against being ruined by competitive conflicts among powers beyond one's control. The decline of an organization, occupation, or group inevitably causes hardships to its members, but they do not suffer irreparable damage if they can readily get another job, pursue another line of work, join another party, build another union. It is precisely this mobility, however, that is impeded by the attachments and loyalties organizations and groups require. A conspicuous example is the occupational immobility consequent to the investments made in an occupation. The great investment men have in their occupation and their job make the wage bargain fundamentally different from other economic exchanges and distinguish its significance for the employee from that which it has for the employer. Whereas the employer buys labor power, just as he buys raw materials, by investing money to make a money profit, the employee's income represents his whole livelihood, not simply one of many profitable transactions, and what he invests is not money at all but a good part of his life. "The worker may be selling humiliation, dependence, and self-respect as well as plowing and hoeing," in the words of Boulding.[32]

"The employer is really exchanging commodity (or money) for commodity. . . . The worker is exchanging life for income; the transaction involves him in status, prestige, his standing in the eyes of his

---

[32] *Ibid.,* p. 214.

family and of the community, and his whole position as a man." [33]
The vital significance their job has for men makes the immobility
resulting from occupational and organizational attachments a particularly serious threat for those caught up in the vicissitudes of competitive conflict between powerful firms. It is the unjust fate of some
individuals to have to pay the price for the benefits the community
obtains from competition.

Conclusions

The expectations of people govern the satisfactions they find in
social life and hence their reactions to social experiences. Depending
on expectations, the same achievement may be experienced as a
gratifying success by some and as a frustrating failure by others.
The attainment of minimum expectations is of great significance,
but as increasingly higher levels of expectations and aspirations are
reached, the significance of attaining still further rewards declines.
These changes in the significance of rewards follow the principle of
the eventually diminishing marginal utility of increasing amounts of
a given benefit. Expectations, however, do not remain constant. The
achievement of what were originally high aspirations tends to turn
them into minimum needs and to give rise to new higher levels of
aspirations. Although the attainment of increasing amounts of rewards
decreases the value of further increments, therefore, this manifestation of the marginal principle is mitigated by the rise of expectations
consequent to attainments, which again increases the value of further
rewards.

Aside from these "general" expectations, which define overall needs
and aspirations regardless of the source from which they are met,
individuals also have "particular" expectations of specific associates.
The impression a person conveys that he has various attractive qualities gives rise to expectations that associating with him will furnish
certain rewards, and these particular expectations guide the social
interaction of others with him. The proximity between an individual's
general and particular expectations determines his initial attraction
to another. That is, if he expects the other to furnish rewards of a
certain kind, whether professional assistance or social support, that
fully meet his general expectations, he will be more attracted than
if he expects rewards that fall far short of meeting his needs. An
individual's particular expectations of various associates differ, de-

---

[33] *Ibid.*, p. 211.

pending on his impression of their qualifications and inclinations to provide him with social rewards. In contrast, his "comparative" expectations of profiting from social experiences constitute a common standard, which indicates the returns he expects to realize from his investments, and which permits him to choose between various potential associates. Lasting attractions develop in those social associations that are most profitable.

The expectations of individuals are not only influenced by their own past attainments but also by the attainments of others who constitute significant reference groups for them and by the common values and norms in the society, which also serve as reference standards. Shared social experiences of groups exert an especially pronounced influence on social expectations. Thus, factory workers who were treated very favorably by their previous manager tend to have higher expectations of his successor than those who had a less rewarding experience under their former manager. Whether or not a given approach of a succeeding manager is experienced by them as rewarding and earns their loyalty depends on whether it exceeds or falls short of the expectations his predecessor's treatment has created. A manager may conceive of his treatment of subordinates as most generous and rewarding in terms of his reference standard and expect favorable reactions from them, whereas their different reference standards, based on their past experience, may lead them to expect more of him and hence to react unfavorably to his treatment. Differences in the expectations that define the significance of given social transactions are a potential source of conflict.

Shared experiences in groups induce members to consider their investments to be similar and to expect similar returns, with the result that the average reward received by group members becomes the standard of expectation that governs the value of rewards. Given this standard of expectation, the same reward—for example, a certain rank and pay grade in the army—is typically experienced as more gratifying in groups where it is rare than in those where it is prevalent. Strangely enough, therefore, the more rewards, such as promotions to higher grades, the members of a group receive, the less satisfaction are these rewards likely to produce. This phenomenon of relative deprivation, as Stouffer and his colleagues termed it, can be conceived of as a principle of diminishing *collective* marginal utility. The relative significance of a social reward declines the more of it has been distributed in a collectivity, just as the significance of a dollar diminishes the more money a man has.

The long-term investments required to furnish various services in demand in a community give rise to social norms that govern what a fair return for rendering these services is. The social disapproval of individuals who take advantage of others in social transactions in violation of these common norms of fairness is a cost to them that discourages such behavior. Nevertheless, many individuals cannot obtain fair returns for their investments. The conditions of supply and demand in particular groups exert an independent influence on exchange transactions and on the going rates of exchange between social benefits that become established. The relationship between the fair rate and the going rate in social exchange roughly corresponds to that between the normal price and the average price in economic markets. The normal price influences the average price in the long run, but its immediate influence is strongly modified by the direct impact conditions of supply and demand have on the going rate of exchange. Hence, many individuals cannot realize a fair return in their transactions. Indeed, many cannot even realize the going rate of exchange. An important reason for this is that social attachments produce immobilities that prevent individuals from taking advantage of alternative opportunities.

A fundamental problem is created by the fact that the effective achievement of collective goals requires organizations with committed and loyal members, but attachments to organizations preclude the mobility necessary for individuals to safeguard their investments and receive a fair return for them. While some organizations and groups must decline in the course of the competition that enables the community to select those for whose services there is a continuing need, this would not have disastrous effects for their individual members as long as they can readily move to other organizations or groups. But effective competition also requires that individuals become committed to occupational pursuits and to particular organizations, and these commitments impede mobility. As a result, some men, due to no fault of their own, cannot obtain a fair return for the major investments of their lives. The unfair deal they receive as the victims of competitive processes beyond their control is likely to make them alienated from and hostile to their society. Social welfare legislation that compensates them in part for their losses is designed to forestall their potential opposition.

SEVEN

The Dynamics of Change
and Adjustment in Groups

Any social order requires a hierarchy of superordinations and sub-ordinations, even if only for technical reasons. Therefore, equality in the sense of justice can only be the exact correspondence of personal qualification with position in this hierarchy. Yet, this harmonious correspondence is in principle impossible for the very simple reason that there always are more persons qualified for superior positions than there are superior positions.

GEORG SIMMEL, *The Sociology of Georg Simmel*

In this chapter, an attempt is made to apply marginal analysis to processes of social exchange in groups.[1] The aim is to explore whether the economic principles of marginal analysis, appropriately adapted to social exchange, can help clarify the changes and adjustments of group structure that occur in the course of social interaction and social differentiation.

The example chosen for this purpose is the pattern of consultation in work groups, that is, the exchange of advice for social status. The

---

[1] One inspiration for doing so was Kenneth E. Boulding's statement in his review of Homans' book that "there is a useful apparatus of indifference curves, contract curves, bargaining paths, Pareto optima, and the like, all of which is highly relevant to Homans' problem, but which he refers to only in passing." The attempt to show in this chapter that specific predictions can be derived from this type of theory was partly motivated by James A. Davis's criticism, in the same double-review article, that it is impossible "to make predictions about empirical events from the theory alone, which unfortunately is the aim of Homans' book." "Two Critiques of Homans' *Social Behavior: Its Elementary Forms*," *American Journal of Sociology*, 67 (1962), 459, 458.

assumption is that advice is a typical service and that its exchange for social status illustrates general principles of social differentiation in groups, although it is important to note that these processes are modified if a group has distinctive common objectives of its own. Two individuals might initially exchange favors, perhaps one advising the other, who may reciprocate with some other favors. But if advice on problems of one's work is the most valuable service, as it often is in work groups, other favors are insufficient to discharge one's obligations for it, and it becomes necessary to reciprocate for advice with respect and compliance. This is the situation that serves as the starting point for the analysis. Concern is with the ways in which exchanges in pairs proliferate into exchange processes throughout the group; with the social differentiation that develops and the changes and adjustments that occur in the group structure in response to internally generated and external stimuli; and with the imperfections of this "social market" that must be taken into account in the analysis of processes of social exchange and of the development of a differentiated structure.

The application of conceptions of economic theory to the study of group structure is intended to yield propositions that can be tested in empirical research and thus to demonstrate that the theoretical model here advanced is capable of generating precise operational hypotheses. Some of the hypotheses derived from the theoretical analysis are: Changes in the number of experts in a work group will affect the volume of consultation if the task is relatively easy but not, or much less, if it is very difficult. Contrary to what common sense would lead one to expect, the supply of advice in a work group will influence the amount of consultation *less* if task performance is of great importance to group members than if it is of little importance relative to informal status. Newcomers to a work group who increase the demand for advice will produce a permanent increase in the volume of consultations, which will persist to some extent even after the newcomers have become experienced oldtimers.

The basic principle underlying marginal analysis, and exchange generally, is that of the eventually diminishing marginal utility. Increasing amounts of benefits of a given kind produce possibly first an increase but in the long run always a decrease in their marginal value, that is, the value another unit has for an individual.[2] This

---

[2] Rising expectations consequent to increasing attainments mitigate the negative effect of increasing attainments on marginal utility, as noted in the last chapter, but they rarely obliterate this effect completely.

principle is the ultimate source of the divergence of attitudes without which exchanges would not take place. The reason two men engage in a voluntary exchange transaction is that both benefit from it. Both can benefit *only if* they have divergent attitudes, which means that the person who trades, for example, an apple for a pear values the apple less than the pear, whereas the one with whom he trades values the apple more than the pear. This difference in preferences would exist even though the two persons have identical tastes if the first has many apples and few pears and the second has many pears and few apples. Since the marginal utility of increasing possessions is relatively smaller, all benefit as "everybody gives up what he has too much of in return for what he has too little of." [3] Specialization provides each man with more of some resources than he can use and fewer of others than he needs. It therefore necessitates exchange. "Exchange without specialization is impossible; specialization without exchange is silly." [4]

The advice of the most expert members of a work group with fairly complex duties constitutes a specialized service, and the less competent members have a need for this service, since they tend to be reluctant to expose their ignorance to supervisors by frequently consulting them. This divergence of attitudes, which makes some "eager sellers" and others "eager buyers" of advice, constitutes the basis for exchange transactions that benefit both parties; [5] one profits from the advice that enables him to perform his duties better, and the other profits from the superior status he is accorded in exchange for his expert advice. The compliance of others, on which superior status rests, can be considered a generalized means of social exchange, similar to money in economic exchange (except that it is far less liquid than money), since a person's command of the compliance of others enables him to obtain a variety of benefits, just as his possession of money does. But when advice is exchanged in mutual partnerships, as it often is between individuals whose competence is about the same, there would seem to be no divergence of preferences that enables both to profit from the transactions. Both do profit, however, because the anxiety aroused by decisions on the basis of which one's performance is evaluated by supervisors often interferes with a person's decision-making on his own cases but not with his decision-

---

[3] Boulding, *Conflict and Defense*, New York: Harper, 1962, p. 193.

[4] Boulding, *Economic Analysis* (3d ed.), New York: Harper, 1955, p. 20 (original in italics).

[5] See *ibid.*, pp. 68–70.

making on a colleague's cases. Hence, the advice two colleagues exchange tends to be superior to their decisions on their own cases. The consequent divergence of attitudes, with each partner preferring the less anxiety-distorted decisions of the other to his own, permits both to benefit from their mutual exchange of advice.

Bilateral Monopoly and Proliferation

As a starting point, each consulting relationship in a work group engaged in mental tasks of a minimum degree of complexity is concentualized as a case of bilateral monopoly, and the analysis will then proceed to the pressures created in these pairs to explore alternative opportunities and to the resulting proliferation of exchange processes. When a consultant is more and more frequently asked for advice by a colleague, the value of the respect and compliance he receives in return for his advice declines. Simultaneously the cost in time of giving advice rises for him as the time he must devote to it increasingly impinges on the time he has left for doing his own work and engaging in other activities. Given these two marginal processes, the marginal rate of substitution, that is, the worth (utility) of the subordination he receives in terms of the worth of the cost in time he incurs, decreases at an accelerated rate with increasing consultations. Initially, the status enhancement he obtains is presumably more valuable for him than the time he must devote to consulting; this is the reason he supplies advice. But the declining value of further status enhancement and the rising value of further time costs reach a point, with more frequent consultations, where the two are equal, and this is the amount of consultation from which the consultant profits most and to which he should adhere if no other considerations influence his conduct. Similarly, the cost of status deflation to the questioner looms larger and larger the more often he must admit, to a man formally his peer, his helplessness and dependence, and his need for advice also diminishes as more of his questions have already been answered, so that he too reaches a point where he no longer profits from further consultations.

The relationship between the subjective worth or utility of two commodities can be represented with the aid of indifference curves. Any point on an indifference curve indicates that the individual is indifferent to whether he possesses the specified amount of the first or the specified amount of the second commodity, that is, that the two have the same value for him. If an individual derives the same pleasure from spending ten dollars on going to the theater or on having dinner at a restaurant, he might not care whether he goes to the theater twice a week and not to a restaurant, goes once to each, or goes twice to a restaurant and not to the theater; all these points would be on one indifference curve. To be sure, he probably would prefer dining out twice a week and also going twice to the theater, but whether he does this or engages in any other combination of going out four times may again not make any difference to him; these points would lie on a higher indifference curve for him. So far, we have assumed that the indifference curves are straight lines on a graph with the frequencies of dining out on one axis and those of going to the theater on the other, but this assumption is obviously unrealistic. The individual who likes both equally on the average and has already dined out six times in a given week surely will prefer a theater to a restaurant on the seventh evening, which means that the more often he has dined out already, the lower becomes the value of dining out relative to that of going to the theater for him, in accordance with the marginal principle.

Indifference curves, therefore, typically have changing slopes (they are curved, not straight), which indicate that the amount of one commodity that is equivalent in utility to a given amount of the other depends on the proportion of the two under consideration, as shown in Figure 1.[6] The individual is indifferent toward any combination of X and Y that lies on I_1, whereas he has increasingly higher preferences toward the combinations that lie on successively higher indifference curves (toward the upper right), being again indifferent toward any that lie on the same curve. The line AB is the opportunity line, that is, it shows the resources available to him to obtain the two commodities. He can purchase OB of Y and no X, OA of X and no Y, or any other combination on the opportunity line. The most preferable combination is the one where the opportunity line is tangent to the highest indifference curve, which is at P, where he obtains OD of Y and OC of X. Other attainable combinations, such as those at M and N, are less preferable, since they lie on lower indifference curves.

Let X represent the benefits an expert obtains from devoting the time he can spare from his own work to relaxation and sociability; Y, the status enhancement that accrues to him as the result of using this time for advising others (both in terms of utility to him); and the line AB, his total extra time. The point P would then show that division of his spare time between relaxation and helping others that

---

[6] Figure 1 is reproduced from George J. Stigler, *The Theory of Competitive Price*, New York: Macmillan, 1942, p. 73.

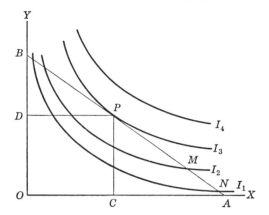

FIGURE 1. Indifference curves.

yields him most utility. The average slope of the indifference curves would reveal his status consciousness, specifically, how significant it is for him to achieve superior status among colleagues relative to the significance that relaxation and sociability have for him. If X represents the benefits a man receives from devoting time to performing his own work (rather than from his leisure time), the average slope of the indifference curves would indicate the degree to which he is oriented to colleagues as a reference group rather than to his instrumental tasks and the superiors who evaluate his performance. One would expect, for example, that social cohesion makes these indifference curves less steep, indicating the increased significance of colleague approval and informal status (Y).

The exchange process in bilateral monopoly can be represented in a box diagram with two facing pairs of coordinates, as in Figure 2.[7] O_a is the origin for the consultant; O_b for the colleague who consults him. K indicates problem-solving ability, which is conceived as the time devoted to problem solving weighted by the competence applied to the task. O_aY (or O_bX) is the total problem-solving ability available in the pair, with O_aK_a representing the greater ability of the expert and O_bK_b the lesser one of the colleague at the initial point P_0, before any consultation takes place. H indicates the compliance each is willing to express to raise the other's status, and the assumption is made that the expert's superior status makes him less inclined

---

[7] Figure 2 is reproduced from Boulding, *op. cit.*, p. 811. The following discussion is adapted from *ibid.*, pp. 810–813.

to subordinate himself to the other for any conceivable benefit than the other is to subordinate himself to the expert, which means that the expert has, in effect, less resources of willing compliance (O_aH_a) than his colleague (O_bH_b). (A different assumption could, of course, be made.) Consultations would be reflected by movements from the initial point P_0 toward the bottom, showing that the expert applies some of his time and ability to the problems of the colleague, and toward the right, showing that the expert's status is raised by the compliance with which the colleague reciprocates for the advice. The solid indifference curves are those of the expert, with higher preferences indicated by the successsive curves toward the upper right, and the dotted ones are those of the colleague, with higher preferences indicated by successive curves toward the lower left. Any movement toward higher indifference curves from A_0 and B_0, respectively, is an improvement. As long as both can move toward higher indifference curves, both profit from increasing consultations.

A fair rate of exchange, based on accepted social norms of what is a fair return for expert advice, is represented by the exchange opportunity line $P_0E_bE_a$. As long as these norms of fairness are adhered to, movements can occur only along this line, the slope of which indicates the degree of compliance expected per unit of expert advice. If exchange proceeds up to the point E_b, it brings both parties to higher indifference curves (from A_0 to A_1 and from B_0 to B_1), which means that both profit from the exchange. The consultant now furnishes P_0L units of advice in exchange for LE_b units of compliance. A move to point E_a, where he would furnish more advice at the same rate, would be to his advantage, since it would bring him to a still higher indifference curve, but it would not be in the interest of the colleague, since it would move him to a lower indifference curve. A change from E_b to E_c, on the other hand, would be to the advantage of both, inasmuch as it would move both to higher indifference curves. At E_c, however, the consultant receives less compliance per unit of advice than the fair rate requires (the line P_0E_c is closer to being vertical than the line P_0E_b, and a vertical line would show that he gives advice free). Even in bilateral monopoly, therefore, it may be, and often is, to the advantage of both parties to depart from the fair rate of exchange.

As long as an increase in the volume of consultation, at whatever exchange rate, is possible that moves both parties to higher indifference curves, it is to the advantage of both to expand their exchange relation. But once a point of tangency of the indifference curves of the two parties is reached, as it is at point E_c, "no further movement

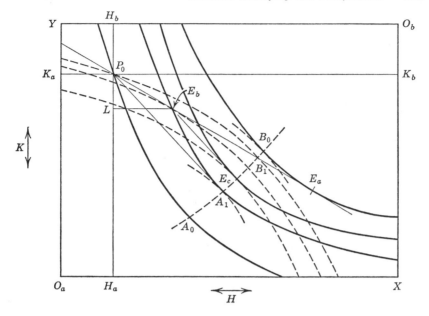

FIGURE 2. Exchange in bilateral monopoly.

can be made which will benefit both parties, no matter what the price."[8] The line that connects all the points of mutual tangency, $A_0E_cB_0$, is called the contract curve or "Paretian optimum," meaning the condition that maximizes the joint advantage of both parties. Whereas moves that profit both parties are possible from any point that is not on the contract curve; once they are on the contract curve no move is possible that does not disadvantage one of the two (or both). A move along the contract curve from A_0 toward B_0 would benefit the consultant at the expense of his colleague, and a move in opposite direction would benefit the latter at the expense of the former. The point on the contract curve that is reached depends on the bargaining strength of the two parties, in other words, on factors outside the theoretical model.

To be sure, there is only a single point that fulfills Pareto's condition of joint optimum and also satisfies the social norm of fairness, namely, the point B_1, where the contract curve is intersected by the opportunity line, which represents the fair rate. Whether this point is reached or not, however, depends on the so-called "bargaining

[8] *Ibid.*, p. 812.

path" of the two parties, that is, the earlier explorations in which they settle the terms of their exchange. If they initially settle at the rate of E_b, in conformity with the standard of a fair rate, they are unlikely ever to get to B_1, since doing so would require the colleague who consults to accept more disadvantageous terms than he already has (to move to a lower indifference curve), whereas there are many opportunities that increase the advantage of the consultant as well as his own. The point reached on the contract curve is influenced by the personal relation between the consultant and the consulting colleague, the skills of each in concealing how much he would be willing to return for the benefits obtained if he had to, and in particular the other benefits that one or both derive from their social interaction. The man who reveals his great need for advice may have to pay more compliance for it than the one who successfully conceals it. The consultant who expresses a supportive interest in helping colleagues tends to earn more appreciation and willing compliance than the one who extends assistance only grudgingly.[9] The man afraid to go to the supervisor for advice may have to pay a higher price for advice from colleagues than the one known sometimes to avail himself of this alternative resource. Generally, available alternatives strengthen a man's bargaining power, and the major alternatives accessible in work groups are other colleagues.

The consulting relations in a work group do not exist in isolation from each other. An individual may not be able to get as much advice as he needs from his consultant at a price he is willing to pay or, for that matter, at any price, and a consultant may not be able to obtain the superior status he feels he deserves from a single colleague. The very existence of alternative opportunities invites their exploration, and as some workers explore various exchange opportunities they tempt others who have already become relatively settled in consulting relations with promises of more profitable alternatives. In consequence of this proliferation of exchange, experts must compete for the compliance of colleagues and for superior status in the group,

---

[9] The significance of such other benefits can be taken into account in more complex theoretical models, but these have a disadvantage in that it becomes increasingly difficult, if not impossible, to operationalize them for empirical research. The simpler models that contain only the most important benefits exchanged, and which can be more easily translated into operational terms, should suffice for statistical predictions. That is, if the most salient benefits are taken into account in the model, even though not all benefits exchanged are, the predictions derived from it should be confirmed in a statistically significant proportion of cases, though not in all of them.

and those in need of advice must compete for the consulting time of experts. In the course of this double competition, an approximate going rate of compliance for advice becomes established in the group.[10] Social norms of fairness influence this going rate, but since the conditions of supply and demand in the group exert an independent influence on it, the going rate often deviates from the fair rate, as noted previously.

Exchange processes proliferate from bilateral monopolies into wider circles not only as a result of the search for more profitable opportunities but also because of limitations of resources. A person can obtain a service in return for either another service or compliance, that is, subordination. Since the workers in need of expert advice usually have nothing else to offer that the consultant needs, they must repay him for it by complying with his wishes. As they consult him more and more, the cost in compliance and self-respect mounts for them. Ultimately, of course, their need for advice also diminishes with increasing consultation, but the problem of those in need of much advice is precisely that they continue to need advice at the point when its cost has become prohibitive, either because their self-respect would suffer too much from further subordination, or because no amount of subordination on their part would profit the consultant sufficiently to devote more time to advising them.

In brief, the maximum amount of compliance with the requests of an expert consultant that workers can pay may not yield them the minimum amount of advice that they need. In this situation, they are likely to do what people generally do when their resources are not adequate to get them the kinds of goods they want, namely, substitute goods of lesser quality that they can afford. The less competent members of a work group often establish partnerships of mutual consultation, in which they obtain advice of poorer quality than that of experts at lower costs. Mutual consultation does not involve subordination for either partner. Each pays for the advice he gets, not with compliance, which he can ill afford, but with consultation time devoted to the other's problems, which is a cheap price, inasmuch as little demand is made on his consultation time and he enjoys the regard for his judgment implicit in the other's asking for his advice. These partnerships, which decrease the demand made on the time of experts, again make expert consulting time

---

[10] "It can be demonstrated that the length of the contract curve decreases as the number of bargainers increases, and that with very many buyers or sellers or both, it reduces to a single point." Stigler, *op. cit.,* p. 81.

available to workers when they need advice on their most difficult problems.[11] Reciprocal exchange relations of this sort decrease the differentiation of social status in groups, since they diminish the dependence of the less resourceful members on the more resourceful ones.

The expert consultants, too, have reasons for not confining their exchange transactions to one colleague but expanding their consulting relations. As the marginal utility or value that the increasing compliance of a colleague has for an expert declines, the value of the compliance of others does not similarly decline; quite the contrary, it increases by comparison. The technical reason for this is that acts of compliance of different persons are not equivalent and interchangeable. The theoretical reason is that superior status in a group requires that many others acknowledge their subordinate position, not simply that one exhibits a very high degree of deference. While there are advantages to having one person completely dependent on onself, the significance of superior social status in a group makes the lesser dependence of most members typically preferable. To achieve superior status, experts are likely to distribute their consulting time among many colleagues rather than to devote all of it to one person.

There is an interesting asymmetry in the effects the marginal processes experienced by the consultants and by those who consult them, respectively, have on the group structure. Changes in the marginal rate of substitution of the benefits obtained in terms of the costs incurred with increasing consultations in a given consulting relation prompt both the expert and the colleague whom he advises to turn to other consulting relations, as we have seen. The fact that a consultant does not sufficiently profit from advising a single colleague leads consultants to try to broaden the scope of their advice-giving to include numerous colleagues, which promotes the differentiation of social status in the group. In contrast, the fact that a man in need of advice cannot obtain sufficient assistance to meet his need from a single colleague leads to the establishment of partnerships of mutual consultation, which reduces the differentiation of social status in the group.

These internally generated forces, which partly operate in opposite directions, produce a differentiated group structure. The characteristics of this social structure govern the modifications and adjustments

---

[11] For the analysis of an empirical case, see Blau, *The Dynamics of Bureaucracy* (2d ed.), University of Chicago Press, 1963, pp. 127–132, 137–138.

that occur in it in response to externally imposed changes in conditions.

Structural Adjustment to Changing Conditions

The concept of elasticity, which economists use in the study of market structures, can be applied in the analysis of changes in group structure. There is a close relationship between the demand for a good or service, the supply of it, and its price. Changes in any one of these three factors produce changes in the other two. The exact nature of these interrelations is governed by the elasticity of the quantity of supply or demand. "The *elasticity* measures the degree to which price is effective in calling forth or holding back the quantity." [12] A rise or fall in *demand* produces initially a corresponding change in price; if supply is elastic, changes in it absorb most of the changes in demand, and the ultimate price is little affected, but if it is inelastic, the change in demand effects a considerable, enduring change in price. Similarly, an increase or decrease in *supply* produces initially an inverse change in price; if demand is elastic, changes in it absorb most of the changes in supply, and the ultimate effect on price is small, but if it is inelastic, the change in demand has a lasting and pronounced impact on price. The application of these principles to the exchange of advice for social status in work groups makes it possible to advance hypotheses concerning the changes and adjustments that occur in the social structure in response to varying conditions.

The impact of changes in the supply of expert advice in a work group depends on the elasticity of the demand for advice. The elasticity of demand is primarily governed by the steepness of the marginal utility curve; "the faster marginal utility declines with increasing consumption, the faster will the marginal rate of substitution decline and the less elastic will be the demand of the consumer for the commodity in question." [13] The vital need for a given commodity, the lack of available substitutes, and the fact that its cost uses up only a small proportion of an individual's total investments are three main factors that make the demand for the commodity relatively unresponsive to changes in its price, that is, inelastic. In respect to advice, demand will be less elastic if the complexity of the task makes it difficult to reach decisions and important to consult col-

---

[12] Boulding, *op. cit.*, p. 119 (italics in original).
[13] *Ibid.*, p. 699.

leagues in doubtful cases than if any easy task makes consulting merely a convenience individuals can do without should it be too costly.[14] Besides, if workers are reluctant to consult the supervisor and if they cannot themselves look up answers to the questions they ask colleagues, demand for colleague advice will be less elastic than if such substitutes for it are readily accessible. Finally, the less investment workers have in their social standing among colleagues compared to that they have in performing their task well and advancing their careers, the less elastic will demand for advice be. This is because the small significance of the cost of advice in subordination makes demand for advice less responsive to its cost than would be the case were its cost to play a greater role in the workers' total investments.

Let us assume that two or three experts have been removed by superiors from a work group and examine how the impact of this decrease in the supply of colleague advice is conditioned by variations in the elasticity of the demand for it. Now twice as many workers than before come to each of the two or three remaining experts for advice, increasing the pressure on the experts and the competition for their consultation time among the rest, thus probably increasing the price in compliance others will offer for advice. If the task is not very difficult and workers can easily look up the information that they previously requested from experts simply to save time, or if the significance of their status among colleagues is great, or that of the quality of their performance is not very great, others will consult experts less rather than subordinate themselves more to them in order to obtain their advice. Under these conditions of elastic demand, a decrease in the supply of advice is expected to reduce the volume of consultation without having pronounced effects on differences in social status.[15] If, however, the difficulty of the task or other factors make getting advice from expert colleagues a necessity for most workers and make their demand for it inelastic, they will have to offer more compliance to induce the few remaining experts to

---

[14] If the task is entirely routine, the demand for advice is probably also inelastic (and virtually zero), but such routine tasks are excluded from consideration here.

[15] Changes in the volume of consultation also influence status differences—if others consult experts less, they are less obligated to comply with their wishes— but changes in volume have less pronounced effects on the differentiation of status than do changes in the rate of compliance required to obtain advice, as shown in greater detail at the end of this section on Structural Adjustment to Changing Conditions.

devote sufficient time to supplying them the advice they need. Under conditions of inelastic demand, a decrease in the supply of advice is expected to intensify status differences and have comparatively little influence on the volume of consultation.

The conclusion that can be derived is that the impact of a change in the number of experts in a work group on its social structure is contingent on the difficulty of the tasks and other factors that affect the elasticity of the demand for advice. A series of hypotheses subject to empirical testing can be inferred from this conclusion and the considerations in the preceding paragraph. If the task is complex, a decrease in the number of experts will intensify status differences, an increase in the number of experts will lessen status differences, and neither will affect the volume of consultation very much. If the task is relatively simple, a change in the number of experts will have little effect on the existing differentiation of status, but it will give rise to parallel changes in the volume of consultation. Similarly, the less easily available substitute sources of advice and information are, the more of an impact will changes in the number of experts have on the status structure, and the less of an impact will they have on the volume of consultation. Moreover, the less significant status in the work group is for its members, the more will changes in the number of experts be reflected in changes in social distance between consultants and others rather than in changes in the volume of consultation. Finally, if the quality of the performance of tasks is of great significance, changes in the number of experts will primarily affect status differences and not the volume of consultation, whereas they will have the opposite effects if task performance is less significant.

The impact of changes in the demand for colleague advice in a work group is contingent on the elasticity of its supply. The elasticity of supply depends essentially on the ease with which existing suppliers can expand their output (which, in turn, depends on the slope of their marginal cost curves, that is, on the fact that an increase in output raises marginal cost little) and on the ease with which others can join the ranks of suppliers. The supply of advice in a group is more elastic if experts are not under time pressure than if the pressure of their own work restrains them from expanding the time devoted to consulting. Besides, the less difficult it is for other workers to become expert consultants, the more elastic is the supply of advice. This depends in the long run on the abilities and training required to become an expert, but in the short run it depends primarily on the difference in competence between the experts who are often consulted and others who are only rarely consulted except in mutual partnerships. Lack of time pressure on experts and the existence of workers who are rarely consulted though they are nearly as competent as experts, then, are the two main factors that increase the elasticity of the supply of advice in a group.

When several inexperienced newcomers are assigned to a work group, the demand for advice is likely to rise. As there are more workers now than before who compete for the consulting time of the experts, the rise in demand, just as the drop in supply previously discussed, probably will initially raise the price in compliance that workers will offer for advice. The elasticity of supply will determine the consequences of this increase in the rate of compliance for advice. If experts are not under time pressure, the fact that giving advice is now more profitable than it was before will provide incentives for them to devote more time to doing so. If several others are nearly as competent as experts, the greater profitability of giving advice is likely to induce them to join the ranks of consultants and the greater demand for advice is likely to induce others to consult these persons even though their counsel is not of the highest quality. The resulting expansion of the supply of advice will counteract the initial rise in its price. Given such an elastic supply of advice, a growing demand for it is expected to increase the amount of consultation without having much influence on the degree of status differentiation produced by consultation. However, if time pressures on consultants and the absence of competent others who can join the ranks of consultants limit the amount of advice available in the group, those in need of advice must compete for it by continuing to offer much compliance to experts in exchange. In a situation where supply is inelastic, a growing demand is expected to intensify status differences but have comparatively little effect on the volume of consultation.

These changes produced by a relatively inelastic supply of advice, however, tend to have further repercussions, particularly if the increased demand for advice due to the addition of newcomers is relatively inelastic too. Since there are many workers who need advice badly and not enough expert consultants to meet the entire need, *some* substitute for advice from expert colleagues must be found although no really satisfactory one is available. Workers may have to overcome their reluctance to go frequently to the supervisor with their problems. But as his time is also limited, consulting the supervisor may still not meet all the need for advice. Partnerships of mutual consultation can meet this need. Experienced professionals or skilled workers of any kind often seek confirmation of tentative decisions they have made to dispel their doubts and anxieties about them rather than help with problems they cannot cope with at all. This type of assistance can be furnished by a fellow professional or worker whose competence is no greater than one's own, especially since a person's lesser anxiety concerning the decisions on his colleagues' cases tends to make the advice of both partners superior to the decisions they make on their own cases, as noted in the introduction of this chapter.

Some of these inferences are supported by empirical data from a study of caseworkers in twelve work groups (with about five members each) in a public welfare agency, a third of whom were newcomers with less than one year of experience.[16] It has been hypothesized that work pressure makes the supply of advice inelastic and that inelastic supply promotes partnerships of reciprocal consultation when many newcomers intensify a strong need for advice. Indeed, the amount of work pressure was directly associated with the degree to which the consultations in a work group involved reciprocal partnerships.[17]

The significance of mutual partnerships is indicated by the finding that in groups where they were rare caseworkers under pressure from a heavy load of new cases consulted *less* than those without such pressure, while in groups with many reciprocal partnerships, the individuals who worked under much pressure consulted *more* than the ones who worked under little pressure. The fact that an individual has many new cases indicates that he encounters many new problems on which he might need advice if he is not very experienced, that is, it implies a greater demand for advice. Hence, when the supply of advice was relatively inelastic, because the limited consulting time of experts was not supplemented by that available in mutual partnerships, the volume of consultation did not rise with the growing demand for advice implied by a larger number of new cases. On the contrary, in this situation where workers had to consult experts they seemed to do so primarily when freedom from work pressure permitted them to afford the luxury of getting advice rather than when their need for it was greatest. When reciprocal partnerships made

---

[16] Blau and W. Richard Scott, *Formal Organizations,* San Francisco: Chandler, 1962, pp. 134–136.

[17] The actual measure of consultation partnerships was *perceived* reciprocity in consultation, that is, the number of colleagues whom a worker named in answer to *both* the question about whom he consults and the question of who consults him. The measure of work pressure was the number of new cases, which entailed much work, assigned per month.

the supply of advice more abundant and elastic, however, the amount of consultation did depend on the need for advice created by new problems. The implication is that changes in demand for advice were reflected in the volume of consultation *only if* supply was elastic, in accordance with the inference derived from the theory.

Once newcomers gain experience and acquire skills, the demand for advice drops off again. The significance of the resulting decline in the price of advice depends on the elasticity of its supply. The contracting supply of a commodity tends to be less elastic than its expanding supply if long-term investments are needed to produce it. A rise in price must be sufficient to justify the investment costs required to expand production and thus supply, but a subsequent drop in price to its previous level does not as readily decrease production and supply, since the investments that permit a larger output have already been made.[18] Workers who have made the effort to improve their competence and to become consultants when the demand for advice in the group increased are likely to want to continue to earn some respect and compliance of colleagues by giving them advice despite a declining demand for it.

After the investments necessary to become an expert have been made, it is easy for consultants to supply advice, and they have incentives to do so even though the rate of compliance they receive in return for it drops below an earlier level or below a fair rate of return. Given this inelasticity of the contracting supply of advice, a decrease in the demand for advice in a group is expected to reduce status differences considerably, more so than a previous increase in demand of the same magnitude intensified them, and to reduce the amount of consultation relatively little. Specifically, when newcomers have acquired experience and competence, the differentiation of status in a work group is expected to become less pronounced but the volume of consultation is expected to remain high. Another hypothesis implicit here is that the addition of inexperienced newcomers to a work group produces a permanent increase in the amount of consultation, which persists to some extent after the newcomers have become experienced oldtimers.[19]

Although the contracting supply of advice tends to be less elastic

---

[18] Boulding, *op. cit.*, p. 572.

[19] This hypothesis corresponds to the conclusion Herbert A. Simon derives from his formalization of Homans' theory that it requires less environmental pressure to sustain group life than to bring it into existence; "A Formal Theory of Interaction in Social Groups," *American Sociological Review*, 17 (1947), 202–211.

than the expanding supply, due to the investments made in attaining expertness as a consultant, there are variations in its relative elasticity. The time pressure under which experts work who feel that they already supply as much advice as they can without neglecting their own work or exhausting themselves makes the expanding supply of advice less elastic, as we have seen, but its contracting supply more elastic. Experts who devote as much time as they do to consultations only because of the high rate of compliance they receive in return will be inclined to restrict their consulting activities when the demand for advice and its price decline. The previous conclusion must therefore be qualified to read that a decreasing demand for advice in a group will reduce the volume of consultation little *unless* consultants are under much pressure, in which case it will reduce it considerably.

In sum, the effects of the assignment of inexperienced workers on the structure of a work group are contingent on the elasticity with which the supply of advice responds to the increased demand for it. If other workers are or can readily become sufficiently competent to join the ranks of expert consultants and the existing consultants can easily devote more time to giving advice, the level of consultation in the group will rise while the obligations incurred by consulting will remain about the same. To be sure, the expansion of consultation itself fortifies the superior status of consultants, but in this case their superior status rests on the great efforts they must devote to supplying needed services and not on the high price their powerful position enables them to extract for limited services. If, on the other hand, the competence of other workers is insufficient for them to become consultants and the time pressure on the few experts prevents them from broadening the scope of their consulting activities, the amount of consultation will increase little in response to the growing demand for advice, while the status differences will become intensified, that is, the few expert consultants will gain more power without furnishing any more services than before. The great social distance between experts and others and the high rate of compliance required for advice, in turn, create pressures on the others to find substitute sources of advice and establish partnerships of reciprocal consultation. These partnerships somewhat lessen the pronounced differentiation of status again because they decrease the demand for expert advice, the others' dependence on experts, and the experts' power. Finally, when most newcomers have acquired experience and improved their competence, the consequent decline in the demand for advice further reduces status differences, but the volume of consultation is not likely to drop to the level existing before the demand had increased, since the investment of consultants in their expertness tends to make the contracting supply of advice less elastic than the expanding one was.[20]

The change in demand resulting from a rise in the price of a commodity is due to a substitution and an income effect. First, other commodities will be substituted for the one whose price has increased, decreasing the demand for it. Second, the rise in price reduces the real income of persons, and the fact that they can buy less for their money now decreases their overall demand, usually, though not always, including their demand for the commodity whose price has risen. Thus, if the rate of compliance for advice in a work group increases, workers will exchange advice more in mutual partnerships instead of requesting it from experts, and the greater subordination entailed in consulting experts will further decrease their inclination to consult them, both of which tendencies reduce workers' demand for expert advice. But in the special case of a "poor man's good" and a "rich man's good," in which indifference curves and the so-called standard of life line bend backwards, the pronounced income effect of a rise in the price of the "poor man's good" may actually increase the demand for it.[21] If people were to buy only two commodities, mostly cheap bread and some expensive cake, a rise in the price of bread would diminish their real income and force them to buy less cake and substitute bread for it, thus increasing the demand for bread. Let us assume that needed advice in a work group can be obtained only from expert colleagues, at the cost of losing social standing in their eyes, or from the supervsior, at the much more serious cost of losing standing in his eyes. An increase in the rate of compliance required to obtain advice from expert colleagues might undermine the self-confidence of workers so much that they are too threatened to consult the supervisor at all and actually go more to colleagues for advice than they did formerly. This is an unlikely result, however (just as the case of a "poor man's good" generally is), since reciprocal partnerships probably would develop in such a situation.

In concluding this application of marginal analysis to changes in group structure, the difference between changes in the amount of

---

[20] It should be noted that the elasticity of supply and demand is not necessarily, or typically, constant. Thus, the supply of advice in a group is likely to expand easily up to a point but much less readily later, and the demand for it probably contracts more easily at first than subsequently.

[21] Boulding, *op. cit.*, pp. 803–807.

consultation and changes in the rate of compliance offered for advice should be further clarified. An increase in the rate of compliance per unit of expert advice strengthens the power of experts over others and intensifies the differentiation of social status in the group. This has been contrasted with an increase in the amount of consultation, but the question arises whether such an increase does not also involve an intensification of status differentiation. To answer this question, it is necessary to examine what produced the greater volume of consultation. If it is largely a result of the exchange of advice in mutual partnerships, it evidently does not promote differentiation of social status. If the greater volume of consultation is due to the fact that additional group members have joined the ranks of consultants, the status distribution in the group has changed, but this does not mean that the differences in status between the consultants and those who consult them are greater than before; as a matter of fact, status differences may have become smaller as more experts compete for the compliance of others. If the greater volume of consultation is the result of the expanding scope of the consulting activities of existing experts, it does indicate that experts command more power and that their superior status in the group is more firmly established than before. Even in this case, the superiority of experts is contingent on their furnishing more extensive services, whereas an increase in the rate of compliance raises their status without requiring them to supply more services in return. Nevertheless, the juxtaposition of changes in the amount of consultation and changes in status differences should be qualified by stating that changes in the amount of consultation sometimes also entail modifications of status differences.

Imperfections

The assumption in marginal analysis is that the principle of equal advantage governs the allocation of resources. "If the owners of any resources think that they can be put to better advantage in some other use than the one in which they are employed, these resources will be transferred from the less advantageous to the more advantageous use." [22] The equimarginal principle expresses this more precisely. To quote Boulding again: "In dividing a fixed quantity of anything among a number of different uses, just so much will be apportioned to each use to cause the gain involved by transferring a unit of dividend into one use to be just equal to the loss involved in the

---

[22] *Ibid.*, p. 69.

uses from which the unit of dividend is withdrawn." [23] Knight puts it more simply by stating that "we tend to apportion our resources among the alternative uses that are open in such a way that equal amounts of resources yield equivalent return in all fields." [24]

An expert in a work group, for example, may have the alternatives of spending his lunch hours either socializing with friends or advising colleagues and thereby improving his status among them. The cost of sociability is the status enhancement foregone by devoting time to it, and the cost of improved status is the sociability foregone to attain it. The more respect and compliance an expert commands among colleagues, the less valuable will a further increment of these manifestations of his superior status be to him, in accordance with the marginal principle, and eventually his gains from devoting more time to consultations will no longer be worth the cost in sociability to him. Similarly, the pleasures of sociability wane as more and more time is spent socializing with companions, until a point is reached when time would be more profitably spent securing one's social status. If no other considerations were to influence his decisions, the expert would divide his lunch hours between sociability and consultations in the manner that gives him as much gratification from the last hour of sociability as he gets from the increment in status produced by the last hour of consultation.

Alternative costs govern the allocation of resources in accordance with the principle of equal advantage. This principle applies to long-term investments as well as to short-run choices. How much time and energy to invest in improving one's competence depends on the gains expected from doing so. Competence promises three advantages: it makes a person less dependent on the advice of others, it enables him to give others advice and receive their respect and compliance in return, and it advances his career by improving his performance of tasks. But the marginal revenue product of increasing competence decreases, that is, the more competent a person has already become, the less difference further increases in his competence are likely to make for gaining more of these rewards. When the costs of the alternatives foregone by devoting more time to training and learning equal the advantages anticipated from further expansions of skills

---

[23] *Ibid.*, p. 688. In technical terms: "The 'best' division of expenditures is that at which the weighted marginal utilities in all lines of expenditure are equal." *Ibid.*, p. 687 (original in italics).

[24] Frank H. Knight, *Risk, Uncertainty and Profit* (2d ed.), Boston: Houghton Mifflin, 1933, p. 65 (original in italics).

and knowledge, a person has no reason to continue to improve his abilities. Of course, individuals usually do not have sufficient information to make these predictions accurately. This may create serious hardships for them, and it constitutes an important limitation of the theoretical model.

Alternative costs, since they underlie the allocation of resources by individuals, determine in principle the exchange ratio between goods and services. If the resources required to produce either of two goods are the same, their prices should be the same, for if one commands a higher price, individuals who produce the other have incentives to reallocate their resources to the first until the ratio of exchange of the two equals the ratio of invested resources or alternative costs. Unless the advantages highly competent workers obtain from advising colleagues equal those they obtain from devoting the same amount of time to their own work (or other pursuits), they have incentives to reallocate their resources until the benefits derived from various activities are proportionate to the time and energy spent on them. This reallocation assumes, however, not only that these individuals have full information about present and future advantages to be gained from various alternatives but also that no other considerations influence their decisions, such as their personal relations with the colleagues who seek their advice. These are clearly unrealistic assumptions for social exchange, but so are those made by the theoretical model for economic exchange, as Boulding has pointed out. "The extremely abstract assumptions of the above argument [that alternative costs determine the exchange ratio] must be noted carefully. It assumes full employment and perfect mobility." [25] The presence of too many experts in a work group may make some "unemployed" as consultants, and the commitments to established social relations restrict mobility, just as the social attachments discussed in chapter six do.

Two comments ought to be made concerning the limitations of the theoretical model of social exchange, one regarding its usefulness despite limitations, and the other regarding the need to modify the most unrealistic assumptions. First, while the model abstracts a few social forces and ignores other factors that influence the processes of social interaction under consideration, this makes it neither incorrect nor inapplicable to empirical research provided that the forces selected are significant ones. The application of the theoretical model to the analysis of social processes yields statistical predictions that

---

[25] Boulding, *op. cit.*, p. 29.

can be tested, although the fact that conditions ignored by the model do influence these processes makes it impossible to advance fully deterministic rather than merely probabilistic predictions. If it is true, as here suggested, that concern with advice and social status exerts a predominant influence on social interaction in work groups, and if elasticity is actually governed by the factors considered, research would confirm the hypotheses advanced in the last section as well as others implicit in the discussion. Should empirical data require the rejection of these hypotheses, it would disprove the theory advanced in this chapter but not necessarily the underlying model. For it might well be that the wrong variables have been selected in applying the model, for example, that social support rather than superior status or advice is what members of work groups primarily seek in their social associations. By including other factors, or several at once, in the model, it might yield accurate predictions. To be sure, if no factors that can be considered would make it possible to derive correct hypotheses from the model, one would have to conclude that the model itself is deficient. Second, however, it is necessary to refine the theory as much as possible by taking account of and removing the unrealistic assumptions made by the model in its simplest form. The basic assumption that must be questioned is that of "perfect competition."

The conception that the rates of exchange are governed by alternative costs rests on the assumption that there is perfect competition (as well as on the assumption that there is no unemployment and no immobility). Perfect competition is an abstraction and does not exist in reality, because the various conditions that would be required for it cannot be fully realized, only approximated. Variations in these conditions determine the degree of competition that actually prevails. The more imperfect competition is, the fewer checks there are on the domination of the powerless by the powerful.

The first requirement of perfect competition is that the products or services available from different suppliers are completely homogeneous, so that those of one can be substituted for those of another and considerations of price alone affect exchange decisions. Some goods, such as wheat of a given grade, are very homogeneous, but many, such as cars from different manufacturers, are not, and services from different persons, whether lawyers or barbers, are necessarily at least somewhat heterogeneous. A second condition of perfect competition is that the number of competitors is sufficiently large and that the proportionate size of the strongest is sufficiently small to prevent the transactions of any one from influencing the price of the commodity appreciably. Since the process of competition often leads to the expansion of the most successful and the elimination of the least successful competitors, it tends to destroy the very conditions necessary for it to thrive. Particularly in industries with a high capital investment, the persistences of even a minimum degree of competition is precarious unless protected through noneconomic institutions, such as antimonopoly legislation. A third fundamental requirement of free competition is perfect communication among all members of the exchange system that provides each with complete information about the actual and potential decisions of all others. Knight has strongly stressed the importance of this assumption: "Chief among the simplifications of reality prerequisites to the achievement of perfect competition is, as has been emphasized all along, the assumption of practical omniscience on the part of every member of the competitive system." [26]

These three main imperfections of competition—due to product heterogeneity, to the limited number of competitors, and to insufficient knowledge and communication—are manifest in the social interaction in groups in which contributions are exchanged for superior status. The contributions various members make are usually somewhat heterogeneous, and often very much so. Variations in quality make the advice from different experts not easily comparable. Even when implicit standards for grading these qualitative differences have been developed in a work group, there are other differences that defy strict comparison. One consultant's advice may be superior to that of another, but the first gives it in a gruff manner whereas the other is hospitable and friendly when being consulted, and a third may be matter-of-fact, and a fourth may furnish instructive explanations as well as answer questions. These other benefits or costs become confounded with the advice itself, making the total benefits obtained from various experts a heterogeneous product. This lack of homogeneity and the commitments to established consulting relations restrict freedom of movement and competition, inasmuch as the degree of compliance expected by different consultants for advice of a given quality is not the sole factor that governs the choices of their colleagues between them. Such restriction of competition is inevitable in social exchange, an inherent character of which is that transactions involving specific services are not completely insulated from other aspects of and other benefits derived from the exchange relations.

---

[26] Knight, *op. cit.*, p. 197.

There are, however, differences in the degree of heterogeneity of the contributions needed by and made in a group. In work groups where the major concern is with the performance of specific tasks, the assistance supplied by expert colleagues to others constitutes a *comparatively* homogeneous service. The more differentiated the tasks of group members are, the more varied will be the contributions for which there is a demand in the group. In multipurpose groups whose members engage in a variety of specialized activities and have a number of objectives, many diverse contributions that cannot be compared are in demand. The lesser heterogeneity of the needed services in work groups with specified duties, compared to that of the needed contributions in multipurpose groups, should intensify competition for status in the groups with specified duties, though other differences between these two kinds of groups, notably in the significance of informal status, have the opposite effect, as we shall see.

The number of members in a face-to-face group is, by definition, too small to meet the second requirement of perfect competition, since the transactions of one member *do* affect the conditions of exchange. The decisions of each one of a handful of expert consultants have a pronounced impact on the supply of advice and on its price in compliance, and the decisions of each one of the consulting colleagues have a considerable, though probably less pronounced, effect on the demand for advice and its price. The experts constitute an oligopoly. Of course, workers could obtain advice from colleagues outside their own work group, but they often do not have enough information about most of them. This situation corresponds to that in which inhabitants of a small town used to find themselves, whose range of choice was also largely confined to the few merchants in town, until national advertising provided them with information about outside merchants and expanded the scope of their choice. Special institutions, such as advertising and the stock market, are necessary to furnish the communication networks without which competition is restricted to only a few buyers and sellers and hence remains very imperfect.

An important difference between work groups, whose members do not pursue a common objective of their own, and groups that do have such collective objectives is that the oligopoly inherent in small size is not likely to become a monopoly in the former but is likely to do so in the latter. Except in very small work groups, a single expert cannot easily meet the entire demand for advice. The fact that each expert's consulting time is limited and cannot be expanded indefinitely tends to prevent each from monopolizing consultations and to encourage the survival of some competition between several of them.[27] The same fact also discourages the development of informal leadership in work groups, because limitations of consulting time make it virtually impossible for a single expert to obligate all other members of the group to accept his dominance over them. For an individual to become the informal leader of a group, he must have a monopoly of major obligations, that is, the entire group must be obligated to comply with his directives. If a group has no common goals, this would require that he obligate each member separately by helping each with his tasks, but time limitations typically preclude his doing so. If a group has common goals, however, the superior contributions an individual makes to the achievement of these goals obligate all members to him and thus become a source of power over all of them for him. Whether he solves the puzzle of the laboratory group, effectively organizes the warfare of a gang, or successfully negotiates a union contract with employers, his single course of action benefits and obligates the entire membership.

Common goals in a group, therefore, not only create a need for a leader who can coordinate activities but also create the possibility for a single person to obligate simultaneously large groups of people— indeed, entire nations—to himself by contributing to their common welfare, which is impossible in the absence of a common purpose. The inference is that work groups, and other groups without a common purpose, typically do not have informal leaders and a centralized status structure, although status differences exist in them,[28] whereas groups with collective goals do, including those that are of much shorter duration, considerably smaller, and of much less significance to members than work groups. One would also expect that the greater import of superior status in groups with collective objectives, where it promises the reward of informal leadership, will make the initial competition for status more intense there than in comparable work groups; but that this competition subsides in groups with common objectives while more of it persists in work groups, both because the centralization of power is less pronounced and because the services in demand are less heterogeneous in work groups. (It is evident that

---

[27] The degree of possible expandability of competing units may well be a fundamental condition that determines whether monopoly and dominance develop; see Blau and Scott, *op. cit.*, pp. 214–217.

[28] A member of a work group may achieve a degree of informal leadership by making contributions to the common welfare, for example, by becoming the group's spokesman who represents its interest in relation to superiors; see, for instance, Blau, *op. cit.*, p. 150.

the supervisor has been excluded from consideration in the references to work groups.) These hypotheses should be tested in empirical research.

Finally, the absence of complete communication and information makes perfect competition impossible. "The main condition of perfect exchange not realized in real life is that of 'perfect intercommunication,' which is to say perfect knowledge of what they are doing on the part of all exchangers." [29] Knight goes on to show that the lack of complete knowledge of the future as well as the present preferences of all marketers, which is assumed in the model of perfect competition, is what necessitates taking risks and what is responsible for profits. Of special importance is the fact that the amount of knowledge different individuals have is not the same but generally varies with their social status. The more extensive information typically at the disposal of those with superior status facilitates assuming responsibility for risky decisions and thereby gives them a competitive advantage in earning still greater power and higher status in return for taking such risks.

A crystallized structure of differential status interferes with free competition and communication. A formal status hierarchy imposed on the group by outside authority, for example, makes winning the respect of other group members less significant and makes commanding their compliance most difficult for those who do not occupy positions of formal authority. Entrenched differences in power have similar implications. The inability of group members under these conditions to bestow superior status on those of their own choice prevents them from utilizing changes in status to elicit contributions. Competition for social standing subsides in groups in which the salient status differences have already become fixed, and the status hierarchy creates obstacles to the free flow of communication, often with deleterious consequences for the performance of tasks. [30] These disadvantages of a status hierarchy constitute the cost of the contributions it makes to the effective coordination of tasks.

Conclusions

When some members of a work group are in need of assistance with their work and others have the competence to supply this

---

[29] Knight, *op. cit.*, p. 86.

[30] See Blau and Scott, *op. cit.*, pp. 116–128, where relevant empirical studies are summarized.

assistance, consulting relations tend to develop, in which advice and help are exchanged for respect and compliance. The initial consulting relations that develop can be thought of as cases of bilateral monopoly, in which the two parties move toward an implicit agreement on how much advice one will render and how much compliance the other will return for it, at a point of optimum joint advantage on the contract curve. The presence of many workers who need advice and several consultants in the group encourages the exploration of alternative opportunities. A consultant has an interest in fortifying his status in the group and extending his power of influence by supplying advice and thus obligating not merely one colleague but as many as his time permits. The tendency of consultants to expand the scope of their consulting activities increases the differentiation of status in the group. Workers in need of assistance may not be able to obtain all the advice they want from experts, at least, not without excessive cost to their self-respect and social standing. As a result, they often establish partnerships of mutual consultation, in which they obtain advice, though of poorer quality, at no loss in self-respect, since they pay for it not by subordinating themselves to another but by giving the partner advice in turn. These partnerships lessen the differentiation of status in the group, although they may create distinct social strata if there are sharp differences in competence. Once group members become committed to certain consulting relations and mutual partnerships, the situation again resembles that of bilateral monopolies.

The concept of elasticity of supply or demand, which refers to the ease with which either expands or contracts, has been applied to the analysis of changes in group structure under various conditions. The implications of differences in elasticity can be tersely summarized as follows: a change in the supply of or demand for a commodity produces primarily a change in the same direction in its demand or its supply, respectively, *if* the latter quantity is elastic, but if it is inelastic, a change in supply produces primarily an inverse change in price, and a change in demand, a parallel change in price. Elasticity, therefore, determines the extent to which changes in supply or in demand affect the volume of transactions rather than the price of a commodity. In the analysis of consultation, the volume of transactions is reflected in the amount of consultation in a group, and the price refers to the rate at which advice is exchanged for compliance and superior status.

The elasticity of the supply of advice in a work group depends directly on the number of nonconsultants with sufficient competence to join the ranks of consultants, should conditions warrant it, and inversely on the time pressure under which the existing consultants work. If the supply of advice is elastic and can easily expand, an increase in the demand for it, which might be the result of the assignment of inexperienced workers or a new supervisor with stricter minimum requirements, will increase the amount of consultation in the group. This growth in the volume of consultation will exert some influence on the status structure, but it will not intensify the differentiation of status as much as would an increase in the demand for advice if its supply is inelastic. For in this case, when no other workers are capable of complementing the existing number of expert consultants and these experts themselves cannot easily devote more time to consulting, the rate of compliance colleagues have to offer consultants in order to obtain advice will increase, with the result that the power of experts over others increases *without* their having to furnish more services. The investment that consultants have in their expertness tends to make the contracting supply of advice less elastic than its expanding supply. Unless consultants are under heavy time pressure, they typically profit more from earning some superiority, little though it may be, by giving advice than from not giving advice at all. When the demand for advice declines after new workers have gained experience, therefore, the status differences produced by consultation are expected to diminish but the level of consultation is expected to be less affected and to remain higher than it originally had been.

The elasticity of the demand for colleague advice in a work group depends largely on the lack of difficulty workers experience with their tasks, the availability of substitute sources of advice and information, and the significance of informal status relative to that of task performance. If the difficulties are not great, substitutes exist, and standing among colleagues is relatively important, demand for advice is elastic, and a change in supply, possibly due to a change in the number of experts in the group, will be primarily reflected in a corresponding change in the volume of consultation, and it will have relatively little influence on the status enhancement consultants achieve by giving a certain amount of advice. But if the demand for advice is inelastic—for example, because the complex task creates unrelenting needs for advice—the volume of consultation will not be very responsive to changes in its supply and price. A decrease in the supply of advice in this situation will have a lasting impact on the rate of compliance required to obtain advice, which will be reflected in a more pronounced differentiation of status in the group. These altered conditions, however, have further repercussions. The high price of advice and the great social distance between expert consultants and others put workers in need of much advice under pressure to find some substitute for the assistance from expert colleagues. These workers often create their own substitute by establishing partnerships of reciprocal consultation, in which they obtain advice of sufficient quality for their less complex problems, and which enable them to reserve the resources needed to obtain expert counsel for their most difficult problems.

The analysis of structural differentiation and its modifications presented in this chapter serves to show that the conception that power over others rests on services furnished to them does *not* imply that the superior power of some is morally justified or deserved by the services they render. Large differences in power occur without corresponding differences in services. Depending on social conditions, suppliers of services may receive an unfair return for their investments or an excessive return. Even were there no initial imperfections in the regulating mechanisms of social exchange, the superior power achieved by furnishing needed services would create such imperfections.

Sufficient power enables individuals to monopolize resources and to make others increasingly dependent on themselves. While the perpetuation of their power is contingent on their continuing to provide *some* benefits to others, if only by refraining from punishing them, it is evident that the very power that makes others dependent for these "benefits" cannot be considered in any sense to constitute a deserved reward for supplying services or an incentive necessary to produce them. In short, once superior power has been attained by furnishing services, it can be sustained without furnishing these same services. This self-perpetuating element of power is still more evident in the class structure of entire societies than in the differentiation of status in small groups, and failure to take it into account is a serious shortcoming of functional conceptions of social stratification.[31]

Finally, there is an important difference between collectivities with a common purpose that must be achieved by the members together

---

[31] See Kingsley Davis and Wilbert E. Moore, "Some Principles of Stratification," *American Sociological Review*, 10 (1945), 242–249. For a revised formulation that notes these implications of power differences, if only in passing, see Wilbert E. Moore, "But Some Are More Equal than Others," *American Sociological Review*, 28 (1963), 13–18, esp. p. 17.

and collectivities whose members are engaged in separate pursuits without collaborating to attain a common objective. Conditions in the common-purpose collectivities not only create a need for leadership but also facilitate its development. To achieve a position of leadership in a group, a person must obligate all or most other members to accept him as their superior. In a group whose members work on separate tasks, obligating the entire membership requires furnishing services to each one separately, which time limitations make impossible except in very small groups. In groups that have common objectives, by contrast, the individual who makes the major contributions to their attainment obligates all members to accept him as their superior in return for the advantages they all derive from his efforts. Leaders are expected to emerge, therefore, in groups that have common goals and not in others. Regardless of how large a collectivity is, common objectives make it possible for an individual to benefit the entire membership and to achieve a position of leadership in exchange for his contributions to the commonweal. Whether a collectivity is characterized by a centralized hierarchy of status or merely by differences in social status—a distinction that is exemplified by that between the official hierarchy in an organization and the class structure in a community—depends primarily on whether there are explicit collective objectives or not. When hierarchies of power exist, processes of legitimation often transform them into hierarchies of authority, as the next chapter will show.

EIGHT

Legitimation and Organization

A just ruler seems to make nothing out of his office; for he does not allot to himself a larger share of things generally good, unless it be proportionate to his merits; so that he labours for others, which accounts for the saying mentioned above, that "Justice is the good of others." Consequently some recompense has to be given him, in the shape of honour and dignity. It is those whom such rewards do not satisfy who make themselves tyrants.

ARISTOTLE, *The Nicomachean Ethics*

Organization involves the coordination of collective effort. Some form of social organization emerges implicitly in collectivities as the result of the processes of exchange and competition, in which the patterns of conduct of individuals and groups and the relations between them become adjusted. These processes have already been discussed. But other organizations are explicitly established for the purpose of achieving specified objectives, whether they are manufacturing goods that can be sold for a profit, participating in bowling tournaments, collective bargaining, or winning political victory. In these formal organizations, special mechanisms exist to effect the coordination of tasks of various members in the pursuit of given objectives. Such coordination of efforts, particularly on a large scale, requires some centralized direction. Power is the resource that makes it possible to direct and coordinate the activities of men.

Stable organizing power requires legitimation. To be sure, men can be made to work and to obey commands through coercion, but the coercive use of power engenders resistance and sometimes active opposition. Power conflicts in and between societies are characterized by resistance and opposition, and while the latter also occur within organizations, effective operations necessitate that they be kept at a minimum there and, especially, that members do not exhibit resistance in discharging their daily duties but perform them and comply with directives from superiors *willingly*. Only legitimate power commands willing compliance.

Legitimate power is authority, which Weber defines as "the probability that certain commands (or all commands) from a given source will be obeyed by a given group of persons." He adds that a basic criterion of authority "is a certain minimum of voluntary submission," although the specific motives for the obedience to commands may vary.[1] His analysis of three types of authority centers on the value orientations that cause people voluntarily to submit to orders from an authority they accept as legitimate.[2] What is left implicit in this analysis is the specific criterion in terms of which authority can be distinguished from other forms of influence to which individuals voluntarily submit. Indeed, the emphasis on voluntarism is misleading without further specification, since an authoritative command is one a subordinate cannot dismiss at will.

It may be suggested that the distinctive feature of authority is that social norms accepted and enforced by the collectivity of subordinates constrain its individual members to comply with directives of a superior. Compliance is voluntary for the collectivity, but social constraints make it compelling for the individual. In contrast to other forms of influence and power, the pressure to follow suggestions and orders does not come from the superior who gives them but from the collectivity of subordinates. These normative constraints may be institutionalized and pervade the entire society, or they may emerge in a group in social interaction. The latter emergent norms define leadership, which, therefore, is considered a type of authority. The authority in formal organizations entails a combination of institutionalized and leadership elements.

Leadership

Furnishing needed contributions in a group empowers a man to effect compliance with his demands. The exercise of power exerts re-

---

[1] Max Weber, *The Theory of Social and Economic Organization*, New York: Oxford University Press, 1947, p. 324.
[2] *Ibid.*, pp. 329–363.

straints, which are, in effect, inescapable if the need for the contributions is great and no alternative sources for them are available. Compliance is a cost that is judged on the basis of social norms of fairness. Excessive demands in terms of these social standards, though those subject to the power may not be able to refuse them, engender disapproval. A person whose demands on others are fair and modest relative to the great contribution he makes to their welfare, however, earns their approval. For example, a laboratory study of small groups found that the emergent leader was more apt to be liked by the rest if the initiative he took in social interaction was accompanied by a high rate of response from others, that is, by their frequently agreeing with him and turning to him with comments and questions, than if the rate of such feedback was low.[3] This may be interpreted to imply that excessive demands by a leader, as indicated by a low rate of feedback, create disapproval that make him less liked.

Compliance can be enforced with sufficient power, but approval cannot be forced regardless of how great the power. Yet the effectiveness and stability of leadership depend on the social approval of subordinates, as several studies have shown. Thus, the results of two experiments demonstrated that leaders who were accepted and approved by subordinates were more effective in exerting influence on them than superiors who were not.[4] A study of army leadership found that trainees who approved of their officers and noncommissioned officers were less likely to express various forms of aggression, such as going "AWOL" (absent without leave), "blowing their top," drunkenness, and gripe sessions, than those who described their superiors as arbitrary or weak.[5] The findings of another experiment indicated that group leaders whose suggestions and directives engendered a disproportionate amount of resistance and disagreement were relatively unstable, that is, they were more likely than others to be displaced as leaders in subsequent experimental periods.[6] The dis-

---

[3] Robert F. Bales, "Task Status and Likability as a Function of Talking and Listening in Decision-making Groups," in Leonard D. White, *The State of the Social Sciences,* University of Chicago Press, 1956, pp. 148–161.

[4] John R. P. French, Jr., and Richard Snyder, "Leadership and Interpersonal Power," in Dorwin Cartwright, *Studies in Social Power,* Ann Arbor: Institute for Social Research, University of Michigan, 1959, pp. 118–149.

[5] Hannan C. Selvin, *The Effects of Leadership,* Glencoe: Free Press, 1960, chapter v.

[6] Elihu Katz, Peter M. Blau, Morton L. Brown, and Fred L. Strodtbeck, "Leadership Stability and Social Change," *Sociometry,* 20 (1957), 36–50, esp. pp. 44–46.

approval some leadership practices evoke among followers impede a leader's effectiveness because they create resistance, aggression, and possibly opposition that may lead to the downfall of an informal leader.

Collective approval, in contrast, legitimates leadership. The abilities that enable a person to make major contributions to the achievement of a group's goals command respect. The respect of others for him prompts them to follow his suggestion, since they expect to benefit from doing so more than from following the suggestion of someone whose abilities are less respected. The actual contributions to their welfare resulting from following his guidance not only validate the others' respect for such a person but also obligate them to comply with his directives regardless of whether doing so is in their personal self-interest. It is their obligation to comply with his directives, not simply their respect, that bestows leadership upon a person and empowers him to coordinate the activities of the members of a group, which involves directing individuals to do things that are not to their own immediate advantage. The effective coordination of effort produces rewards, and the leader's power enables him to exert a predominant influence on their distribution—how much of the honor and glory of the winning team will reflect on the rest rather than on himself, or how large a share of the material benefits goes to others and how much remains in his hands. It is this distribution of rewards that most directly effects the legitimation of leadership.

If the benefits followers derive from a leader's guidance exceed their expectations of a fair return for the costs they have incurred, both by performing services and by complying with directives, their collective approval of his leadership legitimates it. Their joint obligations for his contributions to their welfare and their common approval of his fairness, reinforced by their consensus concerning the respect his abilities deserve, generate group pressures that enforce compliance with his directives. These social pressures constrain individual group members who for personal reasons are inclined to resist the leader's guidance to submit to it lest they draw on themselves the social disapproval of their peers. Legitimate leaders command willing compliance, which obviates the need for sanctions to compel or induce others to comply with directives, because the group of subordinates exerts pressures on its members to follow the leader's orders and suggestions.

The social approval of followers that legitimates leadership is distinct from the respect they may have for the leader's abilities. Although the two go often together, a person in power may have abilities that command the respect of subordinates yet make oppressive demands on them to which they react with disapproval. Respect probably does, however, act as a catalyst of legitimate leadership, since it seems to make compliance with a person's directives less burdensome. Indirect support for this statement is provided by some findings from a study of sixty caseworkers in a welfare agency.[7] Generally, the factors that distinguished workers who were often consulted from those who were rarely consulted also distinguished those who were highly respected from those who were not. But some kinds of workers, such as oldtimers, were often consulted without being highly respected. The obligation incurred to consultants inhibited informal sociability with them if the consultants were not particularly respected, but it did not inhibit sociability if they were. This finding suggests that respect for a person legitimates the obligation to comply with his wishes and thus makes this obligation less of an impediment to informal intercourse with him.

Stable leadership rests on power over others and their legitimating approval of that power. The dilemma of leadership is that the attainment of power and the attainment of social approval make somewhat incompatible demands on a person. To achieve power over others requires not only furnishing services that make them dependent but also remaining independent of any services they might offer in return. To legitimate a position of power and leadership, however, requires that a leader be concerned with earning the social approval of his followers, which means that he does not maintain complete independence of them. An individual's refusal to accept offers of favors from others who are in his debt and his insistence on remaining entirely independent of them are usually experienced as rejections and evoke their disapproval. By asserting his dominance over the rest of the group in the process of becoming their leader and exercising his leadership, a person can hardly help antagonizing at least some of them, thereby endangering his chances of having his leadership legitimated by social approval. Conversely, preoccupation with the approval of followers interferes with a leader's ability to command their respect and compliance by making the greatest contribution to their welfare he can, because concern with being liked prevents him from basing his decisions consistently on criteria of effectiveness alone. Such preoccupation, in other words, induces a leader sometimes to refrain from making what is the best decision in his judgment for fear of antagonizing subordinates.

---

[7] Blau, "Patterns of Choice in Interpersonal Relations," *American Sociological Review*, 27 (1962), 41–55, esp. pp. 50–51, 55.

The dilemma of leadership can be epitomized by saying that its legitimation requires that a leader be magnanimous in the exercise of his power and in the distribution of the rewards that accrue from his leadership, but such magnanimity necessitates that he first mobilize his power and husband the group's resources, that is, act in ways that are the opposite of magnanimous. Once a man has attained much power, however, he can easily make demands that appear only moderate in view of his strength and capacity to supply benefits. In other words, extensive power facilitates obtaining legitimating approval for it.

Two different sets of expectations govern the process of legitimation, since the leader's general expectations define what is extensive or insufficient power, while those of the followers define what are moderate or unfair power demands. The less the leader expects to achieve with his power, the less power will be sufficient to meet his needs and the less demands he will make on those subject to his power. The reactions of the follower's to the leader's demands, in turn, are contingent on their normative expectations of how much a leader can fairly demand in return for his contributions. Small needs for power as well as great power make it easy for a man to exercise his power in ways that elicit legitimating approval from subordinates. The line between exploitative oppression and legitimate leadership is defined by the interplay between the expectations of the man in power that define his needs and the expectations of those subject to his power that define their needs and his complementary rights.

Power must be mobilized before it can be legitimated, because the processes involved in mobilizing it are not compatible with those involved in legitimating it. The dilemma of leadership is resolved by devoting different time periods to coping with its two horns, so to speak. This parallels the conclusion of Bales and Strodtbeck that the dilemma of group problem solving posed by the need for a cognitive orientation to the task and the need for a supportive orientation that reduces tensions, which are incompatible, is resolved by devoting different time phases to meeting these two needs.[8] The potential leader of a gang uses his physical strength first against the other

---

[8] Bales and Strodtbeck, "Phases in Group Problem Solving," *The Journal of Abnormal and Social Psychology*, 46 (1951), 485–495. Another method for resolving the leadership dilemma is a division of labor within the leadership group, that is, having those leaders who exercise power and restraints supported by other leaders who do not and who command the approval and loyalty of followers; see Philip E. Slater, "Role Differentiation in Small Groups," *American Sociological Review*, 20 (1955), 300–310.

members to assert his dominance over them. Only then can he organize their activities and lead them in gang warfare, now using his strength and other resources in behalf of his followers against outsiders. If he is successful, his contributions to their welfare evoke legitimating approval of his leadership, which makes his continuing dominance independent of his use of physical sanctions against followers.

The situation of formal leaders in organizations is different from that of informal leaders who emerge in a group. Resources and institutionalized mechanisms place managers in organizations a priori in a dominant position over subordinates, thereby obviating the need for initially asserting their dominance and facilitating the development of legitimate authority.

Legitimate Authority

The employment contract into which the management of an organization enters with its members is a legal institution that obligates the members to furnish certain services and to follow managerial directives in exchange for a salary or wage.[9] These obligations are reinforced by institutionalized norms in our culture according to which employers have a right to expect their employees to comply with their directives as well as to perform specified duties faithfully. The ultimate source of these obligations, and thus of managerial power, are the organization's resources that enable it to buy the services of employees and to make them dependent on it for their livelihood, the degree of dependence being contingent on employees' investments in their jobs and the alternative employment opportunities available to them. (In organizations whose members are not employees, such as unions and political parties, the power of the leadership rests on the commitments of the members, the benefits they derive from membership, and—notably in the case of some organizations, such as armies—coercive force.) Management's power over dismissals and promotions, which is partly transmitted to lower managers and supervisors through mechanisms like periodic ratings of or *ad hoc* reports on their subordinates, makes the career chances of employees dependent on their performance and compliance.

A manager in an organization has some formal authority over subordinates, since they have accepted the contractual obligation to

---

[9] See John R. Commons, *Legal Foundations of Capitalism*, New York: Macmillan, 1924, pp. 284–286.

perform the tasks he assigns to them, and he has also considerable power over them, since he has official sanctions at his disposal through which he can affect their career chances. The managerial authority that is rooted in the employment contract itself is very limited in scope. It only obligates employees to perform duties assigned to them in accordance with minimum standards. This formal authority does not require them to devote much effort to their work, exercise initiative in carrying it out, or be guided in their performance by the suggestions of superiors. Effective management is impossible within the confines of formal authority alone. A manager may extend his control over subordinates by resorting to his sanctioning power to impose his will upon them, promising rewards for conformity and threatening penalties for disobedience. An alternative strategy a manager can use is to provide services to subordinates that obligate them to comply with his directives. His formal power over subordinates helps him to create joint obligations, in part simply by refraining from exercising it. In this case, the manager relinquishes some of his official power in exchange for greater legitimate authority over subordinates.

The official position and power of the manager give him various opportunities to furnish important services to subordinates that obligate them to him. His superior knowledge and skill, on the basis of which he presumably was selected for his position, enable him to train newcomers and advise oldtimers. His formal status gives him access to top echelons and staff specialists in the organization, making it possible for him to channel needed information to subordinates and to represent their interests with the higher administration. While his official duties as manager *require* him to perform a minimum of these services for subordinates, the extra effort he devotes to benefit them beyond this minimum creates social obligations. Of special significance in this connection are the manager's status prerogatives and formal powers, for he can win the appreciation of his subordinates merely by not exercising these: by not insisting on the deference due his rank, by not enforcing an unpopular housekeeping rule, by ignoring how much time subordinates take for lunch as long as they perform their duties. Every privilege the manager is granted and every rule he is empowered to enforce increase the capital on which he can draw to make subordinates indebted to him. By not using some of his power, he invests it in social obligations. The advantages subordinates derive from his pattern of supervision obligate them to reciprocate by complying with his directives and requests.

In this manner, managerial power is converted into personal influence, but the development of authority depends on a further trans-formation. A manager whose influence over subordinates rests on their *individual* obligations to him does not exercise authority over them, because authority requires social legitimation. Only the shared values of a collectivity can legitimate the power of a superior and thereby transform it into authority. Managerial practices that advance the *collective* interest of subordinates create *joint* obligations. When social consensus develops among subordinates that the practices of the manager contribute to their common welfare and that it is in their common interests to maintain his good will by discharging their obligations to him, shared feelings of loyalty and group norms tend to emerge that make compliance with his directives a *social* obliga-tion that is enforced by the subordinates themselves. The subordi-nates' common approval of managerial practices that benefit them jointly gives rise to social norms that legitimate managerial authority.

Festinger's concept of cognitive dissonance can help explain the underlying process in the legitimation of authority.[10] If individuals must choose between two alternatives one of which is clearly su-perior, their decision entails no doubts and conflicts. But if the two alternatives are both attractive (or unattractive), the choice of one creates cognitive dissonance, that is, the cost incurred by having rejected an attractive opportunity produces doubts concerning the wisdom of the choice made, mental conflicts, and discomfort. Indi-viduals often reduce this dissonance by changing their evaluations of the two alternatives after having committed themselves to one, that is, they resolve their disturbing doubts by inflating the value of the chosen and deflating the value of the rejected benefit. College students asked to choose one of two gifts they would receive for having participated in an experiment, for example, rated the chosen gift more highly and the rejected one less highly after having made the decision than they had done before.[11] Since social consensus on values serves to confirm the valuations of individuals, one would ex-pect these tendencies to be particularly pronounced if they occur in a collective situation, as is the case when a group of subordinates is confronted by a superior who has power over them.

Cognitive dissonance arises only when a manager obligates sub-ordinates to comply with his directives and not when a superior enforces compliance with his orders through sanctions. If a superior

---

[10] Leon Festinger, *A Theory of Cognitive Dissonance,* Evanston: Row, Peter-son, 1957.

[11] *Ibid.*, pp. 61–68.

uses his coercive power to impose his will on subordinates, the serious cost of disobedience makes obedience unequivocally the preferable alternative. Although submission is unpleasant, subordinates have no doubt that the consequences of failure to submit would be more so. There is no cognitive dissonance, and hence no basis for processes of dissonance reduction. But if a manager furnishes services that obligate subordinates to comply with his orders, noncompliance is a possible alternative that is not entirely unreasonable. The assumption is that the advantages of the services contingent on compliance outweigh its cost to subordinates, which is why they choose compliance over noncompliance. Nevertheless, doubts are likely to arise as to whether the benefits of the services are really worth the hardships entailed by following the orders of a superior, particularly in a democratic culture where equality and independence are highly valued. To resolve this cognitive dissonance, individuals are under pressure to appreciate the value of the benefits and depreciate the cost of compliance. They may extol the abilities of the superior and their respect for him and stress that following the guidance of such an expert is objectively the best course of action. They may emphasize that issuing directives is the manager's duty, not his privilege, and that their compliance with these directives does not constitute submission to his will but is simply part of their freely accepted responsibilities, just as issuing the directives is part of his.

These beliefs might be considered rationalizations through which individuals adapt to a subordinate position. Social processes, however, transform the individual rationalizations into common values. Subordinates who find themselves in the same situation are prone to discuss their justifications of their compliance with each other in order to have their doubts relieved and their justifying beliefs confirmed through social agreement. The social consensus that develops among subordinates in the course of their communication that it is right and proper and not at all degrading to follow managerial orders validates these beliefs and converts what might have been individual rationalizations into a common value orientation.

Authority, therefore, rests on the common norms in a collectivity of subordinates that constrain its individual members to conform to the orders of a superior. The joint obligations of subordinates for the benefits they derive from the superior's mode of supervision or leadership are at the roots of these normative constraints, which are reinforced by social values that justify compliance and lessen the onus of it. These norms, like social norms generally, are internalized by group members and socially enforced, with the result that even the potential deviant who for some reason does not feel personally obligated to the superior is under pressure to submit to his authority lest he incur the social disapproval of his peers. A man in authority does not have to enforce compliance with his orders, because the structural constraints that exist among subordinates do so for him. Authority entails voluntary compliance, in contrast to coercion, since the influence of the superior on subordinates rests on their own social norms. But authority entails imperative control, in contrast to persuasion and personal influence, since social norms and group sanctions exert compelling pressures on individual subordinates to follow the superior's directives. Compliance is voluntary from the perspective of the collectivity of subordinates, but it is compulsory from the perspective of its individual members. It is exactly as voluntary as conformity with social norms generally, for example, as our custom of wearing clothes.

The social norms and values of subordinates that legitimate the power of influence of a superior transform it into authority. Simultaneously, indirect processes of social exchange become substituted for the direct exchange transactions between the superior and individual subordinates. Before legitimating norms have developed, subordinates offer compliance with the superior's directive in exchange for services he furnishes, a process essentially similar to that in which consultants achieve compliance with their wishes in exchange for advice. The emergent social norms that legitimate authority give rise to two exchange processes that take the place of this one. Individual subordinates submit to the authority of the superior because group norms require them to do so and failure to conform evokes social disapproval. The individual exchanges compliance with the directives of the superior for social approval from his peers. The collectivity of subordinates exchanges prevailing compliance with the superior's orders, which it has to offer as the result of its social norms that enforce compliance, and which legitimates the superior's authority, for the contribution to the common welfare his leadership furnishes.

The question that arises is whether managerial authority has its ultimate source in the manager's leadership qualities and abilities to assist subordinates or in his official sanctioning power over them. To answer this question, let us assume that these two functions reside in two different persons; a supervisor who provides guidance and counsel but has no formal power of sanction, and an employer who does not guide the work of employees but evaluates its results and decides on promotions and dismissals in accordance with these evaluations. If the supervisor has the qualifications to furnish superior guidance and advice that improve and facilitate the work of subordinates, his contributions to their common welfare create joint obligations that serve as the basis of his authority over them. This situation corresponds essentially to informal leadership. If the employer distributes rewards and punishments purely in terms of objective criteria of performance, these sanctions would provide incentives to perform well but not to comply with his directives (except those specifying the parameters of adequate performance). If, however, he uses his sanctioning power to reward compliance and punish disobedience with his orders, employees may adapt to these conditions by developing social values and norms that justify and enforce their compliance and legitimate his authority. These considerations imply that both effective leadership and sanctioning power can become the sources of an authority structure, but sanctioning power does so at the cost of diverting the incentive system, at least in part, from its major function of encouraging optimum performance by using it to effect obedience. There can be little doubt that the reward systems in organizations are typically used in this manner as instruments of power and aids in the expansion of managerial authority.

Although managerial authority in organizations contains important leadership elements, its distinctive characteristic, which differentiates it from informal leadership, is that it is rooted in the formal powers and sanctions the organization bestows upon managers. Their official position and sanctioning power provide managers with tools that make it easy, even for those with only moderate leadership qualities, to broaden the scope of the limited authority initially invested in them through the employment contract, whereas informal leaders must rely on their own qualities and resources to command the willing compliance of followers. Effective authority, whether in formal organizations or outside, requires both power and legitimating approval, but the one is more problematical for the informal leader, and the other, for the formal leader in an organization.

The crucial problem for the formal leader, with undeniable power, is to win the loyalty and legitimating approval of subordinates, particularly since his power may tempt him to dominate them instead of winning their respect and willing compliance. In contrast, the crucial problem of the informal leader, whose position is evidence of the support and approval of his followers, is to mobilize his power of command and establish sufficient social distance to be able to direct effectively their activities. Fiedler's research indicates this difference.[12] He found that the informal leaders of such groups as

---

[12] Fred E. Fiedler, *Leader Attitudes and Group Effectiveness*, Urbana: University of Illinois Press, 1958, esp. chapter iii.

basketball teams and surveying parties who manifested social distance toward followers were more effective than those who did not, that is, the performance of the groups under the former leaders was superior. The social distance of formal leaders toward subordinates, however, was not generally related to their effectiveness, except when they commanded the loyalty of subordinates and their social distance from subordinates was accompanied by some positive attitudes toward them.

Authority can *arise* only in social structures. The power or personal influence exercised in pair relations can never develop into legitimate authority. For only the common norms of a collectivity of subordinates can legitimate the controlling influence of a superior and effect willing compliance with his directives in the specific sense of making such compliance, since it is enforced by the subordinates themselves, independent of any inducements or enforcement actions of the superior himself. Once authority has become institutionalized and social norms of compliance have become part of the cultural heritage, however, it does find expression in isolated pair relations. A father exercises authority over an only child, because culturally defined role expectations shared by the entire community constrain him to control and guide the child and compel the child to obey him; failure to live up to these expectations draws community disapproval on both of them. Whereas authority typically *has its source* in the power of one individual over a group (or of a group over a larger collectivity), which subsequently becomes legitimated by their social approval and norms, institutionalized authority *is a source* of power, that is, it bestows power over others on individuals or groups occupying a given status.

The institutionalization of authority requires that the social norms that demand compliance with certain orders and the surrounding values that justify and reinforce this compliance become part of the common culture and be transmitted from generation to generation. Children internalize these cultural values and norms in the process of socialization, and the moral obligation to conform to commands from given sources remains part of their personality structure. Paternal, religious, and political authority rest on such cultural orientations. The normative standards underlying institutionalized authority do not emerge in the process of social interaction between superior and subordinates and among subordinates but rather in the process of socialization, to which each one of them is separately exposed in a common culture. The managerial ideologies that have developed in modern societies during the last centuries, which justify and fortify the power of management and the obligation of subordinates to submit to its directives, constitute such an institutionalized value orientation, which legitimates managerial authority in principle.[13] This value orientation, which employees in our culture bring to the organizational context, gives the employment contract salient meaning and serves as the foundation for the social processes in which the authority of specific managers over subordinates is legitimated and expanded. The institutional authority of management and the power its resources give it distinguish legitimating processes in organizations from those characteristic of the emergence of leaders outside an organizational framework.

Institutionalized authority in complex social structures, such as the political authority of a national government, has three distinctive characteristics. First, as just indicated, the people's obligation to comply with the authority's commands does not develop in social exchange as a result of the ruler's contribution to the common welfare but is a moral obligation inculcated by socializing agencies. Whereas disregard for an emergent leader is a sign of disloyalty, disregard for institutionalized authority is a sign of immorality. Second, the political authority is embodied in institutional forms that constitute a historical reality, such as the Congressional form of government in the United States. Third, the differentiated groups in complex structures make it likely that the institutionalized authority accepted by the major groups is not accepted by some entire subgroups and has to be enforced through external restraints on them. Although legitimate authority rests on the social norms and sanctions of the collectivity of subordinates, this does not mean that all groups in a society support institutionalized authority, or even that a majority do. The crucial factor is that important and powerful groups of subordinates enforce the commands of institutionalized authority, putting external pressures to comply on those groups who refuse to do so voluntarily. Governmental authority prevails if the groups who support and enforce it dominate the thinking as well as acting of the rest, so even the deviants recognize that their disobedience is illegitimate. In countries with autocratic traditions, there is, strictly speaking, no public opinion in the sense of all the people's opinion regarding matters of public concern, such as political authority,[14] and the

---

[13] See Reinhard Bendix, *Work and Authority in Industry*, New York: Wiley, 1956.

[14] See Hans Speier, *Social Order and the Risk of War*, New York: Stewart, 1952, pp. 323–338.

elite's support of the ruler suffices to legitimate his authority as long as the *status quo* is accepted by the rest. It is only in countries where democratic values make the population at large concerned with political issues that the institutionalized authority of the legitimate government is in danger unless supported by the majority.

The authority of the government, then, rests on its acceptance as legitimate and its support by the dominant groups of subjects, that is, by the majority of those who participate in political life and are concerned with public matters, not necessarily a majority of the total population. The actual enforcement of the commands of political authority, furthermore, is usually delegated to special agents, such as military and police forces. The groups who support the government express their confidence in it by delegating the power to enforce its commands to agents under its own control. Generally, the political authority of a legitimate government consists of a grant of power "credit" by its supporters, which means that the government has the mandate to use powers vested in the community temporarily at its own discretion without having to account for every single decision.[15] The government that uses its mandate or credit of power to contribute to the welfare of its supporters tends to strengthen their legitimating approval of it, while the ruler who abuses his grant of power is likely to lose the political support that legitimates his rule, and with it his political dominance, unless he resorts to coercion to maintain it. The credit of political support and power on which legitimate governments can draw to enforce compliance, if needed, acts as a deterrent and fortifies their authority to command obedience, thereby having a multiplier effect and extending political control far beyond what could be achieved were it actually necessary to rely on the underlying coercive power.

Organizing Collective Effort

An important function of legitimate authority is to organize collective effort on a large scale in the pursuit of ends commonly accepted. To be sure, this is not the only function of legitimate authority—paternal authority, for example, serves the function of socializing children and thus perpetuating the basic culture. But this is one of its major functions and the one that is manifest in formal organizations, whether they are political, economic, military, or some

---

[15] See Talcott Parsons, "On the Concept of Influence," *Public Opinion Quarterly*, 27 (1963), 59–62, and James S. Coleman, "Comment," *ibid.*, pp. 72–77.

other kind. Using the term "voluntary association" quite broadly to refer to freely established collective organizations generally, de Jouvenel has stated: "By 'authority' I mean the faculty of gaining another man's assent. Or again it may be called, though it comes to the same thing, the efficient cause of voluntary associations. In any voluntary association that comes to my notice I see the work of a force: that force is authority." [16]

Commonly accepted ends are not necessarily common ends. Some organizations, such as unions, are designed to further the common objectives of the membership. The objectives of other organizations, such as business concerns, are those of the owners or of management. The majority of members whose services are bought in order to achieve these goals are expected to accept them as valid guides for operations, although they are not their own objectives. In either case, the members make contributions in exchange for rewards, but whereas the union member's rewards result from and are contingent on the achievement of the union's objectives, those of the firm's employee come from the salary he is paid for his services, which does not *directly* depend on the firm's profits, that is, on the achievement of the organization's objectives.

The difference between these two types of members of organizations corresponds to that between stockholders, who make investments in return for a share of the profits, as union members do, and bondholders, who receive a stipulated return for their investments, as employees do. The ideal expectation is that collective objectives are democratically decided on by the entire membership, while employees or bondholders are not expected to participate in deciding on objectives. In fact, however, objectives and policies are usually not democratically determined either by the union rank-and-file or by corporation stockholders, nor, for that matter, by the membership of any large organization unless special mechanisms, such as a party system, facilitate democratic participation.

The establishment of an organization requires capital investments, often in the form of financial investments, always in the form of social investments.[17] Resources and efforts, which could be spent directly to obtain rewards, must be devoted to building the organization and developing its specialized structure, to recruiting members and contributors, to coordinating their activities and instituting normative

---

[16] Bertrand de Jouvenel, *Sovereignty*, University of Chicago Press, 1957, p. 29.

[17] See George C. Homans, *Social Behavior*, New York: Harcourt, Brace and World, 1961, pp. 385–390.

standards for them to follow. Instead of pursuing their self-interests directly, the members of the organization make contributions to it in conformity with normative expectations and in anticipation of receiving rewards from it. All this entails postponement of gratifications in the hope of greater future gratifications, which requires a surplus of resources beyond those merely sufficient to meet current minimum needs. Hence, only individuals or groups with surplus resources can establish a business, organize a union, or create a political organization.[18]

Knight has emphasized that an organization's profits are the rewards for those who assume ultimate responsibility for entirely uncertain investments:

> Organization involves the concentration of responsibility, placing resources belonging to a large number of individuals under centralized control. Examination shows that the human functions in production involve making decisions, exercising control, but that this control is not final unless combined with assumption of the results of the decisions. The responsible decision relates to men rather than things; the ultimate manager is he who plans the organization, lays out functions, selects men for functions, and appraises their value to the organization as a whole, in competition with all other bidders in the market. For this ultimate management there is but one possible remuneration, the residuum of product remaining after payment is made at rates established in competition with all comers for all services of men or things for which competition exists. This residuum is profit. . . .[19]

Leadership involves assuming responsibility for coordinating the work of others and for the consequences of the common endeavors. To the extent to which specific abilities of leaders make it possible to anticipate the achievements their guidance makes possible, uncertainty is removed. These administrative services of a leader or manager are remunerated by rewards established in competition, just as the rewards of employees are.[20] The leadership of men, however, entails a residue of uncertainty that defies prediction. Success in winning wars or negotiating for peace, in building empires or dominating

---

[18] For example, the workers who are most active in organizing unions and participating in them are not the poorest ones, who need unions most, but those with higher socio-economic status, who have greater resources. See William Spinrad, "Correlates of Trade Union Participation," *American Sociological Review,* 25 (1960), 237–244, esp. p. 239.

[19] Frank H. Knight, *Risk, Uncertainty and Profit* (2d ed.), Boston: Houghton Mifflin, 1933, p. 308.

[20] See *ibid.,* pp. 285–287, 309.

a market, in consolidating unions or winning political campaigns cannot be predicted in advance with any degree of accuracy. The leaders who assumed ultimate responsibility for the decisions and guidance that brought these victories are the ones who reap the profits from them.

While a surplus is necessary to institute an organization, further surpluses are produced in it. The organization of collective effort replaces the free competition for and exchange of benefits among individuals by normatively regulated transactions, although within this framework of regulated transactions there also occur some direct exchanges, such as that of advice for status in work groups. Basically, members of organizations are not free to barter their services but are expected to conform to normative expectations, which involves furnishing services, and receive a return for doing so. The contributions made by employees of an organization, who are compensated for their services, tend to produce a surplus profit at the disposal of management, which it can use at its own discretion, and which is its return for having assumed responsibility for uncertainty by having guaranteed to employees returns for their services.

An organization whose members are not employees compensated for services, such as a union or any organization whose avowed purpose is to advance the common welfare of its membership in some way, also often obtains surplus profits from the contributions of its members. Whereas the members of such an organization are expected to receive this surplus in return for risking their contributions, the power vested in the leadership actually gives it the deciding voice on how to distribute the surplus. This situation is exactly parallel to that in a large corporation, whose stockholders are also expected to receive its surplus profits, but whose management has the power to distribute the surplus as it sees fit, subject only to the restriction that sufficient profits must be distributed to stockholders to attract all the needed capital. This is a severe restriction for weak corporations but not for strong ones, which can pay stockholders interests at a regular rate regardless of the actual profits made in any specific year, treating them, in effect, like bondholders.

Generally, the stronger an organization, the less are the restraints imposed on the leadership by the need to attract members who make contributions, and the greater is the surplus at the leadership's disposal. The leaders of strong unions or the bosses of strong political organizations can furnish sufficient rewards to members to assure their continuing contributions and still retain a surplus for use at their own discretion. This means that the leaders of strong organizations can and do treat members no differently from the way management treats employees, just as strong corporations can treat stockholders as if they were bondholders. For management, too, must distribute enough profits to employees to give them incentives for making contributions to the organization and can retain only the surplus left for its own use. In brief, an organization's great strength combined with its differentiated hierarchical structure tends to destroy the distinction between members, the furthering of whose welfare is presumably its purpose, and employees, whose services are purchased for this purpose. The paradox is that the great contributions made by a large membership, which make any member dispensable, are the very resources that empower the organization's leadership to treat members as if they were merely employees.

The ability to assume responsibility for complex decisions and tasks, which is important and highly prized in organizations, permits individuals to obtain great rewards at little cost to themselves. Jaques has suggested a quantitative measure for the level of responsibility of an organization member, namely, the inverse of the frequency with which his performance is reviewed by his superiors, which may be several times an hour for unskilled workers and once a year for top management.[21] The individual's ability to stand uncertainty for extended periods of time governs the level of responsibility he can easily assume.[22] This ability, which depends on a person's technical competence and tolerance for ambiguity, determines, therefore, whether a certain responsibility is experienced as an enjoyable challenge, which is preferred to a more routine task, or whether it is perceived as an unpleasant threat, which engenders anxieties and a desire to escape from it. In short, the same amount of responsibility may be a gratifying reward for some and a punishing cost for others, and which of these it is determines the reactions of subordinates to supervision, on the one hand, and the power relations among managers, on the other.

Employees who experience their level of responsibility as an unpleasant burden will be grateful to a supervisor who readily offers counsel and guidance and reciprocate for his assistance by complying with his directives. Employees who find their responsibilities challenging, however, will define the same supervisory practices as too

---

[21] Elliott Jaques, *Measurement of Responsibility*, London: Tavistock Publications, 1956, pp. 32–42.

[22] *Ibid.*, pp. 85–106; see also Melville Dalton, *Men Who Manage*, New York: Wiley, 1959, pp. 243–248, 252–255.

close supervision and as unjustified interference with their work rather than as help they appreciate. The manager who supervises his subordinates too closely continually makes demands on them, enabling them to discharge whatever obligations they have to him, whereas the one who does not supervise too closely, but lets subordinates come to him for advice or assistance, recurrently obligates them to reciprocate for his help by complying with his directives, thereby fortifying his authority over them.[23] In brief, the subordinates' orientation toward responsibility governs whether they consider given supervisory practices to be rewarding assistance or demanding interference and whether these practices strengthen or weaken the superior's authority.

Furthermore, a member of an organization who enjoys the challenge of responsibilities can relieve others of duties they dislike and thereby earn their appreciation as well as other rewards at little or no cost to himself. Thus, Crozier noted that the chief engineers in the plants of the bureaucratized French tobacco monopoly exercised more power than their official position warranted, because they were capable of assuming responsibility for maintenance problems with which no one else could cope.[24] Generally, men who discharge important responsibilities are rewarded by their fellows with great honor and power, and they typically make these gains at virtually no cost at all since they enjoy the challenge of their responsibilities.[25]

Risk is an essential element in responsibility, that is, assuming responsibilities entails making decisions whose outcome is uncertain. Frequent reviews of a man's decisions by his superior limit the un-

---

[23] Impersonal mechanisms of control, including such different kinds as assembly-line production and quantitative records of performance, promote the authority of superiors over subordinates in the organization, because these control mechanisms lessen the superior's need to make many demands on subordinates, and because they encourage subordinates to become obligated to their superior by coming to him with requests for help. See Blau, "Formal Organization," *American Journal of Sociology*, 63 (1957), 58–63.

[24] Michel Crozier, *The Bureaucratic Phenomenon*, University of Chicago Press, 1964, pp. 112–174.

[25] To be sure, rendering services entails costs in time, and the ability to provide complex services has been achieved at some investment costs. But given the requisite abilities, assuming greater responsibilities, instead of performing duties that involve lesser ones, does not entail a cost; on the contrary, it is rewarding. Although the social recognition and power men receive who exercise great responsibilities make doing so particularly gratifying, the challenge of responsibilities is inherently gratifying independent of any social rewards obtained for it, as illustrated by the fact that individuals who have the requisite abilities prefer working on difficult rather than easy crossword puzzles even when they are alone.

certainty he must bear but do not entirely eliminate the risks he takes. His judgment may turn out to have been incorrect, and he must suffer the consequences when this is the case. According to Knight, only the entrepreneur who invests capital assumes responsibility for uncertainty and thus earns profits.[26] But in social life, at least, responsibility for uncertainty is not confined to the top of organizations but exists, in varying degrees, throughout their hierarchies. For taking these risks of making uncertain decisions, individuals expect to profit if they are successful, and the approval and power men typically earn for assuming responsibilities can be conceived of as constituting this profit.

The diverse comparisons of rewards between the many groups in a large and complex organization, finally, create special problems for management. The workers in each specialized group are eager to maximize the rewards they receive for their services, and they often engage in concerted union action for this purpose. As management yields to the pressures of one group to avert active opposition in the form of a strike or possible defections to other companies, or as it modifies a group's incentive system in ways that permit its members to increase their earnings, it satisfies the demands of one group but creates dissatisfaction in others. The members of other groups accustomed to comparing themselves with the one to whose demands management yielded experience relative deprivation as the result of the decline in the comparative level of their income and social status, although their absolute earnings and positions have remained the same. Such relative deprivation, no less than any other dissatisfaction, is likely to produce opposition and demands for improvements.[27] Indeed, once earnings have risen sufficiently above the minimum needed for a decent standard of living, relative standing tends to become as important for employees as absolute income. Homans has suggested that this produces a strange paradox for unions: "As for organized labor, the more successful it is in getting the general level of wages raised, the more likely it is to undermine its own unity; for then workers can begin to interest themselves not just in the absolute amount of wages but in wage differentials, and wage differentials are obviously apt to set one group of workers against another."[28]

---

[26] Knight, *op. cit.*, chapter x.

[27] For a report on the reactions of workers to an increase in the earnings of another group of workers, see William F. Whyte, *Money and Motivation*, New York: Harper, 1955, chapter viii.

[28] Homans, *op. cit.*, p. 393.

Some conflict and opposition are inevitable in large organizations with many specialized subgroups, each of which is interested not only in raising its absolute volume of rewards but also its relative standing among others. To pacify the opposition of groups who have effective bargaining power, management may yield to their demands, and by doing so it often evokes the opposition of other groups. The unfavorable comparisons to which most members in large organizations are recurrently exposed create dissatisfaction and opposition that is directed not only against management but also against existing institutions in general. Empirical studies indicate that political radicalism is more pronounced and that work satisfaction is lower among workers in large plants than among those in small ones.[29] To be sure, the success of the enterprise and its expansion mitigate the internal conflicts by putting resources at the disposal of management, which make it possible to increase the benefits of all groups, just as an expanding economy lessens the class conflict in a society, as noted in chapter six. The significance of relative standing among groups, however, is likely to perpetuate conflict and opposition. As some groups gain advantages, the opposition of others is aroused, and as management solves some problems, the new conditions thereby introduced generate new ones. Hence, the process of change in organizations tends to assume a dialectical form,[30] and so does the process of change in social structures generally, as will be shown in subsequent chapters.

Conclusions

The legitimation of patterns of social conduct and social relations requires that common values and norms put the stamp of approval on them and reinforce and perpetuate them. Legitimate organizations and social relations are those of which the community approves, whereas illegitimate ones violate the prevailing values in the community. Many social relations are neither explicitly legitimated by community values nor proscribed by community norms, because social standards only set wide limits within which a range of permissible relations may exist. This is true for exchange relations and power

---

[29] Seymour M. Lipset, Paul F. Lazarsfeld, Allen H. Barton, and Juan Linz, "The Psychology of Voting," in Gardner Lindzey, *Handbook of Social Psychology*, Cambridge: Addison-Wesley, 1954, Vol. II, 1139; and Sergio Talacchi, "Organization Size, Individual Attitudes and Behavior," *Administrative Science Quarterly*, 5 (1960), 398–420, esp. p. 409.

[30] Blau, *op. cit.*, pp. 67–69.

relations. Explicit legitimation entails not merely tolerant approval but the active confirmation and promotion of social patterns by common values, either pre-existing ones or those that emerge in a collectivity in the course of social interaction.

The exercise of power is judged in terms of social norms of fairness by those subject to it and by others witness to it. A powerful individual or group whose demands are moderate in terms of what these norms lead others to expect wins their social approval, which legitimates the authority and fortifies the controlling influence of the powerful. The exploitative use of power, in contrast, provokes social disapproval and opposition. A person who has much power is expected to make great demands, and he therefore can rather easily make demands others consider only fair and thus attain legitimating approval of his power. The conclusion that great power facilitates obtaining legitimating approval of the power must be qualified in two respects. First, if a person has very great needs for power, whether because of objective conditions or for psychological reasons, considerable power over others may still be insufficient for his needs and may not prevent him from using his power exploitatively rather than with moderation. Second, if social approval is irrelevant for a person, it will not restrain him from oppressing others. Legitimating approval is of great importance, however, for stable organizing power. In the context of organized social endeavors, and particularly of formal organization, consequently, it is generally true that great power resources promote fairness in the exercise of power and thus legitimating approval of it, which is one reason why power tends to beget more power.

The dilemma of leadership is that it requires both power over others and their legitimating approval of that power, but the process of gaining ascendency over others and the process of winning their approval are in conflict. An individual who uses his resources to assert his dominance over a group and protects his dominant position by making them dependent on him while refusing to become dependent on them usually creates resentment and fails to earn general social approval. On the other hand, great concern with courting the approval of followers interferes with effective leadership, because it induces the leader to be governed by what followers like rather than by what most furthers the achievement of their common goals. The effective leader must be capable of restraining the immediate desires of individual followers for the sake of their long-run collective interests. Yet, unless he obtains their legitimating approval of his leadership, their desire to escape from his dominance makes his position precarious. Individuals who seek to become the leaders of groups tend to resolve this dilemma by mobilizing their power first and then using it in ways that win them the approval of followers, but as a result of the conflicts that occur in the process only a small proportion of the aspirants to positions of leadership succeed in attaining them. Efficient operations in formal organizations necessitate, however, that men appointed to managerial positions succeed in the majority of cases in establishing effective formal leadership over subordinates, and special mechanisms exist that greatly increase their chances of success in having subordinates accept their legitimate authority.

The institutionalization of the principle of managerial authority in modern societies and the sanctioning power of management, which rests on the organization's resources that enable it to provide recurrent rewards to its members, greatly facilitate the individual manager's task of winning his subordinates' legitimating approval of his authority. A manager's outstanding abilities to contribute to the welfare of subordinates make him a particularly strong formal leader, as is the case for an informal leader, but his formal position and powers make it easy for a manager to benefit his subordinates even if his leadership qualities are limited, and in this respect his situation differs from that of the informal leader. The joint obligations of subordinates, which the manager's contributions to their common welfare have created, tend to find expression in group norms that demand compliance with his directives. These normative constraints of the collectivity of subordinates legitimate the superior's authority over them by effecting *voluntary* compliance with his commands in the specific sense of making such compliance independent of any enforcement action on his part.

Power is the resource that permits an individual or group to coordinate the efforts of many others, and legitimate authority is the resource that makes possible a stable organization of such coordinated effort on a large scale. The leadership of an organization makes contributions to the achievement of its objectives and expects to profit from these investments. The rewards other members receive must compensate them for two kinds of contributions, the instrumental services they render and their compliance with the leadership's directives (though in actual life these two frequently merge). Whereas employees are compensated for their services and are not entitled to a share of the surplus their contributions help to make, other members who risk their investments are expected to receive a share of the profits. This distinction, however, breaks down in very strong organizations, because its leaders can elicit the needed investments from members without giving them a proportionate share of the profits. This means that they treat members who have made investments in the organization, in fact, like management treats employees whose services it purchases. The powerless corporation shareholder and the powerless union rank-and-file are typical illustrations.

The organization of collective effort mobilizes power. The leadership's power over subordinates becomes the basis of the power at its disposal in relation to other segments of the society, and the successful exercise of its external power, in turn, increases its power within the organization. The exercise of power, however, generates conflict and opposition both within the organization and in its external relations. The frequent experience of relative deprivation resulting from the manifold comparisons between groups in large organizations is a source of dissatisfaction and opposition that exists to a lesser extent in small organizations. The commanding position of power leaders of strong organizations hold in the community, finally, is at the root of much social conflict and political opposition.

NINE

Opposition

And if a man cause a blemish in his neighbour; as he hath done, so shall it be done to him; Breach for breach, eye for eye, tooth for tooth: as he has caused a blemish in a man, so shall it be done to him *again*.

Leviticus

Punishment is not a very effective method of influencing behavior, as has become increasingly recognized. Thus Thorndike concluded from his early learning experiments with animals: "The results of all comparisons by all methods tell the same story. Rewarding a connection always strengthened it substantially; punishing it weakened it little or not at all." [1] Later experiments by Skinner and Estes essentially confirmed the conclusion that punishment is a poor reinforcer, especially if it is regularly administered, although if it is administered at irregular intervals it does discourage the behavior that is being punished. [2]

Homans has summarized the implications of these animal experiments: "And the punishment of an activity once found reinforcing leads to an ephemeral fall in its strength: after the punishment has been removed, the activity soon returns to its original probability of emission. . . . It is this characteristic of punishment that makes it so unsatisfactory, because so costly, a way of controlling behavior.

---

[1] E. L. Thorndike, "Reward and Punishment in Animal Learning," *Comparative Psychology Monographs*, 8 (1932), 58, quoted in Ernest R. Hilgard, *Theories of Learning*, New York: Appleton-Century-Crofts, 1948, pp. 26–27.

[2] *Ibid.*, pp. 109–113.

Suppose there is an activity that we find undesirable but that never-theless gets some reinforcement. Unless we are in a position to punish the activity every time it appears, it will soon reinstate itself."[3] The most serious disadvantage of punishment among human beings, which has also been observed among animals, is that it arouses emotional reactions that have undesirable consequences for behavior other than the one it is intended to affect.[4] Although severe punishment of children, particularly physical punishment, may succeed in suppress-ing the misbehavior for which they are penalized, it may simultane-ously produce aggressive tendencies, anxieties, and a weak superego that encourages other forms of misbehavior.[5]

Granted that the effectiveness of punishment as a means of exerting a lasting influence on conduct is highly doubtful, we may ask why people so frequently hurt and punish others not only inadvertently but also intentionally. One reason for doing so is that coercive force, which is the extreme application of negative sanctions, can suppress noxious behavior when all other means for modifying it have failed. The screaming child who cannot be quieted can be prevented from annoying the adults by being locked in its room. Though it has been found impossible to rehabilitate the incorrigible criminal, imprison-ment does prevent him from disrupting life and order in the commu-nity. Of special importance is the fact that groups and societies who are threatened by others are inclined to seek to forestall the danger by preparing punitive measures against potential aggressors, and these preparations are a threat to the suspected aggressors and give them, in turn, reasons to strengthen their deterrent power.[6] The likelihood of overt aggression under these conditions, in which none of the parties want it but all fear it, is great. For example, a systematic content

---

[3] George C. Homans, *Social Behavior*, New York: Harcourt, Brace and World, 1961, p. 26. John W. Thibaut and Harold H. Kelley conceptualized this by indi-cating that effecting conformity through negative sanctions requires surveillance but that effecting it through positive sanctions does not; *The Social Psychology of Groups*, New York: Wiley, 1959, pp. 240–246.

[4] Hilgard, *op. cit.*, p. 113.

[5] For a summary of pertinent research, the results of which are admittedly far from conclusive, see Irvin L. Child, "Socialization," in Gardner Lindzey, *Hand-book of Social Psychology*, Cambridge: Addison-Wesley, 1954, Vol. II, 669–672, 683–686.

[6] For theories on this subject, see Lewis F. Richardson, *Arms and Insecurity*, Pittsburgh: Boxwood, 1960, and *Statistics of Deadly Quarrels*, Chicago: Quad-rangle, 1960; Thomas C. Schelling, *The Strategy of Conflict*, Cambridge: Harvard University Press, 1960; and Kenneth E. Boulding, *Conflict and Defense*, New York: Harper, 1962.

analysis of documents from the weeks immediately preceding the outbreak of World War I found that the key decision-makers of the major participants, particularly Austria-Hungary, Germany, and France, considered themselves friendly and much more the object of aggression than hostile to other nations.[7]

Another reason people resort to punishment is that it seems to be an effective social deterrent even when it has little deterrent effect on the specific individuals that have been punished. The severe punishment of the serious violator of basic moral standards may only confirm him in his aggressive rejection of the mores of the community. But his punishment dramatically symbolizes to the rest of the community the dire consequences of immorality and the vital significance of conformity, thereby fortifying their identification with the prevailing moral principles. "The people demand atonement," psychoanalysts have pointed out, because the punishment of the serious offender helps to empower the superego of law-abiding citizens to continue suppressing the temptation to deviate from normative standards in the pursuit of self-interests.[8] Sociologists have noted that the righteous indignation of the members of a community against the criminal and the discussions of their condemnation of his act occasioned by his trial and punishment serve to unite them in common consensus and reinforce their commitment to the normative standards he has violated.[9] Punishment, since it often makes the punished individuals more confirmed criminals, may be said to sacrifice the conformity of some members of the community for the greater conformity of the rest.

Still other factors that make punishing experiences prevalent have already been mentioned. Recurrent positive sanctions become, in effect, undistinguishable from negative ones, since the cessation of a continuing reward that individuals have come to expect is experienced by them as a punishment. Indeed, even failure to receive expected increments in rewards, such as a regular increase in salary, tends to be considered a penalty. Moreover, the high rewards some persons

---

[7] Ole R. Holsti and Robert C. North, "History as a 'Laboratory' of Conflict," in Elton B. McNeil, *Social Science and Human Conflict*, Englewood Cliffs: Prentice-Hall (forthcoming).

[8] Franz Alexander and Hugo Straub, *The Criminal, the Judge, and the Public*, New York: Macmillan, 1931, pp. 210–217; citation from p. 210.

[9] See Emile Durkheim, *On the Division of Labor in Society*, New York: Macmillan, 1933, pp. 85–96, 108–109; George H. Mead, "The Psychology of Punitive Justice," *American Journal of Sociology*, 23 (1918), 577–602, esp. p. 591; and Kai T. Erikson, "Wayward Puritans," unpublished Ph.D. dissertation, University of Chicago, 1963.

receive engender feelings of relative deprivation in others who think their investments deserve equally great returns. These conditions are punishing without necessarily being intended as penalties by those who produce them, although sometimes they are, but a final factor leads people deliberately to mete out punishment to others.

The desire of human beings to retaliate for harm done to them causes them to seek to punish others. The point here is not that people sometimes employ negative sanctions to gain their own advantage but, quite the contrary, that they sometimes forget their own self-interest due to the strong desire for revenge. When men have been badly hurt or seriously deprived, greatly exploited or strongly oppressed, retaliation for the pain inflicted on them tends to become an end-in-itself, for the sake of which they are willing to sacrifice other advantages. Not only hostility breeds hostility but frustration and deprivation do too, against those who cause the suffering or to whom its cause is attributed.[10] Without being actively hostile or suppressive, groups in power often provoke the animosity of other social classes. If these groups have exploited others to gain advantage or if their superior position rests on conditions in the society that create hardships and deprivations for others, the others will blame them for their misery, and not without justification, since power cannot escape the responsibility for the social conditions in which it is rooted. It is the desire for revenge based on such frustrating experiences out of which opposition and rebellion develop. "And one of the most potent remedies that a prince has against conspiracies, is that of not being hated by the mass of people," [11] stated Machiavelli. He explained in another connection that of "the causes that most easily render a prince odious to his people, the principal one . . . is to deprive them of anything that is advantageous or useful to them; this they never forget, and the least occasion reminds them of it; and as these occur almost daily, their resentment is also daily revived." [12]

Exploitation and Retaliation

Opposition to power arises when those subject to it experience shared feelings of exploitation and oppression. To trace the social

---

[10] See John Dollard, Neal E. Miller, Leonard W. Doob, O. H. Mowrer, and Robert R. Sears, *Frustration and Aggression,* New Haven: Yale University Press, 1939.

[11] Niccolo Machiavelli, *The Prince and the Discourses,* New York: Modern Library, 1940, p. 67 (from *The Prince*).

[12] *Ibid.,* p. 483 (from *The Discourses*). See also Harold Folding, "Functional Analysis in Sociology," *American Sociological Review,* 28 (1963), 10–11.

processes that generate opposition to existing powers, it is necessary to recapitulate the relevant points previously made in different connections. Power over others makes it possible to enforce submission to one's will. Whether it rests on coercive force or on the supply of benefits that meet essential needs and cannot be obtained elsewhere, power can be used to exploit others by forcing them to work in behalf of one's interests. The conditions under which exploitation is experienced depend on two sets of social expectations: those of the group or groups subject to the power, which determine how they react to given demands for obedience, and those of the group in power, which determine the extent of their demands for submission.

Social norms define what power demands are fair and just and which are excessive in relation to the advantages, material or ideological, derived from existing powers. Subjugation by coercive force can hardly be experienced as just, for it offers no compensating advantages for submission. Hence coercion is virtually always resisted and, if possible, actively opposed. But if the power to command services and compliance is derived from the supply of needed benefits, those subject to the power do not necessarily experience their position as disadvantageous, although they may do so. If the benefits obtained are greater than what the social norm of fairness leads subordinates to expect in return for their services and compliance, they will consider their position advantageous and express social approval of the ruling group, which fortifies its power and legitimates its authority. If subordinates' normative expectations are barely met, they will neither feel exploited nor express firm legitimating approval of the group in power. If, however, the demands of the ruling group with a monopoly of vital resources far exceed what social norms define as fair and just, subordinates will feel exploited and seize any opportunity to escape the ruling group's power or to oppose it, inasmuch as their situation is, basically, no different from that of groups subject to coercive force.[13]

Groups in power are also influenced by social norms of fairness, but other considerations may induce them to depart from these standards. Power is a generalized means for the achievement of various ends. The higher a powerful group's expectations of what it wants to

---

[13] The underlying principle has been pointed out by Adam Smith: "That seems blameable which falls short of that ordinary degree of proper beneficence which experience teaches us to expect of everybody; and on the contrary, that seems praise-worthy which goes beyond it. The ordinary degree itself seems neither blameable nor praise-worthy." *The Theory of Moral Sentiments* (2d ed.), London: A. Miller, 1761, pp. 135–136.

accomplish, the greater are its needs for power and the greater is the pressure on the group to mobilize all the power it can in disregard of social norms of justice. The government of a country that aims to dominate its neighbors must mobilize its power over its own subjects for this purpose and frequently demand sacrifices from them in excess of cultural expectations, although such a government typically attempts to solicit social support for its policies with promises that the sacrifices will be amply repaid by the glory and material gains accruing from victory. Should this government be successful and keep its promises, it probably would use its power over other nations exploitatively and employ the resources thereby obtained to earn the legitimating approval of the power it exercises over its own subjects. Generally, since the significance of social approval for the stable organization of collective effort puts restraints on the exercise of power, exploitation and oppression are less pronounced and less prevalent within the context of organizations than outside of them. The power conflicts that are most severe and fought out most ruthlessly are those between groups, organizations, and entire nations, in which cases the rulers with the support of their own followers or subjects strive to dominate other collectivities.

Exploitation and oppression are punishing experiences, which arouse anger, disapproval, and antagonism against those held responsible for them. If the deprivation suffered is severe, the desire to retaliate for it may well become an end-in-itself in the pursuit of which people ignore other considerations. Such emotional reactions to having been hurt appear irrational, and they are indeed if they involve a blind fury that strikes aimlessly at everything in its way. But the endeavors of individuals to retaliate by harming those who have harmed them and their willingness to sacrifice their material welfare to achieve this end are no more irrational than the pursuit of any other objective that is intrinsically valued. Revenge sometimes does become a supreme value in the thinking of people, and its achievement is more rewarding for them than are other rewards they must forego for the sake of it. The jealous husband who shoots his unfaithful wife and her lover only to surrender to the police illustrates this point, and so does the revolutionary who assassinates the tyrant with little hope of escaping death himself. The desire for revenge is seen as a base motive, yet it can be the source of some of the noblest human actions, in which men sacrifice their fortunes and their very lives for ideals that benefit their fellow men.

The wish to punish others in retaliation for having been hurt or disadvantaged by their actions finds expression not only in situations of extreme deprivation but also in everyday social life. Thus those interviewers in a public employment agency many of whose clients were uncooperative and created difficulties for the interviewers penalized clients with sanctions at their disposal not only more often than interviewers with fewer such clients (as would be expected), but *disproportionately* more often.[14] (The ratio of difficult clients in three units was about $1:1\frac{1}{2}:3\frac{1}{2}$, but the ratio of negative sanctions was $1:3:7\frac{1}{2}$.) This finding suggests that the greater the frequency with which interviewers were antagonized by uncooperative clients, the more freely did they penalize clients for transgressions, that is, the more punitive did they become. The tendency to make deviants into scapegoats who are attacked at every opportunity illustrates the same principle. A group member who persistently engages in practices that violate group norms causes displeasure to the other members, and they tend to retaliate by frequently expressing aggression against him, even when he has not done anything wrong at the moment.[15]

Serious social deprivations experienced in a collective situation create, strange as it may seem, a surplus of resources, just as an excess of social rewards does. As long as the benefits received in social transactions merely meet expectations of fairness and basic needs, self-interests tend to govern social exchange. But if rewards exceed expectations and needs, the surplus created permits individuals to be generous and somewhat set aside immediate self-interests.[16] This surplus is the resource that produces social legitimation. Great profits enable management to reward employees generously, and the more than fair returns employees consequently receive for their services promote their legitimating approval of managerial authority. The successful government, similarly, can greatly benefit citizens and thereby earn their appreciation and loyalty, which fortify its political authority.

Rewards that are entirely insufficient to meet expectations of fairness and basic needs paradoxically also create a potential social sur-

---

[14] Blau, *The Dynamics of Bureaucracy* (2d ed.), University of Chicago Press, 1963, pp. 101–106.

[15] See *ibid.*, pp. 198–199. The scapegoat who deviates not so much in his behavior as in his ascribed characteristics, such as the Negro, is punished for causing displeasure by his very presence in a community most of whose members are prejudiced against him.

[16] Homans' reanalysis (*op. cit.*, pp. 170–180) of an empirical study by Joachim Israel suggests that once immediate self-interests are taken care of, the decisions of individuals tend to be guided by their sense of fairness and justice.

plus, and if conditions are favorable for its realization this surplus becomes the resource that produces social opposition. Individuals exploited by existing powers have little to lose by resisting them. The meager rewards they receive for their services, which fall short of standards of fairness, make them less dependent on these powers than individuals whose rewards are fair and satisfactory. Although exploited individuals may have no alternative at the present time, they derive some independence from the fact that the possible alternative of a future change in the power structure is more attractive to them than to those who receive adequate benefits under existing conditions.[17] If their sense of justice is outraged by their oppression and that of their fellows, moreover, retaliation against the oppressors may be more gratifying to them than securing the continuation of their meager rewards. Provided that these conditions of potential opposition are experienced in a collective situation, a revolutionary ideology is likely to develop that helps to realize the potential and activate the opposition. The belief in important ideals makes it rewarding to further their attainment, and the significance of these ideal rewards depreciates the value of material ones by comparison. It is such a revolutionary ideology that effects and completes the transformation of social deprivation into a surplus resource, by making exploited and oppressed groups less dependent on material rewards and thus freeing their energies to fight existing powers.

Social values that legitimate opposition to dominant powers, and thereby solidify it, can emerge only in a collectivity whose members share the experience of being exploited and oppressed, just as social values that legitimate the authority of a superior can develop only in a collectivity of subordinates. Isolated victims of oppression are helpless in their futile anger, but an entire collectivity is not, and its isolation from other segments of the society may actually strengthen its power of resistance against oppression. The insulation of a group from others increases its chances of being exploited and its chances of actively resisting the exploitation. Groups whose geographical isolation, ethnic differences, or distinctive beliefs set them apart from the rest of the community can more easily be exploited by dominant powers, because lack of identification of the majority with these

---

[17] Thibaut and Kelley (*op. cit.*, p. 23) have stressed that it is not a person's dissatisfaction with a social relation but the availability of alternatives that makes him independent of it. Serious deprivations, however, do create a degree of independence, because they make a change in the system of social relations into an attractive alternative worth some sacrifices.

groups has the result that their exploitation is not discouraged by general social disapproval. The relative isolation of these groups promotes extensive intragroup associations and communications, which provide much opportunity for group members to discuss their grievances against the oppressive powers and socially justify their feelings of aggression against them. Isolation also restricts communication with the rest of the community. It therefore lessens the restraints imposed on isolated groups by community norms that legitimate the authority of existing powers and by community disapproval of overt acts of aggression. These conditions make active opposition against exploitation by dominant powers likely, as illustrated by Kerr and Siegel's finding that strikes occurred most often in industries whose work force constituted an "isolated mass," that is, a group whose social and working life separated them from the rest of society, such as miners, sailors, and longshoremen.[18]

The opposition ideology that tends to emerge in the process of communication among the members of an exploited group serves to justify and crystallize the opposition against oppressors in a variety of ways. A desire for revenge, feelings of aggression, and an inclination to resort to violence are culturally tabooed and evoke guilt feelings, particularly if they are motivated by selfish indulgence in one's emotional reaction to deprivation. A revolutionary ideology converts these base tendencies into noble ideals pursued not for selfish reasons but for the sake of relieving the misery of one's fellow men or even for bettering the conditions of humanity at large. Each revolutionary need not be ashamed of wanting to retaliate for the exploitation suffered and to use violence in fighting the oppressors, because he does so to benefit his comrades and not simply himself. His willingness to sacrifice his own material welfare in the interest of advancing the revolutionary cause validates his conviction that it is not selfish indulgence that leads him to violate profound cultural taboos.

The revolutionary ideology activates opposition by legitimating it and intensifies the conflict by transforming it into an unselfish struggle against oppressors. Simmel has noted that

> . . . the parties' consciousness of being mere representatives of supra-individual claims, of fighting not for themselves but only for a cause, can give the conflict a radicalism and mercilessness which find their analogy in the general behavior of certain very selfless and very idealistically

---

[18] Clark Kerr and Abraham Siegel, "The Interindustry Propensity to Strike," in Arthur Kornhauser, Robert Dubin, and Arthur M. Ross, *Industrial Conflict*, New York: McCraw-Hill, 1954, pp. 189–212.

inclined persons. Because they have no consideration for themselves, they have none for others either; they are convinced that they are entitled to make anybody a victim of the idea for which they sacrifice themselves. Such a conflict which is fought out with the strength of the whole person while the victory benefits the cause alone, has a noble character.[19]

Coser, in commenting on this passage, added: "The real difference is whether self-interest is pursued with a good or a bad conscience, in other words, whether its pursuit is considered legitimate by the actor himself and by the collectivity of which he is a part and from which he seeks approval." [20] Social legitimation of the pursuit of collective self-interest by an ideology justifies and fortifies opposition against oppressors.

The opposition ideology, finally, becomes a rallying point, a symbol of group identity, and a new basis of social solidarity. Men who share the experience of being oppressed and the feeling of aggression against the oppressors are drawn to ideals that advocate their overthrow. Common ideals put adherents under pressure to advance the chances of their realization by proselyting and making new converts to the revolutionary cause. Ideological identification becomes a mark of social identity, and ideological conflict defines the boundaries of the opposition movement. "Conflict with other groups contributes to the establishment and reaffirmation of the identity of the group and maintains its boundaries against the surrounding social world." [21] The shared ideology, furthermore, serves as the matrix of social solidarity, superseding personal ties of social attraction as the primary basis of group solidarity. "It is one of the most striking and general features of ideological groups that they frown upon and oppose vehemently any display of personal affective attachments among their members." [22] For personal bonds of intimacy, Nahirny continues, are suspect of impeding pure devotion to the common cause. Only the most intimate personal bonds, however, are discouraged. Generally, shared ideals are a source of social attraction, making it possible for strangers quickly to establish bonds of fellowship. It is by this very process that a shared ideology unites large groups of men, heretofore unknown to each other, in common solidarity.

---

[19] Georg Simmel, *Conflict and The Web of Group-Affiliations,* Glencoe: Free Press, 1955, p. 39.
[20] Lewis A. Coser, *The Functions of Social Conflict,* Glencoe: Free Press, 1956, p. 113.
[21] *Ibid.,* p. 38.
[22] Vladimir C. Nahirny, "Some Observations on Ideological Groups," *American Journal of Sociology,* 67 (1962), 398.

Political Opposition

Downs has presented a rational model based on economic theory for the analysis of political processes.[23] The conduct of government produces advantages for various citizens, or possibly disadvantages. The rational voter in a two-party democracy like ours, according to the model, must compare the utility he derives from the existing government with the utility he expects to derive were the opposition party in power and vote accordingly. If this decision is impossible or too difficult, because there are so many issues on which parties have to be compared, there are two ways of simplifying voting decisions. Instead of comparing parties on all issues, a voter can compare their ideologies and vote for the one whose program appeals to him most and promises to bring him most rewards. Alternatively, he may vote for or against the present government on the basis of whether or not the benefits it furnishes meet his expectations—in the terminology used here, whether or not he receives a fair return for the various investments he has made in his government. The rational government must spend resources to provide rewards for voters "until the marginal vote gain from expenditure equals the marginal vote loss from financing."[24]

A purely rational model of politics has serious limitations. The strictly rational choice of both parties in a two-party system is to become increasingly alike, as the application of the well-known Hotelling principle shows.[25] Since the voters whose ideological position on any issue is to the left of the leftist party can only vote for it or abstain, whereas those whose position is between the leftist or the rightist party may vote for either, the leftist party has an incentive to move closer to the center on all issues, and the same holds true for the rightist party. (Large-scale abstention on the part of extremist voters would somewhat modify these tendencies of the two parties to advocate similar programs.[26]) Besides, it is rational for each party to adopt an ambiguous political ideology, which is not clearly distinct from that of the other party. The similarity and ambiguity of their

---

[23] Anthony Downs, *An Economic Theory of Democracy*, New York: Harper, 1957.

[24] *Ibid.*, p. 73.

[25] Harold Hotelling, "Stability in Competition," *Economic Journal*, 39 (1929), 41–57; see also Arthur Smithies, "Optimum Location in Spatial Competition," *Journal of Political Economy*, 49 (1941), 423–439; and Downs, *op. cit.*, pp. 115–117.

[26] *Ibid.*, pp. 117–120.

programs, however, virtually prevent voters from making rational choices between the two parties. In brief, the most rational course of action of the political parties precludes rational decisions by voters.[27]

Another difficulty inherent in the rational model of political decisions is due to the fact that a single vote exerts very little influence on the outcome of an election. The rational choice of the voter is to incur hardly any cost to vote, since his vote has hardly any impact on his party's chances of victory. It may not even be rational to incur the cost of taking time out to go to the election booth, and it certainly is not rational to incur the cost of acquiring the large amount of political information on the candidates and issues that is necessary to make rational choices between them. In other words, the voter's rational course of action is not to obtain the information he needs to vote rationally. To be sure, people acquire political information incidentally, because they are interested in reading and hearing about politics, but this tendency is outside the theoretical model. Since democratic government depends on citizens who are politically informed and do vote, it is a prerequisite of democracy that many voters, and ideally all, be made to act in ways that are not strictly rational for them.

In a democracy social norms are required that obligate its citizens to keep politically informed and vote and that reward them with social approval for doing so. Conditions in which actions that are in the interest of individuals conflict with the interests of the collectivity always indicate a need for social norms and sanctions, which make it rational for individuals to act in ways that otherwise would be irrational by rewarding them for actions that are not originally in their self-interest and penalizing them for those that are. My nonvoting does not harm me, but yours does harm my self-interest as a democratic citizen—that is, the nonvoting of all of you is contrary to my interest in maintaining democracy. Hence, I and each one of us put pressure on you and, in fact, on everybody to go out and vote. Each one votes not because doing so is in his own self-interest but because conformity to social pressures and internalized normative constraints is. Besides, we legally compel young people to become educated and to receive in the course of their education a minimum of information about our political institutions. Inadequate as this

---

[27] Parties in multiparty systems, by contrast, benefit from adopting clearly distinct political programs, but the coalition governments usually necessary there create other problems for rational voting (although Downs may overemphasize the comparative disadvantages of multiparty systems); *ibid.*, chapter ix.

minimum usually is, the increasing level of education promises to have a salutary impact on democratic participation, as indicated by the well established fact that more educated persons are not only better informed about political issues but also more likely to vote than less educated persons.

Probably the main shortcoming of Downs' rational model of politics is that it cannot account for the growth of opposition parties. The desire to maximize the benefits derived from *government activity* cannot explain the political support received by minor parties with virtually no chance of election in the near future. Two factors ignored by the model can help account for active participation in small, third parties. First, political actions do not rest exclusively on the rational calculation of advantage but sometimes are largely expressive manifestations of people's feelings and values.[28] To be sure, such expressive action is by no means devoid of rewards. However, second, the rewards obtained in political life are not confined to those that the government supplies and that consequently are contingent on election victory but include many directly derived from political participation. These two points require some elaboration.

The political support for an opposition party with a radical ideology gives expression to people's feelings of antagonism to ruling powers and alienation from existing political institutions. The oppressive exercise of power by ruling groups, or a serious depression that prevents large segments of the population from receiving a fair return for their labor, or from receiving any return for the investments they have made in their occupation because of unemployment, tends to create widespread animosity against the groups in power. The collective experience of such deprivations socially reinforces the hostility against the powers held responsible and the desire for retribution. If the major parties have failed either to relieve people's suffering or to satisfy their desire to strike back against their oppressors by depriving them of power, individuals who feel exploited and oppressed are likely to become alienated from these parties.

A political party that receives rewards in the form of election victories without providing the expected return to those who have voted for it by advancing their interests antagonizes them and leads them to withdraw their political support, even though they have no rational alternative since no other major party offers a more satisfactory program. Exploited and oppressed citizens want to retaliate for the

---

[28] In Max Weber's terms, it is *wertrational*, not *zweckrational; The Theory of Social and Economic Organization*, New York: Oxford University Press, 1947, pp. 115–118.

unjust policies of the major political parties, just as they want to retaliate for the unfair treatment they suffer under existing powers.
These two complementary wishes to retaliate make them susceptible
to the appeal of a revolutionary ideology that promises the downfall
of dominant powers and political organizations. Radical political
opposition could hardly emerge were it not for the desire to retaliate
for oppression and injustice, which it gratifies, because there are few
other advantages men obtain from membership in a weak revolutionary sect.

There is some empirical evidence in support of the thesis that extremist opposition is often not a calculated means to gain explicit
rewards but an expressive action signifying antagonism against existing powers, stemming from feelings of deprivation, powerlessness,
and alienation. Anti-fluoridation campaigns exemplify these tendencies.[29] One student of these campaigns concluded that "the opposition
to fluoridation is likely to be concentrated in categories of people
who have a sense of deprivation relative to some reference groups."[30]
Individuals who feel helpless and oppressed by powerful groups apparently seize the opportunity to reject the fluoridation proposals
originated by those in power to vent their aggression against them.
As another investigator of the subject has noted: "It is as if fluoridation somehow symbolized the buffeting one takes in a society where
not even the water one drinks is sacrosanct."[31] A comparative study
of over 200 communities confirmed the hypothesis that a large proportion of persons with weak social attachments to their community,
as indicated by a variety of measures, increased the chances that fluoridation referenda were defeated.[32] Research on two school-bond
referenda similarly found that feelings of powerlessness and political
alienation were associated with opposition to the bond issues.[33] Indi-

---

[29] Most authorities deny that there is a rational basis for opposing the fluoridation of drinking water; for some exceptions, see John Lear, "Documenting the
Case Against Fluoridation," *Saturday Review*, January 4, 1964, pp. 85–92.

[30] Arnold Simmel, "A Signpost for Research on Fluoridation Conflicts," *Journal
of Social Issues*, 17 (1961), 29.

[31] William A. Gamson, "The Fluoridation Dialogue," *Public Opinion Quarterly*,
25 (1961), 536.

[32] Maurice Pinard, "Structural Attachments and Political Support in Urban
Politics," *American Journal of Sociology*, 68 (1963), 513–526.

[33] John E. Horton and Wayne E. Thompson, "Powerlessness and Political Nega-
tivism," *American Journal of Sociology*, 67 (1962), 485–493. For similar findings
on a referendum to create a metropolitan government, see Edward L. McDill and
Jeanne C. Ridley, "Status, Anomia, Political Alienation, and Political Participation," *American Journal of Sociology*, 68 (1962), 205–213.

viduals of low socio-economic status were alienated in disproportionate numbers and opposed the bond issues in disproportionate numbers, but political alienation exerted an influence on opposition that was independent of and greater than the influence of socio-economic status.

The statement that extremist opposition frequently has expressive significance is not meant to imply that the expectation of rewards is irrelevant for the adherents of opposition movements. A radical party, no less than any other association, must furnish rewards to elicit contributions. But the salient rewards of a minor party are those derived from political participation itself and not those contingent on the party's assumption of the power of government, since the chances of political victory are too remote. Clark and Wilson distinguished three types of rewards at the disposal of political parties and other organizations to attract members and induce them to furnish services, which they called "material," "solidary," and "purposive incentives." [34] It is the last of these that is of distinctive importance for the political support of a minor radical party.

The material rewards political parties can offer members in return for contributions are political patronage, actual payments for work done for the party, either occasionally or as a regular job, and candidacy for political office with the possibility of a permanent political career. Solidary incentives refer to the rewarding experience of associating with like-minded people in the course of working for a political organization. The shared opinions of party workers and the social approval and reaffirmation of these opinions in the process of social interaction among them produce a sense of fellowship that is rewarding. In addition, a person who makes outstanding contributions to the party earns the respect of the other members and can attain a position of leadership among them, which is intrinsically rewarding, and which gives him access to the rewards candidacy for political office promise. Purposive or ideological incentives, finally, are the rewards derived from furthering, if in a small way, the achievement of common political ideals and accepted party objectives.

Ideological rewards are of particular significance for a small opposition party. Only a strong party can offer salient material incentives. A party's chances of victory at the polls must be realistic for the promise of political patronage or political office to be a meaningful incentive, and it must have financial resources to pay its officials a

---

[34] Peter B. Clark and James Q. Wilson, "Incentive Systems," *Administrative Science Quarterly*, 6 (1961), 129–166.

salary. While positions of leadership in a small and weak party are also less rewarding than leadership in a large and strong political organization, other solidary rewards do not depend on the party's strength and its chances of victory. But neither do the rewards derived from sociable fellowship among party workers make a specific party preferable to any other, except insofar as the solidary fellowship is rooted in common political ideals. It is the ideological identification with the opposition party's program that makes the social solidarity among its members a distinctive incentive for membership and active participation in *this* party. The common ideology also serves directly as an important incentive for contributing to the party's success, because helping to advance cherished ideals is intrinsically rewarding. A minor party, therefore, must primarily rely on the incentives its ideology gives its members to contribute to the common cause and on the appeal of its ideology to attract new members and contributors.

A deep devotion to radical ideals is characteristic of supporters of small opposition parties because this devotion is the major source of reward for them and anybody devoid of it has little incentive to work for such a party. The small size of an opposition group, moreover, reinforces its radicalism and protects its ideological purity against compromise, as Simmel has noted: "Radicalism [in small groups] is sociological in its very nature. It is necessitated by the unreserved devotion of the individual to the rationale of the group against other nearby groups (a sharpness of demarcation required by the need for the self-preservation of the group), and by the impossibility of taking care of widely varying tendencies and ideas within a narrow social framework." [35] The uncompromising radicalism of the small opposition movement is ultimately rooted in the feelings of aggression and vengeance of its members, without which they would not have been likely to join it. The strong commitments of the group members to the radical ideology is solidified in the social interaction among them. The ideological intolerance of radical sects engenders conflicts among them—for example, among those representing various shades of socialism—and this ideological conflict further increases the intolerance against dissent in each sect, since any deviation from its pure ideology implies defection to another sect. [36]

The firm ideological commitment of the radical opposition con-

---

[35] Georg Simmel, *The Sociology of Georg Simmel*, Glencoe: Free Press, 1950, p. 94.

[36] See Coser's comments on Simmel's insight, *op. cit.*, pp. 102–103.

trasts with the ideological flexibility with which major parties adapt their programs to increase their appeal for the electorate. The psychological process of reducing cognitive dissonance can help explain this difference, just as it was used in the last chapter to help account for the difference between legitimating the authority and submitting to the power of a superior. Members of radical sects incur high costs for their political convictions in the form of general social disapproval and, sometimes, economic and legal sanctions that are invoked against them. Although the ideological rewards these radicals receive from supporting the opposition movement presumably outweigh their costs, doubts are likely to arise in their minds as to whether the rewards are really worth the costs. The resulting cognitive dissonance can be reduced by inflating the value of the rewards and deflating that of the costs, which means in this case emphasizing the great importance of the ideological principles and de-emphasizing the significance of community disapproval and material sacrifices. The fact that these processes occur in a group situation socially confirms the changes in valuations they produce and generates strong commitments to the opposition ideology. Supporters of major parties do not incur similar costs for their political convictions and for the rewards they obtain from engaging in widely approved political activities. Since they have consequently little need for reducing cognitive dissonance through increased valuation of their ideology, their ideological commitments are usually less intense than those of supporters of minor opposition parties.

Extremist political movements typically have their base in collective experiences of serious deprivation, absolute or relative, existing or threatening. Lipset, citing research from many countries, shows that political support for radical opposition parties of the left—Socialists and other parties advocating democratic reforms as well as Communists—comes in disproportionate numbers from the poorest, most deprived social classes, the economically most insecure, and ethnic and religious minorities who suffer status deprivation as the result of discrimination.[37] His analysis also shows, however, that the conclusion that extremist rebellions derive their main support from the most underprivileged social strata is oversimplified and must be qualified in two important respects, one pertaining to the vanguard of radical opposition movements, and the other pertaining to the difference between rightist and leftist extremism.

---

[37] Seymour M. Lipset, *Political Man,* New York: Doubleday, 1960, pp. 220–244.

The political support of the vanguard of an as yet unsuccessful revolutionary movement appears to depend on a combination of intolerance and tolerance. The members of a small radical sect must be intolerant of compromise in their firm conviction that their ideology is the only right one, lest the pervasive social pressures against them lead them to modify their ideals and abandon their fundamental opposition to existing social institutions. On the other hand, they must be capable of tolerating postponement of gratification for long periods of time, since they cannot expect to realize their all-important ideals until, at best, many years in the future. Men who suffer serious economic hardships tend to find postponement of gratification intolerable. The inference is that the lowest socio-economic strata do not furnish the main support of small radical parties but only of larger ones whose chances of winning elections are considerable, whereas the predominant support of small radical parties comes from the upper strata of the working class, whose members have some reason for opposition as well as some resources that make postponement of satisfaction tolerable. Lipset's investigation confirms this inference. "The available evidence from Denmark, Norway, Sweden, Canada, Brazil, and Great Britain . . . , where the Communist party is small and a Labor or Socialist party is much larger, [shows that] Communist support is stronger among the better paid and more skilled workers than it is among the less skilled and poorer strata. In Italy, France, and Finland, where the Communists are the largest party on the left, the lower the income level of workers, the higher their Communist vote."[38]

The political extremism of the right, in contrast to that of the left, does not have its roots in the underprivileged working class. Lipset's research indicates that the growing Nazi party in Germany received its main support from the middle class, who had previously voted for center parties, and neither from the working class, who continued to vote for leftist parties, nor from the upper-class conservatives, who continued to vote for the traditional conservative party.[39] Essentially the same was true for the Nazis in Austria, Poujadism in France, and the support for McCarthy in the United States;[40] they all represent

---

[38] *Ibid.*, p. 123. (The data on Communist support in various states of India reveal a similar pattern; *ibid.*, pp. 124–126). Duncan MacRae, Jr., has criticized the methodology of Lipset's analysis, but his criticism does not affect the conclusion and the illustration cited; see his letter and Lipset's reply, *American Sociological Review*, 27 (1962), 91–92.

[39] Lipset, *Political Man*, pp. 124–126.

[40] *Ibid.*, pp. 154–170.

extremist rebellions by the lower middle class against the *status quo.*

The interpretation these findings suggest is that left-wing opposition is a reaction to serious deprivation experienced by the most underprivileged social strata and that right-wing rebellions are reactions to the serious *relative* deprivation experienced by middle strata whose social standing is threatened. The exploitation and oppression of the poor gives rise to radical opposition movements in the form of leftist parties and unions, which are designed to improve the standard of living and social position of the working class. The success of working-class parties and unions in raising the socio-economic status of workers threatens the social status of the stratum immediately above them. The members of the lower middle class experience relative deprivation as the superiority they have traditionally enjoyed over workers is undermined by the economic improvements workers have achieved through their collective efforts. Lower-middle class persons tend to react to this threat to their relative social standing, particularly if economic conditions intensify their insecurity, by rebelling against the existing order in fascist movements that advocate institutional change often aimed at restoring a glorified past. The hypothesis implied is that economic improvements in the relative position of the working class stimulate the development of rightist extremism.

Political Structure and Ideological Conflict

Politics has been defined by de Jouvenel as the art of "increasing the human energies at our disposal by rallying other men's wills to our cause." [41] It contrasts with and complements economics in human endeavors: "economics is concerned with the use of human resources on the spot, politics with adding to them." [42] This conception of politics as referring to the creation of new resources by mobilizing the energies of men in a common cause is especially apt for the growth of an opposition party. It has already been discussed how the wish to retaliate for oppression suffered, the collective experience of actual or relative deprivation, and the identification with a revolutionary ideology help to produce the human resources required for the development of an opposition movement. Now we turn to examine how conditions in the social structure and the society's political institutions affect political conflict and opposition, and how the dynamics

---

[41] Bertrand de Jouvenel, *Sovereignty,* University of Chicago Press, 1957, p. 18.
[42] *Loc. cit.*

of political contest and ideological conflict influence the chances of a growing opposition party.

Heterogeneity in the social structure tends to promote political conflict between opposing parties. Thus the profound class differences in European societies, compared to the lesser ones in the United States, are apparently reflected in the deep political and ideological cleavages between European parties. These cleavages contrast with the relative lack of conflict over fundamental ideological issues between the Democrats and the Republicans here. But within the United States, too, the extent of competition between parties depends on the degree of heterogeneity in a community, as Key has noted. Political rivalry is generally more intense (in primaries as well as final elections) in the heterogeneous urban areas than in the more homogeneous rural sections of a state. In New England, for example, the proportion of urban and foreign-born residents in an area were correlated with a fairly even split in the two-party vote, which reveals serious rather than merely token election contests.[43] A systematic study of all American cities with a population of over 25,000 found that partisan elections, which, in contrast to nonpartisan ones, are indicative of competition between political parties on the local level, were more prevalent in communities that were heterogeneous either in regard to social class (as measured by a high proportion of the labor force in manufacturing) or in regard to religion (as measured by a considerable proportion of Catholics in the town).[44] This difference in the prevalence of local party contests was most pronounced in states where there was serious competition between the two parties. This is probably because political rivalry in a community depends not only on heterogeneous interests but also on a fair chance of victory for both parties, which hardly exists in states dominated by one party.

Political institutions, although themselves determined by underlying forces and conditions in the social structure, such as the degree of differentiation and heterogeneity, exert an independent influence on political life in a society. Majority rule is evidently impossible in the

---

[43] V. O. Key, Jr., *American State Politics*, New York: Knopf, 1956, esp. pp. 24–26, 177–178, 228–229. Since urban and foreign-born Americans tend to vote Democratic in disproportionate numbers, however, the finding that a large number of them in an area is associated with a high Democratic vote (which is required in Republican New England for a fairly even split) does not constitute clear-cut evidence that *heterogeneity* promotes partisan contests.

[44] Phillips Cutright, "Nonpartisan Electoral Systems in American Cities," *Comparative Studies in Society and History*, 5 (1963), 212–226, esp. pp. 219–223.

absence of democratic institutions. Yet even though these requisite institutions exist, democratic processes cannot prevail in a large society unless permanently organized opposing parties, none of which is completely dominant, provide realistic opportunities for expressing opposition to and for possibly overthrowing the existing government.[45] The specific election procedures that have become institutionalized in a democratic nation also affect the political structure—the number of parties and their chances of growth—which, in turn, influences the program and ideologies of the various parties.

Duverger has pointed out that "the simple-majority single-ballot system favours the two-party system." [46] Nearly all countries with this type of election procedure, which is the one prevalent in the United States, have a two-party system, whereas hardly any countries with different election procedures do. The main reason a simple-majority ballot promotes a two-party system is that it seriously disadvantages third parties, because it results in their being underrepresented in the legislature and, consequently, makes citizens reluctant to "waste" their vote by giving it to third parties.[47] Proportional representation, in contrast, does not disadvantage third parties and hence encourages the development of many parties.[48] Since it accurately reflects changes in public opinion and in the popular vote, proportional representation is sensitive to major shifts in political sentiments and increases the chances of success of opposition movements.[49] The simple-majority system, on the other hand, exaggerates normal variations in opinion by over representing the majority (a slight change in the popular vote may determine which party forms the government) while blunting major shifts in political orientation (a party may attract close to one

---

[45] The importance of permanently and effectively organized political parties for democracy is emphasized by Key, *op. cit., passim,* and *Southern Politics,* New York: Knopf, 1949, esp. chapter xiv. See also Seymour M. Lipset, Martin A. Trow, and James S. Coleman, *Union Democracy,* Glencoe: Free Press, 1956.

[46] Maurice Duverger, *Political Parties* (2d ed.), London: Methuen, 1959, p. 217 (original in italics).

[47] *Ibid.,* pp. 217–227.

[48] *Ibid.,* pp. 245–254. The simple-majority second-ballot system, as exemplified by run-off primaries, also fosters multipartism; *ibid.,* pp. 239–242.

[49] "It is extremely interesting in this connection to observe that the rise of Fascism which occurred throughout Europe in the 'thirties was only visible electorally in the peaceful democracies of the North (Belgium, Holland, and Scandinavia) where it seemed to be much less strong than in France. They had a proportionalist system, France a majority system. In the same way the development of Communism immediately after the Liberation produced a considerable increase in the party only in the proportionalist countries of Europe and not in the Anglo-Saxon simple-majority countries." *Ibid.,* p. 315.

half of the voters in all election districts without gaining any seats in the legislature). In brief, election by simple majority discourages the development of new opposition parties.

The opposition in a two-party system tends to remain more moderate than that in a multiparty system. Major parties that have a good chance to assume responsibility for the government at the next election are restrained, by the possibility of having to implement their policies, from advocating abstract ideals and extreme changes most difficult, if not impossible, to realize in the near future. Inasmuch as minor parties are not subject to these restraints they are likely to adopt radical ideologies or extremist opposition stands, which clearly differentiate them from the major parties they oppose, and even to resort to demagogy.[50] Proportional representation, therefore, fosters the survival of political parties that espouse revolutionary or other extremist ideologies, whereas there is little chance for such parties under the simple-majority system.

The strong identification with their ideology typical of the members of radical opposition movements makes them less dependent on political victory than other party supporters and simultaneously more interested in it. Their idealism makes them less dependent on victory, because it makes participation in the movement rewarding without it, but it makes them more interested in victory, because victory is a prerequisite for realizing their all-important political ideals. The conviction that their ideals point the only true path to a better world tends to induce the movement's members to make converts to their cause and mobilize political support for it. But even when proportional representation protects the growth of an opposition party, the scope of its ideology's appeal poses a basic problem. As long as the appeal of radical opposition ideals is restricted to the most alienated and hostile, the movement cannot muster sufficient support to realize them unless serious upheavals in the society create widespread suffering and discontent. To increase the appeal of an ideology, however, the purity of its ideals and principles must be sacrificed to make concessions to the interests and preferences of various groups in the society.

The distinction Parsons makes between particularistic and universalistic values is relevant here.[51] Particularistic values are those that

---

[50] *Ibid.*, pp. 283–290, 415.

[51] Talcott Parsons, *Essays in Sociological Theory*, Glencoe: Free Press, 1949, pp. 185–199; and Parsons and Edward A. Shils, *Toward a General Theory of Action*, Cambridge: Harvard University Press, 1951, pp. 76–88. Parsons' generic analytical distinction has a variety of specific implications, one of which is singled out for attention here.

the members of a subgroup have in common and that differentiate them from the other subgroups in the collectivity. They furnish the basis for the social attraction between particular persons and segregate subgroups in the community. Thus, a socialist's beliefs make him attractive to another socialist but unattractive to a Republican. Universalistic values, on the other hand, are universally agreed upon by the entire collectivity, and they constitute general standards of judgment. Socialists, Republicans, and members of other parties agree that prosperity is preferable to economic depressions. These are analytical distinctions which apply to ideologies in varying degrees.

The particularistic character of a radical ideology, which unites the members of the opposition group in common solidarity and clearly marks them off from hostile other groups, is essential for their fervent devotion to the cause. But this very particularism also makes the ideology unattractive, indeed, repulsive, to outsiders, except for those who already share the basic sentiments of the ingroup. Expansion requires that the ideology broaden its appeal, which means specifically that it must incorporate features that attract voters who are not emotionally committed to its particular sentiments and who are undecided beween parties or perhaps committed to another party. Only universalistic aspects of political programs make parties comparable and enable voters and potential members to make an intelligent choice between them. If one party favors lower taxes and another higher social security benefits as means to promote prosperity, voters can rationally choose between them in accordance with their interests and preferences, but if one party declares the pronouncements of Stalin or Khrushchev sacrosanct and another makes the same claim for Trotzky's, there is no objective standard of choice. The universalistic features of a party ideology, which make it readily comparable with the programs of other parties, and without which it cannot appeal to the interests of groups as yet uncommitted to it, differ only in degree from corresponding features of other ideologies. These universalistic features therefore pollute the unique, virtually sacred, particularistic nature of the ideology, which is the very foundation of the strong commitments of its most devoted supporters.

This conflict between the particularistic aspects of an ideology, which are the basis of intense commitment to it, and its universalistic aspects, which are the source of its appeal to new adherents, corresponds to Boulding's hypothesis that there is an inverse relationship between the intensity and the appeal of an ideology.[52] The power of

---

[52] Boulding, *op. cit.*, pp. 281–282.

an ideology is a function of both, since the scope of its appeal mobilizes large-scale support, and since the intensity with which it is held promotes great efforts in its behalf. But increasing one weakens the other, because universalistic features of an ideology that widen its appeal destroy the pristine purity that commands intense devotion to it, and particularistic features that strengthen the ingroup's commitment limit its appeal to outsiders.

The success of a radical opposition party in the competition for voters, and ultimately in the contest for winning elections, depends normally on its willingness to widen the appeal of its ideology by modifying it, which entails compromising some ideals. There tends to arise a conflict within the party between the idealists, who hold the political ideals to be sacrosanct and inviolable, and the realists, who favor compromise to strengthen the party. In multiparty systems where the small opposition party has won some seats in parliament, the protagonists in this conflict are frequently the parliamentarians and the militants, as Duverger has noted.[53] The parliamentary representatives, constrained to make concessions by the give and take of political life and by their interest in re-election, tend to be realists willing to make compromises to broaden the ideology's appeal. The militants are idealists anxious to protect the opposition ideology that expresses their political sentiments from being compromised, and they are suspicious of the parliamentary deputies for letting their contacts with the enemy camp weaken their ideological convictions.

The expansion of a small party that appeals to growing segments of the electorate precipitates further changes in its ideology and structure. A third party that succeeds in attracting considerable political support, often after having modified its distinctive ideology and thus diminished its difference from other parties, constrains the major parties to adopt some of its policies in order to undercut its appeal for the voters, which further lessens the difference between it and them. The growth of a party, moreover, raises problems of political apathy and organization. Successful proselyting on a large scale invariably brings into a party many members who do not have a deep commitment to the common cause and are willing to make only token contributions to it.[54] The large membership, though many members are apathetic, makes the informal procedures for conduct-

---

[53] Duverger, *op. cit.*, pp. 190–197.

[54] See Bernard Barber, "Participation and Mass Apathy in Associations," in Alvin W. Gouldner, *Studies in Leadership,* New York: Harper, 1950, pp. 477–504.

ing party affairs that prevailed in the small sect inadequate and creates a need for a more formal organization of political activities.

The main pressure for establishing a strong party organization comes from the need for it in conducting effective political campaigns. The organization's importance for success in political contests often leads to a preoccupation with administrative problems in the course of which the objectives and ideals of the opposition party are lost sight of, as Michels has pointed out.[55] The party leadership is more concerned with strengthening the administrative apparatus than with the political objectives to be pursued, and it is willing to abandon radical ideals if advocating them threatens the organization's survival in a hostile society. Merton has called this process, in which the means intended to achieve given ends become ends-in-themselves that take the place of the original ends, the "displacement of goals."[56] The party organization, designed as an instrument to effect the attainment of political goals, becomes an end-in-itself for the sake of which political goals are sacrificed.

Political parties compete not merely for individual voters but primarily for the support of the major social segments of the society. In order to appeal to large social groups—the farmers, the industrial workers, the Negroes—an opposition party must adopt policies that serve their interests. A group that gives large-scale political support to a party expects, especially if it is organized, to be represented in the party council. Indeed, parties often coopt representatives of interest groups into their policy-making bodies in order to attract their political support.[57] Since unorganized groups are less likely than organized ones to be represented on the party council, the ideology tends to be modified increasingly to reflect the interests of the various organized groups whose political support the party has obtained or hopes to obtain. In the extreme case of a party dominated by one interest group, it becomes, in effect, the political arm of this group, for instance, a farmer's party. This is clearly more likely to happen in small parties than in large ones, but even the major American parties have been accused of being largely the spokesmen of special interest groups—big business in the case of the Republican party, organized labor in the case of the Democratic party.

---

[55] Robert Michels, *Political Parties*, Glencoe: Free Press, 1949.

[56] Robert K. Merton, *Social Theory and Social Structure* (2d ed.), Glencoe: Free Press, 1957, pp. 199–200.

[57] For an analysis of the consequences of cooptation, see Philip Selznick, *TVA and the Grass Roots*, Berkeley: University of California Press, 1959.

The basic principle here is that a political party does not remain a social unit distinct from other social units whose support it attracts but becomes interpenetrated by them. Initially, the party may be conceived of as a separate social group that modifies its ideology in accordance with the interests of various social segments of the society in exchange for their political support. Success in this endeavor, however, destroys the boundary between the party and the other groups, since the party is now largely composed of important elements of these groups. It is no longer meaningful to speak of social exchange between the party and other groups. The appropriate conception is that competition and exchange occur among the elements within the party that represent the interests of various segments of the society, and their objective is to win dominant influence over the party's program and conduct of affairs.[58] In sum, since social groups can interpenetrate, processes of social exchange among them sometimes result in major elements of some becoming integral parts of others.

Once a radical opposition party modifies its ideology to increase its appeal for the electorate, social forces are set into motion that typically lead to further compromises in ideals and an increasingly moderate opposition program. The purpose of these modifications in the ideology is to promote the growth of the party and ultimately to achieve political victory. Since many of the rewards supporters of a party obtain depend on victory in political contests, the promise of impending victory implicit in a growing vote increases their incentives to contribute to the party's success. These rewards are especially important after compromises in the original ideals have greatly reduced the ideological incentives for devoting great effort in behalf of the party, since such compromises alienate the old guard and deprive them as well as other members of a profound cause. Helping to create a new type of society, if in the distant future, can be a sacred cause for men; helping to raise the minimum wage by a quarter, though it may be of greater immediate importance, is not. Basically, however, a third party's chances of winning elections depend on favorable conditions in the society. If economic prosperity creates an unfavorable political climate, even for a moderate opposi-

---

[58] The same principle applies when a community offers tax advantages and other benefits to large business concerns in exchange for the advantages it derives from the concerns' locating within its limits. Once they are located there, the business concerns no longer engage in exchange transactions with the community but are elements of it that enter into competitive and exchange relations with other elements in endeavors to achieve dominant positions in community affairs.

tion program, the compromises the party made in its original ideals will have been to no avail.

The failure of a third party to win political contests and become a major party after it has compromised its ideals is likely—especially in a two-party system—to speed its decline.[59] For it is now robbed of most of the rewards it can offer in exchange for support except the solidary reward of the common fellowship among members. It can provide neither any longer the ideological incentives that motivate members of radical sects to make great sacrifices for their important ideals nor the material rewards promised by impending victory that induce the members of a major party to devote effort to contributing to its success. There is a double contingency under which members of a political party operate. On the one hand, they must offer rewards to groups outside to attract their political support. On the other hand, they need rewards themselves to remain in the party and continue to make contributions to it. If the supply of rewards becomes too low, the present members not only are unable to attract new ones but themselves have reason to leave the party. These considerations imply that a growing third party that has modified its radical ideology to advance its growth must either develop into a major party or it will decline.

Conclusions

Exploitation and oppression may cause serious deprivations and reduce individuals to helplessness, but if they are experienced in a collective situation, they can, paradoxically, produce a social surplus that becomes the source of opposition movements. Power that is exercised with moderation and confers ample benefits in return for submission elicits social approval that legitimates the authority of its commands. The exploitative and oppressive exercise of power, however, provokes social disapproval and, in the extreme case, intense hostility and a desire to retaliate.[60] Isolated victims without social relations among them, though they be many, are helpless in their wrath, but the oppressed collectivity with close social communication among its members tends to be capable of mobilizing some resistance.

---

[59] This is what apparently happened to the C.C.F. in Canada; see Leo Zakuta, "A Becalmed Protest Movement," unpublished Ph.D. dissertation, University of Chicago, 1961.

[60] For a theory of the conflict between groups who exercise power and those subject to their power, see Ralf Dahrendorf, *Class and Class Conflict in Industrial Society,* Stanford University Press, 1959.

As the members of an oppressed collectivity communicate their feelings of outrage, hostility, and revenge to each other, the social consensus that emerges among them legitimates these feelings and reinforces them by absolving individuals from guilt for having such feelings. At this stage, the members of the group are prone to adopt a revolutionary ideology that transforms the struggle against oppressors from a selfish fight rooted in a personal desire for vengeance into a noble cause pursued in the interest of the welfare of one's fellow men. The ideology frees the resources and energies that are necessary to engage in active opposition, because devotion to ideals makes men willing to sacrifice material rewards in the common cause.

Radical political opposition often has expressive significance for participants, and the neglect of this factor is a serious limitation of purely rational models of politics. Extremist ideologies become a rallying point for individuals who feel seriously deprived, and the shared ideals furnish the basis for social solidarity among them. Relative deprivation of status as well as actual economic deprivation promote extremist opposition movements, but of contrasting kinds. The economic deprivation of the poorest social strata tends to find expression in radical opposition of the left, such as Communism, though only after the extremist movement has gathered momentum and become a major party, since the vanguard of radical sects seems generally to be supplied by the higher strata of the working class whose resources facilitate postponement of gratification. The relative deprivation of the lower middle class whose superiority over workers is threatened by the economic improvements the organized opposition of workers in unions and labor parties has achieved, on the other hand, tends to find expression in extremist rebellions of the right, such as Nazism.

The broader social context influences political life in a variety of ways. For democratic processes and majority rule to prevail in large societies, it is not enough to have democratic institutions, but there must also exist permanently organized political parties engaged in serious election contests. Without such partisan conflict between viable political organizations the members of a mass society have no opportunities for expressing their political preferences and thus remain politically impotent, though they may have the right to vote. Plebiscites in one-party states illustrate such political impotence, as do the elections for board members held by corporations and the elections of officials in most unions, because mass voting in the absence of organized opposition groups is meaningless. Partisan conflict, in turn, is more prevalent in heterogeneous than in homogeneous communities. Class, religious, or other social differences in a society foster political conflict and thereby strengthen democracy. Indeed, a typical strategy of the demagogue who wants to eliminate political opposition is to appeal to those characteristics that all members of the society have in common (except possibly a small minority who can be used as scapegoats), such as their "Aryan blood" or their white skin. Political institutions, of course, also affect political processes. Thus the chances that an opposition party will advocate a radical program and that it will survive are greater under proportional representation than under the simple-majority system. The growth of an opposition movement, finally, stimulates changes in its structure and its ideology that have important repercussions for its continuing growth.

An opposition party with aspirations of winning political contests must adapt its ideology to the exigencies of the existing political situation. Unless severe oppression or depressions create favorable predispositions toward the radical ideology among large segments of the population, compromises in ideals must be made to widen their appeal for the electorate. There is a conflict between the particularistic aspects of an ideology, which deepen commitment to it, and its universalistic aspects, which broaden its appeal. An expanding opposition party has no need to modify its radical program, but stagnation creates pressures to do so. Should the attempt to increase the appeal of the ideology by making it more moderate fail to spur the growth of the third party, however, it is likely to hasten the party's decline. For the moderate minor party can furnish neither the ideological incentives of working for profound ideals and a great common cause nor the material incentives promised by impending victory, and without either of these rewards a party has little chance of sustaining political support. If ideological compromise fails, it is apt to be suicidal for an opposition party.

TEN

Mediating Values
in Complex Structures

A society can neither create itself nor recreate itself without at the same time creating an ideal. This creation is not a sort of work of supererogation for it, by which it would complete itself, being already formed; it is the act by which it is periodically made and remade. . . . For a society is not made up merely of the mass of individuals who compose it, the ground which they occupy, the things which they use and the movements which they perform, but above all it is the idea which it forms of itself.

EMILE DURKHEIM, *The Elementary Forms of Religious Life*

The complex social structures that characterize large collectivities differ fundamentally from the simpler structures of small groups. A structure of social relations develops in a small group in the course of social interaction among its members. Since there is no direct social interaction among most members of a large community or entire society, some other mechanism must mediate the structure of social relations among them. Value consensus provides this mediating mechanism. The cultural values and norms that prevail in a society are the matrix that forms the social relations among groups and individuals. These values and norms become institutionalized and perpetuated from generation to generation, although not without modification, and they shape the course of social life in the society and the social patterns that emerge in particular groups. Another distinctive characteristic of macrostructures is that their component elements are interrelated social structures, whereas the elements of microstructures are interrelated individuals, but the treatment of this topic is reserved for chapter eleven. This chapter is devoted to the analysis of the significance of social values and norms for extending the scope of social transactions beyond the range of direct social contacts.

It has been a main thesis of the analysis presented that not all social constraints on human conduct and interaction derive from shared values and norms. The study of complex social structures, therefore, must not be confined to the common values and norms that prevail in them. The power relations between groups, the exchange transactions between organized collectivities, the interdependence between substructures in complex structures, the changes in stratified societies produced by patterns of mobility, and those produced by opposition forces—all these are important problems that must be studied in order to understand complex social structures. An investigation of complex structures ignoring all problems except those directly pertaining to legitimating values is just as inadequate and one-sided as an investigation of social associations that ignores exchange processes and power relations. Although some of the problems mentioned will be briefly examined in the next chapter, the aim in this book is not to develop a full theory of complex social structures but merely to indicate the connections between such a theory and the social processes that have been analyzed in some detail. For this purpose, an emphasis on common value standards appears justified because they provide the connection between the simpler processes in microstructures and the more complex ones in macrostructures. Legitimating values can be said to serve mediating functions methodologically as well as substantively.

Cultural values legitimate the social order and the various arrangements that sustain it. Legitimation entails approving social consensus that endows existing or expected social conditions with value, thereby stabilizing or promoting them. The legitimation of an authority structure and the complex organization of social relations and patterns of conduct associated with it may be considered the prototype of the process of legitimation, whether reference is to a specific formal organization within the society or to the political organization of the society itself. For the core of a legitimate social order is the system of normative orientations that effects social control and compliance with authoritative commands, as Weber has emphasized.[1] Analyti-

---

[1] Max Weber, *The Theory of Social and Economic Organization*, New York, Oxford University Press, 1957, pp. 124–132. After briefly analyzing the concept of the legitimacy of an order in general here, Weber treats the topic more fully in his typology of authority, pp. 324–363.

cally, however, different legitimating beliefs can be distinguished, only one set of which serves directly as the basis of legitimate authority. Standards of fairness in social exchange and other social norms rest on legitimating consensus, as do opposition ideals and other social values that define the goals groups and individuals seek to attain. Commonly agreed upon values and norms serve as media of social life and as mediating links for social transactions. They make indirect social exchange possible, and they govern the processes of social integration and differentiation in complex social structures as well as the development of social organization and reorganization in them.

Social Norms and Indirect Exchange

Normative standards that restrict the range of permissible conduct are essential for social life. Although social exchange serves as a self-regulating mechanism to a considerable extent, since each party advances his own interests by promoting those of others, it must be protected against antisocial practices that would interfere with this very process. Without social norms prohibiting force and fraud, the trust required for social exchange would be jeopardized, and social exchange could not serve as a self-regulating mechanism within the limits of these norms. Moreover, superior power and resources, which often are the result of competitive advantages gained in exchange transactions, make it possible to exploit others. This creates a need for social norms that prohibit at least those forms of exploitation that conflict with fundamental cultural values, such as sexual exploitation.[2] The most dramatic manifestation of the need for social norms is found in social situations where the interests of *all* parties, not only those of most, require protection by social norms because the pursuit of self-interests without normative restraints defeats the self-interests of all parties concerned.

The famous prisoner's dilemma illustrates such a case where both parties cannot realize their own interests in the absence of social norms that protect their self-interests by precluding the very choices that appear to be most rational. Rapoport has summarized the dilemma in these words:

---

[2] See Alvin W. Gouldner, "The Norm of Reciprocity," *American Sociological Review*, 25 (1960), 165–167. Gouldner points out that sexual exploitation is the only form of exploitation that has been extensively analyzed. The reason for this may be that other forms, such as economic exploitation, are less conspicuous because they are not in violation of basic cultural taboos in our society.

Two suspects are questioned separately by the district attorney. They are guilty of the crime of which they are suspected, but the D.A. does not have sufficient evidence to convict either. The state has, however, sufficient evidence to convict both of a lesser offense. The alternatives open to the suspects, A and B, are to confess or not to confess to the serious crime. They are separated and cannot communicate. The outcomes are as follows. If both confess, both get severe sentences, which are, however, somewhat reduced because of the confession. If one confesses (turns state's evidence), the other gets the book thrown at him, and the informer goes scot free. If neither confesses, they cannot be convicted of the serious crime, but will surely be tried and convicted for the lesser offense.[3]

The matrix of negative outcomes (years in prison), with those of A shown in the upper right and those of B in the lower left corner of each cell, would have the following form:

It is evidently to the joint advantage of the two prisoners not to confess and get off with a light sentence of only one year each in jail (lower right cell), but rational calculation of self-interest makes it impossible to achieve this end. A realizes that should B confess he would be better off if he also confesses (eight years in prison) than if he does not (ten years), and should B not confess he again would be better off if he himself confesses (no sentence) than if he does not (one year). In terms of his self-interest, therefore, A must confess, since doing so is to his advantage whether B confesses or not, and as the same considerations apply to B, his self-interest too demands that he confess. Hence, both must confess, with the result that each gets an eight-year sentence (upper left cell), which is the worst joint outcome, nearly as bad as the worst possible outcome for either (ten years), and clearly much more disadvantageous than the one-year sentence they could have received had both kept silent. But how could the prisoners, as rational human beings, decide not to confess?

---

[3] Anatol Rapoport, *Fights, Games, and Debates,* Ann Arbor: University of Michigan Press, 1960, p. 173.

Rapoport suggests that each prisoner should use as the criterion of his decision what is in the collective interest of both rather than what is in his own individual interest.[4] The question that remains, however, is why a prisoner should act in such altruistic and trusting fashion, placing his fate in the hands of another person to whose advantage it is to sell him out. Deutsch's experiment with a variation of the prisoners' dilemma indicates that such trust would, in fact, not be justified, inasmuch as nearly two thirds of the subjects made the distrustful choice which seriously disadvantages the partner should he be trustful.[5] Only a social code among criminals that prohibits confession as a matter of principle does rationally justify the trust Rapoport advocates and enable prisoners held incommunicado to refrain from acting in a selfish manner that actually defeats their own self-interests.

Social norms are necessary to prohibit actions through which individuals can gain advantages at the expense of the common interests of the collectivity. The special case of the prisoner's dilemma merely is an extreme illustration of this general principle. The case of voting in a democracy discussed in chapter nine is more typical. Since democracy cannot be sustained unless citizens participate in it at least by voting, internalized social norms oblige citizens to vote although the cost incurred by doing so is not warranted on strictly rational grounds of purely individual self-interest. The political apathy of many Americans and their failure to vote, which indicate that they do not feel strong political obligations as citizens, constitute a weakness of our democratic system.[6]

The condemnation of rate busters in factories, of apple polishers

---

[4] *Ibid.*, p. 175–177.

[5] Morton Deutsch, "Trust and Suspicion," *Journal of Conflict Resolution*, 2 (1958), 265–279, esp. p. 271. Under the conditions of no communication between partners, with each being instructed to look out for his own interests, 36 per cent of the individuals made the trustful choice, and in only 13 per cent of the cases did both partners do so and thus achieve the outcome that maximized their joint advantage.

[6] The argument sometimes advanced that political apathy and low participation in elections are a healthy sign, because they indicate voters are satisfied, implicitly assumes that voting is governed by self-interest and ignores that low participation reveals a weakness of the normative obligations of democratic citizenship that are necessary to sustain a democratic system. This topic will be more fully discussed in the next chapter. Several authors who advance the above argument are cited in Seymour M. Lipset, *Political Man*, Garden City: Doubleday, 1960, pp. 217–219; see also Bernard K. Berelson, Paul F. Lazarsfeld, and William N. McPhee, *Voting*, University of Chicago Press, 1954, pp. 314–323.

and teacher's pets in schools, of traitors to their country, of stool pigeons and informers in groups of any kind—all these reflect social norms designed to suppress conduct that advances the individual's interest by harming the collective interest. Work groups often discourage competitive endeavors to attain superior rewards, as revealed by restriction of output and social disapproval of rate busting, because competitive conflicts, particularly in a situation of employment insecurity, threaten group cohesion.[7] When competition does not have such deleterious consequences for the group, restriction of output seems to be less pronounced. In a group of civil servants, whose jobs were secure and whose cooperative practices created firm cohesive bonds among them, for example, endeavors to excel evoked little social disapproval, while strong social norms prohibited other practices through which an individual could gain advantages but which simultaneously produced impediments for the work of the rest.[8] The mere fact that the success of some group members limits the chances of success of others does not usually give rise to restrictive group norms. But when a group member's action that furthers his interest, such as informing, directly harms the interest of the rest or of the group as a whole, normative restraints prohibiting this action are likely to develop.

Moral standards that have been internalized and are socially enforced discourage conduct that violates the basic values and interests of the collectivity by changing the rewards and costs of such conduct relative to alternatives. The guilt feelings and social disapproval experienced by an individual whose behavior deviates from moral standards constitute costs that are expected to outweigh the rewards this behavior could bring him. These sanctions convert conduct that otherwise would be irrational into a rational pursuit of self-interest. Men who forego the advantages made possible by cheating do not act contrary to their self-interest *if* the peace of mind and social approval they obtain for their honesty is more rewarding to them than the gains they could make by cheating. For the democratic citizen who takes his political obligations seriously, it is not irrational to keep himself politically informed and to vote, because the satisfaction he

---

[7] See F. J. Roethlisberger and William J. Dickson, *Management and the Worker,* Cambridge: Harvard University Press, 1939, pp. 379–524; and Blau and W. Richard Scott, *Formal Organizations,* San Francisco: Chandler, 1962, pp. 89–93, 191–192, where Roethlisberger and Dickson's case of the Bank Wiring Observation room is further analyzed.

[8] Blau, *The Dynamics of Bureaucracy* (2d ed.), University of Chicago Press, 1963, pp. 187–193.

derives from living up to his obligations are well worth the cost he incurs by doing so. Fully internalized norms serve as a functional alternative for the direct control of individual behavior in the collectivity's interests.[9] Nevertheless, social sanctions through which moral norms are enforced are essential in order to discourage individuals who are not strongly committed to them from deviating from these norms as well as to fortify the moral commitment of those who have made it.

Social norms substitute indirect exchange for direct transactions between individuals. The members of the group receive social approval in exchange for conformity and the contribution to the group their conformity to social expectation makes. Conformity to normative standards often requires that group members refrain from engaging in certain direct exchange transactions with outsiders or among themselves. Moral standards demand that girls do not readily grant sexual favors in exchange for the rewards boys offer in return, that businessmen do not engage in shady dealings in order to reap extra profits, that parents devote time and resources to rearing their children instead of using them to obtain rewards for themselves. By adhering to these moral principles, individuals establish a good reputation, which stands them in good stead in subsequent social interaction. A good reputation in the community is like a high credit rating—for a respectable parent or a girl who is highly thought of as well as for a trustworthy businessman—which enables a person to obtain benefits that are not available to others. Conformity frequently entails sacrificing rewards that could be attained through direct exchange, but it brings other rewards indirectly.

Exchange transactions between the collectivity and its individual members replace some of the transactions between individuals as the result of conformity to normative obligations. In a group of close friends, for example, each one feels obliged to do favors for any of the others without thought of return. There is no direct exchange of favors, but the group norm assures that each friend receives assistance when he needs it. These normative obligations generate indirect chains of exchange, as John does Bill a favor, Bill helps Joe on another occasion, and at still another time Joe has an opportunity to do something for John. Should one of the boys get far ahead of the others in the favors he does for them, the strong social approval he

---

[9] See John W. Thibaut and Harold H. Kelley, *The Social Psychology of Groups*, New York: Wiley, 1959, pp. 127–135.

gets for being such a good friend tends to balance the exchange by giving him a superior reputation in the clique.

The same principle applies to formal organizations. Staff officials do not assist line officials in their work in exchange for rewards received from them, but furnishing this assistance is the official obligation of staff members, and in return for discharging these obligations they receive financial rewards from the company. Long chains of social transactions occur in complex organizations, in which the work of some members contributes to the performance of others, and which typically do not involve reciprocal exchanges. What these chains of transactions do involve is conformity to official obligations on the part of members of the organization in exchange for rewards received from it. In interstitial areas, however, informal direct exchange transactions often arise that supplement these formal indirect ones, as illustrated by consultation among colleagues.

Organized philanthropy provides another example of indirect social exchange. In contrast to the old-fashioned lady bountiful who brought her baskets to the poor and received their gratitude and appreciation, there is no direct contact and no exchange between individual donors and recipients in contemporary organized charity. Wealthy businessmen and members of the upper class make philanthropic contributions to conform with the normative expectations that prevail in their social class and to earn the social approval of their peers, not in order to earn the gratitude of the individuals who benefit from their charity. One student of the subject has emphasized that charitable contributions are largely motivated by the specific rewards they produce for businessmen in the form of furthering their careers in the business world and of maintaining good public relations for the corporations they represent.[10] The upper class rewards its individual members for making contributions to the underprivileged. In addition, there is an implicit exchange between the collectivity of donors and the collectivity of recipients, though not between their individual members.

By assuming the moral obligation to be charitable to the poor, the upper class establishes a claim to moral righteousness and superiority, which ideologically justifies and fortifies its superior social status and power. The social norm of *noblesse oblige* is a two-edged sword, because it implies both that nobility obliges and that being obliging is a sign of nobility. It not only encourages the upper class to assume some

---

[10] Aileen D. Ross, "Philanthropic Activity and the Business Career," *Social Forces*, 32 (1954), 274–280.

obligations for the lower classes but also enables the wealthy and powerful to make a claim to deference on grounds of moral superiority by discharging these obligations. At the same time, the acceptance of charity socially marks an individual as a pauper, as Simmel has noted in a passage previously cited.[11] It transforms him from a poor individual into a member of the social class of underprivileged that depends for support on the charity of higher classes and owes them collective deference for being supported. Middle-class transmitters of charity tend to enforce the deference with which the class of recipients of assistance is expected to repay the contributions of the upper classes. These exchanges between collectivities help to sustain the class structure as well as the system of organized charity.

Professional services involve a still more complex pattern of exchanges among collectivities and between them and their individual members, which replaces direct exchange transactions between individuals that are proscribed by normative standards. Professionals are expected to be governed in their work exclusively by professional standards of performance and conduct and not by considerations of exchange with clients. Although free professionals depend on fees from clients for their livelihood, the professional code of ethics demands that they do not let this fact influence their decisions and that these economic transactions do not affect the social interaction in which professional services are rendered to clients. The professional must refrain from engaging in reciprocal *social* exchange with clients lest his decisions be influenced by the exchange instead of being based only on his best judgment in terms of professional standards.

Parsons' analysis of psychotherapy, which may be considered a prototype of professional services in this respect, illustrates this point.[12] In normal social intercourse, considerations of exchange guide the conduct of participants—friendly overtures tend to be reacted to with friendliness, aggression is typically penalized through withdrawal or counteraggression, and so forth. Psychotherapy requires that a psychiatrist in interaction with a patient abstain from reciprocating in this fashion and instead react to his patient's neurotic behavior purely on the basis of what professional standards indicate to be in the best interest of treatment. The professional detachment of the psychiatrist, which means he is not concerned with obtaining social rewards in his interaction with patients, permits him to refrain

---

[11] Georg Simmel, *Soziologie*, Leipzig: Duncker und Humblot, 1908, pp. 490–491.

[12] Talcott Parsons, *The Social System*, Glencoe: Free Press, 1951, pp. 460–462.

from penalizing a patient for expressing aggression and to reject the friendly overtures of another should effective treatment demand such conduct. The psychiatrist who successfully treats patients in accordance with professional standards receives social approval and respect from his colleagues, which sustain his professional detachment by compensating him for the sacrifice of social rewards in interaction with patients. Professionals in general are primarily oriented to the social approval of colleagues rather than to that of clients, and professional detachment would not be possible otherwise.

A profession renders valued services to the community—protecting its health, administering its laws, educating its youth—in return for which the community gives it exclusive license to perform certain tasks and the mandate to control the work carried out in its area of competence by its own members as well as by others, such as semi-professionals and technicians.[13] The power of self-control is a distinctive characteristic of professions, which differentiates them from other occupations. It consists of two related elements. First, practitioners must acquire expert knowledge in a field and adopt professional standards of conduct that enable them to discharge complex professional responsibilities without supervision. Second, the members of a profession constitute a colleague group of peers, and the only ones considered qualified and entitled to judge the performance of a practitioner are his professional peers. The controlling power of the profession over the recruitment, training, and subsequent fate of its members promotes compliance with professional standards and resistance to pressures to depart from them. Some professions, such as teaching, social work, and nursing, are not dependent on their clients for remuneration, but many practitioners in other professions, such as medicine and law, are paid for their services by their clients. This economic exchange sometimes makes it difficult to adhere to professional standards in disregard of the demands of clients. The consequent need for counterpressure to maintain professional standards may be one of the reasons these free professions, with many self-employed, seem to have been more likely than others to develop strong professional organizations. The expectation is that an indirect chain of exchange replaces direct social transactions based on considerations of reciprocity. The organized profession rewards its individual members for furnishing services to clients in conformity with

---

[13] See Everett C. Hughes, *Men and their Work*, Glencoe: Free Press, 1958, chapter vi; and William J. Goode, "Community within a Community," *American Sociological Review*, 22 (1957), 194–200.

professional standards; the recipients of these services make contributions to the community; and the community bestows superior social status and controlling power upon the profession as a corporate group, which enable it to control and reward its members.

The situation of bureaucratic officials who provide services to clients is similar to that of professionals. Officials in a bureaucracy are expected to treat clients in a detached manner in accordance with official rules, and this requires that officials abstain from exchange relations with clients, because exchange transactions would make them obligated to and dependent for rewards on clients. Even if it is only the gratitude and approval of clients an official wants to earn, his concern with doing so can hardly fail to influence his decisions and may lead him to depart from official procedures.[14] If officials become dependent on clients either for rewards they personally seek or for services of clients the organization needs, they must enter into exchange transactions with clients, which means that they cannot strictly follow bureaucratic procedures in their relation with clients. Two studies found that situations in which officials were dependent on clients engendered debureaucratization, that is, departures from bureaucratic principles.[15]

An essential element of professional and bureaucratic detachment is the absence of exchange relations with clients. Exchange transactions create obligations that make it impossible to conform undeviatingly to professional or bureaucratic standards. Treatment of clients in accordance with these standards suppresses direct exchange with them and substitutes for it a series of indirect social transactions between collectivities and their individual members and sometimes also among collectivities.

Values as Media of Social Transactions

Common values of various types can be conceived of as media of social transactions that expand the compass of social interaction and the structure of social relations through social space and time. Con-

---

[14] The colleague group of officials may—in effect, assuming the role of a professional or bureaucratic organization—promote impersonal treatment of clients by rewarding such impersonal conduct with social approval, thus compensating individual members for the rewards foregone by treating clients impersonally; see Blau, *op. cit.*, pp. 85–86, 106–112.

[15] Elihu Katz and S. N. Eisenstadt, "Some Sociological Observations on the Response of Israeli Organizations to New Immigrants," *Administrative Science Quarterly,* 5 (1960), 113–133; and Blau and Scott, *op. cit.*, pp. 232–233.

sensus on social values serves as the basis for extending the range of social transactions beyond the limits of direct social contacts and for perpetuating social structures beyond the life span of human beings. Value standards can be considered media of social life in two senses of the term: the value context is the medium that molds the form of social relationships; and common values are the mediating links for social associations and transactions on a broad scale. The principle can be illustrated by using social communication as an analogy, although media of communication are, of course, not social values.[16]

All social relations and transactions involve communication. Direct communication between people requires face-to-face contacts, but it is impossible for most members of large collectivities to be in personal contact. Yet social communication is essential to sustain the structure of social relations and the networks of social transactions that integrate large collectivities into a social unit. Hence there is a need for a social mechanism that permits the proliferation of social communication throughout a community and provides mediating links between distant communicators. Media of communication fill this need. They increase the range of communication, making it independent of technical considerations and geographical distance and dependent only on social boundaries. Newspapers and magazines, the radio and television, books and movies, serve as the conveyors of messages to large audiences widely separated in space. Letters and telephones make intercommunication across great distances possible. Cars, trains, and planes permit persons who live far apart to have intermittent direct social contact. By changing the form of social communications, the media of communication affect their nature. Thus the mass media substitute for intercommunication a primarily one-sided transmission of messages from a communication center to a large audience that has little opportunity for feedback communication, as exemplified by newspaper readers and the rare occasions on which members of this group write letters to the editor.

The major function of the media of communication is to broaden the scope of social communication, and a main function of common values is similarly to broaden the scope of social associations and transactions of various kinds. The mass media change the nature of

---

[16] A different conception of symbolic media of social interaction, which also calls attention to their resemblance to communication through language, is presented in Parsons, "On the Concept of Influence," *Public Opinion Quarterly*, 27 (1963), 38–51.

social communication as well as its form, and the complex social structures in communities and societies mediated by social values are also different in fundamental respects from the simpler social structures that emerge in the course of direct social interaction in face-to-face groups. The media of communication serve in part as media or repositories of information that is transmitted to people and helps shape their opinions, as illustrated by newspapers; and they serve in part as intermediaries or intervening links for indirect two-way communication between persons, as exemplified by the telephone. In corresponding fashion, social values partially constitute the medium or context of social life that helps shape the thinking and acting of people, as exemplified by the influence of the common culture on human conduct; and they partially constitute mediators or links for new social associations, as illustrated by the influence of common ideals and opinions on the formation of friendships. Finally, written communications can be preserved through time in exact form. They give a people a written history and make it possible to transmit their cultural heritage and accumulated knowledge to succeeding generations more fully and accurately than can be done through oral traditions. Here again social values have an analogous function, since they play a vital role in the institutionalization of social patterns and their historical perpetuation.

Four types of social values will be analyzed in terms of this principle: particularistic values as media of solidarity, universalistic values as media of exchange and differentiation, legitimating values as media of organization, and opposition ideals as media of reorganization. As a preliminary, it is necessary to clarify the distinction Parsons and Shils make between particularism and universalism.[17] The differentiating criterion is whether the standards that govern people's orientation to each other are *dependent* on or *independent* of the particular relations that exist between them. The latter, universalistic standards are manifest when all candidates for a job are judged on the basis of merit alone, whereas nepotism in hiring practices illustrates particularism, as does a mother's love for her own children regardless of how their qualities or performances compare with those of other children.

One implication of this distinction parallels that made in chapter two between associations that furnish extrinsic rewards and those that are intrinsically rewarding. Extrinsic rewards serve as universal-

---

[17] Parsons and Edward A. Shils, *Toward a General Theory of Action*, Cambridge: Harvard University Press, 1951, pp. 76–88.

istic standards for comparing associates and orienting one's behavior toward them. The fact that an association is intrinsically rewarding, on the other hand, means that the particular features that make it unique and incomparable determine the orientation to it. Here the focus is on psychological dispositions in interpersonal relations. Parsons and Shils explicitly designed their analytical distinction, however, to be applicable not only to the microscopic study of these socio-psychological forces but also to the macroscopic analysis of complex social structures. From the macroscopic perspective, the crucial question is what structural constraints effect the pattern of role relations in the social system, not what inducements dispose individuals to associate with specific others. Another implication of the universalism-particularism dichotomy is most relevant for the analysis of social structure.

In their most explicit definition, Parsons and Shils state that universalistic standards "are defined in completely generalized terms, independent of the particular relationship of the actor's own statuses (qualities or performances, classificatory or relational) to those of the object." Particularistic standards, in contrast, "assert the primacy of the values attached to objects by their particular relations to the actor's properties. . . ." [18] The specific differentiating criterion, therefore, is whether the value standards that govern the orientations and associations among people are *independent or not independent of the relationship between their status attributes.* For instance, if the members of a community, regardless of their own age, express highest regard for the maturity of old age, or if all age groups tend to value youth most highly, age would constitute a universalistic standard. But if most people express a preference for their own age group— the old thinking more highly of older people, and the young, of younger ones—age would constitute a particularistic standard. In other words, attributes that are valued by people regardless of whether they possess them reflect universalistic values, whereas preferences for attributes like one's own reflect particularistic values.

This criterion, which yields an operational measure of the theoretical concepts, refers to the implications of universalism-particularism for the structure of social relations in a collectivity.[19] Universalistic

---

[18] *Ibid.*, p. 82.

[19] See Blau, "Operationalizing a Conceptual Scheme," *American Sociological Review,* 27 (1962), pp. 159–169. Since a man's status affects the impact of his approval, the criterion could be refined by weighing the preferences of each respondent by the significance his evaluations have for the rest.

standards give rise to differentiation of social status, since attributes or performances that are universally valued give prestige and power to those who have them. Particularistic standards produce segregating boundaries between subgroups in the collectivity, because the tendency to value characteristics like one's own unites individuals with given characteristics and separates them from those with others. Occupational achievement and financial success are universalistic values that differentiate social status in our society, and religious beliefs are particularistic values that segregate the members of the different major denominations.[20]

Particularistic social values, the first type, are media of social integration and solidarity. The distinctive values they share unite the members of a collectivity in common social solidarity and extend the scope of integrative bonds far beyond the limits of personal feelings of attraction.[21] These cultural or subcultural beliefs become symbols of group identity that define the boundary between the ingroup and the outgroup. The particular shared values that distinguish a collectivity from others constitute the medium through which its members are bound together into a cohesive community. They serve in this way as functional substitutes for the sentiments of personal attraction that integrate the members of a face-to-face group into a cohesive unit. The common values in a community, however, also mediate personal bonds of attraction, since they constitute particularistic criteria of social attraction that promote the formation of friendly relations among members of the community after short acquaintance. Although particularistic values could not serve their integrating function were they not shared throughout the collectivity, neither could they serve this function were they not defined as distinctive by contrast with the different values in other collectivities. What is common to humanity does not serve as a distinctive symbol of group identity.

---

[20] Value standards, however, do not necessarily remain purely particularistic or universalistic. Thus the fact that Protestants are the high-status majority group in the United States introduces a universalistic element into the otherwise particularistic religious values; there is some general tendency to prefer Protestants that complements the prevailing preferences for the religious ingroup. Similarly, while research skills and teaching ability constitute two universalistic standards among academic scholars, those who are outstanding in one respect tend to emphasize its importance, while those who are outstanding in the other tend to stress its significance, with the result that a particularistic element intrudes upon the universalistic standards.

[21] Reference here is to what Emile Durkheim terms "mechanical solidarity"; *On the Division of Labor in Society*, New York: Macmillan, 1933, pp. 70–110, esp. pp. 79, 109–110.

Particularistic values are characteristic attributes that distinguish collectivities, and simultaneously with uniting the members of each in social solidarity they create segregating boundaries between collectivities.

Second, universalistic values are media of social exchange and differentiation, which expand the range of exchange transactions and status structures beyond the confines of direct social interaction. All exchange ultimately involves the products of the labor of different persons, that is, services that have been performed. Even barter, however, is not limited to the exchange of the services or labor of the two partners themselves, since one can exchange an object he owns that was produced by a third person for the services of the other, for example, a spear for help with hoeing his garden. Exchange itself stimulates the tendency to obtain objects not merely for one's own use but also for use in subsequent barter. When individuals obtain objects in barter that they cannot use themselves, in order to exchange them later for others they can use, indirect exchange has begun. The crucial problem of indirect exchange is that of a generally valid measure of comparative value. The cost a man is willing to incur for an object he wants to use in trade depends on his estimate of what it is worth to others, not on its subjective worth to himself, as would be the case were he only interested in using it himself. For men to make such estimates realistically, there must be universal agreement in a community on a standard of value in terms of which diverse products and services can be compared. A universalistic standard of value, into which the worth of the different products of labor can be translated, serves as a medium of exchange.

The prototype of a medium of exchange is, of course, money, which Boulding defines as "those assets which are customarily exchanged for a wide variety of other assets, and which are wanted mainly because of a belief in their continuing ability so to be exchanged." [22] Modern money is basically not a valuable commodity, such as gold, but a generally agreed upon abstract standard for ascertaining and comparing the value of everything that enters into economic transactions. A tremendous expansion of the network of indirect exchange transactions is made possible by money, because it permits the easy transfer of obligations and credit, and because it is a highly liquid asset that can be readily converted into any other economic valuable. As a medium of exchange, money is a "store of value," [23] which serves

---

[22] Kenneth E. Boulding, *Economic Analysis* (3d ed.), New York: Harper, 1955, p. 312.

[23] *Ibid.*, pp. 310–313.

as a repository of all material value—valuables being either directly transformed into money or translated into money equivalents—and with which profits can be accumulated in the form of capital; that is, the benefits derived from services furnished can be enjoyed or used at some future time. Its transferability makes money the intermediary in a complex system of indirect exchange. Each person renders services to another or to an organization, in return for which he obtains goods and services he wants not from the recipient but from a large number of others, and money mediates these indirect exchange transactions. "The quality of being 'money' is a matter of degree rather than of kind," [24] since money differs from other valuables only in the higher degree of its liquidity, that is, the greater ease with which it can be converted into other commodities.

While there is no exact counterpart of money in social exchange— nothing nearly as liquid—universalistic standards of social contributions and achieved status serve similar functions. Within the scope of social consensus on the relative value of different contributions, indirect exchange is possible, because a person's services directly benefiting some segments of the community, if the entire community defines them as important, earn him general social approval and rewards that often do not come from the same segment. Universalistic values of achievement and approval are the medium of social exchange into which diverse contributions to the collective welfare are translated in the form of social status in the community. This creates a "store of value"—social credit that individuals can draw on to obtain advantages at a later time. Thus common standards of fairness enable individuals to establish a social reputation in exchange transactions that benefit them in later transactions with other partners. Superior social status in the collectivity is the generalized reward for having made contributions to its welfare universally acknowledged as important, and it is the generalized means that makes a large variety of specific social rewards available to individuals.

The differentiation of social status generated by universalistic standards of valued performance serves as a medium of social exchange, that is, as a repository of accumulated social rewards from which future benefits can be derived. The symbols and outward manifestations of generally acknowledged achievement command respect and deference throughout the community. Universalistic standards of performance also furnish mediating links for indirect exchange, since they make it possible for persons to supply services to some and

---

[24] *Ibid.*, pp. 311–312.

receive returns for them from others in the community. As noted in the section on Social Norms and Indirect Exchange, for instance, it is the colleague group or organization that rewards professionals or officials for rendering services to clients in accordance with universalistic standards. The community repays its collective obligation to the profession or organization for its valued services with a mandate of controlling power that enables the corporate group to reward its individual members. Status claims and privileges defined in terms of universalistic standards are not as liquid and transferable an asset as money, but they are an asset of general significance that expands the range of social exchange beyond the limits of direct social contact.

Third, social values that legitimate authority are media of organization, which extend the scope of organized social control. The common values and norms in a collectivity that legitimate the authority of a government or leadership and enforce compliance with its commands constitute a medium of organizing power. They are a repository of the power to command compliance, which is stored in them as the result of the joint social obligations due to the benefits derived from the leadership, and which is available to the leadership in order to organize collective endeavors. The social norms internalized and enforced by the members of a collectivity that effect compliance with the commands of an authority also constitute mediating links in the exercise of power. For these norms mediate between the issue of commands and the compliance with them, whereas other forms of power are not mediated but are directly enforced by the persons or groups who exercise control themselves. Legitimate authority can reside in impersonal principles and offices, which makes it independent of the individuals who administer the principles and occupy the offices. It, consequently, can be transferred from one person to another—from one incumbent of an office to another—and delegated by superiors to subordinates. Legitimating values greatly enlarge the range of controlling power, both directly and indirectly. They make the organizing power of a government or administration independent of the personal influence or obligations its members can establish. It is not the personal influence of the man in the White House but the legitimate authority of the office of President that gives the incumbent such wide powers.[25] Moreover, the legitimate authority of an administration over its own organization bestows on it the entire power of

---

[25] Personal differences in leadership do, of course, affect the scope of the power exercised by the President, but they merely augment the authority that resides in his office.

the organization. Thus the political authority of the government empowers it to mobilize the resources of the nation for use in the power struggle between nations.

Opposition ideals, finally, are media of social change and reorganization. Revolutionary ideologies extend the scope of opposition to existing powers beyond the limits of the influence of individual proselyting to all whose existential conditions predispose them toward these ideals, the world-wide impact of Marx's program being a dramatic example. Opposition ideals constitute a medium of social reorganization, inasmuch as they legitimate the leaders of opposition movements and their organizing power and thus produce a countervailing force against entrenched powers and existing institutions in the society. Revolutionary change or fundamental reforms can occur in a society only if men are inspired by radical ideals for the sake of which they are willing to sacrifice their material welfare. Such ideals also serve as mediating links that bring together men who feel exploited and oppressed and unite them in a common cause.

These four types of social values are reflected in four facets of social structures. Particularistic values and the processes of social integration associated with them are the basis of social solidarity and group loyalty. These values range from those that fortify the cohesiveness of subgroups and simultaneously create segregating boundaries between them to those that encompass all members of a society and unite them in common solidarity.²⁶ Universalistic values and the processes of differentiation to which they give rise find expression in the society's distribution systems, including notably the class structure as the basic manifestation of the differential distribution of major social rewards, the systems of exchange and competition through

---

²⁶ Since particularistic standards can be shared by all members of a society, we may ask what distinguishes them from universalistic standards, which are also shared by all. To answer this question, it is necessary to distinguish the shared standard from the valued attributes or performances to which it refers.   Particularistic standards place a positive value on those attributes of the members of a collectivity, including their beliefs and conduct, that all have in common and that differentiate them from outsiders. Universalistic standards, in contrast, entail social consensus that certain qualities and performances that are *not* characteristic of all members of the collectivity are valuable assets deserving of social recognition, and these standards are often the same in different collectivities. The belief in American ideals, shared by most members of this nation and contrasting with the different ideals of other nations, exemplifies particularism. The belief that high intelligence is a valuable attribute illustrates universalism. Most Americans share this belief but many do not have the valued attribute, and people in other countries also value intelligence.

which social and economic distributions are accomplished, and the functions associated with them, such as division of labor, technology, and training. Legitimating values, which are the foundation of stable organization and centralized authority, are reflected in the political and administrative organization of any collectivity, the society at large, and the various organized collectivities within it. Opposition ideologies and the conflicts they reveal and crystallize, finally, underlie the recurrent patterns of change and reorganization in societies, and these political ideals are particularistic values that constitute new bases of social solidarity and produce realignments as loyalty to the opposition movement supersedes other particularistic allegiances.

Each of the four facets of social structure is manifest in a certain distribution of attributes and pattern of social transactions among the members of the collectivity. Social solidarity rests on the homogeneity of some attributes, notably beliefs, in a population and reciprocal relations in which social support is exchanged among them. Distribution systems involve the heterogeneity of other attributes in the population, which is associated with reciprocal transactions in the exchange system and with unilateral transactions in the system of differentiated status. Organization involves heterogeneity of attributes and transactions coordinated through centralized direction. Opposition implies a dichotomy of attributes in a collectivity and negative reciprocity in social interaction, that is, oppression and retaliation, hostility and counteraggression.

The four syndromes discussed also have implications for a society's collective control over its membership. Specifically, they meet the four conditions necessary to maintain collective power and prevent the usurpation of power by individuals suggested by the schema presented in chapter five, namely: (1) supply of needed rewards, (2) available alternatives, (3) coercive force, and (4) ideals lessening material needs. First, particularistic values and social solidarity become sources of important rewards for individuals that only the collectivity can furnish, thus making individuals dependent on the collectivity. Second, universalistic standards that define the value of contributions to the common welfare and the differential rewards associated with them stimulate competition. If many individuals or segments of a community compete for making needed contributions, the existence of alternative suppliers of essential services makes the community independent of any one of them. In other words, universalistic criteria of rewards promote a multiplicity of suppliers of needed services, none of whom is indispensable, which protects the collectivity from becoming dependent on an indispensable monopolist.

Public education fosters such an abundance of suppliers of important contributions. Third, the political state monopolizes the legitimate use of coercive force in a society,[27] which is available as a last resort to control recalcitrant members, and other organized collectivities also have coercive sanctions at their disposal, such as management's power of dismissal. Finally, common ideals provide incentives for the members of a collectivity to sacrifice material rewards in order to advance its cause. While this is especially important for opposition movements, since support for them entails typically great sacrifices, the patriotic ideals of a nation have the same function.

Institutionalization

Legitimate organizations are faced with the problem of their perpetuation through time. To be sure, all populations, animal as well as human, reproduce themselves, and no special arrangements are necessary to assure the survival of the species for many generations. The survival of a legitimate social order beyond the life span of individuals, however, does require special institutions. The basic cultural values and beliefs that are sacred or virtually sacred to people make them eager to preserve these ideas and ideals for future generations. The investments made in the organized patterns of social life that are legitimated by these values and embody them, and in the knowledge and technology that further the common welfare, make men interested in preserving those too. Formalized arrangements are instituted perpetuating the legitimate order and the social values that sustain it through time by making them independent of individual human beings. The organized community survives total turnover of its membership, often for many generations, as Simmel has noted.[28] What persists are the principles governing social relations and patterns of conduct, and the reason for their persistence is that they have become institutionalized.

Institutionalization involves formalized procedures that perpetuate organizing principles of social life from generation to generation. Establishing a formal procedure requires an investment of resources, and it preserves and rigidifies patterns of social conduct and relations. Merely making explicit a course of action that has become customary entails effort and stabilizes it. Setting up rules to be consistently followed involves further costs and crystallizes the pattern of action

---

[27] Weber, *op. cit.*, pp. 154–157.
[28] Simmel, *op. cit.*, p. 497.

further. The members of organizations sometimes operate under the guidance of superiors and on the basis of precedent without having written procedures to follow. Ascertaining the principles underlying their decisions and producing an official manual of procedures is a difficult task necessitating major investments, which are made in the hope of the future benefits resulting from having such formalized procedures. The explicitly formulated set of procedures, which are expected to govern the decisions of all members of the organization, and which can be readily taught to newcomers, are manifest in a pattern of actions and social interactions that are independent of the specific individuals who carry them out. Formalized rules make an organized pattern of social relations and conduct independent of particular human beings, which is the first requirement of a social institution. Other requirements of institutionalization are that the rules of conduct be legitimated by traditional values and enforced by powerful groups, thereby being made resistant against ready change.

There is a great diversity of social institutions. Examples are the dogma and ritual of a church, the form of government of a country, its laws and courts, the stock exchange that coordinates complex economic transactions, and monogamous marriage. What they all have in common is that legitimating values and formalized procedures perpetuate an organized pattern of social associations. The values that identify men in a society, and the dominant groups in particular, with their institutions and the advantages they derive from them make them interested in preserving these institutions for posterity. Sacred values are more important for the survival of some institutions, such as a church; material advantages are more important for the survival of others, such as a stock exchange; but all are legitimated by some common values. Two complementary social mechanisms preserve the institutions of men though they themselves die, external social arrangements that are historically transmitted and internalized social values that are transmitted in the process of socialization.

Social institutions constitute a historical reality that exists, at least in part, outside and independent of the human beings who make up societies. This historical reality is transmitted through oral traditions in nonliterate societies, but in literate societies it is primarily transmitted through written documents that embody the basic formalized values and norms of the communal life of men—their constitutions and their laws, their bibles and their commandments. To be sure, it is not the parchment or paper on which these documents are written that is of significance but the principles of human conduct they contain. The fact that these principles are written down, however, is of significance, since it assures their survival in fixed form and symbolizes the historical persistence of institutionalized principles of social life, independent of the specific human beings in whom these principles express themselves at any particular time.[29] Although these historical documents must continue to be believed by people to govern social life, they do exert an influence of their own, as Durkheim has noted in his discussion of *written* dogmas and laws:

> However well digested, they would of course remain dead letters if there were no one to conceive their significance and put them into practice. But though they are not self-sufficient, they are none the less in their own way factors of social activity. They have a manner of action of their own. Juridical relations are widely different depending on whether or not the law is written. Where there is a constituted code, jurisprudence is more regular but less flexible. . . . The material forms it assumes are thus not merely ineffective verbal combinations but active realities, since they produce effects which would not occur without their existence. They are not only external to individual consciousness, but this very externality establishes their specific qualities.[30]

Complementary to the historical transmission of the external forms of social institutions is the transmission of the basic cultural values and norms in the process of socialization that give these forms flesh and blood and continuing life, as it were. In the course of rearing their children, people inculcate in them their most profound values and beliefs, often without explicit intent. The dominant values and norms shared by the members of a society or its segments are, therefore, transmitted to succeeding generations. While the rebellion of children against their parents and, especially, the deprivations produced by political oppression or economic exploitation sometimes lead to the rejection of traditional values, only selected political or economic values are usually rejected. The major part of the cultural heritage tends to persist, even in periods of revolutionary transformations. In any case, the process of socialization results in many of the legitimating values of organized community life being passed on to future generations, and these are the institutionalized values that

---

[29] The great importance rituals assume in nonliterate societies, compared to their lesser importance in modern societies, may be the result of a greater need for rituals to perpetuate institutionalized practices in the absence of written codes for doing so.

[30] Durkheim, *Suicide*, Glencoe: Free Press, 1951, pp. 314–315.

sustain and invigorate the external forms of institutions, which without them would be dead skeletons.

A third factor that supplements the other two in sustaining institutions is that they are rooted in the power structure. The cultural values and social arrangements that become institutionalized are those with which the dominant groups in the society are strongly identified, since these groups have the power to make their convictions prevail and to enforce the relevant social norms. Freedom of speech is institutionalized in a society, for example, if powerful groups value and defend it, even if the majority should care little about it or possibly deprecate it; when the powerful are no longer concerned with maintaining free speech its survival as an institution is imperiled. An institution exerts external constraints on succeeding generations in large part because, and as long as, powerful groups that can enforce institutional demands continue to be interested in its preservation. Powerful men and their wives are more likely than others to inculcate traditional values in their children in the process of socialization, inasmuch as the institutional structure embodying these values is the one on which their dominant position rests. Socialization, however, is not confined to childhood but occurs also later in life, notably when individuals join new groups, and members of lower strata who move up into dominant positions tend to be socialized by the established persons there to acquire a proper concern with traditional values and institutions. In brief, institutionalized patterns are typically those with which the dominant groups in a society are most identified, and these groups are the instruments of their historical perpetuation by enforcing the demands necessary for this purpose.[31]

Three conditions, therefore, must be met for aspects of social structures to become institutionalized, that is, to be perpetuated from one generation to the next. Patterns of organized community life must become formalized and part of the historical conditions that persist through time, the social values that legitimate these patterns must be transmitted in the process of socialization, and the society's dominant groups must be especially interested in the survival of these patterns. The historical forms without continued acceptance of the legitimating values become empty shells, and cultural values without institutional forms are ideals yet to be realized; both are required to maintain institutions, and so is their support by powerful groups.

---

[31] I am indebted to Arthur L. Stinchcombe for calling my attention to these points in a private communication.

These factors can be illustrated with our political institutions. On the one hand, our Congressional form of government, the U.S. Constitution and laws, the various branches of government, and the election machinery, are formalized procedures embodied in documents and manifest in many organizations and agencies that persist as part of the historical reality, independent of the particular incumbents of the various offices. On the other hand, democratic and patriotic values, respect for the law and the mores that support it, as well as related values and norms, are transmitted to children in their homes and schools. Americans are born into a historical situation in which certain political forms exist, and they acquire, in their youth, values and norms that legitimate these institutional forms. The foundations of the authority of the law and of political authority are the historical traditions in which they are grounded and the pertinent normative orientations that the members of our society have internalized in the course of socialization as part of their basic personality. The support of the nation's dominant groups, moreover, has sustained the American form of government and legal institutions even in periods when large-scale immigration filled the country with people from other traditions and with different orientations. Institutional constraints generally derive their distinctive force from the combination of being buttressed by the power structure and having twofold historical roots, in the traditions of society and in the childhood socialization experiences of its individual members.

Institutions reflect the historical dimension in social life, the impact of the past on the present. The relationship between institutions and social structure is in some ways parallel to that between social structure and human conduct. Institutions are those aspects of the social structure that persist for long periods of time, and the social structure consists of those patterns of conduct that prevail throughout a collectivity. Yet institutions exert traditional constraints on the social structure that exists at any one time, just as the social structure exerts external constraints on the behavior of individuals. Thus the values and norms shared by most members of a collectivity constitute external structural constraints for each one of them to which he must adapt. Similarly, the traditional values and their external institutional forms constitute a historical framework to which the social structure at any one time must adapt. Men collectively can change the social structure that restrains them, however, and communities in the course of time can change the institutions that confine their social life. In short, institutions impose historical limits on the social structure, which in turn exerts structural constraints on individual conduct.

The typology of social values as mediators of social transactions presented in the preceding section can be employed to classify social institutions. First, integrative institutions perpetuate particularistic values, maintain social solidarity, and preserve the distinctive character and identity of the social structure that differentiates it from others. The core of this institutional complex is the kinship system, which assures every member of the society an integrated position in a network of cohesive social relations and socio-emotional support on the basis of ascribed qualities, and which preserves the distinctive social structure by transmitting cultural values and norms to succeeding generations as well as by reproducing the population biologically. Mate selection in accordance with the incest taboo recurrently establishes new particularistic ties of kinship allegiance between subgroups previously separated by these particularistic boundaries. Religious institutions constitute the second main component of this complex, since moral dogmas and hallowed symbols are fundamental elements of particularism and sacred ceremonies and rituals greatly strengthen commitment to the particularistic values they represent. Inasmuch as most religious bodies in the modern world cut across national boundaries, the common traditions and allegiances they create do too, and separate patriotic doctrines, symbols, and ceremonies—the Declaration of Independence, the Stars and Stripes, Fourth-of-July celebrations—develop to bolster national traditions, solidarity, and loyalty.

A second major type of institution functions to preserve the social arrangements that have been developed for the production and distribution of needed social facilities, contributions, and rewards of various kinds. This type includes, of course, the economic institutions in a society, but it also includes other institutions that are governed by universalistic standards of instrumental value. It encompasses educational institutions, through which technological skills and instrumental knowledge are transmitted to future generations, and which, in their higher branches, simultaneously serve the function of advancing knowledge through research. The stratification system too is part of this institutional complex, insofar as it entails an incentive system for recruiting and channeling men into occupations where they furnish diverse services. It is important in this connection to distinguish two aspects of social stratification.[32] On one hand, the stratification

---

[32] See Walter Buckley, "Social Stratification and the Functional Theory of Social Differentiation," *American Sociological Review*, 23 (1958), 369–375, and Kingsley Davis, "The Abominable Heresy," *American Sociological Review*, 24 (1959), 82–83.

system consists of a hierarchy of social positions, not the persons who occupy them, that yield differential rewards. On the other hand, the class structure consists of actual collectivities of individuals, not abstract positions, who differ in wealth, power, and prestige. The stratification system is an institution, while class structure is not. Although not an institution, the class structure is instrumental in fortifying other institutions, as noted above, and important elements of it typically persist from generation to generation, just as institutions do, because wealth and consequently some aspects of class position can be inherited. The resulting rigidities in the class structure impede the function of the stratification system as a mechanism for distributing human resources, since hereditary status rewards are not effective incentives for achievement.

A third main set of institutions serves to perpetuate the authority and organization necessary to mobilize resources and coordinate collective effort in the pursuit of social objectives. The prototype is the lasting political organization of a society, including not only its form of government and various specific political institutions, such as the legislature, but also such corollary institutions as the judiciary that maintains law and order, the military establishment that protects national security and strength, and the administrative agencies that implement the decisions of the government. To this set of institutions belong also the formal organizations that have become established outside the political arena in a society—like business concerns, unions, and professional associations—and notably the enduring principles of management and administration in terms of which they are governed. Private as well as public organizations are the instruments through which a community attains its social objectives, such as a higher standard of living, and their internal structure corresponds to the executive segment of a political system. Persisting organizations, therefore, are analytically part of the complex of political institutions.[33]

The cultural heritage of a society, finally, contains what may be called a "counterinstitutional component," consisting of those basic values and ideals that have not been realized and have not found expression in explicit institutional forms, and which are the ultimate source of social change. The conflict between these as yet unrealized, but culturally legitimated, ideals and the actual conditions of social existence is at the base of social opposition to existing institutions. For this conflict to become activated typically requires that the dif-

---

[33] See Parsons, *Structure and Process in Modern Societies,* Glencoe: Free Press, 1960, pp. 41–44.

fuse discontent become focused in an opposition ideology. Although some opposition movements formulate revolutionary ideologies that reject many basic values and advocate the complete overthrow of many institutional arrangements, they do so within the framework of some of the ideals and ultimate objectives legitimated by the prevailing culture. Even the most radical revolutionary ideologies are not independent of and receive some legitimation from traditional social values. The very cultural values that legitimate existing institutions contain the seeds of their potential destruction, because the idealized expectations these values raise in the minds of men in order to justify the existing social order cannot be fully met by it and thus may serve as justification, if need be, for opposition to it.[34]

Conclusions

Commonly accepted social values serve as media of social transactions that extend the range of social processes beyond the limits of direct social contacts through large collectivities and long periods of time. Four types of mediating values can be distinguished. Particularistic values serve as media of social solidarity, partly by creating a common unity that substitutes for personal feelings of attraction and partly by mediating bonds of social attraction, although they simultaneously produce segregating boundaries between the solidary subgroups in the larger collectivity. Universalistic standards of social contributions and achievements give rise to differentiation of social status and thereby establish a medium of exchange in the form of status as a generalized reward, which, though far less liquid than money, makes indirect transactions possible. Legitimating values act as the medium for the exercise of authority and the organization of social endeavors on a large scale in the pursuit of collective objectives. Opposition ideals are media of social reorganization and change, since they inspire support for opposition movements and legitimate their leadership.

The complex patterns of social life mediated by common values become institutionalized and thus perpetuated for generations, and sometimes for centuries, if three conditions are met. First, the organizing principles must become embodied in formalized procedures,

---

[34] The schema presented reveals some parallels to Parsons' schema of four functional imperatives—adaptation, goal gratification, integration, and latency— but there are also some fundamental differences; see Parsons and Neil J. Smelser, *Economy and Society,* Glencoe: Free Press, 1956, pp. 16–28 and *passim.*

often in written documents, and find explicit expression in formal social arrangements that are historically transmitted, independent of the human beings who carry them out at any one time, such as the laws and courts in a society, the corporate structures of business concerns, or the dogmas and rituals of religious denominations. Second, the social values that legitimate these institutional forms and keep them alive must be transmitted to succeeding generations in the process of socialization. Third, the dominant groups in the community must be strongly identified with these legitimating values and lend their power to preserve the institutions that express them. Social institutions, therefore, have roots in the power structure and double roots in the past, in the historical tradition of the society, and in the internalized cultural values its members have acquired in childhood. These internalized values adapt men's personalities to fit with ease into the institutions of their society, whereas other social conditions often require difficult adjustments. There is, however, also a counter-institutional component in the cultural heritage, since the ultimate cultural ideals and values are never fully realized in actual life. Opposition to existing institutions tends to arise if the conflict between the social expectations raised by these legitimate ideals and the actual conditions of social existence becomes too great.

Some parallels and contrasts may be drawn between simpler structures of interpersonal relations, complex social structures that consist of substructures, and social institutions that persist through time. Corresponding processes and structural features are found in them, but they take different forms. Processes of social integration rest on sentiments of personal attraction in face-to-face groups, whereas they are mediated by particularistic values that produce a common solidarity in complex structures, and the integration and solidarity of successive generations is established by kinship and religious institutions. Processes of social exchange and differentiation, which involve direct transactions in small groups, are mediated by universalistic standards of performance and achievement in complex structures, and they are perpetuated through the economic and educational institutions and the stratification system of the society. The social approval of the informal leader of a group has its counterpart in the legitimation of authority and organization in large collectivities and in the enduring political institutions of a society. Social disapproval of the exercise of power, which finds direct expression in small groups, leads to opposition ideologies and movements in complex communities, and these may ultimately generate institutional change.

In conclusion, the most distinctive characteristics of complex social structures should be re-emphasized. Since direct social transactions are impossible between most members of a large collectivity, social processes are mediated by common values, and while shared values also influence conduct in small groups, they do not play the crucial role there that they do in complex structures.[35] Moreover, the complex structures of societies become partially institutionalized, and these persisting institutional elements exert traditional constraints on the other elements of community life. Finally, the components of large social structures are also social structures. It is the manifold interdependence of these substructures that reveals the full complexity of social structure and that is a major source of social change, as the following chapter will indicate.

---

[35] This statement is not meant to imply, however, that the impact of common values constitutes the only or the most important structural effect on social patterns.

ELEVEN

The Dynamics of Substructures

Every species of conflict interferes with every other species in society at the same time, save only when their lines of cleavage coincide; in which case they reinforce one another. . . . A society, therefore, which is riven by a dozen oppositions along lines running in every direction, may actually be in less danger of being torn with violence or falling to pieces than one split just along one line. For each new cleavage contributes to narrow the cross clefts, so that one might say that society is *sewn together* by its inner conflicts.

EDWARD A. ROSS, *Principles of Sociology*

The component elements of complex social structures are also social structures. A society consists of the interrelated social groupings and segments, communities and organizations, within it. These interdependent collectivities of various kinds constitute the substructures of the large social structure, both in the sense that they serve as its foundations and that they are its internally structured subunits.

A social structure is comprised of patterned social relations among individuals and groups, including the recurrent conduct in which these relations find expression. The term "microstructure" is used to refer to the interrelations between individuals in a group, and the term "macrostructure," to the interrelations of these groups in a larger collectivity or of these larger collectivities in a still larger one. The elements of macrostructures, therefore, may be either microstructures or themselves macrostructures. The relations between groups and collectivities are manifest in their interdependence, in the mobility of individuals between them, and in the social interaction

283

between their individual members when they act as the representatives of their groups and in their specific roles as group members, whether this involves concerted actions in the pursuit of collective goals or actions oriented toward individual ends that are molded by the conditions in the social structure.

The complex interplay between substructures gives the social structure encompassing them its fundamental characteristics and is the source of the dynamic forces governing it. There are many levels of substructures, as illustrated by the states, counties, communities, districts, and neighborhoods in the country. This image of substructures as concentric circles, with those on each level being mutually exclusive, however, is oversimplified, since many kinds of substructures constitute intersecting circles. Individuals belong simultaneously to many groups and can become part of still others—they are New Yorkers, Negroes, Democrats, employees of a firm, and members of a union all at once, and can join any number of voluntary associations. These groups, consequently, have overlapping memberships, the networks of social relations that define their structures are interpenetrating, and the boundaries between them are neither sharp nor fixed, that is, the groups expand and contract with the mobility of members in and out of them. The differentiation among groups in the larger structure and their internal structures are related. Simmel advanced the principle concerning this relationship that "the elements of differentiated social circles are undifferentiated, those of undifferentiated ones are differentiated." [1] The important additional point he made is that the social differentiation within collectivities produces connecting links between the social elements similarly located in each, as exemplified by the class solidarity of members of the same social class in different communities and even countries,[2] which means that internal structural differentiation generates new intersecting groupings. The dynamics of macrostructures rests on the manifold interdependence between the social forces within and among their substructures.

Macrostructure and Substructures

Different kinds of substructures in a society can be distinguished. First, a population can be divided into social segments or categories

---

[1] Georg Simmel, *Soziologie*, Leipzig: Duncker und Humblot, 1908, p. 715 (my translation).

[2] *Ibid.*, pp. 709–713.

on the basis of any socially relevant attribute, that is, any attribute that actually governs the relations among people and their orientations to each other. Sex is a meaningful social category and so is skin color in our society, while eye color is not. Any one criterion of classification, as long as it is unequivocal, yields mutually exclusive social categories, although several criteria produce, of course, intersecting social segments. Second, communities—in the narrow sense of the term—are collectivities organized in given territories, which typically have their own government and geographical boundaries that preclude their being overlapping, though every community includes smaller and is part of larger territorial organizations. There is no overlap between the population of Manhattan and that of Queens, but the residents of both boroughs are simultaneously New Yorkers and inhabitants of the United States. Third, organized collectivities are associations of people with a distinctive social organization, which may range from a small informal friendship clique to a large bureaucratized formal organization. Individuals belong to numerous organized collectivities, which means that these substructures interpenetrate, and collectivities often have marginal members, which means that their boundaries are fluid and not clearly defined. Finally, abstract social systems consist not of the social relations in specific collectivities but of analytical principles of organization, such as the economy of a society or its political institutions.

Social values have contrasting implications for a social structure and its substructures. The most important substructures for this analysis are organized collectivities and communities. Communities may be considered a special case of collectivities. A community is an organized collectivity with certain distinctive features, notably a territorial base and geographical limits that do not overlap with those of other communities. The boundaries of communities and those of other kinds of organized collectivities, however, do intersect. Organized collectivities have characteristic value orientations, and the four types of values standards discussed in the last chapter often have different consequences for a social structure and its substructures.

Particularistic values create integrative bonds of social solidarity in substructures but simultaneously segregating boundaries between them in the wider social structure. The religious beliefs uniting the members of each church, for instance, divide the society into contrasting and sometimes conflicting religious groups. Social solidarity in macrostructures is always problematical, because the particularistic values that unite ingroups create segregating boundaries between them in the larger collectivity. This raises the question of the compass of particularistic standards—how inclusive the scope of their unifying force is. As a matter of fact, the particularistic standards in a social structure often become universalistic standards in its substructures. Religious beliefs and principles are not only particularistic values uniting the members of each denomination in a common faith but frequently also universalistic standards of conduct that promote a differentiation of status within the religious group, because the most devout who live up to the highest moral standards of their religion command respect and deference among their fellow believers. Political orientations, too, are particularistic standards from the perspective of the society, but within each political camp they act as universalistic standards for differentiating those whose devotion to the cause earns them high respect and superior status from their more apathetic and less highly thought of comrades. Analytically, particularistic standards refer to valued attributes all members of a subcollectivity share, whereas universalistic standards refer to valued attributes that are rare among them. Valued attributes that are reflected in behavior, however, are typically exhibited by different individuals to varying degrees, which confounds the analytical distinction between particularism and universalism.

When the universalistic standards of various substructures in a collectivity conflict, they constitute particularistic standards from the perspective of the encompassing social structure. This point, which is the complement of the one made above, can be clarified with a hypothetical example. The high schools in a community are divided into those where most students are positively oriented toward academic achievement and those where most have a negative orientation toward it. In the former schools, academic achievement is generally admired and associated with superior status among fellow students. In the latter, academic achievement is generally looked down on, and the students who most flagrantly resist academic pressures are accorded highest status. Hence, academic achievement would constitute a universalistic standard in both types of school, though of opposite significance. But from the standpoint of the entire community of high-school students, academic achievement would be a particularistic standard. For a student's social status does not depend on his having academic characteristics that are generally acknowledged as outstanding in the community but on his having the kind of academic orientation that is prevalent among his fellow students, only in more extreme form. Diverse universalistic standards in substructures are particularistic standards in the larger structure they constitute. The distinctive value standards of the members within a subcollectivity, therefore, serve to unite them in common solidarity and simultaneously to differentiate social status among them on the basis of their varying abilities and tendencies to live up to these standards.

Conversely, the universalistic values in a social structure may become the basis of particularistic orientations in its substructures. Universalistic standards of achievement and status promote a differentiated class structure in a society and give the members of each social class some common interests that differ from and often conflict with those of other classes. It is the universally acknowledged significance of financial success that gives the poor in a society the distinctive economic interests they have in common. The shared life chances, conditions of social existence, and interests that differentiate social classes create social distance between them and promote social associations within the boundaries of each, which produce distinctive styles of life that further crystallize the separation between classes. The common interests and orientations toward life of each social class are particularistic values that serve as integrative bonds to unite its members in social solidarity. These particularistic bonds of class solidarity are grounded in the very universalistic standards that differentiate social classes. Identification as an underprivileged worker becomes the mark of the solidarity of the proletariat, which implies that a universalistically defined sign of failure has been transformed into a particularistic social value.

Legitimation of social objectives and the authority to pursue them typically gives rise to explicit organizations with formal procedures for mobilizing resources and coordinating collective endeavors. Centralization of control is a conspicuous feature of these formal organizations, and so are, usually, specialization and departmentalization. The specialized segments that are formally established and legitimated through delegation of authority and serve essential functions for the achievement of organizational objectives tend to acquire some autonomy. The relatively autonomous organizations of substructures can easily conflict with the centralized organization of the larger social structure.[3] Thus operations in the professional departments of a bureaucratic organization are expected to be governed by professional

---

[3] Perhaps this conflict is most likely to occur in federations of originally independent units rather than in organizations whose subunits emerged as the result of internal differentiation. For the distinction, see Amitai Etzioni, "The Epigenesis of Political Communities at the International Level," *American Journal of Sociology*, 68 (1963), 406–421.

standards, but professional requirements recurrently conflict with the administrative requirements of the organization as a whole. The executive departments and agencies constituting elements of a country's political organization sometimes come into conflict with each other and with the central government itself. This occurs because their policies are partly determined by the requirements their specialized functions impose and not exclusively by directives from the central political authority, which means that they have some autonomy. Disagreements among the different branches of the military establishment and between the military establishment and the Administration illustrate this point. The basic principle is that the effectiveness of the total organization depends on the effective discharge of specialized functions by its various departments, which necessitates sufficient functional autonomy of the departments to permit them to organize operations in terms of their own requirements.[4] Hence, the centralized direction in a legitimate organization is generally complemented by a minimum of autonomy of the organization's functional segments. Gouldner has noted that the autonomy of component parts of organized social systems serves as a catalyst for social change, since autonomous substructures are, in effect, exogenous social forces contained within the social structure to which the structure must continually adjust.[5]

Opposition ideals that have wide appeal divide a collectivity into conflicting camps but simultaneously unite many subgroups in a common cause. From the perspective of the social structure, the opposition ideology is a divisive force, and it promotes departures from established social values and norms. From the perspective of the substructures, it is a unifying force not only among the supporters of the opposition movement but also among those who rally to defeat it, and it engenders strict conformity with accepted social values and norms. Radical nonconformists with society's prevailing values are often rigid conformists with the values of their ingroup. While revolutionary ideals and beliefs deny the legitimacy of the existing social order, they also provide a new foundation for legitimate authority and organization in the opposition substructure.

In sum, as soon as social structures and their substructures are considered, it becomes apparent that the analysis of social values must take into account their compass, that is, the range of organized social

---

[4] See Alvin W. Gouldner, "Reciprocity and Autonomy in Functional Theory," in Llewellyn Gross, *Symposium on Sociological Theory,* Evanston: Row, Peterson, 1959, pp. 241–270.

[5] *Ibid.,* pp. 263–266.

relations in the system to which the values refer, because differences in this compass often completely alter the structural implications of the same value standard. Diverse universalistic standards in various groups constitute a particularistic standard in the wider social structure that encompasses them. Universalistic standards of social achievement and status in the broader social structure may become transformed into particularistic symbols of social solidarity in its stratified substructures. The values and norms that legitimate centralized authority and organization and those that legitimate the autonomy of suborganizations frequently come into conflict. Beliefs that constitute deviant opposition ideals from the perspective of the community are legitimating values from the perspective of the opposition movement within it.

The interdependence between the macrostructure and its substructures can be further analyzed by tracing the interrelations among three facets of social structure—integration, differentiation, and organization—on these two levels. Specifically, nine connections will be examined, namely, how integration, differentiation, and organization of substructures is related to each of the same three factors of the macrostructure. The fourth facet of social structure, reorganization through opposition, is singled out for special treatment later in this chapter. The nine relationships to be discussed now can be schematically presented in the following form:

Macrostructure

	Integration	Differentiation	Organization
Substructures			
Integration	1. Personal attraction and particularistic solidarity	2. Attachment versus mobility	3. Subgroup loyalty limiting political obligations
Differentiation	4. Crosscutting ties between social strata	5. Intragroup status and intergroup mobility	6. Political elite and subgroup representation
Organization	7. Organizations integrated by cultural values	8. Internal organization and differential success	9. Autonomy and centralized authority and differential success

(1) Social integration in microstructures rests on personal bonds of social attraction, whereas the integrative bonds of social solidarity in macrostructures rest on shared particularistic values. The particularistic values of the larger community diffuse into the face-to-face groups in it and shape the social relations and patterns of conduct of their members, with the result that the daily social relations in various groups reinforce the particularistic values and bonds of solidarity in the community at large. Stinchcombe has called attention to this: "Penetration of primary groups gives larger groups the capacity to socialize loyalty to themselves into deeper levels of the personality. Rewards of primary group life and loyalties to other members of primary groups become resources at the disposal of the larger group." [6] The intensity and compass of the particularistic values of various larger collectivities determine their impact on group life. "Family culture among Jews is more distinctively Jewish than family culture of Presbyterians is distinctively Presbyterian (though the latter is distinctively 'respectable Protestant')." [7] While the cohesive relations in microstructures, which are molded by the particularistic values of the macrostructure, promote the integration of primary groups and their members into the macrostructure, the particularistic values of the different macrostructures within the society as a whole make competing demands for loyalty and social integration. The subcultures of the Protestants and the Presbyterians, of the South and of Texas, of the middle class and of the professional stratum, and the American culture itself, constitute separate particularistic systems, some parallel and some on different levels. Various combinations of these particularistic circles are reflected in actual group life, and the more definitely Texan group allegiances and patterns are, the less distinctively Presbyterian they tend to be.

(2) The social integration in substructures and the social differentiation in the macrostructure raise the problem of social attachment and mobility. Standards of achievement and success universally accepted in the society make individuals interested in moving up to higher social strata if they can, but particularistic attachments to groups and the limitations imposed by the particular value orientations and economic conditions in the lower classes create obstacles to social mobility. Moreover, success in competition among organizations requires that each recruit members in terms of universalistic

---

[6] Arthur L. Stinchcombe, "Social Structure and Organizations" in James March, *Handbook of Organizations,* Chicago: Rand-McNally (forthcoming).
[7] *Loc. cit.*

criteria of merit and qualifications, but the importance of common values for social solidarity introduces particularistic criteria into the recruitment process. The elite of the officer corps has been traditionally recruited from the nobility in Europe and from the higher classes in the United States, although the pattern has changed in recent decades; [8] senior business executives are expected to have assimilated the values and style of life of the upper class; and ideological identification with union values is demanded of union officials. Finally, the particularistic integration of individuals in microstructures, especially their families and intimate circles of friends, furnishes relief from the strains of universalistic competition in the larger community.

(3) Microstructure integration also has implications for the explicit organization of collective endeavors on the macrostructural level, for instance, the political organization of a society. On one hand, the values and norms that legitimate political authority and prompt men to discharge their political obligations are acquired in the process of socialization in families, which derive their permanence and supportive significance from the particularistic bonds of social integration among their members. On the other hand, the profound and diffuse obligations of men to their families set limits to the obligations the larger organized collectivity can impose on them. Although a nation can demand great sacrifices from its citizens in times of war, it is generally recognized that at other times obligations to their families take precedence over political obligations. Indeed, even in times of war an emergency in his family usually justifies a soldier's leave.

(4) The internal differentiation in substructures promotes crosscutting ties between similarly located strata in the various substructures and thus furnishes new bonds of social integration in the larger social structure. The common situation and interests of manual workers in various communities create bonds of social solidarity among them that unify them into a social class, which is a substructure intersecting communities and other collectivities and consequently produces integrative ties along new lines crisscrossing the old ones. The same is true for members of a given profession in various organizations, who have similar concerns with professional problems, standards, and training, and for all occupational groups and strata in differentiated substructures whose members face similar problems and have some common interests. Crosscutting integrative bonds between col-

---

[8] See Morris Janowitz, *The Professional Soldier,* Glencoe: Free Press, 1960, pp. 89–97.

lectivities fortify the solidarity of the entire society. Social differentiation itself gives corresponding strata in different segments of the society some common interests, as Simmel has pointed out:

> After the process of social differentiation has produced a division between the highs and the lows, the purely formal fact that they occupy a given social position creates a connection between the members of the most varied groups, an internal bond, and often also some external relations. Together with such social differentiation in a group grows the need and inclination to expand beyond its original limits in space and in economic and mental life. The original centripetal force in a group is complemented as individual differences create conflicts between its elements by a centrifugal tendency that establishes bridges with other groups.[9]

(5) The relationship between the social differentiation within substructures and their relative positions in the differentiated macrostructure is at the core of the analysis of the dynamics of complex social structures. It poses the central problems of intergroup mobility and intergroup competition. The status of individuals depends in part on the social stratum in which they are generally accepted and in part on the respect and compliance they command within this stratum. Individuals may be confronted by the alternative of occupying either a higher position in a lower stratum (or weaker organization) or a lower one in a higher stratum (or stronger organization). The opportunity for making such decisions and the prevailing decisions made determine the pattern of mobility between substructures and the fluidity of their boundaries within the encompassing social system. Many groups and organizations also compete for a dominant position in the larger social structure, and success in this competition requires a flexible internal status structure that permits an organized collectivity to attract qualified contributors by rewarding them with superior status. These problems of intergroup relations and mobility are more fully analyzed in the next section.

(6) The social differentiation in substructures serves as a recruitment mechanism for the leadership of the political or administrative organization in the larger social structure. The heads of departments are candidates for top executive positions in the organization. Communities and states elect representatives to the national legislature, and other organized collectivities also endeavor to be represented by outstanding members in the legislative and other branches of the government. The government strengthens its legitimate authority by including in its rank leading representatives of various groups endorsed

---

[9] Simmel, *op. cit.*, p. 711 (my translation).

by their members. Besides, individuals who occupy top positions in business enterprises and other organized collectivities often form a power elite that exercises dominant influence, through formal and informal channels, over the organized political and economic life of the community.[10]

(7) The formally organized substructures are integrated into the macrostructure through its pervasive particularistic values. The cultural values of a society legitimate most organizations established in it and the objectives they pursue, and set them apart from illegitimate organizations based on coercive powers or heretical ideals in contravention of cultural values and norms, such as a crime syndicate or an extremist opposition party. (An extremist opposition is illegitimate only as long as it is so defined by prevailing values, and its success in capturing the allegiance of major groups tends to alter this definition.) The cultural values pervade organizations and are reflected in their structure, as exemplified by the difference between the Prussian and American army. The integration of legitimate organizations into the very fabric of society makes them important contributors to its welfare and important elements in defining its course.

(8) The formal organization of collective endeavors in substructures both stimulates and is stimulated by competition among them for scarce resources and a dominant position in the differentiated macrostructure. The immediate object of the competition is social support in some form—firms compete for customers, parties for voters, and religious denominations for converts. Success in this competition gives an organization a dominant, or at least a superior, position in the macrostructure and also has important implications for its internal structure. Successful competition strengthens the legitimate authority of the organization's leadership by validating the leaders' judgment and guidance and by furnishing rewards to members that justify their compliance and increase their loyalty to the organization and its leadership. Conversely, failure in the competition is likely to undermine the authority of an organization's leaders and may promote internal opposition to them. For instance, opposition factions often arise and sometimes gain dominance in a defeated political party. Failure, moreover, encourages defections of members to other, more successful organizations, further weakening the organization. In brief, the internal organization of substructures is strongly affected by their competitive position in the differentiated larger social structure.

---

[10] See Floyd Hunter, *Community Power Structure*, Chapel Hill: University of North Carolina Press, 1953.

(9) Finally, the main problem concerning the relationship between the organized units within a larger system and its overall organization under a central authority is that of the degree of autonomy of the units and the degree of centralized control exercised over them. The autonomy of an organization depends on freedom from domination by other organizations as well as by superordinate authorities. Centralized political authority is often exercised to limit the autonomy of some organizations in order to protect that of others, as exemplified by antimonopoly legislation, or to prevent an organized authority from suppressing the legitimate autonomy of its subordinate units, as illustrated by actions of the federal government and courts prohibiting states from interfering with the civil rights of Negroes or other minorities. The conflict between the legitimate political authority of the macrostructure and that of its major substructures resembles and can easily turn into a conflict between legitimate organization and organized opposition to it; an example was the States Rights party formed in 1948 that crystallized the opposition of Southern states.

Even this simplified analysis of the relationships between social integration, differentiation, and organization on only two levels of social structure indicates the complex interdependence between substructures. The problems outlined are intended merely as illustrations of the type of analysis that would be required, in much more extensive form, for the development of a systematic theory of macrostructures.

Intergroup Relations and Mobility

The relations between groups differ, of course, from those between individuals. One fundamental distinction is illustrated by the difference in implications between the rejection of a group by other groups and the rejection of an individual by other individuals. The isolated individual who is ostracized by his fellows is seriously penalized by being deprived of social companionship and rewards and is under strong pressure to find some social acceptance either in other groups or by modifying his behavior and becoming reintegrated in this one, if possible. The minority group toward which the other groups in the community express hostility, however, is not penalized in this form, whatever other disadvantages the discrimination of the majority against it may have. To be sure, the individual member of the minority group rejected by the members of other groups also is in need of alternative sources of social companionship and support, but these are readily available to him from other members of his own group. Hence, integrative ties of social cohesion tend to be particularly strong in rejected groups, fortifying resistance against majority pressure in these minorities, in contrast to the situation of the isolated individual deprived of social ties, whose vulnerable position weakens resistance against majority pressure unless he can find some new social support.[11] As Durkheim has pointed out, ". . . when religious intolerance is very pronounced, it often produces an opposite effect. Instead of exciting the dissenters to respect opinion more, it accustoms them to disregard it." [12] Sumner's famous observation that ingroup solidarity is associated with hostility toward the outgroup [13] may actually often be a spurious correlation due to the fact that the hosility of the outgroup toward the ingroup fosters both ingroup cohesion and counter-hostility toward the outgroup.

Another distinctive characteristic of intergroup relations is that they involve mobility of individuals from group to group. Many collectivities have fluid boundaries; they expand and contract with the flow of members and supporters into and out of them. Employees are laid off by some firms and hired by others; workers join unions; voters shift political support to another party; customers frequent different stores; successful individuals rise to higher social strata, and unsuccessful ones drop to lower strata. The major patterns of these movements redefine the boundaries of the substructures in the macrostructure and modify their internal structures. The origin of these patterns of mobility is also found in the interrelated status structures.

Membership in various collectivities is not equally rewarding, which is one factor that promotes mobility between them. The rewards derived from group membership can be analytically divided into two components, the basic advantages that accrue to all members, and the additional rewards that are differentially distributed within the group. The basic rewards offered by various collectivities differ. For instance, living conditions are more pleasant in some communities than in others, the prestige that acceptance in a social stratum commands in the community at large varies with the rank of the stratum, the wage rates of all firms are not the same, membership in some management groups gives a person more power than that in others,

---

[11] Solomon E. Asch's well-known experiment indicates that even social support from one other person strengthens resistance to majority pressures; *Social Psychology*, New York: Prentice-Hall, 1952, chapter xvi, esp. pp. 477–479.

[12] Emile Durkheim, *Suicide*, Glencoe: Free Press, 1951, p. 156.

[13] William G. Sumner, *Folkways*, Boston: Ginn, 1907, pp. 12–13. See also Robert K. Merton's criticism of Sumner's dictum, *Social Theory and Social Structure* (2d ed.), Glencoe: Free Press, 1957, pp. 297–299.

and even the social support obtained in informal fellowship depends on a group's cohesion. In terms of this factor alone, all individuals have equal incentives to move to the most rewarding collectivity in which they can find acceptance.

The differential distribution of rewards associated with the status structure in a collectivity, however, alters the situation, creating differences in incentives for mobility between members. The superior rewards received by high-status members give them least incentive to leave their present collectivity for another, and the inferior rewards received by low-status members give them most incentive to do so. In terms of these conditions, assuming others for the moment to be constant, the pattern of mobility between collectivities would be governed by the relationship between the rewards low-status members obtain in their present collectivities and those they could obtain for the same contributions in others. This situation is analogous to the movement of firms between industries depending on whether the profits in any one are above or below the general norm. "If the profits of the least profitable firm are less than normal, this firm and others in like case will eventually leave the industry. . . . If, on the other hand, the least profitable firm is making profits above normal, . . . there will be a tendency for new firms to come in, and the industry will expand." [14] Correspondingly, collectivities in which minimum rewards are less than they are elsewhere are likely to lose members, and those in which minimum contributions command greater rewards than elsewhere are likely to attract members from other collectivities.

The actual mobility of individuals depends, of course, not only on their incentives to move but also on their capabilities of doing so. While inferior status in a collectivity gives members most reason to want to leave it for another, superior status in it creates the greatest opportunities and potentialities for moving into another collectivity that promises higher rewards. The access the leaders and others of superior rank, who represent a collectivity in its relations with others, have to other collectivities,[15] and their superior qualifications, to which their position testifies, give them disproportionate chances of rising to and being welcomed in more desirable collectivities than their present one. The superior position the group bestows on some of its

---

[14] Kenneth E. Boulding, *Economic Analysis* (3d ed.), New York: Harper, 1955, p. 566.

[15] On the tendency of leaders to associate with leaders of other groups, see William F. Whyte, *Street Corner Society* (2d ed.), University of Chicago Press, 1955, p. 214.

members helps them to move out of it into other groups of higher standing in the community. The middle stratum in a collectivity, therefore, tends to constitute its solid core of members who neither have much reason for wanting to leave it nor much tempting potential for doing so. Whether members in top or bottom positions are most likely to move voluntarily from one collectivity to others depends on the type of value standard that governs its status structure.

The internal differentiation of status and the associated distribution of rewards in substructures may be based on standards that are, from the perspective of the encompassing social structure, universalistic or particularistic, although these standards are, by definition, universalistic within the narrower compass of each substructure, that is, they are generally accepted criteria of achievement *within the subgroup*. If internal status in substructures is governed by standards universally accepted as valid throughout the macrostructure, as is typical for criteria of instrumental performance, superior internal status indicates assets that are valued in other collectivities too. Hence, individuals in superior positions within collectivities have the best chance of moving to more desirable collectivities, and those in inferior positions move only when they are pushed out and down. The mobility of successful managers of smaller concerns to larger ones illustrates this, as does vertical mobility between socio-economic strata. If, however, internal status in substructures rests on diverse standards that are particularistic from the perspective of the macrostructure, the higher a person's status is in one collectivity, the less likely are his qualifications to make him acceptable in another with different value standards. Not the most devoted Republican but the most alienated one makes the best candidate for the Socialist party. The very behavior that stamps a person a poor Catholic makes him attractive among atheists. Under these conditions, the individuals who command little social recognition and few rewards in their own collectivities have the best chance of improving their situation by moving to other collectivities with contrasting value standards and are most likely to do so of their own volition.

Vertical mobility between social strata that are internally differentiated and hierarchically ranked in the macrostructure in terms of the same universalistic standards of achievement and status regularly confronts individuals with the choice of being either a big fish in a little pond or a little fish in a big pond. The alternatives are whether to use one's capacities and achievements in order to sustain a superordinate rather than a subordinate position in daily social intercourse or in order to attain and maintain social affiliation with the highest hierarchical stratum possible. Some full professors associate extensively with their junior colleagues, thereby loosening their affiliation with the senior faculty but increasing the respect and deference they receive in recurrent social interaction. The juniors who associate with them gain social, and sometimes material, advantages from this affiliation with high-status colleagues but must assume a subordinate role in much of their social life, which they would not have to do were they to associate mostly with their own peers. Whyte showed that some corner boys in the Italian slum he studied used their money and resources to achieve a superordinate position in their gang, and others used their resources to increase their chances of moving up to a higher social stratum.[16] A person who changes his class affiliation to his own advantage tends thereby to change his prevailing pattern of social interaction to his disadvantage, and the person who is willing to assume a more disadvantageous stratum position typically improves his role in his everyday life.

The fundamental choice underlying the question of the relative size of fish and pond is the one between the privileges affiliation with a superior social stratum bestows on individuals and the rewards they derive from assuming a superordinate role in recurrent social intercourse. Occupational achievement and success enable a person to command a position of respect and power among his old associates, whom he can obligate to defer to his wishes with his generosity. His superordinate role in interaction with them continually rewards him for his achievement and reminds him of his success by contrast with their less fortunate position.[17] These advantages must be foregone in large part by persons who want to use their economic achievements to become affiliated with a more privileged social stratum than that in which they originated. Affiliation with a higher stratum requires that a person gain acceptance among its members by adopting their style of life and that he associate mostly with them rather than with his old friends. But in these new associations he does not occupy a

---

[16] *Ibid.*, pp. 104–108.

[17] Marcel Proust has called attention to the significance of maintaining some old social ties in order to keep the experience of successful social mobility alive: ". . . she knew that a great deal of the pleasure which a woman finds in entering a class of society different from that in which she has previously lived would be lacking if she had no means of keeping her old associates informed of those others, relatively more brilliant, with whom she has replaced them. Therefore, she requires an eye-witness who may be allowed to penetrate this new, delicious world. . . ." *Remembrance of Things Past*, New York: Random House, 1934, Vol. I, 394.

superordinate position and may have to take a subordinate one, at least, initially, inasmuch as the economic resources of his new associates are generally as large as his and their social position is of longer standing and more firmly established than his.

Occupational failure confronts individuals with parallel alternatives. The advantages of continued affiliation with their original social stratum must be paid for by individuals who cannot any longer properly repay social obligations in these circles by assuming a subordinate role in social life and being recurrently reminded of their deprivation and failure. These hardships are avoided by economically unsuccessful persons who cut their social ties and associate mostly with members of a less privileged stratum than that in which they originated, and this is a compensating advantage for the cost entailed in downward social mobility. To be sure, the alternatives of the successful entail two kinds of social gratification, and those of the unsuccessful, two kinds of social deprivation, but both must choose between greater stratum privileges and greater rewards from daily social intercourse. Another factor to be taken into consideration is the cost of social mobility itself, regardless of direction, which involves abandoning established social attachments and adapting to new social situations.

The receiving collectivity has an interest in accepting the upwardly mobile for two reasons. First, it seeks to recruit new members with the qualifications to make contributions to its welfare. This is of evident importance in groups organized to accomplish instrumental tasks, such as management groups of business concerns, but other social segments typically contain instrumental components that make it also relevant. Thus upwardly mobile individuals often gain initial entry into the upper class by making contributions to its instrumental activities, for instance, by contributing to its philanthropic and charitable enterprises. Second, the deferential role individuals who have recently moved up into a higher social stratum generally must assume in interaction with its established members, to gain full social acceptance, is a significant source of social reward for the established members. This deference fortifies the superiority of the higher stratum by furnishing continual evidence of the high price others are willing to pay for acceptance in this stratum.[18] Large-scale upward mobility

---

[18] The downwardly mobile are not recruited into the social class or segment that receives them, but its members may also derive advantages from accepting them in their midst and associating with them. Those with superior education and qualifications who for some reason have been downwardly mobile may make

into a privileged stratum, however, may endanger the privileged position of its established families and, consequently, tends to be resisted by them. A typical manifestation of this resistance is the Brahmin's complaint against the vulgarization of the cultivated tastes and manners of the upper class by the *nouveau riche*.

The free flow of intergroup mobility adjusts the substructures in a macrostructure. Collectivities that have excessive resources for rewarding members for their contributions attract new members and expand, and those with insufficient resources for adequate rewards repel some of their own members and contract. The differentiation of power that is an essential element of the stratified structure, however, impedes these processes, because powerful individuals and groups tend to have the desire and capacity to perpetuate their positions and transfer them to their progeny by restricting access to these positions, if only by giving their children disproportionately great chances of occupying them. The actual situation, therefore, is intermediate between the model of completely free mobility and the polar case of absolutely rigid boundaries that preclude all mobility. Castes come close to this last extreme, and so do most total societies today, since mobility between them is inconsequential.

Adjustment in a social structure with rigid boundaries differs fundamentally from that in one where mobility out of and into it occurs. If there are insufficient rewards for the contributions its members are capable of making in a collectivity from which they cannot move to another, internal adjustments are the only ones possible. The situation is analogous to an economic depression, when consumption plus investment fail to absorb the entire capacity to produce and unemployment results. Classical economic theory assumes these conditions will depress prices and thus lead to automatic adjustments. Keynes, in contrast, held that active intervention by the government in the form of economic investments having multiplier effects is necessary for adjustments to occur and for employment to rise.[19] Keynes' theory has interesting implications for social structure.

If the members of a society, or any collectivity with rigid boundaries, cannot obtain sufficient rewards for their contributions, actual

---

superior contributions and provide opposition leadership for the less privileged group; indeed, the opportunity to do so may have prompted their downward mobility. Besides, many individuals derive satisfaction from associating with a person of superior social origins, say, with a former member of the nobility who still uses his title though it has been abolished.

[19] See Boulding, *op. cit.*, pp. 300–305; the original reference is John M. Keynes, *General Theory of Employment, Interest and Money*, New York: Harcourt, Brace, 1936.

or potential, some adjustments have to be made internally. According to classical theory, individuals will furnish contributions for lesser rewards and thus promote adjustments. According to Keynes, however, the situation will become aggravated and stagnation will result unless new investments that stimulate growth are made through the intervention of an agency outside the system. Since concern is with an entire society, the agency that introjects the new stimuli can be outside the system only in an analytical sense. In the case of the economy in a depression, it is the political system of the same society that introduces the new investments. In the case of a social structure with insufficient rewards for contributions, it is the emergence of an opposition movement that produces new investments. Opposition ideals generate new investments within the society though analytically originating outside the existing social system, because they create new social rewards, new social resources by inspiring men with fresh energies, and a new organized collectivity for mobilizing these resources within the society. A major opposition movement, therefore, can be considered an external investment designed to regenerate a stagnant social structure, just as major governmental expenditures are external investments designed to reactivate a depressed economy.

Opposition as Regenerative Force

Opposition is a regenerative force that introjects new vitality into a social structure and becomes the basis of social reorganization. It serves as a catalyst or starting mechanism of social change, which is sometimes carried out in large part by others rather than those active in the opposition that stimulated it. There are tendencies toward change in social structures that do not depend on opposition movements, such as those generated by technological developments. But there are also structural rigidities due to vested interests and powers, organizational commitments, and traditional institutions. These defy modification and adjustment except through social conflict and opposition. What Merton has said about bureaucracy applies, to a lesser degree, to the institutionalized sentiments and forces that sustain the traditional social order in general. "There is a margin of safety, so to speak, in the pressure exerted by these sentiments upon the bureaucrat to conform to his patterned obligations, in much the same sense that added allowances (precautionary overestimations) are made by the engineer in designing the supports of a bridge." [20]

---

[20] Merton, *op. cit.*, p. 199.

Institutionalized patterns, in their form as internalized sentiments and in their external manifestations invested with power, assure the stability and survival of the existing social order with a great margin of safety, which prevents adjustments and adaptations when new circumstances call for them. Traditional values often transform social arrangements instituted for a specific purpose under given historical conditions into sacred symbols that must be preserved, even though they can no longer serve this purpose effectively under different conditions. Powers with vested interests in such obsolete arrangements—for instance, the electoral college for choosing the U.S. President—are greatly aided in their defense of them by these legitimating institutional values. This process through which means become ends-in-themselves illustrates the displacement of goals, which Merton described for bureaucracies in the passage immediately following the one just quoted. Opposition movements constitute countervailing forces against these institutional rigidities, rooted in vested powers as well as traditional values, and they are essential for speeding social change.

Opposition is here conceived as a generic social force, which takes many different forms, a revolutionary political movement being only one of them. It is a type of conflict, differing from other types in that one of the parties represents "The Establishment" and holds the dominant legitimate power against which the other or others struggle. A fundamentally new style in the arts and a new school of thought in a scholarly discipline illustrate forms of opposition; so do innovating firms that challenge the dominant powers in a market, movements of civic reform, challenges of a stockholder group against the corporation management, factions challenging the union leadership, as well as more or less extremist rebellions against the political order. The distinctive characteristic of social opposition is organized collective dissent and action against an established order.

On an abstract theoretical level, opposition can be conceptualized in terms of the conflict between autonomy and interdependence of substructures in a macrostructure. Gouldner has stressed that varying degrees of both autonomy and interdependence must be taken into account in the analysis of parts in a social system.[21] This important point should be refined by explicitly distinguishing two kinds of interrelations within a system. First, substructures are dependent on each other, which means that changes in one lead to changes in the others. This kind of interdependence has its source in the relative

---

[21] Gouldner, *op. cit.*, pp. 254–259.

autonomy of substructures and does not conflict with such autonomy, except when one of them becomes a dominant power that can and does organize the others in accordance with its interests. This situation resembles analytically the second kind of interdependence, which involves the dependence of the substructures, not on each other, but on the larger social structure, because a centralized authority in the larger collectivity coordinates and directs the major courses of action in its subgroups.[22] It is this second type of interdependence of the component parts due to centralized control in the system that directly conflicts with their autonomy. The conflict is inevitable, since both some centralized coordination and some autonomy of parts are necessary for organized collectivities. Movements that mobilize opposition to the established organization by drawing together dissatisfied elements into a new substructure are grounded in the latent opposition of existing subgroups inherent in this conflict.

On a less abstract level, the social conditions that give rise to active opposition forces have already been discussed and need only be briefly summarized here. Organizing collective effort involves exerting constraints and may easily lead to the oppression of some groups in the interest of the larger collectivity or its dominant members. Powerful groups and organizations can exploit others, and great social distances encourage them to take advantage of this ability. The actual rewards of most people frequently fall short of the high expectations of achievement and success created by cultural values in the process of legitimating existing institutions, which produces frustrations and deprivations. The common experience of oppression and exploitation in a group, notably one somewhat isolated from the rest of the community, promotes communications that socially justify and reinforce the feeling of outrage and the desire to retaliate against the powers held responsible for the frustrations and deprivations suffered. The

---

[22] The difference between these two types of relations between social structures in a macrostructure corresponds to two types of functional relationships between variables that Lazarsfeld has distinguished—a direct causal relationship between two variables and a spurious correlation due to the causal influence of a third. In the first type of interdependence, substructures exert a causal influence on each other. In the second type, however, the relations between them are spurious in a technical sense, that is, they are not due to direct causal influences among them but to the causal influence of the coordinating authority in the macrostructure on all of them. (Needless to add, the distinction is an analytical one, and both types of interdependence occur simultaneously.) See Patricia L. Kendall and Paul F. Lazarsfeld, "Problems of Survey Analysis," in Merton and Lazarsfeld, *Continuities of Social Research,* Glencoe: Free Press, 1950, pp. 147–167.

group in which such orientations crystallize and develop into an opposition ideology may become the core of an opposition movement to which others with similar social experiences rally.

This, however, is only the extreme case of opposition, which is duplicated in a large variety of milder forms whenever individuals and groups who share feelings of dissatisfaction with existing conditions join together in common endeavors to improve these conditions by opposing the powers that perpetuate them and by advocating reforms to alleviate the dissatisfactions.[23] Whereas revolutionary movements occasionally produce profound upheavals and transformations, it is the multitude of recurrently emerging and subsiding, less extreme, oppositions of diverse sorts that produces continual social change and reorganization in societies. Opposition activates conflict by giving overt social expression to latent disagreements and hostilities, but it also helps to remove the sources of these conflicts. It is a disturbing and divisive force that ultimately contributes to social stability and cohesion. For major cleavages that fundamentally disrupt society are most likely to occur precisely when recurrent oppositions have been suppressed and conflicts have smoldered. Ross has called attention to this:

> In a way, *open opposition preserves society*. . . . Protest affords relief, gives us the feeling that we are not completely crushed in a relationship which otherwise we would find unendurable, and from which we should extricate ourselves at any cost. In any volunteer association the corking up by the dominant element of the protest and opposition of the rest is likely to lead to the splitting of the group. Shrewd statesmen realize that it is well to tolerate criticism of government in parliament and in the press as a vaccine against revolt. Free remonstrance is a safety valve, letting off steam which, if confined, might blow up the boiler.[24]

The new social arrangements instituted by successful opposition forces, or by established authorities in self-defense against the gathering opposition, typically create new dissatisfactions in due course, stimulating opposition anew. Social change is a dialectical process, because any form of social organization is likely to engender problems and conflicts that call for some reorganization. Oppositions arise, successful ones reorganize patterns of social life in accordance with their

---

[23] Oppression and exploitation are held here to be important sources of opposition, but it is not assumed that all opposition is a reaction to oppression and exploitation.

[24] Edward A. Ross, *Principles of Sociology* (2d ed.), New York: Century, 1930, p. 151 (italics in original).

program and interests, the reformed social order has disadvantageous consequences for other groups, and sometimes even unanticipated disadvantages for parts of the very groups that have instituted it, providing incentives for fresh oppositions. The process, however, is not circular, because social reorganizations never fully recreate the past, although they often incorporate elements of previously existing forms of organization. The government of Western Germany resembles the Weimar Republic more than the Nazi regime, but it differs from both.

A crucial problem is posed by the fact that an opposition that achieves success, perhaps only after extended struggle imposing serious hardships on its members, has a strong interest in protecting the power it finally has attained by suppressing opposition to it. This tendency is particularly pronounced in collectivities engaged in conflict with others. Union leaders justify their suppression of opposition factions by the need for solidarity in the struggles with employers, and governments of nations at war similarly justify their suppression of dissent and civil liberties by the need for unity in the face of common danger. Generally, the freedom of opposition and dissent can only persevere under firm institutional protection, since the dominant group gains advantages from and thus has an interest in suppressing resistance and opposition.

Democracy entails the institutionalization of opposition forces in the political arena, which perpetuates stable mechanisms for expressing political conflict and instituting social change. It is a paradoxical institution, inasmuch as it preserves stable forms of political arrangements designed to facilitate recurrent modifications in political and social arrangements. The basic paradox is that the freedom of dissent and opposition constituting the very foundation of democracy must surely include the right to advocate the suppression of dissent and opposition. Whereas the freedom to advocate such totalitarian principles cannot be denied without surrendering the basic premise of democracy, democracy cannot survive unless the electorate denies those who advocate them access to political power. Hence, the persistence of democratic institutions depends, to a still greater degree than that of other institutions, on being supported by moral values and norms that are deeply ingrained in the consciousness of the people. Even the most democratic constitution and other external institutions are to no avail if unsupported by profound democratic values accepted throughout the society, as history has often shown, the Weimar Republic being a conspicuous example. Another mainstay of stable democracy is the existence of many cross-cutting conflicts and overlapping oppositions in the society.

Multigroup affiliations of the members of a society promote many intersecting conflicts and opposition forces, which forestall the development of intense hostility between two opposing camps that might easily tear the society asunder and lead to the destruction of democratic institutions. Coleman has analyzed the implications for conflict of the existence of many voluntary associations and organized groups with interlocking memberships in a community.[25] Conflict over social issues in modern communities occurs largely between organized groups, not between isolated individuals, and if the issue is of wide significance, most organized collectivities are under pressure to take a stand. The greater the density of associations and organizations in a community, therefore, the greater the chances are that a large proportion of the population will be drawn into conflicts of various sorts. At the same time, however, a high organizational density implies that most men in the community belong to several organizations, and these interlocking memberships mitigate the severity of conflict, particularly if many organizations have memberships from diverse social segments and classes in the community.

When organized groups take opposing sides in a controversy, interlocking memberships make it likely that many individuals are pulled toward both sides by different associations to which they belong. Under these conditions, several associations on both sides include some members who have considerable sympathy for the opposing viewpoint, because they also belong to groups that have taken the opposite stand. The mental conflict experienced by individuals under cross pressure from different organizations of which they are members and that have taken opposite stands on an issue dissipates, so to speak, part of the conflict between the two sides and makes it less intense, and so does the conflict that occurs within the various groups on each side. A collectivity is restrained from viewing the opposition with great hostility and from taking extreme action against it if some of its own members have close associates in the opposition and, in some respects, belong themselves to it. Without cross affiliations, conflicts tend to be cumulative as many involve the same split in the community, and the predominant communications within each opposition camp may lead to intense hostility and endeavors not merely to defeat the opposition but to destroy it.

---

[25] James S. Coleman, *Community Conflict*, Glencoe: Free Press, 1957, pp. 21–23. See also Lewis A. Coser, *The Functions of Social Conflict*, Glencoe: Free Press, 1956, pp. 72–80. See also Ralf Dahrendorf, *Class and Class Conflict in Industrial Society*, Stanford University Press, 1959, esp. pp. 206–218.

Many intersecting organized collectivities in a society, then, create diverse crisscrossing conflicts that discourage deep cleavages for several reasons. As a large proportion of the adults in a society are recurrently drawn into conflicts by their organizational affiliations, deep-seated resentments are less likely to accumulate. If both sides in a conflict include numerous individuals with close associates and group affiliations on the other side, each side is constrained to grant the legitimacy of the opponent and to conduct the contest according to rules of fair play, whereas the absence of social ties and communication between adversaries often leads to a social image of the opponent as a worthless enemy of society and an orientation of all-out war in which the ends justify the means. Lipset has noted the importance of such crosscutting social ties between major political parties and between them and various social segments for political tolerance and stable democracy.[26] Overlapping conflicts that recurrently regroup the community into opposing factions along different lines prevent its division into two antagonistic camps that come to take opposite stands on virtually every issue as a matter of principle. The likely results of such a split into two antagonistic camps would be that grievances become cumulative and reinforce each other, hostilities grow more and more intense, and there is increasing social pressure to the effect that any means is justified to vanquish the enemy, which is the very orientation that is incompatible with the survival of democratic institutions.[27] Cross pressures, finally, lessen partisan involvement, incline individuals to arbitrate controversies, and make conflicts generally less severe.

The cross pressures of multigroup affiliations and the cross currents of conflicts that reduce the intensity and violence of opposition forces protect democratic institutions against destruction by heated partisanship, but they simultaneously protect other institutions and the existing power structure from being fundamentally transformed by a radical opposition movement with a firmly committed membership. Overlapping oppositions that deter a major opposition force from gathering strength serve important functions for stable democracy. They do so, however, at a social cost that is paid by the most oppressed social classes who would benefit from radical changes in the

---

[26] Seymour M. Lipset, *Political Man,* Garden City: Doubleday, 1960, pp. 31–32, 88–92.

[27] Major dysfunctions of the caste-like segregation between Negroes and whites in the South are that it prevents cross-affiliations, makes conflicts cumulative, and leads to their suppression until they finally explode in violent battles that threaten law and order as well as democratic processes.

status quo. Cross pressures reduce democratic participation in elec-tions,[28] and lower socio-economic strata vote in smaller proportions than higher strata, quite possibly because the lower strata are subject to greater cross pressures than the higher. Lipset has suggested that ". . . the lower strata in every society are influenced by their life experiences and their class organizations to favor those parties which advocate social and economic reforms, but at the same time they are exposed to strong upper-class and conservative influences through the press, radio, schools, churches, and so forth. . . . Members of the more well-to-do classes, on the other hand, are seldom exposed to equivalent sets of cross-pressures." [29]

Low election turnout reflects the absence of intense partisanship and violent opposition sentiments. It is, therefore, a sign of underlying forces that further the stability of democratic institutions, although the low political participation itself does undoubtedly not contribute to democracy. The argument that a low rate of voting indicates satis-faction with political and social conditions seems utterly untenable in view of the fact that voting is more prevalent in higher than in lower social classes (quite aside from the point previously made that such a low rate reveals a weakness of the political obligations of democratic citizenship). For if it were satisfaction that primarily prompts people to stay away from the polls, the richer people would do so in greater numbers than the poorer ones, whereas the reverse is actually the case. The low political participation of sharecroppers and farm laborers can hardly be attributed to the satisfactory condi-tions under which they live. The cross pressures manifest in weak partisanship and low turnout in elections do serve important functions for democratic stability, but the fact that they disproportionately affect the lower socio-economic strata creates undemocratic inequities in political representation.[30] Those segments in the society that have

---

[28] For several empirical studies demonstrating this conclusion, see *ibid.,* pp. 203–216.

[29] *Ibid.,* p. 205. Although organizational affiliations are more prevalent in the middle class than in the working class, middle-class affiliations are more likely to reinforce each other rather than create crosspressures.

[30] Edgar Litt found that civics courses and leaders in a working-class commu-nity emphasized less than those in a middle-class community the importance of political participation and the significance of politics as a process of power through which conflicts between groups are resolved and that, consequently, these courses produced a more realistic attitude to politics in students only in the middle-class town; "Civic Education, Community Norms, and Political Indoc-trination," *American Sociological Review,* 28 (1963), 69–75.

most reason to be dissatisfied and to favor changes in the *status quo* are most discouraged by these pressures from giving political expression to their views. Crosscutting conflicts fortify democratic institutions at the expense of the most oppressed social strata, whose political influence they diminish.

Conclusions

A systematic theory of social structure must analyze the interrelations between attributes of a macrostructure and those of its substructures on different levels. At this point, it was only possible to adumbrate the general directions such a theory would be expected to follow. One principle suggested is that the structural implications of given value standards depend on the compass of organized social relations they include. Particularistic standards integrate substructures and create segregating boundaries between them in the macrostructure. What is a particularistic criterion from the perspective of the macrostructure may constitute diverse universalistic criteria within the narrower compass of its substructures. Universalistic values differentiating social strata in the macrostructure often become the basis of particularistic values that further social integration and solidarity within each stratum. There is a conflict between the legitimate centralized authority in organizations and the legitimate autonomy of its component parts. Deviant opposition ideals constitute legitimate values from the narrower perspective of the opposition movement itself and, if it is successful, also from the long-range perspective of the future.[31]

The interrelations between three facets of social structure—integration, differentiation, and organization—on two levels have been outlined. Without recapitulating the nine interrelations discussed and summarized in a chart (p. 289), the basic ways in which this analysis needs to be extended should be pointed out. A larger number of more refined attributes of social structure than these few broad categories should be taken into account. More than two levels of structure and substructures should be considered. Structural constraints that do not emanate from social values should be dealt with to a much greater extent. Of special importance would be the treatment of more complex relationships between attributes, notably the significance of the

---

[31] Karl Mannheim's concept "utopia" refers to opposition ideals that are actually to be realized in the future and become the basis of a new legitimate social order; *Ideology and Utopia*, New York: Harcourt, Brace, 1936, pp. 173–179.

variance between and within substructures in respect to a given attribute for the larger structure, and the interaction effects of several attributes on one level for attributes on another level, which would indicate the significance of the *Gestalt* of one level for the other. These conceptual formulations must, of course, be tested in empirical research.

The mobility of individuals between social segments and organizations in a society may be considered the core of the relations between substructures in a macrostructure, through which the internal structures as well as their boundaries in the larger system are continually modified. Differences between collectivities in the rewards furnished for comparable contributions provide incentives for mobility, although social attachments and the restrictions powerful groups impose on entry create restraints that depress mobility below the extent that would exist under perfect competition. If the standards of performance governing the internal differentiation of status in a collectivity are particularistic from the perspective of the larger social system, as is the case for religious groups, low-status members are most likely to move, but if they are universalistic throughout the system, as exemplified by instrumental achievement or financial success, high-status members are most likely to move voluntarily, and low-status ones do so only involuntarily. The latter situation of vertical social mobility often confronts individuals with the choice between a superior position within a lower social stratum or an inferior position within a higher one. The underlying alternatives are, on the one hand, the rewards derived from occupying a superordinate position in recurrent social interaction and, on the other, the greater advantages obtained from membership in a higher social stratum, the cost of which is that a subordinate position must be assumed in daily social life.

Opposition is a regenerative social force. It acts as a countervailing power against institutional rigidities and serves as a catalyst for social change and reorganization. A major opposition movement can be analytically conceived of as an external investment that reinvigorates an ossified social structure, just as major governmental expenditures are external investments that stimulate activity in a stagnant economy. The crosscutting conflicts and oppositions in complex modern societies, with many intersecting organized collectivities and interlocking memberships in them, are a continual source of social reorganization and change. The pattern of change is dialectical, since each basic reorganization has wide repercussions that create new problems and stimulate fresh oppositions.

The cross pressures resulting from multigroup affiliations and the recurrent realignments of overlapping collectivities in different controversies prevent conflicts over issues from becoming cumulative and producing a deep cleavage between two hostile camps. The intense animosity generated between two strong opposition forces that are isolated from one another and have accumulated grievances endangers democratic institutions, because it encourages an orientation that denies the legitimacy of the opposition, an inclination to resort to violence, and a willingness to sacrifice democratic principles and other moral standards in the all-important struggle. The cross pressures and cross currents of conflicts that forestall such a deep split in the society, therefore, protect its democratic institutions, but they do so at the expense of the most disadvantaged social classes. For the political participation of the lower socio-economic strata is most adversely affected by cross pressures, robbing the very groups most in need of giving voice to opposition sentiments of much of their power to do so.

Dialectical Forces

Thus dialectics reduced itself to the science of the general laws of motion—both of the external world and of human thought—two sets of laws which are identical in substance, but differ in their expression in so far as the human mind can apply them consciously, while in nature and also up to now for the most part in human history, these laws assert themselves unconsciously in the form of external necessity in the midst of an endless series of seeming accidents. Thereby the dialectic of the concept itself became merely the conscious reflex of the dialectical motion of the real world and the dialectic of Hegel was placed upon its head; or rather turned off its head, on which it was standing before, and placed upon its feet again.

FRIEDRICH ENGELS, *Ludwig Feuerbach*

Two fundamental questions can be asked in the analysis of inter-personal relations, what attracts individuals to the association and whether their transactions are symmetrical or not. The first distinction is that between associations that participants experience as intrinsi-cally rewarding, as in love relations, and social interactions in which individuals engage to obtain some extrinsic benefits, as in instrumen-tal cooperation. Extrinsic benefits are, in principle, detachable from their social source—that is, the persons who supply them—and thus furnish external criteria for choosing between associates, for example, for deciding which colleague to ask for advice. No such objective criteria of comparison exist when an association is an end-in-itself, since the fused rewards that make it intrinsically attractive cannot be separated from the association itself. The second distinction is that

312

between reciprocal and unilateral social transactions. Cross classification of these two dimensions yields four types of associations between persons:

	Intrinsic	*Extrinsic*
Reciprocal	Mutual attraction	Exchange
Unilateral	One–sided attachment	Power

The structures of social associations in groups and societies can also be analyzed in terms of two underlying dimensions. In this case, the first question is whether particularistic or universalistic standards govern the pattern of social relations and orientations in a collectivity. That is, whether the structure of social relations reveals preferences among persons with similar status attributes or universal preferences throughout the collectivity for persons with given attributes. Particularistic standards refer to status attributes that are valued only by the ingroup, such as religious or political beliefs, whereas universalistic standards refer to attributes that are generally valued, by those who do not have them as well as by those who do, such as wealth or competence. The second question is whether the patterns of social interaction under consideration are the emergent aggregate result of the diverse endeavors of the members of the collectivity, or whether they are organized and explicitly focused on some common, immediate or ultimate, objectives. Cross classification of these two dimensions yields four facets of social structure:

	Particularism	*Universalism*
Emergent	Integration	Differentiation
Goal–focused	Opposition	Legitimation

These two schemas reflect the main topics discussed in this book. In short, two pairs of conceptual dimensions provide the framework for the analysis presented. A serious limitation of such typologies derived from underlying dimensions, however, is that they imply a static conception of social life and social structure. Although the explicit inclusion of opposition, a major generator of social change, as one of the types is an attempt to overcome this limitation, the schemas still fail to indicate the manifold conflicts between social forces and the dynamic processes of social change. The prime significance of the contrast between reciprocity and imbalance, for example, is not as a

dimension for classifying social associations but as a dynamic force
that transforms simple into increasingly complex social processes and
that serves as a catalyst of ubiquitous change in social structures.
There is a strain toward reciprocity in social associations, but reciprocity on one level creates imbalances on others, giving rise to recurrent pressures for re-equilibration and social change. In complex
social structures with many interdependent, and often interpenetrating, substructures, particularly, every movement toward equilibrium
precipitates disturbances and disequilibria and thus new dynamic
processes. The perennial adjustments and counteradjustments find
expression in a dialectical pattern of social change.

In this concluding chapter, those points of the preceding discussion
that pertain to the dialectical forces of social change will be reviewed.
Dilemmas of social life and the conditions that produce them will be
analyzed. The progressive differentiation of status in social structures
and its implications will be examined. The dynamic interrelations
between emergent exchange processes and the explicit organization
of collectivities will be briefly investigated. Finally, a dialectical conception of structural change will be formulated.

Dilemmas

Social exchange is the basic concept in terms of which the associations between persons have been analyzed. The prototype is the
reciprocal exchange of *extrinsic* benefits. People often do favors for
their associates, and by doing so they obligate them to return favors.
The anticipation that an association will be a rewarding experience
is what initially attracts individuals to it, and the exchange of various
rewarding services cements the social bonds between associates.
Either dimension of "pure" exchange can become modified, however,
yielding the two special cases of intrinsic attraction and power based
on unilateral services. When an association is intrinsically rewarding,
as in love, the exchange of extrinsic benefits is merely a means to
attain and sustain the ultimate reward of reciprocated attraction. The
supply of recurrent unilateral services is a source of power, since it
obliges those who cannot reciprocate in kind to discharge their obligations to the supplier by complying with his wishes.

There are a number of similarities between social exchange and
economic exchange. Individuals who do favors for others expect a
return, at the very least in the form of expressions of gratitude and
appreciation, just as merchants expect repayment for economic services. Individuals must be compensated for social rewards lest they

cease to supply them, because they incur costs by doing so, notably the cost of the alternatives foregone by devoting time to the association. The principle of the eventually diminishing marginal utility applies to social as well as economic commodities. Thus the social approval of the first few colleagues is usually more important to a newcomer in a work group than that of the last few after the rest have already accepted him. In addition to these similarities, however, there are also fundamental differences between social and strictly economic exchange.

In contrast to economic transactions, in which an explicit or implicit formal contract stipulates in advance the precise obligations incurred by both parties, social exchange entails unspecified obligations. There is no contract, and there is no exact price. A person to whom others are indebted for favors performed has the general expectation that they will discharge their obligations by doing things for him, but he must leave the exact nature of the return up to them. He cannot bargain with them over how much his favors are worth, and he has no recourse if they fail to reciprocate altogether, except, of course, that he can, and probably will, discontinue to do favors for them. Since there is no contract that can be enforced, social exchange requires trust. But little trust is required for the minor transactions with which exchange relations typically start, and the gradual expansion of the exchange permits the partners to prove their trustworthiness to each other. Processes of social exchange, consequently, generate trust in social relations. The mutual trust between committed exchange partners encourages them to engage in a variety of transactions—to exchange advice, help, social support, and companionship—and these diffuse transactions give the partnership some intrinsic significance. Only impersonal economic exchange remains exclusively focused on specific extrinsic benefits, whereas in social exchange the association itself invariably assumes a minimum of intrinsic significance.

Exchange can be considered a mixed game, in which the partners have some common and some conflicting interests. This is the case for each transaction and for the enduring partnership. If both partners profit from a transaction, they have a common interest in effecting it, but their interests conflict concerning the ratio at which they exchange services. Moreover, both have a common interest in maintaining a stable exchange partnership. The more committed individuals are to an exchange relation, the more stable it is. The person who is less committed to the partnership gains a special advantage, since the other's commitment stabilizes the relationship, and since his lesser commitment permits him, more so than the other, to explore alternative opportunities. Hence, aside from their common interest in assuring that there is sufficient commitment, the two partners also have conflicting interests, because each is interested in having the other make the greater commitment. This situation poses the dilemma for each partner that he must put pressure on the other to make the greater commitment by withholding his own commitment up to the point where it would endanger the relationship but not beyond this point.

Social life is full of dilemmas of this type and others. Whenever two individuals are attracted to one another, either is confronted by the dilemma of waiting until the other makes the greater commitment first, thereby possibly endangering the continuation of the relationship, or committing himself before the other, thereby worsening his position in the relationship. Another dilemma faces the individual seeking to become integrated into a group. For an individual's endeavors to impress the rest of the group with his outstanding qualities in order to prove himself attractive to them and gain their social acceptance simultaneously poses a status threat for these others that tends to antagonize them. The very outstanding qualities that make an individual differentially attractive as an associate also raise fears of dependence that inhibit easy sociability and thus make him unattractive as a sociable companion.

Social approval poses dilemmas, and so does love. People seek the approval of those they respect, and they also seek their help with improving their own performance. But the two are not compatible, inasmuch as supportive approval fails to furnish an instrumental basis for improvements and critical appraisals imply disapproval. By being supportive through his praise of others, a person gains their appreciation but fails to earn their respect, and by offering incisive criticisms, he earns their respect but often also their dislike, since they are predisposed to consider his criticism too severe. If others value a person's approval, moreover, he is under pressure to offer it, yet approval that is offered freely, not only for outstanding performances but also for mediocre ones, depreciates in value. The demand for approval and the need to withhold it to protect its value create cross pressures. Lovers, too, are under cross pressure to furnish emotional support and express affection for one another, on the one hand, and to withhold excessive demonstrations of affection and premature commitments, on the other, because the free expression of affection and commitment depreciates their value.

The achievement of a position of leadership in a group entails a dilemma, since it requires that a person command power over others and receive their legitimating approval of this power, but many of the steps necessary to attain dominance tend to antagonize others and evoke their disapproval. To mobilize his power a leader must remain independent of his followers and husband his resources; to receive their legitimating approval, however, he must acknowledge his dependence on them and freely use the resources available to him to furnish rewards to followers as evidence of the advantages that accrue to them from his leadership. Another dilemma confronts the members of emergent radical opposition movements that fail to expand rapidly. Unless they modify their extremist ideology to increase its appeal, they have little chance to make new converts and achieve success, yet if they do modify it, they surrender in advance the very ideals they aspired to realize, and they alienate the most devoted members of the movement. The opposition to a growing opposition movement, too, is faced with a dilemma, because intolerant resistance is required to suppress it, but such intolerance publicly acknowledges that the powerful threat of the opposition must be taken seriously and may create a bandwagon effect that further strengthens it.

One source of the dilemmas of social associations is the conflict of interests in mixed-game situations. If two individuals are attracted to one another, the first choice of either is to have the other make the greater commitment, but each prefers to make the commitment himself rather than let the relationship perish. The dilemma is how far to go in putting pressure on the other to make his commitment first, inasmuch as withholding commitment too long in order to gain a superior position in the relationship may endanger the relationship itself. A second source of dilemmas is that two interdependent contradictory forces govern the impact of social rewards on social interaction.

The abundance of social rewards depreciates their value, with the result that furnishing rewards has contradictory implications for social conduct. The more gratification an individual experiences in a social association, for example, the more likely he is to become committed to it. His gratification is a function of both the actual rewards he receives in the relationship and the value he places on these rewards. The more of a certain reward he receives, however, the less value further increments have for him, in accordance with the principle of eventually diminishing marginal utility. By furnishing an increasing amount of rewards to an individual to enhance his incentives to become committed, therefore, one depreciates the value of these rewards and hence their impact as incentives for commitment. The dilemma is how much to offer—how much approval, how much emotional support, how much help—before the deflated value of the rewards outweighs the significance of their increasing volume.

The marginal principle reflects different forces in social life.[1] There is not only the psychological process that, as individuals reach higher and higher levels of expectations and aspirations, the significance of further attainments declines, but there are also social forces that deflate the value of abundant social rewards. The value of most rewards rests not so much on their inherent utility as on the social demand for them. Since goods in great demand tend to be scarce, scarcity itself becomes a symbol of social value. The fact that most men seek to attain a social reward and few succeed in doing so typically raises its social value. The approval of the man who rarely gives it is most precious, and so is the affection of the woman that cannot easily be won. Moreover, reference groups serve as standards of comparisons in terms of which individuals judge the value of their own rewards. The average amount of reward in a group, consequently, tends to become the baseline that governs whether individuals feel relatively gratified or relatively deprived by the rewards they receive for their contributions. Regardless of the size of the income of a man, he is likely to feel deprived if most members of his reference groups earn more than he does. Whereas promoted soldiers were, on the average, more satisfied with promotion chances in the army than privates, the more frequent promotions were in an outfit, the less satisfied were its members with promotions.[2] This pattern of relative deprivation, as Stouffer called it, reflects a principle of diminishing *collective* marginal utility. By distributing more rewards in a collectivity, the baseline of expectations is raised, and the value of increments in rewards to the collectivity declines.

A final important source of dilemmas is the existence of incom-

---

[1] The marginal principle in economics also reflects different underlying forces. The principle of the eventually diminishing marginal utility of increasing possessions of a commodity rests either on satiation or on the fact that rewards necessary to meet expectations and aspirations are more significant than further increments in rewards. The so-called law of diminishing returns, that is, the principle of the eventually diminishing marginal physical productivity, on the other hand, is due to the fact that it takes a combination of inputs to produce a certain output. Increases in a single input without corresponding increases in others fail to raise the output proportionately. See Kenneth E. Boulding, *Economic Analysis* (3d ed.), New York: Harper, 1955, pp. 682–683, 588–590.

[2] Samuel A. Stouffer, Edward A. Suchman, Leland C. DeVinney, Shirley A. Star, and Robin M. Williams, Jr., *The American Soldier*, Princeton University Press, 1949, Vol. I, 250–253.

patible requirements of goal states. Social actions have multiple consequences, and actions designed to attain one goal often have consequences that impede the attainment of another, or actions that meet one requirement for accomplishing a given objective interfere with meeting another requirement for accomplishing the same objective. Two prerequisites of leadership are a position of dominance and the legitimating approval of followers, but the practices through which a man achieves dominance over others frequently inspire more fear than love, that is, create obstacles to obtaining the approval of followers.[3] For an ideology to have a strong impact requires that it command intense devotion and that it have a wide appeal; lofty ideals that command intense devotion, however, tend to appeal only to restricted segments of a community.

The manifold interdependence between interpenetrating substructures on numerous levels in complex social structures produces many incompatibilities, that is, social conditions that have been established or have developed to meet some requirement of goal states become impediments for meeting others. For example, the effective achievement of social objectives in large societies requires formal organizations with committed and loyal members. It also requires that the members of these organizations have made investments in acquiring occupational skills and have become committed to occupational careers. To have incentives to make such investments, men must receive a fair return for them. Opportunity for mobility is a basic prerequisite for receiving a fair return for one's services, since without it individuals who do not receive a fair return cannot better their position. The attachments of men to occupations and organizations, however, which are necessary in modern societies, restrict the mobility that alone can assure that most men receive a fair return for their services. Another illustration of these incompatibilities is the dilemma between centralization and departmental autonomy in large organizations. The autonomy required for effective operations in the major segments of an organization and the centralized direction required for effective coordination of the various segments often come into conflict, and many practices instituted to further one impede the other. The prototype is the perennial conflict between professional

---

[3] The dilemma is revealed in Niccolo Machiavelli's famous phrase that a prince "ought to be both feared and loved, but as it is difficult for the two to go together, it is much safer to be feared than loved, if one of the two has to be wanting." *The Prince and the Discourses*, New York: Modern Library, 1940, p. 61 (from *The Prince*).

and administrative requirements in bureaucracies with professional personnel.

The dilemmas posed by incompatible requirements demand more than compromise. Each requirement must be attended to. Individuals confronted by such dilemmas generally shift their strategies from taking care of one horn to taking care of the other, so to speak. To become an integrated member of a group, for instance, requires that an individual demonstrate both his attractiveness and his approachability, but outstanding qualities that make him attractive also make him unapproachable. To overcome this dilemma and meet these incompatible requirements, individuals usually first seek to impress others to prove themselves attractive companions and then shift to expressions of self-depreciating modesty to counteract the status threat their impressive demeanor has created and prove themselves easily approachable sociable companions. Incompatible requirements in social structures lead to recurrent reorganizations. Thus, as professional problems become acute in an organization, the professional staff is given more autonomy to cope with them, and as this reorganization produces new administrative problems, administrative reforms are instituted in an attempt to meet them. In this manner, dilemmas that confront organized collectivities promote a dialectical pattern of change, which may entail fundamental transformations *of* the social structure itself as well as lesser adjustments *within* it.[4]

The differentiation of status that develops in groups and societies resolves some of the dilemmas of individuals which occur primarily in unstructured situations, but it simultaneously produces new dialectical forces of change. Once a man commands respect and compliance in a group and his superior status is generally acknowledged among the other members, integration no longer poses a serious dilemma for him. If there is social consensus in the rest of the group concerning the importance of his contributions and their indebtedness to him, moreover, this superior can afford to be generous and modest in his conduct, thereby earning the group's legitimating approval of his leadership. The differentiation in the group, however, which emerges to provide incentives for making significant contributions to its welfare and objectives, intensifies the need for integrative bonds

---

[4] Talcott Parsons and Neil J. Smelser (*Economy and Society*, Glencoe: Free Press, 1956, pp. 247–249) distinguish between processes of change *in* a structure and processes of equilibrium *within* it, but the distinction is one of degree rather than a clear dichotomy, since hardly any adjustments merely restore a pre-existing equilibrium.

to fortify group cohesion. Generally, integrative and differentiating processes come into conflict, as do legitimate organizations and the opposition provoked by the constraints they exert, and so do the diverse implications value standards have for the social structure and its component substructures. Such conflicting social forces give rise to alternating patterns of structural change.

Differentiation

Structural differentiation occurs along different lines in collectivities. Competition for scarce resources, whether it involves speaking time in discussion groups, material resources in communities, or superior status in collectivities of all kinds, leads to a differential allocation of these resources initially in accordance with the valued contributions the various members of the collectivity make or are expected to make. Differentiation in respect arises when individuals demonstrate variations in relevant abilities, and the high regard of his fellows gives an individual a competitive advantage in the subsequent differentiation of power and competition for dominance and leadership. As several aspects of status become successively differentiated, exchange relations also become differentiated from competitive ones, since only those successful in the earlier competition can continue to compete for dominant positions and leadership, whereas the unsuccessful become exchange partners of the successful in this competition. Role specialization develops as leaders use their authority to assign different tasks to followers and as other members seek to gain status by making new kinds of contributions. The division of labor becomes the basis of further differentiation into subgroups of many different types in large collectivities.

Superior status securely rooted in the social structure leads to the expansion of power. With the exception of the special case of coercive force, power has its origin in unilateral exchange transactions. A person who has services or resources at his disposal that others need and who is independent of any with which the others could reciprocate can gain power over them by making the supply of his services or resources contingent on their compliance with his directives. People who become indebted to a person for essential benefits are obligated to accede to his wishes lest he cease to furnish these benefits. An individual who distributes gifts and services to others makes a claim to superiority over them. If they properly repay him or possibly even make excessive returns, they challenge this claim and invite him to enter into a peer relation of mutual exchange. If they are unable to reciprocate, however, they validate his claim to superiority. The continuing unilateral supply of needed services to others creates a backlog of obligations on which the supplier can draw at his discretion, and these accumulated obligations to accede to his demands give him power over the others.

The possession of resources enabling a person to satisfy important needs of others, however, is not a sufficient condition for achieving power over them. Four other conditions must also be met, that is, there are four conditions that make it possible for others to remain independent of a person or group with such resources. First, if others have resources that permit them to reciprocate for his services by furnishing him with benefits he needs, they remain his equals. Second, if there are many alternative suppliers in competition from whom others can obtain the needed services, they do not become dependent on any. Third, if they have the power to force the person to give them what they want, they maintain their independence of him. Fourth, if people learn to get along without the benefits they originally considered necessary, a person's ability to dispense these benefits no longer gives him power over them. Within the framework of these limiting conditions, however, the person who can supply essential benefits to others has an undeniable claim to power over them. Unless one of these four possibilities is open to them, individuals who want benefits at the disposal of another have no choice but to submit to his power as an incentive for him to provide these benefits.

Superior status, like capital, is an accumulated resource, which an individual can draw on to obtain advantages, which is expanded in use, and which can be invested at risk to increase it. A person to whom others are obligated can ask them to do things whenever it is to his advantage, but his making such requests gives them an opportunity to discharge their obligations. Once they are no longer indebted to him he has no more power over them, unless he has replenished his power by furnishing more services, thus keeping them under obligation. The sheer reminder that they owe him a service indicates that he is dependent on their doing things for him, just as they are dependent on his doing things for them, and this evidence of interdependence weakens his power over them. The man with great power, however, needs no reminders of this sort, because others are eager to discharge some of their obligations to him to maintain his good will without ever being able to discharge all of them. Power over an entire group, moreover, enables a man to live on his interests, as it were, benefiting from his power without using it up, because a man in such a position can coordinate the activities of group members to further the achievement of common objectives and thereby continually renew their indebtedness to him for his effective guidance. Assuming responsibility for coordination involves a risk, since unsuccessful direction of the activities of others typically entails the loss of power over them. The rewards that accrue to group members from successful guidance, however, increase their obligations to the leader and fortify his position of leadership. In addition, the compliance the leader commands among his followers extends his power over outsiders.

Two factors secure a person's superior status and create a basis for additional improvements in it—multiple supports in the social structure and joint support by subordinates. The multiple supports of the power of a man who has the resources to command the compliance of one hundred others make his power not only one hundred times as great but also immeasurably more secure than is the power of a man who only commands the compliance of one other. The basic reason is that power over many others enables a man to spread the risk of defections from his rule by taking into account the cost of such defections and insuring himself against their disadvantageous consequences, in accordance with the principles of eliminating uncertainty through insurance as advanced by Knight.[5] The employer of a single employee depends on his services, just as the employee depends on the employer's wages, the degree of dependence of each being contingent on the alternative opportunities available to him for obtaining as good a worker or as good a job, respectively. The employer of one thousand employees, in contrast, is not dependent on any of them, although they are dependent on his wages, since he can calculate on the basis of past experience the amount of turnover expected and insure himself against it by taking into account the cost of regularly having to replace a certain proportion of employees.[6] The major limitation of power is the superior's uncertainty as to when subordinates will be willing to forego the advantages he can provide and escape from his command. Power over sufficient numbers to estimate the statistical probability of such defections eliminates this uncertainty and makes protection against defections possible, though at some cost. Besides, power over many others enables a man to use his power to bring those into line who might want to escape from his rule. Alternative supports make power independent of any one of them, and hence

---

[5] Frank H. Knight, *Risk, Uncertainty and Profit* (2d ed.), Boston: Houghton Mifflin, 1933, esp. chapter viii.

[6] Concerted action by employees, notably in the form of collective bargaining through unions, makes large employers as dependent on employees as small ones are, since it deprives the large employers of independent alternatives.

reinforce it far beyond their additive effect, just as alternative sources of needed benefits make individuals independent of any one of them.

Multiple supports of superior status that are transformed into a joint social support in the course of interaction among subordinates solidify this status still further. When agreement develops in a group that the abilities of one of its members deserve high respect, even newcomers and others who have no personal basis for judging him are likely to accord him respect. If a person's contributions to the welfare of a collectivity create joint obligations among its members and consensus emerges in their social interaction concerning their indebtedness to him, social norms and sanctions tend to develop through which compliance with his directives is enforced. This makes his controlling power over the entire membership independent of the personal feelings of obligations of any one of them and independent of any enforcement actions on his part. Multiple status supports that become joined through shared social acknowledgment and consequent collective action firmly root superior status in the social structure.

The significance of multiple and joint supports is not confined to power but extends to other aspects of status. A man who is not known in a group can only impress others by telling them about his achievements and abilities, whereas the one whose achievements are generally known and acknowledged can modestly belittle his accomplishments and thereby be the more impressive. The individual who accepts gifts or services from others without reciprocating becomes subordinate to them, but the chief whose institutional authority is firmly established can accept tributes from his subjects without in the least endangering his position. The unpopular girl is fearful lest she does not please the boy enough who takes her out and also wary lest her eager show of affection reveal her lack of popularity and depreciate her value in his eyes. But the girl known to be popular among boys need have no such fears and can act more freely in accordance with her inclinations. A professional who manifests high respect and praise for a colleague implicitly subordinates himself to the other, unless he is a renowned authority widely respected in his field, in which case his praise of the colleague is a magnanimous gesture that does not at all reflect adversely on his own standing. Withholding approval may antagonize others and giving it freely may depreciate its value, and these consequences of his own evaluations can hardly help but distort the decisions of the one who makes them; the status of the expert whose excellent judgment is publicly recognized, however, is largely immune to such threats, which permits him to be less disturbed and more accurate in his evaluations. In brief, many dilemmas that confront individuals dissolve once status is firmly grounded in the social structure.

The dilemmas people face in unstructured social situations debilitate them in social interaction, and the resolution of dilemmas resulting from status being secured in the social structure strengthens them. Individuals whose social status is precarious must eagerly guard it in social interaction against any infringement, whereas those whose superior prestige or power are well established can afford to risk some of it to gain more. This is in accordance with the marginal principle that the greater an individual's possessions of any kind, the less important is the last increment of these possessions to him. But there is also another factor, namely, that status securely supported in the social structure is not at all endangered by actions that would endanger insecure status. The person whose position in a social class is insecure needs to protect it by refraining from socializing with others of lower status and by asserting his superiority over them when the situation requires him to have some contact with them. The person whose social position is firmly anchored, on the other hand, tends to be less reluctant to enter into sociable intercourse with attractive companions of inferior status and tends to be more egalitarian in interaction with them, which enables him to gain various social rewards from them. Social insecurity hampers involvement in work and in play, while a minimum of security fosters it.

The man who commands little power is more likely to take full advantage of it, other conditions being equal, than the one who has much power. Furthermore, only controlling influence over an entire collectivity enables a man to organize the activities of its members for the purpose of attaining greater rewards than they could attain singly. The additional rewards they derive from his successful leadership help to legitimate and enhance his control over them. In formal organizations, finally, the ability of a manager to direct the work of subordinates is not left to chance or his leadership skills. His position in the social structure places official powers at the manager's disposal that assure him controlling influence over subordinates and make it relatively easy for him to earn their approval and command their willing compliance.

Structural supports of status promote tolerance, while insecure status due to their absence engenders rigidities and intolerance. Lower-class whites in the South, whose social standing is most threatened by any advancements of Negroes, are most intolerant toward them. Southern whites from higher social strata are less resistant against improvements in the conditions and social status of

Negroes, which pose little threat for them.[7] Men firmly established in their profession are more likely to be tolerant and accepting of members of lower professions than those who feel insecure about their own standing.[8] Generally, members of lower social strata are more intolerant of deviant opinions than those of higher ones.[9] Weak extremist sects are most rigid and intolerant in their ideological commitments. The strong superior can allow those subject to his control a degree of freedom that the weaker one is usually afraid to permit. The man with great power can easily make demands that appear moderate in terms of the expectations his strength arouses, and he can thereby earn legitimating approval of his authority. This is the principle on which managerial authority in formal organizations rests. The considerable formal powers the organization puts at the command of a manager enable him to discharge his responsibilities without imposing all controls available to him upon subordinates and to permit them more freedom of action than formal procedures led them to expect and even to tolerate departures from official rules. These conditions greatly enhance the manager's chances of winning the loyalty of subordinates and establishing effective authority over them.

Superior status secured by multiple structural supports makes men relatively independent of others. It is this independence that is the source of the tolerance of powerful men, but the same independence also makes it possible for them intolerantly to exploit and oppress others when they have reason for doing so. Great power is more likely than little power to be ample for the purposes of the individuals or groups who have it, which allows them to be moderate and permissive in exercising control over others. Should, however, their power, regardless of how great it is in absolute terms, fall short of their needs, that is, be insufficient to accomplish the objectives to which they aspire, they are likely to exploit all the power they have fully, and their very independence of the members of inferior social strata enables them to exercise their power oppressively without fear of retaliation. But this independence of the very powerful is only relative and not irrevocable. Excessive exploitation and oppression provoke

---

[7] An exception is the Southern politician who seeks to benefit from the support of lower-class whites by expressing extreme intolerance against Negroes.

[8] See Alvin Zander, Arthur R. Cohen, and Ezra Stotland, "Power and the Relations Among Professions," in Dorwin Cartwright, *Studies in Social Power,* Ann Arbor: Institute for Social Research, University of Michigan, 1959, pp. 15–34.

[9] See Samuel A. Stouffer, *Communism, Conformity, and Civil Liberties,* New York: Doubleday, 1955, p. 139.

opposition movements that, if they spread and are successful, may overthrow existing powers. For a successful opposition, by uniting the different groups of oppressed in a common endeavor, deprives the ruling group of the multiple supports on which their independence and power rests, inasmuch as such alternative supports persist only as long as subordinates act independently and collapse once they act in unison.

Opposition forces have paradoxical implications. The strong can afford to tolerate some opposition; the weak cannot for fear that it crush them. By tolerating an opposition movement, and possibly even laughing it off, people demonstrate that their own strength is immune to it, and this social evidence that the opposition does not have to be taken seriously undermines its strength by discouraging potential supporters from joining such a movement presumably doomed to failure. An opposition that poses a serious threat, however, must be taken seriously, which means that it will be intolerantly opposed. But intolerant resistance against the opposition and unrelenting endeavors to fight it publicly acknowledge that it constitutes an important force and grave danger. They thus may actually reinforce the opposition by encouraging individuals to join it for fear of its power or in anticipation of its victory. In short, the intolerance directed against it may strengthen the opposition, and the clash between opposition forces intensifies intolerance on both sides. The typical result of fierce battles between two hostile camps is the suppression of the vanquished by the victor. The toleration of opposition is difficult, but it is essential in a democracy, for it dulls the edge of opposition forces and thereby prevents fights to the finish that lead to the suppression of opposition and to the end of democratic institutions.

Dynamics

Four facets of social structures have been distinguished—integration, differentiation, organization, and opposition. The first two emerge in the course of social transactions without any explicit design, whereas the last two are the result of organized efforts focused on some collective objectives or ideals. Integration and opposition rest on particularistic values that unite ingroups and divide them from outgroups. Differentiation and legitimation are governed by universalistic standards that specify the achievements and qualities that are generally valued within the compass of the collectivity under consideration and that bestow superior status on those who exhibit them. Two of these four facets of social structure can be directly derived from an analysis of exchange, and the other two, more indirectly.

Social exchange has been defined by two criteria, associations oriented largely to extrinsic rather than purely intrinsic rewards and reciprocal rather than unilateral transactions. In the course of recurrent reciprocal exchange of extrinsic benefits, partnerships of mutual trust develop that assume some intrinsic significance for the partners, introjecting an intrinsic element into social interaction. At the same time, some individuals can supply important services to others for which the latter cannot appropriately reciprocate, and the unilateral transactions that consequently take place give rise to differentiation of status. Exchange processes, therefore, lead to the emergence of bonds of intrinsic attraction and social integration, on the one hand, and of unilateral services and social differentiation, on the other.

The development of social integration and differentiation in a collectivity creates a fertile soil for the establishment of an organization designed to coordinate endeavors in the pursuit of common objectives. Integrative bonds provide opportunities for communication about common problems, some of which can only be solved through concerted action, and in these social communications agreement on collective goals tends to arise. In the process of social differentiation, some individuals have demonstrated their ability to make outstanding contributions to the welfare of the rest, and these become apparent candidates for directing collective endeavors, that is, for leadership. Agreement on social objectives is a prerequisite for organization and leadership in a collectivity, because common objectives are the incentives for organizing and coordinating the activities of various members, and because they provide the conditions that permit leaders to arise. For a leader to be able to guide the activities in a collectivity, all or most members must be obliged to comply with his directives. A common purpose makes it possible for a man, by making crucial contributions to its achievement, to obligate all members simultaneously and thus command the compliance of all of them. In groups without a common purpose, a man commands the compliance of others by contributing to their individual ends, and this makes it impossible, except in very small groups, for leadership to evolve, since no man has the time to furnish services to a large number of men singly.[10]

---

[10] Reference here is to direct services rendered by a person to others. The situation is different if a man has the resources to pay wages to many others. Such financial resources are a major source of extensive power over large numbers of men, since money as a general medium of exchange makes indirect transactions on a large scale possible.

Formal organizations are explicitly instituted to achieve given objectives. Their full establishment requires that the objectives they are intended to serve and the authority of their leadership become legitimated by social values. The contributions effective leadership makes to the welfare of the rest create joint obligations and social approval, which give rise to social norms among followers that demand compliance with the orders of leaders and effectuate their authority. The enforcement of compliance with the directives of superiors *by the collectivity of subordinates* is the distinctive characteristic of legitimate authority. Some organizations, such as voluntary associations and unions, consist mostly of members, whose ends the organization is designed to serve, and who are expected to receive a share of the profits. Other organizations, such as business concerns, consist mostly of employees, who are compensated for services that further the ends of others, and who are not entitled to a share of the profits. In strong voluntary organizations with powerful leaders, however, this distinction becomes obscured, since leaders need to distribute only sufficient rewards to members to act as incentives for compliance and contributions and can keep the rest at their own disposal, which means that they treat members, in effect, as management treats employees.

Within the organization, indirect exchange processes become substituted for direct ones, although direct ones persist in interstitial areas, such as informal cooperation among colleagues. The development of authority illustrates the transformation of direct into indirect exchange transactions. As long as subordinates obey the orders of a superior primarily because they are obligated to him for services he has rendered and favors he has done for them individually, he does not actually exercise authority over the subordinates, and there is a direct exchange between him and them, of the type involving unilateral services. The establishment of authority means that normative constraints that originate among the subordinates themselves effect their compliance with the orders of the superior—partly through public pressure and partly through enforcement actions by the dominant groups among subordinates—and indirect exchanges now take the place of the former direct ones. The individual subordinate offers compliance to the superior in exchange for approval from his colleagues; the collectivity of subordinates enforces compliance with the superior's directives to repay its joint obligations to the superior; and the superior makes contributions to the collectivity in exchange for the self-enforced voluntary compliance of its members on which his authority rests.

The performance of many duties in formal organizations entails indirect exchange. Supervisors and staff personnel have the official duty to provide assistance to operating employees, in return for which they are compensated, not by these employees, but by the organization, which ultimately benefits from their contributions to the work of others. Officials in bureaucratic organizations are expected to treat clients impersonally in accordance with the rules, which requires that they refrain from engaging in exchange transactions with them. They must, of course, not accept bribes or gratuities, and neither must they reward clients with more favorable treatment for expressions of gratitude and appreciation lest impartial service to all clients in conformity with official procedures suffer. In return for offering services to clients without accepting rewards from them, officials receive material rewards from the organization and colleague approval for conforming with accepted standards. The clients make contributions to the community, which furnishes the resources to the organization that enable it to reward its members. Professional service involves a similar chain of indirect exchange, the central link of which is colleague approval for service to clients in accordance with professional standards and hence in disregard of considerations of social exchange. The obligations created in exchange transactions would make undeviating adherence to impersonal bureaucratic or professional standards impossible. The absence of exchange transactions with clients is a prerequisite of bureaucratic or professional detachment toward them. To maintain such detachment, therefore, requires that colleague approval or other rewards compensate practitioners for the advantages foregone by refraining from entering into exchanges with clients.

Indirect transactions are characteristic of the complex structures in large collectivities generally. Since direct contact between most members in a large collectivity is not possible, the interrelations between them uniting them in a social structure are primarily indirect, and social values serve as the media of these indirect links and transactions. Particularistic values create a common solidarity and integrative ties that unify the members of the collectivity and divide them from other collectivities, functioning both as substitutes for the personal bonds of attraction that solidify face-to-face groups and as a basis for such bonds in the collectivity and its subgroups. Universalistic standards define achievements and qualifications that are generally acknowledged as valuable, making indirect exchange transactions possible, notably in the form of enabling individuals and groups to accumulate social status and power in one setting and gain advantages from them in another. Legitimating values expand the scope of social control beyond the limits of personal influence by establishing authority that commands willing compliance enforced by the subordinates themselves, and these values become the foundation for organizing collective effort on a large scale. Opposition ideals serve as rallying points of opposition movements and as catalysts of social change and reorganization. These four types of value standards constitute media of social associations and transactions; they are the social context that molds social relations, and they act as mediating links for indirect connections in the social structure.

One characteristic that distinguishes macrostructures from microstructures is that social processes in the macrostructures are mediated by prevailing values. Another differentiating criterion is that macrostructures are composed of interrelated social structures, whereas the constituent elements of microstructures are interrelated individuals in direct social contact. Furthermore, parts of the complex social structures in societies assume enduring form as institutions. Institutionalization involves two complementary social mechanisms through which social patterns are perpetuated from generation to generation. On the one hand, external social arrangements are historically transmitted, partly through written documents that circumscribe and preserve them, as exemplified by the form of government in a society resting on its constitution and laws. On the other hand, internalized cultural values are transmitted in processes of socialization and give the traditional external manifestations of institutions continuing meaning and significance. These institutional mechanisms are implemented by the power structure, since the powerful groups in a society tend to be most identified with its institutions, and since they tend to use their power to preserve the traditional institutions.

Once organized collectivities have developed, social transactions occur between them. A basic distinction can be made between two major types of processes that characterize the transactions of organized collectivities—as well as those of individuals, for that matter—competitive processes reflecting endeavors to maximize scarce resources and exchange processes reflecting some form of interdependence. Competition occurs only among like social units that have the same objective and not among unlike units with different objectives—among political parties and among business concerns but not between a party and a firm—whereas exchange occurs only between unlike units—between a political party and various interest groups but not among the different parties (except when two form a coalition and thus cease to be two independent political units). Competition promotes hierarchical differentiation between the more and the less successful organizations, and exchange promotes horizontal differentiation between specialized organizations of diverse sorts. Extensive hierarchical differentiation, however, makes formerly alike units unlike in important respects and unlike ones alike in their power and opportunity to attain a dominant position. Hence, exchange relations may develop between units that once were alike as the result of differential success in competition, and competition for dominance may develop among unlike units made alike by their success. The first of these developments is illustrated by the exchange relation between a giant manufacturing concern and an unsuccessful competitor who becomes the other's supplier of parts, and the second, by the competition among major business concerns, strong unions, and other organized interest groups for a position of dominant influence in the community.

Competition among collectivities that belong in some respect to the same general type is manifest in patterns of mobility of individuals from one to another, which continually modify their boundaries and internal structure. Organized collectivities typically compete for members and contributors—for experienced executives, skilled employees, customers, voters, religious converts, and so forth. Successful competition provides more resources for rewarding members and thus spells further success, since the greater rewards discourage members of the collectivity from defecting from it to others and encourage members of other collectivities to leave them for it. The internal differentiation of status and consequent differential distribution of rewards in a collectivity, however, create differences in incentives for mobility among its members. If different value standards prevail in the various social groupings, as is the case for religious denominations or political parties, the marginal members of low standing in one collectivity have most incentive to move to another. But if social groupings are hierarchically ranked in terms of the same universalistic standards that prevail throughout all of them, as is the case for social classes, individuals with high social standing within a social stratum have most incentive to leave it, since they have the best chance of moving up to a higher one. The typical patterns of mobility under these conditions are from a superior position in a lower stratum to an inferior position in a higher one and vice versa. The opportunity for such movements confronts individuals with the choice between being a big fish in a little pond and a little fish in a big pond, which entails the alternatives of either deriving social rewards from occupying a superordinate position in daily social intercourse or obtaining the advantages and privileges that accrue from membership in a higher social class at the cost of having to assume a subordinate role in recurrent social interaction.

The interdependent organizations in a society engage in exchange and various related transactions.[11] Formal organizations often exchange services. For example, welfare and health organizations refer clients to each other,[12] parties adopt programs that serve the interests of various groups in exchange for political support, and, of course, firms exchange a large variety of products and services for a price. Many organizational exchanges are mediated through the community. Thus, the police provides protection to the members of the community, schools furnish training for the young, universities supply research knowledge, hospitals render health services, and they all receive support from the community in exchange for their services. Organizations sometimes form coalitions committing them to joint decisions and actions. Small parties unite forces in a political campaign, for instance, several unions agree to carry out a strike together, and churches join in an ecumenical council. Coalitions among organizations may become mergers that destroy the former boundaries between them. But even without complete mergers, transactions between organized collectivities often lead to their interpenetration and obscure their boundaries. A political party that is primarily supported by two occupational groupings, for example, cannot be said to constitute a social entity distinct from these groups that engages in exchange relations with them. Rather, representative segments of these occupational groups are constituent elements of the party, and competition and bargaining occur between them within the party as each seeks to influence its political program and course of action.

Transactions among organized collectivities, then, may give rise to social ties that unite them, just as social exchange among individuals tends to produce integrative bonds. These transactions also differentiate competing organizations and may result in the elimination or absorption of competitors and the dominance of one or a few organizations—a few giant corporations, two major parties, a universal church—just as unilateral transactions and competition among individuals generate hierarchical differentiation and may result in the

---

[11] For a typology of relations among organizations, see James D. Thompson and William J. McEwen, "Organization Goals and Environment," *American Sociological Review*, 23 (1958), 23–31.

[12] See Sol Levine and Paul E. White, "Exchange as a Conceptual Framework for the Study of Interorganizational Relationships," *Administrative Science Quarterly*, 5 (1961), 583–601.

dominance of one or a few leaders in a group. The existence of a differentiated structure of relations among organized collectivities creates the conditions for its formalization and the explicit establishment of an overall political organization in order to maintain order and protect the power of the organizations and ruling groups, which rests on the distribution of needed benefits, against being overthrown by violence, which is the major threat to it. For a political organization to become instituted in a society, however, requires that social values legitimate its objectives and invest it with authority. This process is again analogous to the development of a single organization when the emergent social integration and differentiation in a collectivity are complemented by social values that legitimate common endeavors and the authority to pursue them. No claim is made that the conception outlined represents the actual historical evolution of social organization. It is merely a theoretical model, in which political organization is analytically derived from transactions among organized collectivities and these organizations, in turn, are traced back to simpler processes of social exchange. This model can be schematically presented in the following form:

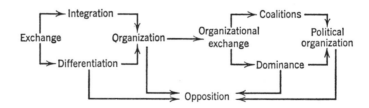

The dynamics of organized social life has its source in opposition forces. The dominant power of individuals, groups, or organizations over others makes it possible for them to establish legitimate authority by exercising their power fairly and with moderation and by making it profitable for others to remain under their protective influence. Dominant power, however, also makes it possible to exploit others and thereby gain advantages, and it consequently is often exercised oppressively. Serious deprivations caused by the unfair exercise of power tend to engender a desire for retaliation. If the exploitation is experienced in a group situation, particularly in a group comparatively isolated from the rest of the community, communication among the oppressed socially justifies and reinforces their feeling of hostility against existing powers by giving rise to an opposition ideology that transforms this hostility from a selfish expression of revenge into a noble cause pursued to further the welfare of one's fellow men. While oppression is not the sole reason for opposition, ideological identification with a cause is essential for the support of radical movements, inasmuch as existing powers have the sanctions to assure that such support harms a man's self-interest and thus is not warranted on purely rational grounds. Opposition ideals create a surplus of resources, since devotion to them frees social energies by making men willing to sacrifice material welfare for their sake, and the opposition movement they inspire constitutes a new social investment that brings about social change and reorganization.

Vested interests and powers create rigidities in social structures, and so does the institutionalization of social arrangements through which they are perpetuated beyond the life span of individuals. Social institutions are crystallized forms of organized social life that have their base in historical traditions and that are supported by major cultural values internalized in childhood and passed on from generation to generation. Traditional institutions, endowed by profound values with symbolic significance, tend to defy innovation and reform even when changes in social conditions have made them obsolete. Powerful groups whose interests are served by existing institutional arrangements defend them against attack and fortify them. Institutions meet the need for social order and stability in a society at the cost of rigidities and inequities that often cause serious hardships. Vigorous social opposition is required to produce a change in institutions, and it constitutes a countervailing force against institutional rigidities.

Not all opposition takes the form of radical rebellions. Conditions in complex social structures with their interlaced substructures recurrently engender opposing forces. Particularistic values integrate the members of collectivities into solidary units and simultaneously produce divisive boundaries between them that frequently create problems of social solidarity in the encompassing social structure. Universalistic standards of achievement give rise to differentiated social strata in which vested powers and particularistic allegiances restrict upward mobility on the basis of universalistic criteria of achievement alone. Legitimate centralized authority and the autonomy of its component organizations often come into conflict. Even the reorganizations effected by successful opposition movements tend to have repercussions that cause fresh problems and new needs for reorganization. Moreover, the many intersecting organized collectivities with interlocking memberships typical of modern society stimulate a multitude of crisscrossing conflicts, since many issues arise among organized groups, and since individuals are drawn by their organizational affiliations into these controversies. Cross-cutting conflicts that periodically realign opposition forces prevent conflicts from becoming cumulative and dividing the community into two hostile camps, and they are manifest in dialectical patterns of change and reorganization.

Dialectic

There is a dialectic in social life, for it is governed by many contradictory forces. The dilemmas of social associations reflect this dialectic, and so does the character of social change.[13] To conceive of change in social structures as dialectical implies that it involves neither evolutionary progress in a straight line nor recurring cycles but alternating patterns of intermittent social reorganization along different lines. The analysis of the relationship between reciprocity and imbalance illustrates the underlying conception.

Reciprocity is an equilibrating force, the assumption being that every social action is balanced by some appropriate counteraction. Individuals who receive needed benefits from others are obligated, lest the supply of benefits cease, to reciprocate in some form, whether through expressions of gratitude, approval, material rewards, services, or compliance. Reciprocity on one level, however, entails imbalances on others. If persons are obligated to accede to another's wishes because he renders essential services to them for which they cannot otherwise compensate him, their compliance reciprocates for the unilateral services they obtain and in this sense restores balance, but it also creates an imbalance of power. The reactions to the exercise of power superimpose a secondary exchange upon the primary one. The exercise of power with fairness and moderation earns a man social approval, whereas the oppressive use of power evokes disapproval. The social approval that rewards rulers for not taking full advantage of their power and the social disapproval that penalizes them for taking excessive advantage of it equilibrate the scales, so to speak. Simultaneously, however, the collective approval of subordinates legitimates the governing group's authority over them and thus reinforces the imbalance of power, and the collective disapproval of the oppressed tends to give rise to opposition forces that disturb social

---

[13] For a theoretical conception of dialectical change, which has similarities with the one presented, but which unfortunately was published too late for full discussion here, see Pierre L. van der Berghe, "Dialectic and Functionalism," *American Sociological Review*, 28 (1963), 695–705.

equilibrium and stimulate reorganizations in the social structure. Every social process restoring equilibrium engenders some new imbalances.

Social forces often have contradictory implications. One reason for this is that the conditions produced by a social force may provoke the emergence of another force in the opposite direction. Processes of social integration, in which group members impress each other with their outstanding qualities, give rise to differentiation of status, and social differentiation reinforces the need for processes that effect social integration. Inelastic supply of advice that is in high demand in a work group intensifies status differences, since experts gain much status in exchange for their counsel, but the high price of advice encourages the formation of mutual partnerships of consultation, which lessen the status differences in the group. The very increase in rewards intended to elicit greater contributions depreciates the value of these rewards as incentives for making contributions. By increasing the number of promotions in a company, for example, the level of expectations is raised, with the result that the same promotion no longer creates the same satisfaction as before. The deprivation of the underprivileged prompts them to organize unions and leftist opposition parties in order to improve their conditions, and the relative deprivation of the lower-middle class consequent to success in these endeavors fosters the development of rightist opposition movements.

The multiple consequences of a social force are another reason it may have contradictory repercussions in the social structure. The forces set in motion to restore equilibrium in one respect, or in one segment of the social structure, are typically disequilibrating forces in other respects, or in other segments. For supply and demand to reach an equilibrium, established exchange relations must be upset. The equilibrium in an organization is disturbed by membership turnover and promoted by a stable membership committed to the organization and their occupational careers in it, but these organizational attachments impede the mobility of individuals that is necessary for occupational investments and the returns received for them to attain a state of equilibrium. The success of some organized collectivities in competition, which produces optimum conditions for meeting internal requirements, spells the failure of others, with consequent internal disruptions and possible failure to survive altogether. Conditions established to further centralized planning and coordination in an organization interfere with the departmental autonomy required for effective operations. Many incompatible requirements exist in complex social structures, and given the interdependence between substructures, social processes that meet some requirements frequently create impediments for meeting others, stimulating the emergence of different social processes to meet these other requirements.

There is much resistance to social change in societies. Vested interests and powers, established practices and organizations, traditional values and institutions, and other kinds of social investments are forces of stability and resistance to basic social innovations and reorganizations. New problems and social needs continually arise, but they often persist for long periods of time before the adjustments necessary to meet them occur, since due to these forces of resistance considerable pressure toward change must build up before it is realized. Changes in major social institutions supported by interested powers as well as traditional values, in particular, require strenuous and prolonged struggles by strong opposition movements. Oppression and hardships must be severe and widespread for men to be likely to make social investments in a radical opposition movement and for the movement to have the wide appeal required for its ultimate success. The lesser opposition forces that crisscross complex social structures, overlapping and going in diverse directions, must also gather some momentum before they can produce readjustments. The existence of conflicting forces that pull in different directions itself would be reflected in social change in the direction of the resultant force, but in combination with the need for a latency period before opposition forces can realize their potential, it leads to structural change characterized not so much by continuous adjustments as by intermittent reorganizations.

Structural change, therefore, assumes a dialectical pattern. While social structures are governed by equilibrating forces, given the complex interdependence and incompatible requirements of intersecting substructures in a society, virtually every equilibrating force generates disequilibrium on other levels. In the process of creating readjustments in one respect, other dislocations are typically produced that necessitate further readjustments. Social imbalances may persist for prolonged periods, and social equilibrium is not constantly maintained, because a latency period intervenes before opposition forces have mobilized sufficient strength to effect adjustments. The recurrent disequilibrating and re-equilibrating forces on many levels of social structure are reflected in the dialectical nature of structural change.

Name Index

Subject Index